ARMY GROUP NORTH
The Wehrmacht in Russia
1941-1945

Also by Werner Haupt
ASSAULT ON MOSCOW 1941

ARMY GROUP NORTH

The Wehrmacht in Russia
1941-1945

WERNER HAUPT

Schiffer Military History
Atglen, PA

Book Design by Robert Biondi.
Translated from the German by Joseph G. Welsh.

This book was originally published under the title,
Heeresgruppe Nord,
by Podzun-Pallas Verlag, Friedberg.

Copyright © 1997 by Schiffer Publishing Ltd.
Library of Congress Catalog Number: 96-69819.

All rights reserved. No part of this work may be reproduced or used in any forms or by
any means – graphic, electronic or mechanical, including photocopying or information
storage and retrieval systems – without written permission from the copyright holder.

Printed in the United States of America.
ISBN: 0-7643-0182-9

We are interested in hearing from authors with book ideas on related topics.

Published by Schiffer Publishing Ltd.
77 Lower Valley Road
Atglen, PA 19310
Phone: (610) 593-1777
FAX: (610) 593-2002
Please write for a free catalog.
This book may be purchased from the publisher.
Please include $2.95 postage.
Try your bookstore first.

Contents

Preface

The military history of the Second World War cannot be completely described, because of the lack of essential German documents. One cannot assume to find publications in a Reich archives, as one may when concerned with the First World War. Therefore, the written German combat history is confined to battle descriptions, memoirs, and troop histories.

After long years of studying sources and literature, the author is making a first attempt to describe the military history of one of the larger theaters of the war. It must be established from the beginning that this work has no political or ideological interpretation, since it is based only on the military facts from both of the combating powers.

The completion of the history of "Army Group North" is the result of the author's utilization of all available German and Russian literature, as well as those combat diaries and documents of the committed troop units, that are available in German archives. In addition, the author was assisted in clearing up several questions by the advice of former members of the army group — from commanders to drivers.

The author — who himself served in the war as a soldier and officer in the northern sector of the Eastern Front — wishes to thank all of the institutes, libraries, and private individuals that helped him in describing this chapter of the Second World War.

Werner Haupt
Waiblingen, Summer 1966

7

1

THE THEATER OF WAR
The Land - The People - The History

The war in the east — 1941 to 1945 — burst asunder the former military settlement of the states. The struggle was not played out on the battlefield alone, though, but also on economic and ideological plains as well. In addition, the arena not only focused on mechanical, technological, and political power, it also had to deal with the immense land and its peculiarities.

The theater of war in the north of the Eastern Front encompassed three geographic areas, which were governed by their terrain conditions and their historically varied natures. These were the Baltic Provinces, Ingermanland, and the Volkhov/Lake Ilmen region.

These important terrain complexes extended into the west from the waters of the Baltic Sea. The boundary in the north is the Neva river and Lake Ladoga. Volkhov and Lake Ilmen close off the region to the east. The boundary to the southwest ran along the former German Reich border, while to the southeast it crossed the land in the swamps and moors of Volhynies.

The entire region lies in the area of an ice age moraine. There is only a small coastal strip offering any arable land all the way up to the sandy precipices and rocky inlets of Estonia. A moraine topography extends into the interior. Here, it changes into unending forests, with lovely meadows, fruitful fields, sandy plains, blue lakes, and bottomless marshes.

The Baltic Provinces are formed from the three states bordering on the Baltic Sea; Lithuania, Latvia, and Estonia. The land and people of these once independent republics belongs to Eastern Europe, while their culture and history tend toward Middle Europe. The geographic structure of the Baltic Provinces is the connecting link between these two major European regions. The hilly land, which, with the Munamaeggi in southern Estonia and the Gaising in northern Latvia, does not exceed an elevation of 300 meters, is reminiscent of East Prussia. Pine, spruce, oak, elm, and ash grow in its forests. The further one goes to the east the more desolate the land becomes, with marshes, sand, moors, primeval forests, and scanty settlements. There is no distinct transition into central Russia.

The major lines of communication run generally in an east-west direction. The main roads lead from Riga through Duenaburg to Moscow, and from Schaulen through Riga to Pleskau. The rail lines run parallel to these roads. The only large waterway on which ships can traffic is the Duena. This river cuts its way through a deep valley, which forms the boundary between Kurland and Livonia. The arterial roads are not usable for operations, since the majority of them terminate at sea ports.

The Baltic lands and the states that took form here, sandwiched between the sparsely populated regions of Eastern Europe and the thickly settled regions of Middle Europe, have been a point of discord between these antagonists since the dawn of history. The Baltic Provinces became historically important with the arrival of the Hanseatic merchants in the 12th Century. At this time, the land was occupied by Fino-Estonians and Baltic-Indogermans (Lettish, Selens, Semgauls, Lithuanians, Kurens, and Prussians). These people were constantly warring with one another. The eastern region, populated by Latvians, was the booty of the princes of Polozk and Pleskau, while the south was coveted by the Lithuanians.

German merchants in search of the trading metropolis of Novgorod reached the confluence of the Duena and established the first Christian church there in 1184. 17 years later, they founded the city of Riga. The struggle to Christianize and subjugate the people living here continued for two centuries, until the "German Order of Knights" [Teutons] ruled over the land from the Weichsel to the Gulf of Finland. A small Lithuanian wedge was between the Prussian and Livonian possessions, thus preventing a solid contact between the Baltic and German states.

The discord between the sovereigns — the Teutons, the bishops, and the city of Riga — was utilized by the princes of Moscow, who invaded from their fortress of Ivangorod. The "Teutons" were able to repulse the Russian Army in 1502. They were finally defeated, however, by the assault from the east in 1560. Estonia fell to Sweden, Livonia to Poland, and Kurland became an independent duchy.

Sweden, the strongest power in the Baltic Sea at the time, extended its sovereignty up to the Duena. Russia, which was becoming more powerful, finally occupied all of the Baltic Provinces after the battle of Poltava. Livonia and Estonia were Russian in 1721, and Kurland followed in 1795. The Tsar did not meddle in the internal affairs of the areas, which were represented by a Land Marshal in Livonia, a Captain of Knights in Estonia, and a Plenipotentiary in Kurland. These actually promoted an increase in German immigration, predominantly merchants and academics.

The Russification of the Baltic Provinces began under the reign of Tsar Nicholas I. Religion, education, law, and administration gradually took on Russian characteristics. The German influence, which was detected particularly in the spirit and culture of the area, noticeably decreased. On the other hand, the Russians recognized the slowly changing national consciousness of the Baltic people, and thus stimulated it and offered it in contrast to the German upper classes.

These developments received impetus from the outbreak of the 1st World War and the war in the Baltic Provinces. From 1915 to 1917, German troops occupied the land up to the Duena, as well as the Baltic islands. After the fall of the Tsar, a reorganization of the Baltic Provinces had to be conducted. However, German, Baltic, and Russian interests collided, either from the government in Berlin or the new dictators in Leningrad.

With the help of the western powers, Lithuania, Latvia, and Estonia were constituted as independent republics, and this was also recognized by the Soviet Union in 1920. Their independence lasted two decades. Then, the 2nd World War began, and the intrigues of the great powers of Germany and the USSR contrived to again occupy this region. Finally, on 17/

6/1940, the Soviets made the surprise occupation of the Baltic Provinces a "fait accompli", which changed the political balance in the Baltic Sea region with one blow.

The history of the Ingermanland is no less diversified. The wide area between Lakes Peipus, Ladoga, and Ilmen received its name from Ingegard, a daughter of a Swedish King. It was her dowry after her marriage to the crown prince of Novgorod.

The population of this region was of Finnish descent. The many waterways made early contact with other peoples possible. Since it was inevitable that squabbles and wars could not be avoided, the original Finnish population was gradually decimated. From the 7th Century on, the Slavs pressured from the south. They eventually out-populated the Vikings, which had established themselves on Lakes Ladoga and Ilmen in the 9th Century.

The city of Novgorod, at the confluence of the Volkhov into Lake Ilmen, grew into a political and trade center, and finally dominated all of Ingermanland. This sovereignty lasted four centuries, until the great prince of Moscow subjugated the land in 1478.

History changed when the Teuton state collapsed and the Swedes pressured further to the east from Estonia. In 1617, King Gustaf Adolf forced the Russians to cede their Baltic possessions, and the Ingermanland became Swedish. However, the new sovereigns could not extend their influence in politics and culture, even with the help of the Lutheran Church, to the small peasants, which remained true to their Orthodox Faith and their Russian customs.

In 1703, Tsar Peter the Great won the region back. He founded Petersburg as a gateway to the sea and the West. This city, now a metropolis of the great Russian Empire, shaped the land and its people until the 1st World War. The Tsars treated Ingermanland as an occupied territory, expelling the local aristocracy and enslaving the peasants. In spite of these draconian measures, the population was not Russified. As late as 1926, the resident Finns, Estonians, Jews, and Germans constituted 42% of the population between the Neva and Lake Ladoga!

Petersburg, which was renamed Leningrad in 1917, lost its political importance under Soviet hegemony. The population decreased from 2.3

million in 1914 to 700,000 in 1922. The city's favorable location on the sea and, therefore, to the West, provided the impetus for a new enormous increase in trade. By the outbreak of the 2nd World War, the population of Leningrad increased to 3.2 million. Its 700,000 industrial workers accounted for 12.5% of the entire industrial output of the Soviet Union.

Like a sponge, Leningrad absorbed men with technical and intellectual ability. Therefore, the vast area between Lakes Ladoga and Ilmen — independent of the cities and the lines of communication — maintained its natural state as it had for centuries.

The terrain was formed from the sediment of ice age glaciers. The marshy lowlands were interspersed with forested hills. The highest elevation registered in this area is the 321 meter forested highlands southeast of Lake Ilmen. The highlands are the source of the Volga, Dnepr, and Duena. These rivers are not only navigable to the Caspian Sea, the Black Sea, and the Baltic Sea, but are also the lifelines for the expansion of Russian authority in this area!

In the 20th Century, the rivers became insignificant. There was no industry or trade in the Volkhov/Lake Ilmen region. The cities of Novgorod and Staraya Russa, north and south of Lake Ilmen, once a launching pad for Russian influence, had decreased to mid-sized European cities. By the beginning of the eastern campaign, they seemed archaic.

Primeval forests, moors, and marshes covered 4/5 of the entire surface area. The towns and throughways were located along the many rivers. The entire area on either side of the Volkhov and south of Lake Ilmen was a vast flat marsh with a few dry places.

The settlements were poor and dreary, the houses small and rickety. They were built of wood, furnished by the forests. The people lived for and from the land. They planted flax, which gave them linen for shirts and frocks. The skins from their butchered animals were worked into shoes and furs. The alluvial plains of the rivers brought the loam to make hearths and chimneys, and the forests provided material for furniture, wagons, and tools.

In the summer, the land was open and friendly, but in spring and fall it sank into the mud, and in winter it turned to ice and snow.

2

THE DEPLOYMENT
German and Soviet Measures

After the failure of his "Peace Initiatives" toward Great Britain shortly after the conclusion of the Western Campaign, Adolf Hitler determined to cut the island kingdom off at the knees. He had to work quickly, because time was working against the German Reich. The government of the United States would side with England sooner or later, and the extension of the power of the Soviet Union into Middle Europe was, at the same time, an acute threat.

The occupation of the Baltic Provinces by the Soviet 3rd, 8th, and 11th Soviet Armies, and the annexation of the Lithuanian, Latvian, and Estonian republics into the USSR, would eventually pose a threat to German shipping routes connecting them to Scandinavia and its important metals for the conduct of the war. Moscow's demand to annex Bessarabia had to be viewed as a desire for the Rumanian oil fields, which were also a war necessity for the German Reich.

In the summer of 1940, Hitler believed he could no longer accommodate the Soviet Union. He bluntly refused Moscow's request for more influence in Finland and Rumania. He now devised a plan to eliminate the Soviet Union as a power in Europe.

During a situation briefing on 13/7/1940, the senior commanders of the Wehrmacht reported to Hitler on the military situation on the eastern

German border. Eight days later, he ordered the OKH to "attack the Russian problem." On 29/7/1940, the Chief of Wehrmacht Operations received the mission, "...to eliminate the Bolshevik threat!" On the same day, the commander of the 18th Army, which was the senior German commander in East Prussia at that time, was commissioned with working out a study for an offensive against the USSR.

The "Marcks Plan" — named after its author — foresaw an offensive against the USSR in four phases. This study was turned down. The Senior Quartermaster of the OKH, Major General Paulus (later Field Marshal), worked on an operations plan until February 1941, which was completed that summer.

The military, economic, and political plans for the campaign against Eastern Europe were worked out in the winter of 1940/41 under the utmost secrecy at the highest levels. It is not our task here to describe these plans. We will only concern ourselves with the German forces, which later fought on the northern sector of the Eastern Front.

From the fall of 1940, Hitler energetically pressed for the military plans — the transfer of troops from France to East Prussia and the General-gouvernment, the establishment of supply bases, etc. — and their rapid execution. The plans were not confined to German territory alone. Thus, in October, Hitler ordered the commander of the Luftwaffe to conduct extensive reconnaissance in the Soviet Union.

The Luftwaffe organized a long range reconnaissance formation under Lieutenant Colonel Rowehl, which was tasked with photographing western Russia from high altitude. Two of the four squadrons, which began operations in the winter, were stationed in East Prussia (Seerappen, Insterburg). The 1st Squadron, equipped with type He-111 aircraft, which were outfitted with special high altitude engines, began photographing Soviet troop concentrations, installations, lines of communications, etc. The region from the Memel to Lake Ilmen was the operations area of the 2nd Squadron, which flew in Do-215B aircraft at 9000 meters.

It was not yet half a year since Hitler's first orders to the General Staff, when the first operations directives for "Barbarossa" — the attack on the Soviet Union — were endorsed. Order Nr. 21 (OKW/WFSt/.Abt. L (I) Nr.

33 408/40) of 19/12/1940 gave the following line of direction for the army group assigned on the north of the front:

"...the army group operating in the north will destroy enemy forces located in the Baltic Provinces from East Prussia in the general direction of Leningrad. After accomplishing this priority task, the occupation of Leningrad and Kronstadt must follow..."

This order only sketchily outlined the mission of the German armies set against Leningrad. On 31/1/1941, it was further defined by the final deployment instructions:

"Army Group North has the mission of destroying the enemy forces in the Baltic Provinces and, by occupying the Baltic ports, including Leningrad and Kronstadt, denying the Russian fleet their harbors. Together with Army Group Center, they will drive on Smolensk, with mobile forces timely provided by the OKH.

In conjunction with this mission, Army Group North breaks through the enemy front, with the main effort in the direction of Duenaburg, and drives its reinforced right flank — mobile troops crossing the Duena — as soon as possible into the area northeast of Opochka, in order to prevent the withdrawal of combat capable Russian forces from the Baltic Provinces to the east and to create the prerequisite for a further rapid advance in the direction of Leningrad."

Therefore, it was established that Army Group North was not the main emphasis of the offensive. This was assigned to Army Group Center and the capture of Moscow. The formations operating in the northern region had to provide flank protection. These tasks could only be accomplished in conjunction with the Navy, because they could not secure the occupation of the harbors alone.

The Navy had to follow the advance of the Army and achieve superiority in the eastern Baltic Sea. The OKM (Naval High Command) was not fond of these plans. The Navy, especially its commander, believed that it was more important to suppress the British supply lines in the Mediterranean Sea and North Africa. All of the Navy's efforts were directed at conducting war with Great Britain. An offensive commitment in the Baltic Sea and in the Black Sea would necessitate their splitting up of assets and further weakening their already limited fleet formations.

These thoughts are reflected in a situation report from Naval Operations:

"Even during an Eastern Campaign, the emphasis of the Navy remains directed against Great Britain. The missions in the Baltic Sea are the securing of the friendly coast, preventing the Russian strike forces from breaking out into the Baltic Sea; this requires a larger naval operation. ...the securing of all of the sea routes in the Baltic Sea and the supply by sea of the northern army flank. ..."

The preparations for the planned commitment of the Navy is, therefore, described in its own chapter, which involved the German and Soviet Pact of 1939. The cruiser "Luetzow", which was launched from Stapel in 1939, went to the Soviet Union in 1939 for further construction and was still there. In addition, the German Reich still had a lot of equipment, including construction assets (skilled ship workers, machinery, electronics, weapons, and administrators) and assembly assets (6 engineers, 15 supervisors, and 56 mechanics) on the "Baltischen Werft" in Leningrad. (The cruiser "Luetzow" was later used as a floating fortress during the defense of the city.)

The Navy maintained a defensive posture during the offensive against the Soviet Union — occupying the Baltic islands, conducting mine warfare in the Gulf of Finland, etc. — until the autumn of 1944.

The preparations of the Army went into high gear. From January 1941, the railroad deployments were increased. The deployment of German divisions along the entire eastern border increased from month to month. While there were 17 large formations committed here in June 1940, they increased to 38 in February 1941, to 56 in April, and to 72 in May.

On 1/3, Hitler ordered that the command authorities be organized about four weeks before the start of the operation. In the East Prussian deployment area, the 18th Army and the staff of "Sub-sector East Prussia" were the command authorities. On 1/4/1941, Army Command Group "C" received the designation Army Command Group North and was assigned the northern sector area of operations. The staff arrived in Elbing on 22/4 and took command over the troops stationed there.

The organization at this point in time was as follows:

> Sub-sector East Prussia (HQ Bartenstein
>> II Army Corps (HQ Gumbinnen)
>>> 32nd, 121st ID
>> X Army Corps (HQ Hethberg)
>>> 122nd, 123rd. 126th, 206th, 253rd ID
> 18th Army (HQ Koenigsberg)
>> I Army Corps (HQ Koenigsberg)
>>> 1st, 11th, 21st, 254th, 290th ID
>> XXVI Army Corps (HQ Tilsit)
>>> 61st, 217th, 269th, 291st ID
> Staff XXXVIII Corps (HQ Elbing)
> Staff XXIII (HQ Marienburg)
> Panzer Group 4 (HQ Allenstein)
>> 1st, 6th Panzer Divisions
> 101st Rear Area Command (HQ Stargard)
>> 207th, 281st, 285th Security Divisions

By mid-April 1941, the army group had 16 infantry, 3 security, and 2 panzer divisions available. The commitment area covered East Prussia and the interior of Danzig Bay. The border sector of 230 kilometers was guarded by four infantry divisions. The additional divisions committed here were still further behind the border. They had only outposts and patrols up on the border.

The troops in East Prussia were reinforced further. New army formations arrived from the Reich and were inserted on the front. The border security was increased. The division frontages were shortened. By mid June, the army group had increased to 6 corps, 3 fortification, 20 infantry, 3 panzer, 3 security, 2 motorized, and 1 SS division.

Chapter 2: The Deployment

Luftwaffe units supporting the army group were subordinated to Luftflotte 1 (HQ Norkitten). The commander of the I Air Corps commanded the air formations. Additionally, 4 air communications and 3 air defense regiments belonged to the Luftflotte. The air units were distributed across the entire breadth of the army group, depending upon the situation, while the reconnaissance and courier squadrons were assigned with the two armies and the panzer group.

The Navy began to take up its deployment positions in the second half of June. The cruiser commanders were responsible for laying mines and for U and S Boat actions. Security Strike Forces East was responsible for taking measures to prevent the break out of the Russian fleet from the Baltic Sea. The cooperation of the Finish Navy was guaranteed in negotiations on 6 June. The Commander of Torpedo Boats went to Helsinki as commander of German naval forces in Finland, from where he conducted the war in the Gulf of Finland.

The military war preparations and the deployment of stronger German forces along the western border of the Soviet Union could not be kept secret from the government in Moscow. On 1/8/1940, the Supreme Soviet issued the decree to "institute mobilization of the national reserves." These measures, which were conducted throughout 1940 — after the occupation of the Baltic Provinces and North Bukovina — were indications of a threat of war.

The construction of western fortifications along the courses of rivers and the former Polish border ("Stalin Line") were undertaken, and border guard troops were reinforced. A reorganization of the Army and Navy — the Air Force was not a separate branch of service — followed in December of 1940, according to the experiences of the Soviet-Finish Winter War and lessons learned during the Western Campaign. In February 1941, the Navy received its first directives for an imminent confrontation with Germany.

In March, the deployment of the German Wehrmacht was reported by the Soviet spy organization "Red Band" to the Soviet government by radio from Switzerland, and they even informed them of the date of the attack — to within two days!

The Soviets, from this time on, directed their political efforts to a wartime footing. In March, the Vice President of the Comintern, Manuilskiy, spoke of the inevitability of war. On 2/5, the German embassy reported the increase of tension in Moscow and the rumors of imminent war. By this time, the British Prime Minister and the American President had already informed the Moscow government that German troops were standing on the Soviet western border in combat readiness!

On 5/5, Stalin gave a remarkable speech to the officers of the senior commands. The following is an extract:

"We must count on a German attack in the near future. Therefore, be prepared! ...The Red Army is still not strong enough to defeat the Germans. ...The Soviet government will try to delay the conflict until autumn. ...In any case, we will be at war in 1942. ..."

Soviet headquarters prepared for a German attack after troop transports to Sweden and Finland were established and the Luftwaffe had flown reconnaissance flights far into the Baltic Sea. Since the beginning of May, naval elements were delivering men and war materials to Scandinavia. Up to mid June, a total of 43,000 men were transported across the Baltic from Stettin, Oslo, and Aalsborg.

The "Baltic Red Banner Fleet" — the strongest naval unit in the Soviet Navy — reported these movements. There was intensive construction at the naval bases in Reval, Libau, and Hango, and fortifications were expanded on the Baltic islands and along the Gulf of Finland. The ports on the islands and Libau were organized into the "Baltic Naval Base" and, in May, were subordinated to the Baltic Special Military District.

At this time, control over the land forces was exercised by the Soviet 8th Army. The disposition of the army was placed on alert by the express order of Stalin. The majority of the troops were withdrawn to a distance of 100 kilometers behind the border. Only two rifle divisions remained along the coast between Reval and Libau, while there were three rifle divisions stationed on the islands. The forces deployed on the border, which were still taking up positions during the weeks of May, had to secure and defend the border. The stronger formations located further to the rear, including the mechanized and tank brigades, were to attack the enemy forces in the flank as they broke through and destroy them.

The 8th Army, subordinated to the Baltic Special Military District, controlled 10 rifle divisions, 1 tank, and 4 mechanized brigades in Lithuania; and 8 rifle, 2 cavalry divisions, 2 tank, and 2 mechanized brigades in Latvia by the beginning of June 1941. The commander of the military district had a reserve, including the I Tank Corps, assembled in the Pleskau-Ostrov-Dno area. 650,000 Soviet soldiers, although not armed as well as their future enemy, stood ready.

The German deployment continued in mid June. After 14/6, no German ship put to sail in the middle and eastern Baltic Sea. On the other hand, 40 Russian ships were still in German harbors.

The Baltic Sea was already a war zone, even before the first shot was fired! The Chief of Naval Operations had ordered mines to be laid between Oeland and the Lithuanian-Latvian border, even before the outbreak of hostilities.

On the afternoon of 18/6, the mine ships "Pruessen", "Grille", "Skagerrak", and "Versailles" set out from Pillau with 3300 mines on board. The placing of these first mines of the Eastern Campaign (Wartburg mine field) occurred, as planned, during the night of 19/6. During the next two nights, the mine field was even expanded, and the last mine was placed during the night before the start of the war.

New minefields were laid in the Gulf of Finland. In addition, since 12/6, the Navy had been dispatching naval units to Finland. Two naval groups — Group COBRA (Korvettenkapitaen Dr. Brill) with the mine layers "Cobra", Kaiser", and "Koenigin Luise"; and Group NORD (Fregattenkapitaen von Schoenermark) with the mine layers "Tannenberg", "Brummer", and "Hansestadt Danzig" — laid the Apolda mine field during the night of 12/6 in the region between Fano-Fjord and the northern tip of Dago, as well as the Corbetha mine field in the area between Kallabada-Grund and Pakerort.

Soviet naval units observed these operations without interfering. Finally, a reconnaissance aircraft shot at the mine layer "Brummer" and the mine sweeper "R-35" northwest of Dago, but did not cause any damage. The first shots of the Eastern Campaign, which had still not begun, had been fired.

The war was kindled at sea. The commander of the "Baltic Red Banner Fleet", in view of the expected German operations, had ordered the withdrawal of his units afloat. Light naval forces and submarine elements set out from Libau. Ships of the line transferred from Reval to Kronstadt. These measures were taken on the basis of instructions from the Peoples' Commissar for the Red Navy dated 6/19. On 21 June at 2337 hours — as German mines were already falling into the water in the Gulf of Finland and the eastern Baltic Sea — the secret mobilization level was upgraded to full combat readiness.

Four submarines, "M-97", "M-81", "M-83", and "L-3", took up positions in front of Libau. The mine sweeper "Fuges" laid mines in front of the harbor entrance. "L-3" (Captain 3rd Rank Griscenko) made course for Memel. This first commitment of Russian submarines to the German coast was in preparation for the mining of the Memel harbor entrance.

As at sea, the die on the land was also cast. Throughout East Prussia, the sounds of tank engines, the stomping of hooves, and the tramp of many soldiers' boots were heard. On 6/18, Army Group North completed its deployment, and the divisions moved closer to the border.

50 vehicle columns and 10 motorized supply companies moved forward ammunition, rations, and equipment during these nights. The supply for the army group was distributed in two large sectors, each controlled by supply commanders subordinate to the General Quartermaster.

The northern supply area (Tilsit) had available:

> 14,949 tons of ammunition
> 18,435 tons of rations
> 19,671 cubic meters of fuel.

The southern supply area (Gumbinnen) had available:

> 12,854 tons of ammunition
> 26,223 tons of rations
> 20,228 cubic meters of fuel.

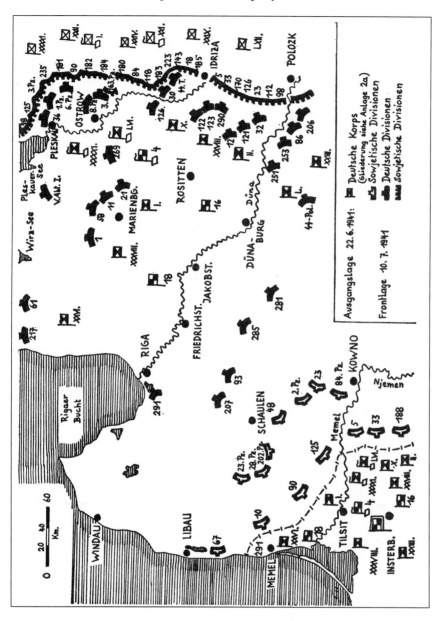

In addition, to each supply district were assigned engineer, infantry, artillery, communications, and equipment parks. Medical and veterinary bases were established in Koenigsberg. The large transport area for ammunition, rations, and fuel was located in the area west of Koenigsberg, Elbing, and Mohrungen.

On 21 June at 1300 hours, radio and telephone stations of the army group received the code word "Duesseldorf." Commanders, adjutants, and orderlies lifted their hands to their steel helmets. The order was given. Watch officers hung up their telephones, the wheels of couriers sprung to life, and orderlies scattered on their horses.

The order arrived! The order which extinguished all of the anxiety of the past days and weeks. The order which assured war with the Soviet Union!

As the evening of this sultry summer day ended in the Memel valley, the Romintener Heide, and on Lake Masurischen, the German Eastern Army set in march. Tank engines roared, trucks rattled, horses whinnied, the tracks of the heavy machines creaked, metal and weapons clinked, and orders were given in soto voice. Security posts on and behind the border loaded their sub-machine-guns and rifles, and they guided the engineers through the shrubbery with their flame throwers and rafts. The first shells were loaded into the tubes.

On the other side, however, only a few meters beyond the rivers and forests, the night was likewise not quiet.

On 6/22 at 0030 hours, the senior command of the Red Army issued instructions to the commanders of the military districts and fleets. This stated that troops located in the border area must be ready to defend:

> "During the night of 6/22/1941, the fire positions of the fortified zones on the national border are to be inconspicuously occupied.
>
> Before the dawn of 6/22/1941, all airfields, including the attached troop formations, will be camouflaged.
>
> All units are to come to combat readiness. The troops are to be dispersed and camouflaged.
>
> Air defenses are to be brought to combat readiness. All measures will be taken to black out cities and installations.

No other measures are to be taken without special approval. ..."

At this point in time, in spite of all of the intelligence received from agents and the reports from front commanders, Stalin and his senior command did not believe that the German Army was prepared to attack. The instructions from Moscow — which were received after midnight — to increase the readiness levels did not hint at an impending attack. With these instructions, the commanders on the front could not begin to take the measures which were necessary.

Already the motors of the German combat vehicles were started.

Already the tank engines had warmed up.

Already the breeches on the guns had snapped shut.

Already the German assault troop commanders were eying the dials on their wrist watches.

The ringing of the telephones in the Soviet headquarters' shelters and the ticking of the morse equipment in the Soviet radio stations continued. It was 0232 hours when the last order from Moscow arrived:

"No provocations will be made, which could lead to complications ... meet a surprise German attack with all forces available."

The morning of 22 June 1941 was dawning.

3

THE ATTACK

The German Offensive 1941

It was still dark in the forests, meadows, and valleys as, on 22 June 1941 at 0305 hours, the German guns opened their fire strike and rained iron and death down upon Russia. The fire strike on the 230 kilometer wide front of the army group lasted only several minutes. Then, the infantrymen and engineers rose up out of their shelters and assaulted across the border against an unknown enemy.

At the same time, the air was filled with droning German aircraft making their way to the east. Luftflotte 1 set out with 270 combat and 110 fighter aircraft. Their mission was to destroy Soviet strong points, aircraft, and lines of communication between Memel and Duena. The 54th Fighter [Regiment] had the following tasks: 1. gain air superiority, 2. escort the combat squadrons, 3. engage targets of opportunity, and 4. conduct deep attacks on columns and later engage shipping.

The army group set out with 18 divisions on the entire front. The main effort was obviously in the 4th Panzer Group area and especially in the XLI Motorized Army Corps area. The panzer group was reinforced by 5 artillery battalions, 3 anti-tank, 3 air defense batteries, and 3 engineer battalions. However, before the motorized forces could be committed, the infantry had to clear the way.

Chapter 3: The Attack

The Soviet border positions were almost all thrown back, and the border was crossed without resistance. Only where determined officers and commissars commanded was there any bitter resistance. The 7/501 Infantry Regiment ran into a Soviet outpost north of Memel which stubbornly defended. Lieutenant Weinrowski fell in the first minutes of the campaign, and he was the first soldier lost in the army group!

By 0400 hours, German operations staffs were able to paint a picture of the situation. At 0440 hours, the army group commander received an orientation report from the armies and the panzer group. At 0600 hours, the situation of the army group showed:

16th Army:
12th ID about 7.5 kilometers east of Schlossberg;
32nd ID penetrating into the forest 5 kilometers east of Vistytis;
121st ID directly west of Wirballen, in house to house combat in Kybartei;
122nd and 123rd ID on line 3 kilometers east of Naumiestis - 8 kilometers northwest of Sintautai;
126th ID 12 kilometers west-southwest of Sakiai;
30th ID 3 kilometers southwest of Jurbarkas.

4th Panzer Group:
8th Panzer Division had taken Jurbarkas;
290th ID advancing through Mitva 12 kilometers northwest of Jurbarkas;
269th ID 12 kilometers north of Wischwill;
6th Panzer Division 4 kilometers south of Tauroggen;
1st Panzer Division directly west of Tauroggen.

18th Army:
11th ID had taken Naumiestis;
61st ID had taken the bridge near Gargzdai;
291st ID was in urban combat in Kretinga.

Three hours after the start of the attack, the army group had received reports from the majority of its divisions. The 18th Army had reported the situation of only three divisions. Here, the picture reflected: the 21st ID — the army's main effort, reinforced by a motorized artillery battalion, an army air defense battalion, and an assault gun battalion — was fighting on a 8 kilometer front toward Tauroggen and had too subdue considerable resistance. The left neighboring 1st ID split the seam between the 90th and 125th Rifle Divisions and was quickly advancing. Contact between the I and XXVI Army Corps was secured by the 374th Infantry Regiment (207th Security Division). The regiment crossed the border with six strong assault troops to screen the main effort.

The Soviets reflected surprise at the mass of the attacking German divisions, which, by 0600 hours, had penetrated 12 kilometers into Russian territory! The aircraft of the Red Air Force burst under the bombs of the German combat aircraft in the early hours of this summer day. On the morning of 6/22, the Soviets lost approximately 100 aircraft!

Only the bravest of enemy pilots were able to reach the German areas at two locations. At 0545 hours, eight aircraft attacked the bridge near Wischwill and the railroad station at Eydtkau without causing any damage. At 0715 hours, the Soviet 8th Army ordered its air elements:

> "...to launch a powerful attack, with bombers and fighter-bombers, on the enemy airfields and the main groupings of ground forces and destroy them. The air attack is to be directed into the depth of German territory, up to 100-150 kilometers. Koenigsberg and Memel are to be destroyed with bombs..."

This did not occur, of course, because the German advance rolled on! In some locations, the Soviet defense stiffened from hour to hour, however, they could not stop the tanks and infantrymen at any one location. By noon, the border defenses had been broken at all locations. The divisions aimed toward their objectives of the day.

The attack developed very favorably in dry, hot weather, particularly in the LVI Motorized Army Corps area (General of Infantry von Manstein). The 8th Panzer Division (Major General Brandenberger) reached the

Dubyssa in the course of the afternoon and established the first bridgehead down stream from Ariogala. Therefore, by the evening of this day, the division was located 80 kilometers within enemy territory.

The center of the army group had advanced the furthest. However, the extreme left flank of the advance developed just as rapidly. The considerably reinforced 291st ID (Lieutenant General Herzog), which was directly subordinate to the 18th Army, quickly overcame the resistance of the border troops near the coast. The 505th Infantry Regiment (Colonel Lohmeyer) broke through the lines of the Soviet 67th Rifle Division during the morning and assaulted to the north, disregarding their flanks. By noon, the regiment reached their objective of the day, the occupation of Skuodas, and was the first unit of the army group to cross the Latvian border. The East Prussian infantrymen had successfully fought their way 65 kilometers in one day!

On 6/22, German air reconnaissance still had no clue as to the disposition of the Red Army and their eventual countermeasures. They only established fortification works along the Duena between Duenaburg and Jakobstadt, and therefore, the Chief of the General Staff, General Halder, wrote in his diary:

> "The Russians are prepared to withdraw behind the Duena. Possibly because we are claiming Lithuania according to agreement..."

Air reconnaissance did not uncover any troop movement north of the Duena. Truck columns were discovered south of the river southwest of Schaulen, northwest of Telsche and Kedainiai, as well as south of Riga. Bombing attacks were immediately committed, destroying 40 trucks near Schaulen and demolishing the 48th Rifle Division, which became the first Soviet division to be almost completely wiped out.

On the evening of 22 June, the Soviet High Command ordered both the 8th Army and 11th Army (Major General Sobennikov, Lieutenant General Morosov) to stop the enemy advance. General Kuznetsov, commander of the "Baltic Special Military District", recognized the danger presented by the breakthrough of the German LVI Motorized Army Corps to the Dubyssa. Here, the 8th Panzer Division had overcome both armies during the night!

The first Soviet army report was issued at 2200 hours. It was short and concise:

"During the day, regular German army troops attacked our border troops and achieved small successes in several sectors. In the afternoon, as reserve forces of the Red Army arrived on the front, the attack of the German troops was repulsed in most sectors, with heavy losses suffered by the enemy!"

This army report did not refer to the situation in the northern front. No Soviet reserves had arrived here to throw back the Germans. In the meantime, the senior command in Riga had overcome its initial surprise. It ordered an attack into the flanks of the lead German tank elements to destroy them. The XII Mechanized Corps was to attack out of the Schaulen area to the southeast, while the III Mechanized Corps had to attack from Kedainiai to the northwest. As the order went out to the corps, the command in Riga did not know that the XII Mechanized Corps had already been so battered by German combat aircraft that it could not prepare for the planned attack!

On the evening of the first day of combat, the commander of Army Group North clarified the situation in both friendly and enemy sectors. Enemy forces in front of the 16th Army were fighting on a continuous line. On the other hand, the Soviets in front of the 4th Panzer Group and 18th Army appeared to be splintered. Therefore, the army group commander issued the following order:

"The army group is to continue to attack in its present order to fix the withdrawing enemy still forward of the Duena and destroy them!"

The night was short. The intensity of the combat did not decrease. As the morning of 6/23 dawned, reconnaissance aircraft lingered over the enemy area. The pilots reported the withdrawal of Soviet forces along the entire front. They also reported motorized columns on the Jonava — Kedainiai road and from Schaulen to the north. However, an exact strength of these columns could not be determined, so the army group arrived at an incorrect situation estimate, which became apparent 24 hours later. The

German command posts concluded that these were withdrawing tank formations.

In the meantime, the advance continued along the entire breadth. Tanks, armored personnel carries, artillerymen, infantrymen, engineers, and communicators followed on the heels of the enemy. There were delaying battles in several sectors. However, the defenders were successfully thrown back. The XLI Motorized Army Corps, which was somewhat delayed by combat around Tauroggen and on the Jura sector, made contact with the LVI Motorized Army Corps after a 100 kilometer advance. In spite of terrain and route difficulties, the infantrymen kept pace with the motorized battalions.

"The Lithuanians greeted us with shouts of "Swieks gyos" and offered us flowers. In front of the houses they loaded tables with milk, coffee, eggs, bread, and butter and cakes for snacking. And the Landser had learned to say thank you in their native tongue: Swieks gyos, Marijana!"[1]

The Eastern Campaign to many of the German soldiers, though at the start, appeared to be a "Blumenkrieg" [war of flowers]. The Russian soldier soon learned. Energetic officers and commissars rallied the men to fight to their last bullet in some locations. Few prisoners were taken! Large formations withdrew in disorder away from the roads.

Thus, the Soviet XVI Rifle Corps, with the 5th and 33rd Rifle Divisions, withdrew before the pursuing II Army Corps (General of Infantry Count von Brockdorff-Ahlefeldt) on the extreme right flank of the army group. After conquering Marjampol, the corps had formed an advance detachment under Colonel Holm. They attacked as quickly as possible toward Kovno. However, the Soviet resistance stiffened here. The infantrymen, anti-tankers, and wheeled vehicle troops bogged down 18 kilometers in front of the city.

The Lithuanian population began to rebel against the Soviet occupation troops. Turbulent scenes resulted. Some civilians attacked the Red Army troops with weapons. On 6/23, local volunteers succeeded in occupying a transmitting station. At 1930 hours, a representative of the "Lithuanian Army

Command" broadcast a plea to the German High Command to bomb the city of Kovno and the withdrawing Soviets in the city!

At noon the next day the Soviet formations withdrew further. An assault troop of the 123rd Reconnaissance Battalion, under Lieutenant Floret, had already penetrated enemy lines to Kovno during the morning. Here, they were able to make contact with the Lithuanian volunteers and occupy the radio transmitter! At 1715 hours, the forward detachment of Colonel Holm reached Kovno and was greeted in friendship by the population.

Shortly after that, the 89th Infantry Regiment and the 405th Infantry Regiment, as well as the 121st Reconnaissance Battalion, entered the Lithuanian capital. On 6/26, the Kovno transmitter was already in the hands of the 501st Propaganda Company, which broadcast a program in the German language on the same day.

On the third day of the war, the 16th Army had torn a gap in the enemy front. Their II and XXVIII Army Corps crossed the Nieman on either side of Kovno and set out to advance further to the northeast.

As on the right flank, the German offensive in the center of the front also advanced. However, they now paid for their false situation estimate. The XLI Motorized Army Corps (General of Panzer Troops Reinhardt) had just thrown back the Soviet 125th Rifle Division, when suddenly enemy tanks appeared. The III Mechanized Corps (Major General Kurkin) attacked into the flank of the lead German panzer elements, along with the 2nd Tank Brigade and the 48th Rifle Division. It was on 6/24 at 1500 hours when the steel colossus rolled forward.

"The Kv-I and II, 46 ton tanks raged forward! Our company opened fire at about 800 meters: it had no effect. The enemy advanced closer and closer, without flagging. After a short time, they were 50 to 100 meters in front of us. A furious fire fight ensued, without any noticeable German success. The Russian tanks advanced further. All of our anti-tank shells bounced off of them... The Russian tanks rolled through the ranks of the 1st Panzer Regiment and into our rear. The panzer regiment turned about and moved to high ground."[2]

Chapter 3: The Attack

The first tank battle in the Army Group North sector had begun! It was the first tank battle of the Eastern Campaign! At the same time, it was the only tank battle that occurred in the northern sector of the Eastern Front between strong friendly and enemy tank formations!

On 24 June, the Soviets had an important advantage. Their tanks were very heavy in relation to those on the German side. It was impossible to cause damage to these steel colossi with the available anti-tank weapons. The 3.7 cm anti-tank gun shells merely bounced off of the steel walls. The Russian combat vehicles advanced unhindered by this defensive fire, over-running the anti-tank gunners and penetrating into the artillery positions. Only there, where the 8.8 cm air defense guns were deployed, or where there were several friendly P-III and P-IV tanks to oppose the Soviets, could they overcome the colossi.

The enemy leadership could take advantage of this superiority. The attack did not strike the flank of the XLI Army Corps as intended, but the front. Here, the advanced elements of the 6th Panzer Division (Major General Landgraf) were in a bit of a fix, but they were not thrown back.

General of Panzer Troops Reinhardt immediately set his remaining divisions to counterattack, in order to eventually outflank the enemy forces. The 1st Panzer Division (Lieutenant General Kirchner), which was already east of the Dubyssa, was stopped and turned around 180 degrees. The 36th Motorized Infantry Division (Lieutenant General Ottenbacher) was inserted in the northwest and took over flank protection. The 269th ID (Major General von Leyser) moved behind the 6th Panzer Division to the east across the Dubyssa and attacked to the north. Therefore, the maneuvers to encircle the Soviet corps were initiated.

On 6/25, the battle see-sawed. However, slowly the Germans gained the upper hand. The 1st Panzer Regiment (Lieutenant Colonel Kopp) and the 1/113 Security Regiment (Major Dr. Eckinger) initiated a decisive breakthrough on the following day at 0400 hours. The tanks of the 1st and 6th Panzer Divisions met near Sokaiciai at 0838 hours. The ring was closed!

The first tank battle of the Eastern Campaign ended in a Soviet defeat. They had to abandon 186 tanks — including 29 type Kv-I — 77 guns, 23 anti-tank guns, and about 600 vehicles as wrecks. However, the victory had its down side. The XLI Army Corps was tied up for two days by the III

Mechanized Corps. Therefore, contact with the LVI Motorized Army Corps was lost.

On the second day of the campaign, the 4th Panzer Group had already ordered its two corps to take the Duenaburg area as quickly as possible. Because the XLI Motorized Army Corps was engaged in combat with the enemy, only General Manstein's mobile troops could advance further. They executed a "Hussar Charge" that was reminiscent of an old cavalry attack.

On 6/24, the lead elements of the corps reached the area around Wilkomierz. The advance detachment of the 8th Panzer Division reached the road to Duenaburg after repulsing a weak enemy counterattack. Suddenly, the Soviets withdrew to the north and east. Therefore, the regiments of the 3rd Motorized Infantry Division (Lieutenant General Jahn) could closely pursue them. On 6/25, the 8th Panzer Division and 3rd Motorized Infantry Division made it to Ukmerge and further!

Duenaburg lay at the feet of the German soldiers.

A special group of the 8th "Brandenburg" Training Regiment (a regiment of the German Abwehr), under Colonel Knaak, reported to Major General Brandenberger during the night. They set two small groups of bold men, which were dressed in Russian uniforms, off the next morning in two captured trucks. The daring operation succeeded! Colonel Knaak reached the two large Duena bridges by driving right through the middle of the Soviet columns with his people. Here, the Landser jumped from their trucks, assaulted the Russian bridge guards, and took up positions.

They held out until 0500 hours, when the lead elements of the 5th Battalion of the 8th Panzer Division, under Major Wolff (one each rifle, tank, self-propelled weapon, and engineer company), arrived. Lieutenant Colonel Schneider, commander of the 3/59 Engineer Battalion, took over the command on the bridge. The railroad bridge was burning. The men with the black collar tabs fought to put out the fire for two hours, in spite of enemy counter fire, and saved the bridge.

As the bulk of the 8th Panzer Division rolled on at noon, tanks, armored personnel carriers, prime movers, and wheeled vehicles crossed the Duena undisturbed. The lead elements of Manstein's corps were 300 kilometers beyond the Reich border. The first bridgehead on the Duena was established!

Chapter 3: The Attack

On 6/26, the army group commander ordered:

> "The army group maintains a bridgehead near Duenaburg. The left flank of the 4th Panzer Group (XLI Motorized Army Corps) is attacking across a line Raguva-Panevezys and across the Duena. The armies are continuing the attack in the direction of the Duena. 16th Army with their main effort on the Kovno-Duenaburg road, 18th Army with the right flank moving generally to the east, the left flank pursuing the withdrawing enemy west of the Schaulen-Mitau road."

To this point in time, the Soviet border troops were being thrown back. The commander of the "Baltic Special Military District" was just as amazed at the speed of the German advance as was Stalin in Moscow. Because unified leadership was lacking, the two armies operated separately. The 8th Army unilaterally withdrew to the north in the direction of Duena, while the formations of the 11th Army moved to the east toward Drissa.

The Soviet High Command energetically set out to correct these uncoordinated operations and to stop the advance of the Germans through the gaps. The 27th Army (Major General Bersarin), which was still in reserve, was sent forward. In addition, the I Mechanized Corps — the former reserve of the military district — was attached to them. The 27th Army was to secure the Duena from Lievenhof to Duenaburg. However, before they could arrive, Manstein's tanks were already there!

This threatening situation was now also recognized by Moscow. Stalin ordered the 22nd Army (Lieutenant General Jerschakov), which was in the Vitebsk area, to advance in the direction of Kovno. Here, the new army was to intercept the retreating troops of the 11th Army and occupy a blocking position in the marsh land forward of the Duena.

The Soviet front stiffened noticeably in front of the advancing divisions of the 16th German Army. Because of this, General Busch had to gradually turn his corps to the east, instead of leading them to the north behind the advanced tank troops.

On the other hand, the infantrymen were able to clear the path on the extreme left flank. On the second day of the war, the East Prussians of the 291st ID were already 50 kilometers in front of Libau. There, the enemy's defense stiffened considerably, so that Colonel Lohmeyer was forced to await the 291st ID to close with his regiment.

On 6/25 at 0130 hours, Lieutenant General Herzog set his division to assault Libau. The Soviets, with elements of the 67th Rifle Division and marine infantry, defended so tenaciously that the attack had to be suspended in the morning. The enemy weighted a breakout attempt to the north and northeast. They were not hampered by the uncoordinated maneuvers of the 2/504 Infantry Regiment and the 3/504 Infantry Regiment, but were finally bogged down in the direct fire of the 291st Artillery Regiment. The Soviets did not give up and, on 6/27, repeated their breakout attempt. They were able to break out small groups, although suffering heavy losses, into the free Kurland area. The majority of the 67th Rifle Division, however, was stopped by the East Prussian soldiers and systematically forced back into the city. The 505th Infantry Regiment (Colonel Lohmeyer), the marine assault battalion (Kapitaenleutnant von Diest), and the Special Marine Command (Kapitaenleutnant Bigler) penetrated the fortifications of Libau from the south.

"The house and street battle was very bitterly fought. Enemy machine-gun fire spat from camouflaged port holes. The resistance could only be broken by heavy infantry guns firing from open positions and the shells of heavy field howitzers and mortars."[3]

The fierce and bitter combat around Libau, which was finally occupied on 6/28, made the army group realize for the first time that the Russian soldier was prepared to fight fanatically and selflessly!

The capture of Libau won the Navy an important base. The staff of Naval Command "C" (Konteradmiral Claasen) took over the administration here several days later. The commander of the sea defenses and the harbor commander were established, and a naval detachment (Korvettenkapitaen Glaeser) and the 1st Naval Communications Battalion (Korvettenkapitaen Neuendorff) assumed their new posts.

The first Soviet ships were now able to be salvaged from destruction or damage. They worked on the heavily damaged destroyer "Lenin", as well as the submarines "S-1", "M-76", "M-83", "Ronis", and "Spidola", which were scuttled by their own crews. The "Baltic Red Banner Fleet" had already bemoaned the loss of nine new submarines in addition to these five.

The war in the east at first did not involve any offensive operations by the two fleets. The Germans operated with only mine sweepers and motor torpedo boats, while U Boats U-140, U-142, U-144, U-145, and U-149 took up positions between Memel and the Baltic islands.

At the beginning of the war, the Soviets began to mine their waters. The majority of the mining ships were committed at the exits from the Gulf of Finland. The cruisers "Maxim Gorkiy" and the destroyers "Gnevniy", "Gordiy", and "Staregushchiy" were assigned to cover these operations. On 6/23, the destroyer "Gnevniy" ran into a mine field, was heavily damaged, and later sank. The cruiser "Maxim Gorkiy" also ran into a mine and could only reach Kronstadt with difficulty.

These early losses were not the only ones. On 6/23, the German U Boat U-144 (Kapitaenleutnant von Mittelstedt) sank the Soviet submarine "M-78" west of Windau with a torpedo hit. The motor torpedo boat "S-35" destroyed "S-3" with a depth charge; likewise, German motor torpedo boats sank "S-10" with depth charges, while the fourth submarine to sink was "M-80", when it ran into a mine.

The Soviet fleet command surrendered the Kurland coast during the first weeks of the war. The units still afloat were withdrawn to the Baltic islands or into the Gulf of Finland. Kurland lay open to the German soldiers.

In the meantime, the army group commander had set the divisions of the second echelon, the 58th, 86th, 206th, 251st, 253rd, and 254th ID, in to march across the Reich border. "As we crossed the border, it was like we entered another world. The roads were poor, the forests on either side of the road were unattended and overrun with shrubbery, the houses of the villages were poor and run down."[4] The 86th and 206th ID of the L Army Corps — formerly the army reserve — was shifted to the right flank of the 16th Army. Here, the resistance of the Soviets was tenacious.

The advance under the burning sun and in clouds of dust went well for the remainder of the army group front. Luftflotte 1 had achieved air superiority and forced the Soviet air formations onto the defensive, because they often had to evacuate their airfields quickly. Thus, among others, the

2/21 Engineer Battalion, and the 1st and 14th Companies of the 3rd Infantry Regiment (all from the 21st ID) captured 40 operational Soviet aircraft on the Schaulen airfield. On 6/27, the combat groups began to bombard enemy lines of communication north of the Duena, because there were no longer any good targets south of the river. The main emphasis of the air sorties slowly preceded the front of the 18th Army and concentrated on the installations around Riga.

In the first days, the Soviet air formations had no successes to speak of, except during the night of 6/24 when they dropped 50 air mines into Memel harbor. The enemy fighter pilots were powerless against the constant German air attacks, in spite of all of their efforts. Junior Lieutenants Zhukov, Sdorpwzew, and Kharitonov, all stationed at a Leningrad fighter formation, were the first members of the Red Army to receive the award of "Hero of the Soviet Union."

On the sixth day of combat, the situation in front of the army group indicated that the Soviet front had been split into two parts. The commander of the "Baltic Special Military District" realized the situation. The most threatened point was at Duenaburg, where the heaviest combat was developing.

On 6/27, Hitler ordered the OKH to concentrate the 4th Panzer Group in the direction of Duenaburg. At this time, the panzer group was almost neutralized, because the army group had ordered a several hour halt in order to give the X Army Corps, with the 30th, 122nd, and 126th ID, the opportunity to cross the march route.

The 8th Panzer Division was now the only large formation in the Duenaburg bridgehead. Only the 3rd Motorized Infantry Division (Lieutenant General Jahn) slowly advanced to the river. On the other hand, the 290th ID (Lieutenant General Baron von Wrede) and the SS "Totenkopf" Division were ordered to halt and could not catch up.

The combat around the bridgehead, which was expanded to a depth of 10 kilometers with the help of the 3rd ID, became more difficult. The Soviets directed the V Air Land Corps (Major General Shadov) and the XXI Mechanized Corps (Major General Lelyushenko), with the support of the 8th Air and 61st Fighter Brigades, to counterattack. General von Manstein's soldiers tenaciously defended themselves. On 6/28, they destroyed 74 enemy tanks, but they also suffered heavy casualties. During this combat, the SS "Totenkopf" Division lost a third of its combat strength and later had to disband one regiment!

The LVI Motorized Army Corps alone remained on the Duena. The two follow-on infantry corps — the X and XXVIII Army Corps — were still far behind. The XLI Motorized Army Corps was not following in the direction of Duenaburg. After the Kedainiai tank battle, the corps reorganized, crossed the Lithuanian-Latvian border on 6/27, and advanced in the direction of Jakobstadt without running into great resistance. The city fell into the hands of the 1st Panzer Division (Lieutenant General Kirchner) on 6/28.

They did not capture the Duena bridge. A battalion of the "Brandenburg" Training Regiment showed up a minute too late. The bridge blew into the air before the eyes of the Germans. The 2/113 Infantry Regiment (Major von Kittel) crossed on rafts, in spite of enemy fire. The soldiers of the 37th Engineer Battalion and 26th Bridge Construction Battalion constructed a 20 ton bridge across the 166 meter wide Duena in 9 1/2 hours. Infantrymen, anti-tankers, and engineers advanced and widened the bridgehead further. Two days later, the advance detachment of the 6th Panzer Division (Major General Landgraf) established another bridgehead near Lievenhof.

Therefore, Army Group North had achieved its first offensive objective on a wide front. The Soviets were withdrawing in front of the army group. Up to this time, the enemy in the 16th and 18th Army sectors lost a total of 478 tanks, 190 guns, and 6200 prisoners (including the commanders of the 67th and 90th Rifle Divisions).

The army group commander decided to permit the enemy no rest. He issued instructions to the panzer group:

"4th Panzer Group prepares to continue the advance through Opochka-Ostrov into the area northeast of Opochka. By achieving this objective, they will prevent the further retreat of enemy elements from the west, south of Lake Peipus!"

The two army corps were ordered to speed up the advance in the direction of Duena. On 6/27, the 18th Army had already organized a combat group from the I Army Corps, under Colonel Lasch, which was to block the river crossing near Riga. The combat group left Schaulen on the same day. An advance detachment consisting of the 3/43 Infantry Regiment, 402nd Wheeled Battalion, 536th Heavy Artillery Battalion, 185th Assault Gun Battalion, and the 2/604 Air Defence battalion crossed the Musa sector and penetrated into Bauske.

The assault on Riga began on the morning of 6/29 at 0310 hours. In spite of enemy resistance, the three march groups stormed into the Latvian capital.

The lead elements of the group — five assault guns of the 3/185 Assault Gun Battalion under Lieutenant Colonel Geissler, three air defense guns, one 3.7 cm anti-tank gun, one group of the 10th Company of the 43rd Infantry Regiment, and a group of engineers from the 43rd Infantry Regiment — rushed over the 600 meter long railroad bridge, taking the enemy bank... then the bridge was blown into the air behind them. The follow-on combat group (Major Helbig) could not close with them. They had to set up a hasty defense on their side of the Duena.

Then the Soviets attacked. It was elements of the 10th, 11th, and 90th Security Divisions, which now placed Colonel Lasch's advanced soldiers in a critical situation. The isolated German combat group repulsed the fierce Soviet counterattack. 9 officers and 82 non-commissioned officers and men fell in the street battle in Riga.

Then elements of the I Army Corps, 5th Battalion of the 61st ID (Lieutenant General Haenicke) and elements of the 667th Engineer Regiment (Colonel Ullersperger) reached the Duena. During the night of 7/1, the engineers crossed the river in assault boats and ferries.

There were no enemy forces in the city. The Soviets had evacuated Riga during the night. The Latvian population lined the streets and greeted the entering German troops as liberators. The city itself looked as if it had been fought over. The landmarks of the city — the Schwartzhaeupterhaus, the Arthaus, and St Peter's Church — were burning like torches.

At the beginning of July, the army group stood near Riga, Jakobstadt, and Duenaburg, and had crossed the Duena. The enemy's withdrawal route was severed, although the infantry divisions had not reached the river on a wide front. Several enemy groups could no longer make it to the northern bank of the Duena. These groups did not disintegrate behind the German front, but tried to continue the fight.

The commander of the army rear area immediately dispatched a security division to clear the area behind the armies. These were remnants of the 67th Rifle Division, which had, in the meantime, been able to occupy Skuodas. The 207th Security Division (Lieutenant General von Tiedemann) took over the protection of the rear area of the 18th Army. The 281st Security Division (Lieutenant General Bayer) followed behind the 16th Army on the Eydtkau-Kovno road.

The army group commander, which had, in the meantime, re-deployed his main headquarters to Kovno, ordered preparations to attack out of the Duena bridgehead. At this time, the 4th Panzer Group had to repulse a fierce attack in the Duenaburg direction. Soviet air formations repeatedly joined in the combat. On 6/30, the 54th Fighter [Squadron] (Major Trautloft), with its 2nd and 3rd Groups, were transferred to an airfield south of the city. The Soviets continued their air attacks on 7/1. However, this time they ran into the "Me 109." Eight times the aircraft with the iron crosses repulsed the superior enemy bomber squadrons. As evening covered the land on this day, 65 Soviet combat aircraft lay wrecked on the banks of the Duena! The air space over the LVI Motorized Army Corps was cleared!

The first phase of the Army Group North offensive ended on 1 July 1941. The Duena was reached. The enemy was driven out of Lithuania and Kurland. The coast near Riga was solidly in German hands. The Soviet naval forces, which at this time lost the destroyer "Smely", the escort ship "Tsiklon", the mine sweeper "T-299", and the submarine "M-81", evacuated the region in front of the Kurland coast.

They remained close on the heels of the enemy forces forward of the Duena. Preparations for the second phase of the offensive were being made. Supply distribution points were set up on the two most important lines of communications for the 18th Army (Tilsit-Tauroggen-Schaulen-Bauske) and the 16th Army (Eydtkau-Kovno-Ukmerge-Duenaburg). The motorized supply columns were soon able to take the burden off of the initial transport trains. Already on 6/24 the first train had left Tauroggen for Schaulen, and on 6/27, the railroad station in Kovno was captured.

The Soviet government was, for the time being, surprised and shocked by the power of the German offensive. However, the surprise soon wore off. Moscow undertook concrete measures in order to meet the threatening danger. On 6/29, the Council of the Peoples Commissars of the USSR and the Central Committee of the Communist Party of the Soviet Union issued a secret directive, which ran:

> "The treacherous attack of fascist Germany on the Soviet Union continues. The objective of this attack is the destruction of Soviet society, the conquest of Soviet territory, the enslavement of the peoples of the Soviet Union, the plundering of our land... The enemy has already penetrated far into Soviet territory, having conquered a large portion of Lithuania and Latvia...
>
> From each of you we require:
>
> The defense of every foot of Soviet territory in relentless combat against the enemy; to fight for our cities and towns with our last drop of blood..."

The Moscow government, party agencies, and military commands began, partially through draconian measures, to mobilize the entire population for defense, to secure industrial installations, hasten the organization of reserve and militia units, and deploy them into combat. The civilian population constructed defensive walls along the rivers and in front of the large cities. The first partisan units were formed behind the front.

Was there a strong will and a plan available?

What about the German side?

Hitler was so impressed by the rapid occupation of Duenaburg that he ordered priority to be granted Army Group North's operations and that they be reinforced with mobile forces from Army Group Center as soon as possible. In this manner, Hitler wanted to achieve three objectives: the elimination of the Soviet Baltic Sea Fleet, the facilitation of the Finish advance, and the freeing up of the left flank of the army group for a later advance on Moscow.

As Army Group North began preparing for the second phase of the offensive, they were not aware of these thoughts of Hitler. Naturally, there was no time to stop all of the units to prepare them for the new deployment. The attack, had to practically take place on the move.

The situation of the army group during the night of 2 July was as follows:

18th Army (HQ Birsen)
> XXVI Army Corps was at Riga with the 61st and 217th ID,
> I Army Corps was at Friedrichtstadt with 1st, 11th, 21st ID.

4th Panzer Group (HQ Utena)
> XLI Motorized Army Corps stopped in the Jakobstadt - Lievenhof area with the 1st, 6th Panzer Divisions and 36th Motorized Infantry Division,
> The LVI Motorized Army Corps, with the 8th Panzer Division, 3rd Motorized Infantry Division, SS "Totenkopf" Division and 290th ID, was fighting in the Duenaburg bridgehead.

On the morning of 7/2, these troops were all in combat with the enemy. The 16th Army was advancing to the Duena almost without contacting the enemy. Only one combat group of the II Army Corps was detached toward Lake Druksiu as flank security. The L Army Corps, which was formerly on the right flank, was withdrawn. Their two divisions — 86th and 206th ID — left the northern sector and transferred to Army Group Center.

The main emphasis of the offensive was, obviously, in the 4th Panzer Group area. On 7/1, Field Marshal Ritter von Leeb arrived at the panzer group command post. After General Hoepner described his attack sector, the commander of the army group observed:

> "Then we must approach this task with the panzer group as the eastern cornerstone of the entire attack east of Lake Ilmen!"

This observation was in contrast to that of the panzer group, whose advance in the former direction through Opochka-Ostrov had had the long range objective of Leningrad. The leadership of the panzer group was not flustered and, on 7/2 at 0300 hours, began to execute the army group order.

There was no Luftwaffe support available on this day, because rain from the previous night had turned the airfields into muddy roads. The weeks of constant hot and sunny weather, which made such a rapid advance possible, ended with the coming rain and muddy roads.

In the last two weeks, the enemy had considerably reinforced his front. Reserves were committed from the Moscow-Staraya Russa area. Four armies now stood in front of Army Group North, after which the Soviet 22nd Army (Lieutenant General Yershakov), along with the LI and LXXII Rifle Corps, was inserted left of the 11th Army in the Polozk area. The command of the Soviet troops in the northern sector was taken over by Major General Sobennikov, who transferred the 8th Army to Lieutenant General Ivanov. The former commander of the "Baltic Special Military District", General Kuznetsov, was relieved of his post.

Soviet resistance was concentrated on the Duenaburg-Rositten road and in front of Kraslawa. The 8th Panzer Division and the SS "Totenkopf" Division could, therefore, gain no ground. After the 6th Panzer Division was diverted from the neighboring corps to Rositten and attacked the enemy in the rear, the Russians gave it up.

The XLI Motorized Army Corps (General of Panzer troops Reinhardt) ran into no resistance worth mentioning. The 1st Panzer Division attacked west of Lake Lubaner and, after a march of 100 kilometers, captured Balvi. The 5th Battalion advanced 50 kilometers toward Ostrov by evening! The German companies were ready to move into the city when the streets and roads turned to mud. Traffic everywhere was effected — a new enemy had emerged: mud!

The next day brought better weather, and the fierceness of the combat continued. The right flank of the LVI Motorized Army Corps could not advance. The adjacent 121st ID was quickly crossed over the Duena to assist the SS "Totenkopf" Division. The commander of the 121st ID, Major General Lancelle, fell during this operation. He was the first General of the army group to fall.

On the afternoon of 7/3, the enemy's resistance collapsed. Major General Brandenberger's 8th Panzer Division exploited the situation and immediately attacked toward Rositten. The 3rd Motorized Infantry Division advanced 25 kilometers before night and took Ludsen.

Chapter 3: The Attack

The majority of the day's success could be claimed by the XLI Motorized Army Corps. The 6th Panzer Division advanced west of the road to Opochka and cut off the withdrawing Soviets from their withdrawal route near Karsava and Gauri. The 1st Panzer Division approached to within 12 kilometers of Ostrov. One of their combat groups captured the Velikaya bridge near Tizhina, 10 kilometers west of Ostrov. The old Russian border was crossed!

The Soviets did recognize the threat of the German attack, but were not in a situation to stop it. The I Mechanized Corps (Major General Cheryavskiy), which was formerly held in reserve to the military district, was hastily thrown into the Pleskau area, along with the XLI Rifle Corps (Major General Korssobutskiy) in order to attack Reinhardt's tanks in the flank, and with the XX Mechanized Corps which was already fighting there.

The ponderous nature of Russian leadership and the slowness of troop mobility allowed the 1st Panzer Division to reach Ostrov and capture the railroad and road bridges. The 6th Panzer Division overcame the Soviet defensive positions around Gauri in 15 hours and, on the afternoon of 7/5, established contact with the 1st Panzer Division here.

The division had already set Combat Group Colonel Krueger toward Pleskau, and they came under enemy counterattack. The Russian tanks overran our anti-tank guns and could only be repulsed by the guns of the 3/73 Artillery Regiment (Major Soeth). Therefore, the attack of the I Mechanized Corps came to an end.

On the other hand, the situation in the neighboring LVI Motorized Army Corps area was much better. Here, there were few enemy forces to offer resistance to the divisions except for the miserable terrain, with its swampy roads, marshy fields, and thick forests. The tanks and armored vehicles advanced only in fits and starts. The infantrymen agonized over each meter through the primeval forests and marshes. Because of this, General Hoepner decided to halt the corps and, with the exception of one division, turn toward Ostrov. The 3rd Motorized ID lead in the new direction, while the 8th Panzer Division slowly worked its way through the marshy terrain to the hills of Krasnoy.

The Soviet High Command wanted badly to eliminate the German bridgehead near Ostrov. Here, Reinhardt's tanks had broken through the so-called "Stalin Line." The enemy directed new troops into the narrow passage between Pleskau and Ostrov. The 1st and 3rd Panzer Brigades, as well as the 143rd, 181st, 183rd, and 184th Rifle Divisions, repeatedly smashed against the defensive positions of the 1st Panzer Division. The situation improved when elements of the 6th Panzer Division and 36th ID arrived.

Time was pressing the Germans for a success. The Soviets — the 11th Army took over the Pleskau sector — were becoming noticeably stronger. The XLI Motorized Army Corps still stood alone. Only the 3rd Motorized Infantry Division from Manstein's corps had arrived on the battlefield. General von Manstein even received the SS "Totenkopf" Division and advanced in the general direction of Sebesh. SS Gruppenfuehrer Eicke was to find a weak spot in the enemy front here!

The division failed to take Ostrov. It could advance no further. Therefore, the German leadership was forced to dispatch the second echelon 290th ID toward Sebesh.

On 7/6, as the Soviet resistance began to weaken near Pleskau, General Hoepner believed the XLI Motorized Army Corps alone could attack the city. On the morning of 7/7, the 1st and 6th Panzer Divisions set out. At the same time, the first battalions of the 3rd Motorized Infantry Division took over flank protection near Ostrov.

Tanks and armored personnel carriers of the 1st Panzer Division rolled on either side of the road to Pleskau. The lead elements of the group under Colonel Westhoven approached to within 12 kilometers of the city and captured the airfield. The combat groups of the 6th Panzer Division took the road fork near Solotukhina, halfway between Ostrov and Porkhov. The 36th Motorized Infantry Division, echeloned to the rear and far to the left, closed on the attack of the panzer divisions and, with its advance detachment, reached the area 40 kilometers southwest of Pleskau.

The enemy's defensive strength noticeably slackened. Since the weather again became sunny and warm, the German attack could be continued. The 36th Motorized Infantry Division executed a forced march from the west to Pleskau and occupied the city! The 118th Motorized Infantry Regiment (Colonel Casper), which had distinguished itself for some time, was out front. Nevertheless, the Soviets succeeded in blowing the 200 meter long

Vilikaya bridge up. The 1st Panzer Division, which was attacking to the northeast, southeast of the city, also quickly advanced. By evening, the division rested 20 kilometers east of Pleskau. The 1st Rifle Brigade, under Colonel Krueger, captured the undamaged bridge across the Tserjoha. The 6th Panzer Division advanced in the same direction, although they had to repulse a fierce attack by the Soviet 3rd Tank Brigade.

On the evening of 8 July, the 4th Panzer Group stood at Lake Peipus! Therefore, they had achieved their subsequent operational objective. The "Stalin Line" was broken through! Air reconnaissance showed no indications of a second fortification line further to the east or north. Russian resistance, with local exceptions, appeared to be weakening.

Army Group North had found a departure position from which it could achieve its operational objective of Leningrad. Field Marshal Ritter von Leeb issued the following order on 8/7:

Commander of Army Group North
Ia Nr. 1660/41 g.Kdos.

Army Group Order

1. The enemy attempt to construct a new defensive front on the former Russian border failed. It has been broken through.

2. Army Group North attacks further in the direction of Leningrad and captures Leningrad.

3. ...

4. 4th Panzer Group prepares to attack Leningrad between Lake Ilmen and Pleskau. ...

a) They isolate Leningrad between Lake Ladoga and Kronstadt Bay.

b) Until the arrival of the 16th Army, they will have to secure their own rear area against enemy forces east of Lake Ilmen.

c) By occupying the Narva crossings... they prevent the escape of enemy forces from Estonia.

5. 16th Army attacks further to the northeast to protect the eastern flank and the rear of the 4th Panzer Group, reaches the Kholm-Porkhov area and dispatches the right flank in the direction of Velikie Luki.

6. If necessary, 18th Army joins in the attack of the 4th Panzer Group near and south of Pleskau. They wheel around to the north, east of Peipus, after reaching the region west of the Ostrov-Pleskau road, in order to follow behind the left flank of the 4th Panzer Group. The mission of clearing Estonia and the routes from Reval and the Baltic port stands..."

This order recognized that the two armies could not keep pace with the panzer group and, at this time, were still lagging far behind. The 18th Army, with its three corps — I, XXVI, and XXXVIII — was advancing in rapid march from Riga and Stockmannsdorf to the northeast. The infantrymen had to deal more with the poor roads, thick forests, and the kilometer-long dusty trails, than with the enemy.

The XXVI Army Corps (General of Artillery Wodrig) broke off from the advance route directly behind Riga and moved to the north, with its two divisions, in order to "clear" Estonia. (That this "mopping up operation" would lead to a weeks-long bitter battle, was not known by the German soldiers at this time.) The 217th ID (Lieutenant General Baltzer) marched along the coast of the Gulf of Riga with the objective of Pernau. A motorized advance detachment of the division reached the area south of the harbor on the evening of 7/7. Senior Lieutenant Stephani, commander of 3/ 600 Engineer Battalion, under enemy fire, cut the burning fuse of a bridge and, therefore, facilitated the rapid advance of the advance battalion.

The East Prussian 61st ID (Lieutenant General Haenicke) left the Pleskau road behind Venden and also moved to the north. On 7/7, the division reached Volmar and drove its advance detachment up to the hills of Lake Virz. There were still no enemy to be found...

Chapter 3: The Attack

The I Army Corps (General of Infantry von Both) followed the XLI Motorized Army Corps in constant march. The 11th (Lieutenant General von Boeckmann) and 21st ID (Major General Sponheimer) advanced 350 kilometers in eleven days, however, could not be of help to the far advanced panzer formations in their battle around Pleskau. The XXXVIII Army Corps (General of Infantry Chappuis) followed with the 1st (Major General Kleffel), 58th (Lieutenant General Heunert), and 254th ID (Lieutenant General Behschnitt).

The divisions of the 16th Army followed the quickly moving panzer troops. They could not, however, keep pace with the motorized formations. The X Army Corps (General of Artillery Hansen) fought their way to Ostrov. However, halfway between Duena and Ostrov the corps, with its two divisions — the 126th ID on the left (Lieutenant General Laux) and the 30th ID on the right (Lieutenant General von Tippelskirch) — had to turn to the east, in order to provide flank protection for the panzer group.

The XXVIII Army Corps (General of Infantry Wiktorin) long had its front in this direction. The 122nd ID (Major General Machholz) and the 123rd ID (Lieutenant General Lichel) repulsed the first large attacks of the newly arrived elements of the Soviet 22nd Army. The II Army Corps (General of Infantry Count von Brockdorff-Ahlefeldt) marched with all three divisions — from left to right: 12th ID (Major General von Seydlitz-Kurzbach), 121st ID (Major General Wandel), and 32nd ID (Major General Bohnstedt) — north of the Duena, also with its front to the east. The 32nd ID rested its flank on the steep river bank.

The strongest enemy resistance proved to be on the right flank. The 22nd Soviet Army established a deep defense between Idritsa and Polozk and prevented the northern divisions of Army Group Center from breaking through. Because the mission of the 16th Army was not to lose contact with this army group, additional forces were inserted on the right flank. This was done with the L Army Corps (General of Cavalry Lindemann), along with the 251st (Lieutenant General Kratzert) and the 253rd ID (Lieutenant General Schellert).

In the first week of July, the front of Army Group North was already so wide that the committed air formations of Luftflotte 1 could only be utilized on the main efforts of the offensive. The main objectives of the I Air

Corps were the same as before: enemy airfields. From 7/1-8, the Soviets lost a total of 209 aircraft in air combat; on the German side, 12 aircraft were lost.

The Luftflotte followed the army troops and had established provisional airfields between Kovno-Duenaburg-Ostrov-Schaulen. The majority of the air defense battalions were in the sector of the 4th Panzer Group. Only two battalions each were in the areas of the two armies. The 1/51 and 1/111 remained with the 18th Army; the 1/13 and the 1/411 fought on the right flank of the 16th Army.

With the occupation of the coast up to the Duena, the Navy area of operations expanded. The 31st Mine Sweeper Flotilla (Korvettenkapitaen Conrad) reported that the route to Libau was free of mines on 7/3. The 5th Mine Sweeper Flotilla (Korvettenkapitaen Klug), with the "6" and "11" blockade breakers, cleared the way to Windau on the following day. Blockade breakers "11" and "36" fought their way to the entrance to the mouth of the Duena on 7/6, although they first had to repulse the attack of two Soviet destroyers, the "Serditiy" and "Silniy."

On 7/11, Naval Command "C" established its administration in Riga. Its priority mission was to secure traffic over the Baltic Sea. The army group requested the OKM to ship their supplies by sea, because the deployment routes for the friendly supply columns had become unusable due to rainy weather.

During mid July, the Navy established the "Chief of Convoys East" (Korvettenkapitaen Schroeder). His mission was to secure sea transport between Germany and the Kurland harbors, including Riga. The 3rd Patrol Boat, 15th and 17th Mine Sweeper, and 11th Anti-submarine Flotillas were assigned as security forces.

The army group recognized the termination of the second phase of operations, which could no longer quickly achieve the objective of Leningrad. At the beginning of July, the situation changed for the worse for the Germans. The Soviets had indeed lost the important communication centers of Pleskau and Ostrov; however, air reconnaissance showed that before Leningrad — in the so-called Luga sector — new fortification lines were being constructed. Above all, the front situation worsened on the right flank. Here, the 16th Army was already inferior in personnel and equipment.

"This war is the great war of the entire Soviet people!" That was the most prominent theme of a radio address of Stalin on 3 July, with which he roused all of the people of the USSR to resistance. In Moscow four days before, all political and military power was concentrated in the newly established National Defense Committee. New commands were established on the front, in order to reinforce defensive measures.

Marshal Voroshilov took command of the Red Army in the Baltic Provinces and northwestern Russia. The Northwestern Command — whose headquarters was transferred to Novgorod — took control over all Soviet Army, Navy, and Air Force formations in northern Russia, northwestern Russia, and the North Sea on 7/10.

From this point on, the Russian forces were better organized. The 8th Army, which was assigned to cooperate with the commander of the "Baltic Red Banner Fleet", was to defend Estonia with the X and XI Rifle Corps. Therefore, the army was to secure the operations of the naval forces in the eastern Baltic Sea. Medium and small naval formations continued to attack ships in Riga Bay. A destroyer formation, under Fregattenkapitaen Abashvili, even laid a mine field within the bay.

For the time being, the German commands could not eliminate these standing threats from the sea. The occupation of additional coastal forces and even the capture of the Baltic islands were planned many times. However, they had to be put off for a later time, due to friendly force adjustments. The army group commander would not permit splitting the formations, but held to the ordered attack on Leningrad.

The main emphasis still lay in the Pleskau area. The Soviets had likewise deployed the bulk of their corps here. The 11th Army controlled the I Mechanized Corps, as well as the XXII, XXIV, and XLI Rifle Corps, which were committed between Pleskau and Novorchev.

Simultaneously, with the reorganization of the Red Army, the striking power of the Air Force was improved. The air forces not only received their independent command, but were completely reorganized. The air formations were organized into air divisions of two regiments each. Major General Novikov, commander of the air forces in the Northwestern Command area of operations, now controlled the PVO [Anti-aircraft Defense] fighter corps, which was being reinforced and was stationed in the Leningrad area.

Lieutenant General Popov, commander of the Northwest Front, was tasked with the defense of a 250 kilometer long defensive strip along the Luga. It was difficult terrain, with many forests and numerous streams, along with defensive trenches, anti-tank ditches, and gun positions. This so-called "Luga Position" was only the first portion of a defensive system that would grow up around Leningrad in subsequent weeks and months.

The line stretched from Staraya Russa through Shimsk and Luga to Narva. A second position was constructed between Krasnovardeisk and Sluzk, and a third ran directly to the national border from Leningrad. Soldiers, men, women, and children built, within two months, a 900 kilometer long defensive position, which protected Leningrad from the attack of the Germans. The soldiers and civilians did not construct these trenches, bunkers, and positions under duress. Propaganda had described to them the horrible dangers which would befall them if the German soldiers appeared. Hitler himself ordered the Luftwaffe to level Moscow and Leningrad on 7/8!

The Soviet Northwestern Command established "Operational Group Luga" under Lieutenant General Pyadyshev. This army group was inserted to the right behind the 11th Army, in order to hold and defend the Luga positions. On 10 July, the first four rifle divisions and three newly formed peoples' defense divisions entered the defensive positions. The VII Fighter Corps took over the air defense.

This was the situation — which was not known to the German command — as the army group began the third phase of the offensive. The instructions of the 4th Panzer Group were short and to the point:

"It is now time to complete the breakthrough and reach Leningrad!"

The 4th Panzer Group, at this point in time, was with its divisions east and northeast of Pleskau and Ostrov. The I Army Corps followed as quickly as the poor road conditions allowed, but the East Prussian regiments could not arrive in the next five days. The commander of Army Group North was compelled to insert the XXXVIII Army Corps behind the I Army Corps, in order to reinforce the infantry forces of the panzer group as best as possible. A forward detachment of the I Army Corps was already located directly west of Pleskau.

At this time, the OKH made a decision interfering in the offensive, which imposed a limitation on the army group. The OKH saw fit not to subordinate any further divisions to the army group and, on 7/9, issued a directive:

> "... commit additional forces in Estonia, utilizing the forces already available, without assistance from the mobile forces of Army Group Center. The 4th Panzer Group is to be along the Volkhov on the right flank!"

The main emphasis of the new offensive was placed on the right flank. This also meant that the panzer group had to plan for the attack of one corps in the direction of Lake Ilmen-Volkhov. Because later a second corps had to be committed here, it required the lengthening of the already long front of the 16th Army, which was not permitted to lose contact. These considerations lead the commander of the panzer group to search for a better way.

Colonel Charles de Beaulieu, Chief of Staff of the panzer group, realized, after intensive map studies, that the terrain on the right flank was completely unsuitable for tanks. General Hoepner agreed with his Chief of Staff and decided to attack his group on the left side of the front. The 1st and 6th Panzer Divisions, which were already advancing on Luga, were halted and turned to the north. The divisions wallowed through marshy stretches of road in the new direction for almost 180 kilometers. The 1/113 Infantry Regiment (major Dr. Eckinger) had already assaulted the first Luga bridge near Sabsk.

The commander of the army group agreed with the panzer group, even though they were not in accord with the OKH directive. While the panzer and motorized divisions were assembling for a new offensive on the lower Luga, the OKH again interfered. The Chief of the General Staff, General Halder, noted in his diary:

"The information from Hoepner's left flank, which is advancing on Narva, is incomprehensible, while the right flank is advancing on Novgorod at the same time...."

The OKH stopped the preparations and demanded the establishment of the main effort on the right immediately. Leningrad would not be taken, but would, instead, be by-passed from the southeast along the Volkhov and encircled! Hitler categorically forbid the transfer of the LVI Motorized Army Corps behind the XLI Motorized Army Corps!

At this time, the 4th Panzer Group was split up. This was the moment that the Soviet formations on the "Luga Front", including the peoples' defense divisions, broke. The XLI Motorized Army Corps found no enemy forces in front of it. 1st and 6th Panzer Divisions had already established a bridgehead over the Luga, which, therefore, formed a departure base for an attack. The von Manstein Corps, in the meantime, marched in another direction. The 3rd Motorized Infantry Division took Porkhov on 7/11 and advanced further to the north toward Borovichi. The following 8th Panzer Division quickly took the Szitnja sector, 20 kilometers west of Zholtsy. The LVI Motorized Army Corps had very little breadth, because the two divisions advanced with only one assault group.

The right flank of the corps and, therefore, the panzer group lay open! Contact with the 16th Army was completely lost. The army was situated with its strongest formations on the right flank in combat with a strong enemy force in front of the seam between the two German army groups. The only division located in this gap was the SS "Totenkopf" Division, which was laboriously working its way to the communications center of Dno. The X Army Corps, which was still fighting far to the south, had, in the meantime, turned completely to the east.

During these days, the 16th Army fought with all four corps in a bitter battle against the Soviet 22nd Army, which had established itself in the "Stalin Line" between Dno and Polozk. The L Army Corps on the right only slowly gained ground to the east, although the enemy was fighting in an inverted front here, because the XXXIX Motorized Army Corps of Army Group Center had advanced into their rear. The II Army Corps crossed the Saryanka to the east. The XXVIII Army Corps established themselves around Sebesh. The town, a center on the Riga-Moscow and Pleskau-Polozk rail lines, was strongly reinforced by the Soviets. The 290th ID, which had relieved the SS "Totenkopf" Division here, had to overcome the resistance of the 113th, 163rd, 170th, and 185th Rifle Divisions in order to continue the advance. The 122nd and 123rd ID could not help the northern German soldiers of Lieutenant General Baron von Wrede, because the narrow lake passage would not allow their commitment. Therefore, both divisions were inserted in the north. The X Army Corps — the flanking corps, which was charged with maintaining contact with the panzer group — ran into enemy forces on either side of Opochka on the Velikaya. The 126th ID marched in the direction of Orsha. The division was to cut off enemy forces retreating from the 30th ID. The division — lead by the 426th Infantry Regiment (Lieutenant Colonel Hemmann) — occupied Orsha and Novorshev. The enemy forces, which were almost encircled between Orsha and Pushkinskie Gory (once home to the Russian writer Pushkin), did not give up.

"The day began at 0500 hours, with an unexpected attack by the Russians, supported by several 52 ton tanks, out of the open northeastern flank against the bridge position near Ossinkina ...The valiant commitment of the 4/126 Artillery Regiment (Captain Jost), which engaged the enemy in direct fire ...and the 3/126 Engineer battalion ...succeeded in halting the enemy long enough for elements of the 422nd Infantry Regiment of Colonel Tauch and the 126th Reconnaissance Battalion to establish a solid front in the morning ...Particularly troublesome was the loss of contact with our supply troops ...if the enemy had realized this and attacked immediately, they would have threatened the majority of our formations on the Velikaya with encirclement."[5]

The 30th ID, which was coming from the south, ran into this attack. The 46th Infantry Regiment (Colonel Sieler), which was in the lead, had to fight for every meter of ground for two hours, in order to bring the Soviets to a standstill. On the following day, the 30th ID set out further. "The tenaciously and bitterly fighting enemy had to be overcome in difficult hand-to-hand combat, stretching over a main battlefield of almost 10 kilometers. However, without awaiting the re-deployment of the artillery, the resistance of the tightly packed infantry was broken as the strong barrage fire of the Russian artillery could not stop the pressure of the attack, although it caused considerable losses."[6]

The bitter Soviet resistance, which had to be overcome by either flame throwers or by the air bombardment of their positions, fettered the 16th Army from week to week. It did not allow for room to conduct offensive operations in the marshy terrain between Orsha and Polozk. Instead, it required the taking of one town after the next, of forest by forest and road by road. The distance from the left flank of the army to the LVI Motorized Army Corps was not reduced.

It was somewhat better on the flank of the XLI Motorized Army Corps. Here, in the meantime, the I and XXXVIII Army Corps of the 18th Army had arrived. The XXXVIII Army Corps reached Pleskau on 7/12, with the 1st and 58th ID. The 58th ID (Lieutenant General Heunert) made their way on the bottomless, sandy routes along the eastern coast of Lake Peipus to the north. They were followed on the right by the 1st ID and the 36th Motorized Infantry Division, which were, in turn, followed by the 6th Panzer Division, already fighting southeast of Narva. The I Army Corps advanced south of Pleskau in the direction of Dno, along with the 11th and 21st ID.

The I Army Corps was attached to the march of the panzer group and ordered not to go to Pleskau — as originally planned — but through Porkhov. The 11th and 12th ID were to attack near the southern flank of the LVI Army Corps, which was advancing north and northeast of Dno, in order to relieve them. This brought some relief to the panzer group on both flanks, although the gap to the 16th Army still totaled some 50 kilometers.

The situation for the panzer group — which advanced on a wide front between Narva and Lake Ilmen — worsened, because the Soviet leadership succeeded in bringing forward more divisions from the interior. The enemy gained air superiority from week to week. On 7/13 alone there were 354 enemy aircraft over the front, and this was more than the Soviets had in the Baltic provinces at the start of the war. The commitment of Luftflotte 1 had to be split up more and more. German combat aircraft attacked sea targets, fired on enemy positions in Estonia, dropped bombs on the Luga positions, engaged transport trains on Lake Ilmen, flew air reconnaissance up to the Waldai Hills, and fought in deep attack over the marshes of Kholm.

Chapter 3: The Attack

On 7/15 at 0300 hours, the following radio message arrived at the command post of the panzer group:

> "Rear area services of the 8th Panzer Division, 3 kilometers east of Borovichi, are defending against an enemy attack with machine-guns and mortars."

Contact with the 8th Panzer Division was torn asunder. The panzer group did not know where they were. The corps only requested the quick deployment of the SS "Totenkopf" Division. The situation of the 8th Panzer Division was not enviable. Strong enemy forces were attacking Soltsy from the north, while at the same time a new enemy was crossing the Zhelon from the south into the city. The division withdrew from Soltsy and established a defense.

On 7/16, a mobile regiment of the SS "Totenkopf" Division arrived. The SS men immediately advanced bravely against the Soviets and cleared up the situation on the Zhelon. The enemy was so strong that the corps — even after the 3rd Motorized Infantry Division was committed to the defense — bogged down. The right flank of the 4th Panzer Group still ran in front of Lake Ilmen!

Since the beginning of the campaign, the panzer group had registered the following losses:

Dead: 2,025, including 150 officers,
Wounded: 6,450, including 280 officers,
Missing: 315, including 6 officers.

In spite of these local set-backs, General Hoepner was optimistic about making a decisive attack on Leningrad. The XLI Motorized Army Corps had achieved a point of departure after establishing the first Luga bridgehead. The 1st Panzer Division was being relieved by the rapidly deploying 269th ID (Major General von Leyser) and moved closer to the 6th Panzer Division. General Hoepner decided on 7/15 to cover the 100 kilometer distance to Leningrad with the XLI Motorized Army Corps alone, while the LVI Motorized Army Corps could be freed up and take over flank protection. Because the two corps of the 18th Army were to be echeloned in the rear, there was concern for the eventual infantry protection.

The OKH energetically followed up their directive on setting the main emphasis on the right. In spite of all of the plans of the panzer group, the commander of the army group gave in. Field Marshal Ritter von Leeb turned up at the panzer group command post on 7/16 in order to examine the possibility of an attack in the direction of Leningrad. He disapproved of the commitment of the XLI Motorized Army Corps near Narva. However, he also did not wish to remove the LVI Motorized Army Corps from Lake Ilmen.

At this time, the I Army Corps arrived and was subordinated to the panzer group. The corps was tasked with the flank security to the southeast. On 7/17 at 1500 hours, the two East Prussian divisions set out to attack east of Porkhov. They were able to immediately break the initial resistance. The 21st ID won ground directly south of Dno on the following day.

The two divisions did not lessen the pressure of their attack. The enemy's last rear guard was driven out of their trenches. At many locations, the Soviets had no opportunity for an organized withdrawal. The command post of the XXII Rifle Corps near Dno was captured in an assault. Here, only the corps' 415th Communications Battalion, under Commissar Meri, continued to offer resistance (Meri was awarded "Hero of the Soviet Union").

The communications center of Dno was reached on the morning of 7/19 and occupied by the 3rd Infantry Regiment (Colonel Becker). The 11th ID advanced even further and approached the Zhelon over Soltsy. This 200 meter wide river, which flowed into the southwest tip of Lake Ilmen, proved to be an obstacle for a short period of time. On 7/21, the 11th ID crossed over and then captured Soltsy on the following day.

The attack of these infantry divisions freed Manstein's panzer troops from their threatened situation. The SS "Totenkopf" Division, which had, in the meantime, also arrived, relieved the hard pressed 8th Panzer Division and joined in the battle on the north bank of the Zhelon. The German advance bogged down. The Soviets threw new troops into the battle. The I

Army Corps had to cross over to the defense and gradually withdraw. Ryelbitsy was lost.

The threat to the right flank of the panzer group was, nevertheless, blocked. Since 7/21, the X Army Corps of the 16th Army had broken away from the enemy and was able to quickly advance to the north. The 126th ID crossed through Dno to Ryelbitsy, while the right neighboring 30th ID took Morina. The gap to the 16th Army was closed!

The assembly areas on the left flank of the panzer group were now captured. The 269th ID had to repulse a strong counterattack and give up Plyussa. When elements of the 1st Panzer Division and the 118th Motorized Infantry Regiment (36th Motorized Infantry Division) were committed, the battle fizzled out. There was no contact on the left through the rough forested terrain. An 80 kilometer wide gap yawned in front of the 1st Panzer Division! This vacant area was secured from 7/14, when the 36th Motorized Infantry Division closed ranks.

For the time being, 1st and 6th Panzer Divisions stood alone in the small Luga bridgehead south of the Krasnovardeisk-Narva rail line. The Soviets understood the danger posed by this bridgehead and deployed what troops they could here. The transport trains moved on the rail line under the fire of German artillery. The troops unloaded on a free stretch and attacked the positions of the panzer divisions. The cadets and midshipmen of the Leningrad Infantry School, as well as the reservists of the 2nd Peoples' Defense Division, put up a brave effort.

The situation on Lake Peipus improved quickly. The XXXVIII Army Corps had directed its two divisions to the north. The 58th ID attacked Gdov. The reinforced 158th Reconnaissance battalion forced its way into the city on 7/17. The 118th Rifle Division courageously defended the blocks of houses and fell back only when elements of the 36th Motorized Infantry Division joined in the street battle after capturing the airfield on the previous day.

The 36th Motorized Infantry Division moved into the gap between the 269th ID and 1st Panzer Division after capturing Gdov. The 58th ID remained in the city.

"Supply from Pleskau is unthinkable because of the poor road conditions. The division had to rely on its own means. They succeeded in putting a motorized mill in operation, which supplied the division, as well as the civilian population, with bread; however, the baker could not get rid of the taste of oil. The Russians soaked everything in oil that they had to abandon. It is a good thing that there is a salt installation on Lake Peipus, oily bread without salt would have been unbearable."[7]

The 58th ID stood alone on the eastern bank of Lake Peipus. The 1st ID was in combat far to the right in difficult forested terrain. Both of the divisions had the mission to work their way to Narva on the left next to the 6th Panzer Division. On 7/19, the 58th ID set out to the north, committing the 1/209 Infantry Regiment (Major Hartte) to the west. The battalion, reinforced by the 8th Battery of the 158th Artillery Regiment (Lieutenant Colonel Gohde), was to occupy positions on the Narva River and prevent the withdrawal of Soviet troops from Estonia.

The division fought further to the north. Therefore, the western flank became further extended. Thus, additional infantry and artillery battalions took up positions on the Narva. The lead attack elements became smaller and weaker after their reconnaissance battalion was dispatched to the marshy terrain to the east in order to secure that area. The continuation of the march against strong resistance, especially on the Plyussa, became extremely wearisome.

The month of July and its sunny, warm weather came slowly to an end. An attack on Leningrad — desired by the officers and soldiers — did not come about. The OKH itself delayed it. On 7/23, it ordered the main emphasis transferred to the right and the elements removed from the Luga bridgehead. Field Marshal Ritter von Leeb did not pass on these instructions. He compromised and ordered General Hoepner to set the attack of the LVI Motorized Army Corps, which was assembled southeast of Luga, more to the northeast toward Lyuban-Chudovo, instead of to the north.

The LVI Motorized Army Corps fought its way to the Mshaga sector. The I Army Corps closed on this attack. In the meantime, the enemy had become so strong that neither the 3rd Motorized Infantry Division, the SS "Totenkopf" Division, nor the two East Prussian divisions advanced. The

21st ID, advancing on the right, launched a surprise attack on Shimsk on 7/ 22 which did not succeed. Losses increased from day to day, ammunition decreased, and the necessary supply of men and equipment bogged down. The 21st ID, between 7/15 and 7/27, registered losses of 11 officers and 155 soldiers dead, 24 officers and 643 soldiers wounded, and 36 missing.

For the first time, on 27 July, the situation on the entire front between Narva and lake Ilmen somewhat stabilized. Therefore, the army group could again think about continuing the offensive against Leningrad. They organized three attack groups, as follows:

Group Shimsk: I Army Corps, with 11th, 21st ID and elements of the 126th ID; XXVIII Army Corps, with the 121st,
122nd ID, SS "Totenkopf" Division; the 96th ID was held in reserve.

Group Luga: LVI Motorized Army Corps, with 3rd Motorized Infantry Division; SS Police Division, 269th ID.

Group North: XLI Motorized Army Corps, with the 1st, 6th, 8th Panzer Divisions, 36th Motorized Infantry Division and the newly subordinated 1st ID; XXXVIII Army Corps, with 58th ID.

The order of the army group for the resumption of the offensive was issued on this day. In extract form, it ran:

"Commander Army Group North   HQ, 27/7/1941
Ia Nr. 1770/41 g.Kdos.

1. The enemy in front of 16th Army has been destroyed. The remnants are withdrawing through the marshy terrain south of lake Ilmen to the east. 4th Panzer Group is pushing back those enemy forces to its front to the northeast. The 18th Army is defeating enemy forces in the area north of Dorpat.

2. The army group attacks further against the Leningrad area...

3. ...

4. 16th Army ... takes over the right flank of 4th Panzer Group ... Besides occupying the Moscow-Leningrad rail line, it is also important to occupy the road leading from Chudovo to the southeast as soon as possible.

5. 4th Panzer Group ... gives up I Army Corps to the 16th Army. ... They commit the XXVIII Army Corps on their right flank. ... The objective of the 4th Panzer Group is to isolate the area from Leningrad. In addition, they reach the Neva from Schluesselburg to Ivanovskoe, further to the line Marjino — forward of Krasnovardeisk -Taitsy-Vyssotskoe-Peterhov. The mobile forces are to win an advantage and hold on to it until the infantry closes ranks.

6. The attack in the entire area between Lakes Ilmen and Peipus will be uniformly executed, as soon as the XXVIII Army Corps is inserted. In the meantime, attempts are to be made to prepare the most favorable departure positions for the attack as possible.

7. 18th Army: The missions for this army remain unchanged..."

The main emphasis for the new offensive — the last, as many soldiers believed — was ordered. The objective was Leningrad. 4th Panzer Group was to advance as the attack wedge, while the 16th Army had to follow to provide flank protection on the Volkhov. The 18th Army was not to advance on Leningrad. Its mission was the clearing and occupation of Estonia.

On 7/7, the first formations of the army were advancing toward Estonia. The XXVI Army Corps formed an advance detachment on this day whose mission was to move through Fellin toward the north as fast as possible, in order to prevent the Soviets from establishing a defense here. The advance detachment (3/151 Infantry Regiment, 10th Machine-gun Battalion, 2/58 Artillery Regiment, 633rd Heavy Artillery Battalion, 12th Observation Battalion, 161st Engineer Battalion, 1/660 Engineer Battalion, 1/563 Anti-tank Battalion, 4/111 Air Defense Battalion, and 2/161 Medical Battalion) occupied the city of Fellin on 7/8. At the same time, an additional advance detachment, under Colonel Ullersperger, advanced along the Baltic Sea coast and captured Pernau.

Air reconnaissance revealed no enemy forces in the southern portion of Estonia, so they were able to advance quickly to Reval. The 61st and 217th ID left the 18th Army march route and turned to the north to occupy this territory. The XXVI Army Corps remained alone, because the OKH prohibited deploying any more troops on 7/9.

The German soldiers were heartily greeted by the Estonian population. Women and children stood along the streets and offered flowers, milk, cakes, and wine. The houses were decorated with blue-black-white national flags. The soldiers were treated as liberators — however, the Estonians wanted to take part in their own liberation from the Soviet power.

Estonian officers and soldiers, which had fled to Finland or Sweden after their country was occupied by the Red Army, were assembled into an Abwehr battalion of the OKW on the Soko peninsula, 40 kilometers west of Helsinki, for intelligence collection purposes. The first group of volunteer Estonians tried to land in Kuma Bay on 7/5, with the support of the German 1st S Boat Flotilla, in order to actively participate in the liberation. The landing failed due to high seas. A second attempt succeeded on 7/7.

The Estonian Colonel Krug and 40 men made it to land. On the way, one group was located by Soviet warships and destroyed. After a third landing attempt was thwarted by enemy guards, the Abwehr gave up further attempts from the sea. The Estonians constructed a provisional airfield in the forest, by means of which the remaining volunteers were landed by German transports.

Therefore, operation "Erna" began. The Estonian volunteers were directed by radio from the 18th Army. They had to report over the radio situation reports about the Soviet troops and insure that the means of communications and military installations fell into the hands of the Germans as undamaged as possible. The direction of the operation was in the hands of Korvettenkapitaen Cellarius.

The Soviet command posts reacted quickly and tried to destroy the individually operating groups. There were five Estonian troops in the middle of the month of July, and of them, one was directly in the neighborhood of the army headquarters in Wesenberg. The volunteers received reinforcement from a partisan element of Colonel Leithamel, who conducted war against the Soviets on his own.

On the night of 7/10, the XXVI Army Corps continued to advance to the north with its two advance detachments. The advance detachment of the 217th ID reached the cost of Moonsundes in Virtsu on the following day. The enemy was surprised by this rapid attack. Their coastal craft fell under the fire of the German anti-tank guns. However, Soviet bombers soon appeared overhead. The guns of the 1/111 Air Defense Regiment took up positions and shot down nine aircraft in the first wave.

The advance detachment of the XXVI Army Corps, under Major General von Selle, was able to take the Navesti bridge, and then bogged down in heavy resistance. They had to wait for the division to close ranks. The 217th ID occupied positions around Pernau, the 61st ID closed on Fellin. Lieutenant General Haenicke dispatched strong scout troops in the direction of Dorpat, which were repulsed by superior enemy forces. Then, the 18th Army commander decided to form an advance detachment to set out for the I Army Corps in Pleskau and Dorpat.

This advance detachment, under Major General Burdach, (1st Reconnaissance Battalion, 11th Reconnaissance Battalion, and 1/2 Infantry Regiment) moved out during the night and entered Dorpat on 7/11. The portion of the city west of the Em was occupied; however, they could not get any further. The Soviets were encircled in Dorpat. The 16th Rifle Division here committed combat groups against the positions of the Burdach detachment, which suffered heavy losses.

The 18th Army commander realized that they would not clear Estonia, because the enemy was willing to fight to defend every meter of ground. The 254th ID, therefore, was halted in its march to the west and also turned to the north. An advance group of this division attacked by Fellin to the east, but was repulsed by the rear guard of the 11th Rifle Division.

The enemy resistance was fierce. The German soldiers had to clear mine fields, road blocks, and take cover from the constant deep air attacks.

German Luftwaffe support was not possible, because the bomber squadrons were committed to the 4th Panzer Division. The situation in the XXVI Army Corps area was other than "rosy."

The Soviets had far more forces in Estonia than German reconnaissance had located. The headquarters of the 8th Army was in Wesenberg. The army had two subordinate corps: the X Rifle Corps, with the 10th Rifle Division and the 11th and 22nd Motorized Rifle Divisions, as well as naval infantry and the XI Rifle Corps with the 16th, 48th, and 125th Rifle Divisions. Only the X Rifle Corps had all of its formations in combat, while the 48th and 125th Rifle Divisions were hastily planning to march in the direction of Dorpat between Narva and Reval.

The situation did not change on the German side. The divisions were committed in heavy defensive combat where they had to give up ground. The 217th ID broke contact with the enemy and withdrew to the east toward Turgel. The 291st ID, therefore, was hurriedly dispatched to Estonia after they had reached Riga, in order to strengthen the combat forces there.

The dry, sunny weather changed to rain on 7/16, which made the roads impassable. Therefore, German movements were again delayed. The gap between the 217th and 61st ID was closed by the 402nd Wheeled Battalion, while the 254th and 291st ID advanced slowly.

The soldiers of the 61st ID reached the Oberpahlen-Weissenstein road. The 217th ID did not enjoy any initial success, because it fell under a strong air attack. Elements of the 254th ID luckily arrived in the Fellin area, while the 291st ID moved to positions around Pernau. For the time being, the division defended a sector 70 kilometers wide, with the 505th Infantry Regiment, 4/291 Artillery Regiment, 291st Anti-tank Battalion, and the 1/31 Air Defense Battalion!

Further attack was canceled on 7/18. It was now clear that they would not achieve any success with the forces on hand. The 18th Army commander ordered the closing of the remaining divisions. The 254th ID assembled in the rear of the 61st ID. The 291st ID evacuated their advanced field positions in order to confine themselves to Pernau. The 93rd ID — the last reserve of the 18th Army — was moved forward.

It was impossible for the XXVI Army Corps to react. Enemy resistance increased from day to day. The Russians burned part of the forest down in order to give the illusion of an attack. The period of bad weather and the enormous supply and transport problems caused by it prevented movement. Since the Soviet naval forces could fire on the German positions from the sea and force the withdrawal of the coastal batteries, which were established in Virtsu, the left flank was in constant danger. The army group requested corresponding assistance from the Navy.

Enemy destroyers, motor torpedo boats, and submarines often appeared in the Gulf of Riga and disrupted the important shipping lanes. The interdiction of the Moon Straight was not accomplished, partially due to the commitment of aircraft. The Navy force landed their transports. On 7/12, in spite of an attack by nine Soviet destroyers, elements of the "Baltic Sea Training Formation" (naval barges, artillery platforms, and coastal motor boats) and mine sweepers fought their way to the mouth of the Duena, although the Russian blockade was not removed.

Naval operations knew that transport by ship could only be achieved at high cost. They decided not to send any more transports into the Gulf of Riga. The transport ships made the round trip in shallow water from Windau to the coast near Riga in 12 hours.

The battle against the boldly operating Soviet destroyers was naturally conducted by small naval units. Friendly losses kept pace with those of the enemy. From 7/10-31 the losses of both fleets were: German = one each U Boat, mine sweeper, and assault boat, while two steamers and two mine sweepers were damaged; Soviets = two motor torpedo boats, one submarine destroyer, and one ice breaker.

The cruiser "Kirov" broke through the Moon Straight. The trip was only made possible by the barges. This extraordinary naval effort resulted in heavy damage of the destroyers "Smetliviy", "Grozjascij", and Stojkij."

The Army also had to fight further without perceptible relief from the Navy. On 7/21, the army group ordered the 18th Army:

"... on 7/22, launch an attack in northern Estonia through the line Oberpahlen-Turgel to the east, tying up the enemy forces on either side of the Em, in order to destroy the enemy forces located north of Dorpat..."

Chapter 3: The Attack

The XXVI Army Corps attacked on 7/22 at 0300 hours, with the 61st and 254th ID. The 61st ID (the main effort) was reinforced with the 185th Assault Gun Battalion, 2/58 Artillery Regiment, 511th and 637th Heavy Artillery Battalion, and the 622nd Engineer Battalion and 402nd Wheeled Battalion. By noon, the division captured Oberpahlen. The Soviets defended the city tenaciously, however, they were forced to withdraw in the afternoon. The 254th ID ran into some resistance and advanced another 20 kilometers northeast through Oberpahlen.

The attack was continued on the next day. The enemy defended bitterly in and around Jogeva in order to keep the road open from Dorpat to the north. The 217th ID joined in the attack on 7/23 and attacked past Turgel to the north. The enemy divisions which were holding Dorpat — the 48th and 125th — were in danger of being pushed into Lake Peipus. They evacuated their positions on the Em. The 93rd Division and Combat Group Burdach pursued the enemy.

The German attack continued. An advance detachment of the 61st ID reached the bank of Lake Peipus during the night of 7/25, 7 kilometers south of Mustvee. The enemy was encircled here from the north! The 254th ID penetrated into Mustvee and strengthened the encirclement. They paved the way for the first great success in Estonia. On 7/25, the army group, therefore, ordered:

"... Destroy the enemy forces encircled north of Dorpat, screening against the enemy forces in northern and northwestern Estonia, and prepare for a concentrated attack on Reval, with the XXVI Army Corps (61st and 254th ID) on the right and the XLII Army Corps (217th and 219th ID) on the left!"

On 7/22, the commander of the XLII Army Corps (General of Panzer Troops Kuntze) was subordinated to the 18th Army commander and ordered, three days later, for commitment in western Estonia. In this manner, the XXVI Army Corps was relieved and an improved unit distribution was made possible. The XLII Army Corps took command of the 291st ID, which, in spite of all attempts, could not gain ground in the difficult forested terrain.

The enemy forces encircled north of Dorpat were compressed during the following two days, and all of their breakout attempts were repulsed. Combat fizzled out on 7/27. 8,794 Soviet soldiers were taken prisoner, and 68 guns, 5 anti-tank guns, 5 air defense guns, 86 machine-guns, and other materials were taken on the battlefield near Lake Peipus.

The lake flank could now be covered by the army coastal batteries. By 7/27, the following batteries had taken up their positions: Libau, Grobin, Windau, Piso, Mazirbe, Rojen, Markgrafen, Engare, Duena, Estuary, and Ikla. The 207th Security Division had, in the meantime, taken over the protection of the rear area and established local commands in the Estonian cities.

Supply distribution points were set up in Fellin, Pernau, Rujen, and Riga. On 7/26 they had lost: 2,423 tons of ammunition, 819 cubic meters of fuel, and 4,285 tons of rations. Vehicle repair stations were located in Pernau, Fellin, Vorbuse, and Seredka. The Riga-Venden-Fellin rollbahn and the Riga-Venden-Volmar-Vello-Verro-Pleskau rail lines were established as supply routes.

After the supply matters were taken care of and the first reinforcements reached the front line troops, the attack could be continued as ordered by the army group. On 7/29, both corps set out on a line Mustvee-Jogeva-Paimure-Turgel to attack to the north. The East Prussian 61st ID, which was again attacking on the main axis, ran into the seam between the 11th and 22nd Rifle Divisions, which they energetically defended. The attack moved to the north, where it became entangled in the wild forests, with its many swamps and lakes. It developed into a bush war, in which the individual Soviet fighters had the advantage.

The XXVI Army Corps penetrated into the front of the enemy after a two day struggle. The 254th ID took the sector around Rakke, while the 61st ID penetrated into Kuuru. To protect the ever stretching eastern flank, the army committed the 402nd Wheeled Battalion and the 10th Machine-gun Battalion. Because the battle around Mustvee ceased on 7/31, the 176th Infantry Regiment (61st ID) returned to its division.

At the beginning of August, the 18th Army again reorganized. The breadth of the area forced them to establish special main axes. The divisions organized combat groups. The character of the commitment of the army group took shape at the beginning of the war and lasted until the surrender: "The War of the Army of Individuals"! The soldiers were dispersed, because of Soviet air superiority.

The positions of the army formations at the beginning of the month were, from left to right, as follows: Combat Group Hippler (formerly 504th Infantry Regiment) secured Pernau; the XLII Army Corps (HQ Weissenstein) controlled the 217th and 61st ID, which were deployed around Turgel. The XXVI Army Corps, with the 254th, 291st, and 93rd ID were in the center of the front, while the newly formed Combat Group Major General Friedrich (271st Infantry Regiment, 402nd Wheeled Battalion, 161st Anti-tank Battalion, 662nd Engineer Battalion, 536th Heavy Artillery Battalion, and 185th Assault Gun Battalion) took over the security of Lake Peipus; and both the 111th Air Defense Battalion and the 51st Air Defense Battalion guaranteed protection against the constant air attacks. At this time, the army only had the 4/21 Reconnaissance Squadron and the 12th Courier Squadron available for air support, but later the 3/54 Fighter Regiment was transferred to the area.

The attack of the XXVI Army Corps split the seam between the X and XI Rifle Corps. The 254th ID (Lieutenant General Behschnitt) immediately passed through and captured Taps on 8/4. Two days later, the division had covered half the distance to the coast. The 291st ID was not left behind and found itself in an all-out advance along the Taps -Vesenberg road. The 61st ID, which was attacking on the left, overpowered the enemy's 16th Rifle Division in Jaerva-Jaani and Lehtse and attacked along the road and rail line in the direction of Reval.

This attack deprived the Soviets on Lake Peipus of room to maneuver, so they hastily withdrew to the north. Combat Group Friedrich pursued and captured 1,812 prisoners by 8/7. The 1/374 Infantry Regiment (207th Security Division) executed the mopping up operations on the lake shore. On 8/13, the Soviets scuttled the last boat from their Lake Peipus fleet.

The situation changed for the better in the XXVI Army Corps area the further east they attacked. The 254th ID reached the Gulf of Finland near Kunda on 8/7. The XI Rifle Corps withdrew to the east toward Narva, while the X Rifle Corps retreated to the west toward Reval. The Soviet troops in Estonia were scattered!

The 291st ID had taken the city of Wesenberg. Here, the Soviet 118th Rifle Division fled the region on the Kunda. Only the 268th Rifle Division offered any resistance. The 93rd ID pushed the 11th Rifle Division across the Kunda. On this day, the corps reported capturing 2,500 prisoners.

The successful attack of the XXVI Army Corps lead the way for the XLII Army Corps. The enemy ground troops withdrew. On the other hand, the Soviet bomber and deep strike squadrons continuously hammered at the German troops. On 8/7, 90 enemy aircraft bombed the harbor of Pernau. Losses were high; a Reichs labor battalion in the harbor area lost 10 dead and 20 injured.

The friendly Luftwaffe formations were too weak to oppose the enemy bombers. Because the squadrons and groups of the I Air Corps were badly needed in the center of the army group, the only units they had available were from the "Baltic Sea Air Command." The 806th Combat Group, a group from the 54th Fighter Regiment and the 3/125 Reconnaissance group, took off from Riga. On 8/8, a combat squadron destroyed the Soviet destroyer "Karl Marx" in Loksa Bay.

Also on 8/8, the XXVI Army Corps turned its divisions to the east. Their objective was Narva. Enemy resistance stiffened. Heavy artillery was established in the Narva passage. They were supported by the guns of the destroyers, which cruised almost undisturbed in the Gulf of Finland. On 8/13, the 502nd Army Coastal Battery, which took up positions around Kunda, brought some relief. The corps stopped the 254th ID in front of Kunda, turned it 180 degrees, and set it against Reval.

The 93rd and 291st ID were plagued by forests, escarpment, marsh, and field positions. Finally, after days of heavy combat, friendly gun fire was heard from out of the southeast. These were the batteries of the 58th ID on the other side of the Narva River. An advance detachment of the 291st ID, under Colonel Lohmeyer, set out on 8/16 to assault Narva and captured the city on the following day. At the same time, the 1/220 Infantry Regiment (Major Courth) of the 58th ID entered Narva from the south. A detached combat group took Hungerburg at the Narva estuary and established a bridgehead.

Chapter 3: The Attack

"The old border lands were reached. From the top of the Hermann fortress the terrain to the east was flat and forested, it was like the beginning of another world. Estonia, with its blue-black-white banners and its friendly people, was behind us; Russia proper, exotic and unknown, lay before the soldiers..."[8]

On 8/20, the XXVI Army Corps crossed the border, while the XLII Army Corps prepared to attack the last positions of the Soviet 8th Army on the same day. The army commander had already left Reval and set up command on the coastal front near Oranienbaum. Admiral Tribuc, commander of the "Baltic Red Banner Fleet", commanded the remaining army, naval, and air units around Reval. The X Rifle Corps, under Major General Nikolaev, had, from left to right: the 22nd, 16th Rifle Divisions, and 10th Motorized Rifle Division. 14 naval and construction battalions were to secure the coast of the Gulf of Riga.

For weeks, the Soviets constructed fortifications around the Estonian capital. 20,000 soldiers and 25,000 civilians worked day and night on the defensive positions covering an area of 25 by 40 kilometers. All of the roads were mined.

General of Panzer Troops Kuntze attacked with the 254th (on the right), 61st (center), and 217th ID (Left). Combat Groups Major General Friedrich and Colonel Hippler covered the left flank from Pernau through northwestern Estonia. In spite of mine fields and field positions, the attack gained ground. On 8/25, the 254th ID stood before the eastern suburbs of Reval. The 61st ID reached Lake Oberem and the Rae marsh, and the 217th ID reached Nomme. The silhouette of Reval was reflected on the horizon by blue-red flames.

"Reval was burning; ...tracers flew here and there at the edge of the city. The towers of the old Hanseatic city stood black in front of the bright night sky. As the morning fog lifted on the morning of 27 August, the heavy air and artillery activity resumed. Russian cruisers and destroyers joined in the land battle from the harbor, and the earth trembled under the impact of 18 cm shells. At 0630 hours, the 176th Infantry Regiment, along with the 151st Infantry Regiment, set out and, in spite of bitter resistance, reached Punane Road at the edge of the city ... In the afternoon, the regiments were able to shift their positions further into the eastern portion of the city; they were directed to spend the night there. ... On 28 August at 0800 hours, after a short fire strike, the attack was resumed and, by 1330 hours, the 2/151 Infantry Regiment reported by radio that they had reached city hall, almost at the same time as did elements of the 217th ID. Reval was taken! Major Driedger and his battalion had already prepared a reception ceremony at the city hall. As the regiments entered the city in the afternoon, they were met by the jubilant population ..."[9]

Since it was senseless to hold it, the Soviets began evacuating the city on 8/27. The embarkation was in full swing as the German flag waved from the city hall tower. The ships were covered by a wall of fog, so they could not be engaged by the field guns. Admiral Tribuc left Reval with two convoys. The cruiser "Kirov", 18 destroyers, 6 torpedo boats, 28 mine sweepers, 6 submarines, one tanker, and 25 merchant ships made up the first convoy; 6 mine sweepers, 12 escorts, and 60 steamers of various sizes followed. The destroyer "Minsk", on which the Chief of Staff of the fleet, Konteradmiral Panteleev, was located, took up security as the rear guard of the convoy.

Not all of the Soviet soldiers and sailors could be evacuated. 11,432 prisoners, 97 guns, 144 air defense guns, 91 armored vehicles, and 304 machine-guns were left behind in Reval. The mine layer "Amut", the submarine "Kalev", and several merchant ships were sunk in the harbor.

The two convoys steamed to the east. Seven Ju-88 bombers of the 2/77 Combat Group, which were returning from an unsuccessful attack on the locks on the White Sea Canal, sighted the convoys. Their bombs disrupted the ship formation. Naval and merchant ships scattered and ran into the "Juminda Blockade."

The German mine layer "Cobra" (Korvettenkapitaen Dr. Brill) had laid the first blockade in this region of the sea on 8/9, which was expanded to 18 further blockades during the next two weeks by the mine layers "Cobra", "Koenigin Luise", "Kaiser", "Roland", "Brummer", the 5th Mine Sweeper Flotilla, and the 1st and 2nd Motor Torpedo Boat Flotillas. The

Soviet motor torpedo boats and coast guard ships repeatedly attacked the German ships.

Naval Captain Buetow, torpedo boat commander, ordered the strengthening of the blockade and the increase of the density and depth of the mines.

The first success of the "Juminda Blockade" occurred on 8/24, when the Soviet destroyer "Engels" ran into a mine and sank. Then the 29th of August dawned.

Admiral Tribuc lead his convoy into the blockade — the existence of which was unknown to him. The first water columns rose high into the air, explosions tore through the bodies of the ships, fire danced over the decks, and steamers sank into the foaming sea. Stubbornly the ships steamed on and reached Kronstadt. Not all of them made it: the destroyers "Sverdlov", "Artem", "Volodarskiy", "Skoriy", "Kalinin", the escort ship "Sneg", the submarines "S-5", "SC-301", and "SC-324", mine sweeper "T-202", training ship "Zeleznorodosnik", and 35 merchant ships did not! They lay torn to pieces at the bottom of the Gulf of Finland. The flag ship cruiser "Kirov" hit a mine, but was able to make it to a protected harbor at the entrance to Leningrad.

The second largest city in the Soviet Union prepared for the battle that would determine if it was to exist or not. Shortly after the beginning of the war, the population was mobilized for its defense. 160,000 men and 32,000 women reported for voluntary military service in the first weeks of the war!

The first volunteer division was sent to the Luga front on 7/4. Several days later followed the 2nd and 3rd Peoples' Defense Divisions. The new commander of the Northwest Front, Marshal Voroshilov, and his war commissar, the Chief of the Central Committee of the Communist Party of the Soviet Union in Leningrad, Zhdanov, issued a proclamation on 7/14:

"The direct threat of an enemy invasion now hangs over Leningrad, the cradle of the proletarian revolution. While the troops of the Northern Front bravely fight the Nazi hoards and the Finish rifle corps on the entire stretch front the Barents Sea to Reval and Hango and defend each inch of our beloved Soviet land, the troops of the Northwest Front are often not in a situation to repulse the enemy attack..."

With brutal candor, the population was called to unconditional commitment. A special commission under party secretary Kuznetsov took responsibility for the construction of a defensive system in front of the densely populated city. Men, women, children, factory workers, and students built 4000 firing positions, 650 machine-gun nests, 24,000 iron-concrete obstacles for blocking tanks, 4600 bunkers, 700 kilometers of anti-tank ditches, 300 kilometers of wooden obstacles, and 17,000 embrasures along rivers and roads, through forests and meadows, on the edges of the city, and towns. Those not capable of being committed, namely the sick and old — about 656,000 — were transported by rail to the east.

By mid August 1941, Leningrad was a fortress!

"Like one man we came to the defense of our city, our homes, families, honor, and freedom. We wanted to fulfill our sacred duty as Soviet patriots and we would not be subdued by the hated enemy. Vigilantly and without mercy we took up the battle against cowards, trouble makers, and deserters. We instituted the strongest revolutionary order in our city. Armed with iron discipline and Bolshevik organization we opposed the enemy and participated in his destruction!"

These words leaped off of placards every day in Leningrad. Marshal Voroshilov and regional commissar Zhdanov issued a proclamation on 8/20 to the Leningrad party members that ran short and concisely:

"Either the working class of Leningrad will be enslaved or we will stop the fascists!"

This was the situation on the Soviet side: a call for the total commitment of all means to conduct the war! At the same time, the first doubts of a swift success hit the German commands. The Chief of the General Staff of the Army noted in his diary:

Chapter 3: The Attack

"Cooperation between the army groups is not functioning properly. (7/22) The army group reports: the Russians cannot be beaten operationally. They must be broken down into small elements tactically by encirclements. (7/26) What we are now doing is the last attempt to avoid bogging down into positional warfare. We have underrated the Russian colossus! (8/11)"

During the three weeks in which the beginning and the end of this encirclement were scheduled, a crisis arose in the chances of the army group to launch a decisive attack on Leningrad. The time of the German attack was postponed several times during this period. General of Panzer Troops Reinhardt, who wanted to resume the offensive on 7/27 with his XLI Motorized Army Corps, tendered his resignation:

"Its dreadful! ... The decisive opportunity has passed!"

By the beginning of the month of August, the army group was advanced far enough to be directed to continue. According to instructions from the OKH, only one defensive flank could be formed south of Lake Ilmen, therefore, the assigned main emphasis on the right could be strengthened. The 16th Army took command of the I and XXVIII Army Corps, which were to advance in a 50 kilometer wide combat lane (the entire breadth of the army totaled about 190 kilometers). The LVI Motorized Army Corps deployed in front of Luga, the XLI Motorized Army Corps was in the two Luga bridgeheads, and the XXXVIII Army Corps was prepared to attack Narva-Kingisepp.

The I Air Corps was committed in front of the 4th Panzer Group, while the VIII Air Corps was to clear the way for the 16th Army. The corps of General of Aviation Baron von Richthofen was particularly suited for ground combat. It was still committed in Army Group Center's area and could not make it to the new operations area in time.

The supply and transport problems in the area of the 16th Army were the reason that the planned start of the offensive had to be changed five times between 7/22 and 8/6. Finally, as the day of the start of the attack (8/7) approached, the weather changed, so that no aircraft could take off.

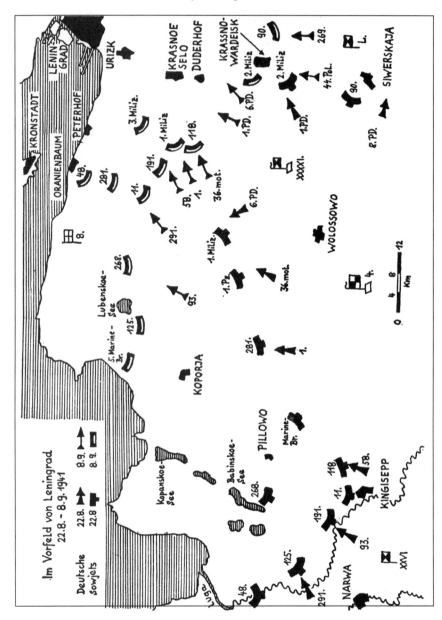

On the battlefield before Leningrad 8/22-9/8/1941

Chapter 3: The Attack

General Hoepner energetically protested against a new delay. The attack preparations in the two Luga bridgeheads were so far advanced that they could not be stopped. The army group yielded to this protest in so far as the XLI Motorized Army Corps was allowed to attack on 8 August, however, the other corps had to wait.

Rain, rain, and more rain characterized the morning of 8 August. Impatiently commanders, officers, and men of the 1st and 6th Panzer Divisions, 36th Motorized Infantry Division, and 1st ID looked at their clocks and at the heavens. Was the attack to be postponed again, because the rain turned all of the roads into mud and no friendly combat aircraft would be able to assist?

At last — several minutes before 0900 hours — a fire strike by the German guns split the gray morning. As the hands of the clocks struck 0900 hours, the infantrymen and engineers rose up. The infantrymen mounted their motorcycles and the tanks began to roll.

The German attack on Leningrad had begun!

The enemy was ready. He was set to defend bitterly, so that, in the first hours of the attack, losses were considerable. Only the 1st Panzer Division was able to gain ground to the northeast. The soldiers of the neighboring 1st ID could only advance a meter at a time. The attack of the 6th Panzer Division and 36th Motorized Infantry Division ran into considerable resistance, which was supported by strong artillery. They were only able to advance 3-5 kilometers, and then they stopped.

The panzer group ordered:

"XLI Motorized Army Corps is to stop at the achieved line and make the necessary arrangements to transition to the defense."

The army group commander intervened and wanted to conduct the attack with the main effort on the right. General Hoepner did not divert from his decision to conduct the main attack with the XLI Motorized Army Corps. Nevertheless, he now had the LVI Motorized Army Corps advance near Luga.

On 8/9, the 1st Panzer Division penetrated into the Soviet front. The division advanced to the north and attacked enemy forces, which were in front of the 6th Panzer Division, in the flank. After two days, the 1st Panzer Division was in open terrain and in the rear of the enemy! The 1st Panzer Division, 6th Panzer Division, and 36th Motorized Infantry Division won some breathing space. The 1st Panzer Division and 6th Panzer Division turned their fronts to the east, while the 36th Motorized Infantry Division moved behind the divisions into the open left flank. The 8th Panzer Division, which was now subordinate to the XLI Motorized Army Corps, moved to the right flank. On 8/14, all of the divisions overcame the forest bottleneck, which cut the Kingisepp- Krasnovardeisk rail line and threw back the enemy.

They were able to continue!

The LVI Motorized Army Corps (from left to right: 269th ID, SS Police Division, and 3rd Motorized ID), which was deployed before Luga, set out with the two divisions on the left on 8/10. After initial gains, the attack bogged down in a well echeloned defensive wall of the Soviet XLI Rifle Corps. Since no progress was made on the following day, the corps halted. The 3rd Motorized Infantry Division was hastily subordinated to the XLI Motorized Army Corps, in order to reinforce the successful breakthrough here.

On 8/15, the commander of the army group arrived at the command post of the panzer group in order to receive a clarification of the mission, which would have the entire panzer group close on Leningrad through Krasnovardeisk. Field Marshal Ritter von Leeb agreed with this view, but refused to deploy any new divisions.

The day was still not over. At 1800 hours, an order arrived which threw all of the plans overboard. The LVI Motorized Army Corps was to make the 3rd Motorized Infantry Division and SS "Totenkopf" Division available to the 16th Army to clear up a crisis situation there. This order, which hit General Hoepner's command post like a bombshell, lead to the following memo:

"During the day, the panzer group had executed the attack with extreme valor, but also with high casualties, on the flank of the group and the enemy withdrew, committing their last reserves. ... Then, for the second time, the panzer group was stopped before reaching its objective, by the army group!"

General Hoepner had to order his divisions to stop and not cross the line Volossovo-Biegunitsy. On 8/16, the 1st Panzer Division occupied Volossovo, 40 kilometers southwest of Krasnovardeisk, with little enemy resistance. Due to the reduction of his combat strength, Reinhardt's corps was only able to cover 10 kilometers a day, although there was no unified Soviet resistance detected.

The 1st Panzer Division, 6th Panzer Division, and 36th Motorized Infantry Division reached the area southwest of Krasnovardeisk on 8/21 and transitioned to the defense on a 150 kilometer wide front. Only the 8th Panzer Division was turned around to the south.

The left flank of the corps was protected as long as the 58th ID was able to make contact with the 1st ID from the south. The 1st ID (Lieutenant General Kleffel) penetrated into Kingisepp from the east on 8/17, while the 209th Infantry Regiment (Lieutenant Colonel Kreipe) of the 58th ID also reached the city from the south. Resistance was stiff; especially valorous were the efforts of the Soviet 263rd Machine-gun Battalion and the sailors of the Fleet Technical School.

On 8/18, the XXXVIII Army Corps was taken from under the panzer group and, with the 1st and 58th ID, assigned to the 18th Army. General von Kuechler's army was to participate in the conquest of Leningrad. They had to form the left flank of the attack wedge.

How were things on the right flank?

At the end of July, the 16th Army had established contact with the panzer group. The I Army Corps (11th and 21st ID) was deployed in the direction of Lake Ilmen. The XXVIII Army Corps, with the 121st and 122nd ID, followed the East Prussian corps in order to slip closer to the panzer group.

Lake Ilmen, the triangle-shaped, fish rich body of water — 659 square kilometers at low tide and 2230 square kilometers at high tide — divided the II and X Army Corps of the 16th Army into a widely separated front. The Soviets knew the importance of this area. The headquarters of Marshal Voroshilov was located in Novgorod, on the northern tip of Lake Ilmen.

The 48th Army of Lieutenant General Akimov was ordered to defend the western bank of the lake. From left to right were deployed the 70th and 237th Rifle Divisions and the 1st People's Defense Division, awaiting the German assault.

The I Army Corps quickly arrived. The 21st ID and the 126th Rheinish Westphalian Infantry Division (the latter belonging to the X Army Corps) reached the southwestern portion of Lake Ilmen at the same time. The 21st ID took Shimsk, while from the 126th ID, only the 424th Infantry Regiment crossed over the Zhelon and worked their way toward the bank of the lake to the north. The entire attack along the coast, with the objective of Novgorod, began on 8/12 at 0500 hours. The 21st ID advanced on the left, while the 424th Infantry Regiment moved to the right of the road. The 11th ID moved still further to the left and, on the third day of the attack, cut the Luga-Novgorod rail line.

The soldiers of the 21st ID (Lieutenant General Sponheimer) and the reinforced 424th Infantry Regiment (Lieutenant Colonel Hoppe) fought their way over the many rivers flowing into Lake Ilmen to the northeast. On the morning of 8/15, the many towers of Novgorod appeared before the eyes of the German soldiers.

Novgorod, one of the oldest settlements of the great Russian Empire, was the objective of the 21st ID. The city was founded by Rurik during the time of Charlemagne and became a free city in the middle ages. It has a rich history and only once — in the 17th Century — was it assaulted by an enemy. On 8/15, the Soviet 48th Army radioed the defenders of Novgorod, the 305th Rifle Division, 128th Motorized Rifle Division, and the 21st Tank Brigade:

"Novgorod is to be held to the last man!"

It was at 1600 hours on this day that General Busch, commander of the 16th Army, arrived at the 424th Infantry Regiment. At the same time, the motors of the stukas began to drone. The aircraft of the VIII Air Corps, which were to bombard the fortifications of Novgorod, raced through the air.

Chapter 3: The Attack

The last stuka squadron flew at 1730 hours. Then smoke and fire billowed. A gray wall appeared in front of the city, blazing up from the explosions. The batteries hurled new fires into mortally wounded Novgorod.

As the clock struck 1800 hours, the infantry assaulted, penetrating into the Russian walls. With fixed bayonets and flinging hand grenades, they fought their way to the entrances to the anti-tank ditches and reached the southern suburb of Troitki.

The I Army Corps decided to leave Novgorod during the night, marching the bulk of their forces to the west toward Chudovo. The 3rd Infantry Regiment (Colonel Becker) of the 21st ID and the 424th Infantry Regiment (Lieutenant Colonel Hoppe) of the 126th ID were to continue the fight for Novgorod. Both commanders thought they should stop their attack.

"The 1/424 Infantry Regiment (Senior Lieutenant Richter) entered Novgorod on 8/16 at 0400 hours and found the main part of the fortress, which was destroyed by the stukas, unoccupied. The companies immediately occupied the interior of the fortress as the Russian rear guard was withdrawing, and Kaufmann and Greven of the Propaganda Company raised the flag at 0700 hours on the main tower. The regiment commander reported to the 21st ID: 424th Infantry Regiment has taken the fortress and Novgorod at 0600 hours!"[10]

The following 3rd Infantry Regiment marched past Novgorod, in order to cross the Volkhov north of the city, establish a bridgehead, and from there occupy the Volkhov island and East Novgorod. This plan failed on 8/17. The 3rd Infantry Regiment crossed the river near Stininka, but two battalions bogged down in front of the northeastern edge of the city, while 1/3 Infantry Regiment secured to the east around Sarele.

The 424th Infantry Regiment and the 2/23 Infantry Regiment were inserted into the bridgehead in order to support the attack on the following day. Preparations were made on 8/18. However, as the time for the attack approached, a storm arrived and caused torrential rains that turned the terrain into mud. Then stukas showed up at 1700 hours. As the last bombs fell, the soldiers, wet and covered in mud, stood up in their trenches and attacked. The 2/424 Infantry Regiment (Major Schilling) and the 2/23 Infantry Regiment (Major Spiethoff) threw the Soviets from their trenches and stood in East Novgorod two hours later. The 3/424 Infantry Regiment (Captain Cappel) took up the flank protection in the east, marched to Mal-Volkhov, and occupied the monastery the following day.

The first Volkhov bridgehead existed! The enemy, especially the 19th Rifle Regiment, attacked the monastery bastion — which was called "Alcazar" — several times in the following days. The German bridgehead near Novgorod held!

The I Army Corps directed the 11th ID, after it had reached Vyachichi on bottomless roads, to follow behind the 21st ID and fan out to the Volkhov. The 11th ID took charge of the Novgorod bridgehead and the area north of it. The 44th Infantry Regiment stood to the right, the 2nd Infantry Regiment in the center, and the 23rd Infantry Regiment in the north.

The Volkhov front was established!

A front, the most wretched in Russia; a front which would know six months of winter and six months of mud; a front which seemed to have been there since the creation of the universe; a front that was held long after the war for Germany was lost!

The 21st ID, lead division of the I Army Corps, marched to the north in order to neutralize the important Leningrad-Moscow rail line near Chudovo. An advanced combat group, under Major von Glasov (21st Reconnaissance Battalion, 2/37 Artillery Regiment, 666th Assault Gun Battery, 272nd Army Air Defense Battalion, 9th Smoke Generation Battalion, 24th Infantry Regiment, and 45th Infantry Regiment), was directed to Chudovo. The 45th Infantry Regiment followed quickly and captured Luka, southeast of the city.

The division assembled in Glushitsa for the final assault on Polisti. The 21st Reconnaissance Battalion assaulted Korpovo on the Keresti and provided flank protection to the west. The 24th Infantry Regiment fought east of Chudovo, while the 45th Infantry Regiment (Colonel Chill) attacked the front of the city. The 2nd Company was the first to the Keresti. Staff Sergeant Feige reached the road bridge with his platoon at noon. Lieutenant Kahle occupied the undamaged railroad bridge. The 24th Infantry Regiment (Colonel Heinrichs) was responsible for the remaining bridges in Chudovo. The 2/45 Infantry Regiment (Lieutenant Colonel Matussik) set out to the east on the afternoon of 8/20, overran the Soviets between Sloboda and Volokhovo, captured the large railroad bridge, and established the second German bridgehead on the eastern bank of the Volkhov!

The Soviet 311th Rifle Regiment could not offer any more resistance and quickly withdrew to Kirishi. The 21st ID, which bore the main brunt of the combat — in the past ten days, they lost 215 dead and 602 wounded — regrouped and moved further. After six days, the Volkhov was reached near Grusino. Here, the division transitioned to the defense. Now, from Novgorod to Grusino stood the 11th, 126th, and 21st ID.

The Volkhov front was fortified. The XXVIII Army Corps followed to the left of the I Army Corps attack. They attacked with the 122nd (Left) and the newly arrived 96th ID (right) to the northwest, while the 121st ID marched to the northeast, cutting the Leningrad-Moscow rail line and occupying Tossno with the 21st ID. Therefore, flank protection to the east for the 4th Panzer Group was secured so that they could now assault Leningrad.

The Soviet High Command saw the danger posed by the attack along the Volkhov, which isolated Leningrad from central Russia. The former North Front — which included the struggle against Finland — was dissolved. The Karelian Front and the Leningrad Front emerged, and the latter had control over the troops in front of Leningrad. Lieutenant General Popov was the commander, and Zhdanov was a member of the war council.

The commander of the Northwest Front was changed. Marshal Voroshilov was pulled out. Major General Sobennikov took command. He was responsible for conducting combat on the Volkhov and in the Lake Ilmen area. To secure the seam between the Leningrad and Northwest Fronts, two new armies were inserted into position. These were the 52nd Army under Lieutenant General Klykov and the 54th Army under Marshal Kulik, who had been the Chief of Staff for Marshal Budenny in the Ukraine. Both of these armies remained directly subordinate to Moscow.

The German side regrouped at the same time. The OKH understood that the army group could not capture Leningrad with the forces available to it. Therefore, on 8/16, it ordered that the XXXIX Motorized Army Corps, with the 12th Panzer Division and 18th and 20th Motorized Infantry Divisions be transferred from Army Group Center to the northern area.

The XXXIX Motorized Army Corps (General of Panzer Troops

Schmidt) arrived in the Army Group North area on 8/24. The 18th Motorized Infantry Division (Major General Herrlein) was the first large formation to make contact with the enemy near Chudovo on this day. The 20th Motorized Infantry Division and the 12th Panzer Division marched between Shimsk and Novgorod.

Thus, the German front in the southeast received considerable reinforcement, which would make it possible to encircle Leningrad and give emphasis on the right, long demanded by the OKH. The plan of Army Group North was as follows: 16th Army closes the front on the Volkhov and south of Lake Ilmen in the Waldai Hills to the east. The newly formed "Group Schmidt" (XXXIX Motorized Army Corps and XXVIII Army Corps) completed the encirclement of Leningrad from the southeast, the 4th Panzer Group from the south, and the 18th Army from the west.

The center of the southern attack front was still lagging behind after the left flank already stood in front of Krasnovardeisk and the right flank near Chudovo. The Soviet formations were still fighting in the Luga positions! A long time passed before the L Army Corps made the preparations for the frontal attack on the Luga positions.

The two divisions — the 269th ID, SS Police Division — were located several kilometers south and southwest of Luga. The SS Police Division (SS Brigadefuehrer Muelverstedt) advanced right up to the Luga next to the city and assaulted several bunkers. To the left of the 269th ID were elements of the 285th Security Division, which maintained contact with the 8th Panzer Division. The 122nd ID of the XXVIII Army Corps had to participate in the first phase of the attack in order to encircle the city of Luga from the east.

The L Army Corps (General of Cavalry Lindemann) began to assault the core of the Luga positions on 8/22. The advance ran into problems. The Soviets had to literally be shot out of their bunkers and defensive positions. The 269th ID (Major General von Leyser) fought its way slowly to the west from Luga into the river bend to the north, while the SS Police Division approached Luga directly.

The Soviet XLI Rifle Corps defended bitterly and launched a counterattack with tanks. The L Army Corps destroyed 43 enemy tanks up to 24 August and assaulted 115 bunkers. The SS Police Division captured the city of Luga on the same day and took 500 prisoners. The losses of the SS Police Division were so high, though, that the division was no longer combat capable to continue the attack on 8/25.

The frontal advance was facilitated by the commitment of the 8th Panzer Division (Major General Brandenberger). The division — itself only at one-third of its original combat strength — reached Siverskaya on the Luga-Krasnovardeisk rail line. The 8th Panzer Division turned almost 180 degrees to the south in order to work opposite the L Army Corps. Simultaneously, the 122nd and 96th ID were coming from the east. The 122nd ID was stopped northeast of Luga on 8/28 in order to continue in the direction of Tossna.

The 96th ID (Lieutenant General Schede) received an order on 8/24 to immediately continue from its Luga bridgehead near Oredesh to the northwest in order to block the withdrawal route of the Soviets, which were retreating from Luga to the north. In spite of pouring rain and completely washed out roads — only the infantry could make it, since vehicles and guns became hopelessly stuck in the mud — the division reached the Novinka railroad station on 8/27 and, therefore, blocked the last withdrawal possibility for the enemy.

The Soviet leadership ordered the three encircled divisions to break through to the north in the direction of Leningrad as best as possible in small groups. The staff of the 8th Panzer Division took control of the battlefield on the German side. The friendly forces for this battle were very weak, because slowly all of the regiments and mobile reconnaissance battalions were removed. Even the supply companies had to be committed to mop up the Luga pocket. The pocket was split on 9/7, and on 9/15 the last resistance collapsed. 20,000 prisoners were taken. The prerequisite for the encirclement of Leningrad was accomplished.

The German armies approached the city of Peter the Great, or the "Cradle of the October Revolution", from three sides. The attack of the XXXIX Motorized Army Corps (General of Panzer Troops Schmidt), which was to be the "death stroke" for Leningrad, did not initially come off. The 18th Motorized Infantry Division had to shift to the north instead of the west. From here, the Soviets attacked the Lyuban-Chudovo rail line with considerable forces in order to reclaim this important life line. The division was subordinated to the I Army Corps to simplify command and control.

Meanwhile, the 12th Panzer Division (Major General Harpe) arrived and attacked through the 121st ID, and occupied Lyuban on 8/25. The infantry division withdrew from the rollbahn in order to free the way for the panzer forces. The 12th Panzer Division still made it to Ishora, and captured the town on 8/28. Then they bogged down. Their forces moved no further.

The third division of the XXXIX Motorized Army Corps — the 20th Motorized Infantry Division (Major General Zorn) — could not give any assistance to the 12th Panzer Division. The division was committed to the north toward the Neva, along with the subordinate 424th Infantry Regiment (126th ID), in order to secure the area opposite Lake Ladoga. It was, therefore, established on 8/31 that, due to the enemy situation, the XXXIX Motorized Army Corps would be omitted from an attack on Leningrad!

The operations area of Army Group North not only included the Baltic Provinces and Ingermanland. The large, partially unknown area south of Lake Ilmen also belonged to them. The right flank of the 16th Army stood, at the beginning of August, on a widely separated front west of Lovati, which ran in an almost perfect north-south direction on the southern portion of Lake Ilmen. On the extreme right flank, the L Army Corps, with the 251st ID and the 253rd ID, advanced north of Nevel (the corps commander was later transferred to the Luga Front, the two infantry divisions went to Army Group Center). The II Army Corps closed on Kholm with its three major formations — the 12th, 32nd, and 123rd ID.

The continuing rain prevented all movement, so that they had to transition to the defense.

The X Army Corps (General of Artillery Hansen) was slowly advancing to the east, south of the lake. The Soviet positions west of Staraya Russa were thought to be strong and deeply echeloned. The XXII Rifle Corps defended the forest and water lands with the 180th, 183rd, 237th and 254th Rifle Divisions, and the 1st Tank Brigade.

The 16th Army commander ordered Staraya Russa to be attacked from the front. The 126th ID (Lieutenant General Laux), 30th ID (Lieutenant General Tippelskirch), and 290th ID (Lieutenant General Baron von Wrede) were to make preparations from the left to the right. The first day of the attack was successful, however, on the second day the infantrymen ran into strong defensive fire. Only the commitment of the VIII Air Corps of General Baron von Richthofen on 8/7 paved the way of the 126th ID into the burning Staraya Russa. The 3/426 Infantry Regiment (Major Bunzel) was the first into the city.

The 126th ID and 30th ID attacked further across the Polisti up to Redya and Lovati. The 290th ID turned to the south in order to provide flank protection. Between here and the II Army Corps, which was still near Kholm, yawned a huge gap. Here the Soviet High Command saw its chance. They subordinated the 34th Army (Major General Kachanov) to the Northwest Front, with the mission of conducting a counterattack through Staraya Russa toward Dno, in order to cut off the entire right flank of Army Group North.

The Soviet 34th Army attacked into the gap on 8/12, with the XXI, XXII, XXIV Rifle Corps, and the XXV Cavalry Corps — in all, eight divisions (3rd, 254th, 259th, 163rd, 257th, 262nd, 202nd, and 245th Rifle Divisions from right to left). In their first assault, these strong forces threw the German security back.

The Soviets not only advanced to the west, but also to the north. After 24 hours, the tanks with the red stars had gained 22 kilometers to the west and halted only 16 kilometers south of Staraya Russa. The X Army Corps was in danger of being encircled.

General of Artillery Hansen immediately ordered his 126th and 30th ID to turn around toward the neighboring 290th ID threatened on their right. This did not do away with the danger. Since 8/15, four new Soviet divisions were shoved into the 80 kilometer wide gap to II Army Corps. On this day, twelve enemy divisions attacked into the open right flank of the 16th Army!

In this threatening situation, the army group commander decided to stop the advance of the panzer group and quickly direct the LVI Motorized Army Corps toward Dno and Staraya Russa. The 3rd Motorized Infantry Division and SS "Totenkopf" Division took four days to cover the 260 kilometer stretch from Luga to Kholm. Then they attacked from the move to the northeast into the flank of the 34th Soviet Army.

The enemy had already split the 30th and 126th ID. Finally, on 8/20, the lead attack elements of the SS "Totenkopf" Division and the 30th ID, which were moving in the opposite direction, took the upper hand! The enemy was destroyed and the X Army Corps freed. More than 10,000 Soviet soldiers were taken prisoner, and 141 tanks and 246 guns — including the first "Stalin Organ" — fell into German hands.

General of Infantry von Manstein continued the attack to the east with his two divisions. The X Army Corps closed with the 30th and 290th ID (The 126th ID was transferred to the Volkhov). It was the army's plan to not only capture the Waldai Hills, but also advance on the eastern side of the Volkhov to the northeast. The II Army Corps was to cover the flank to the east through Kholm.

These plans were disrupted by new rains. The mud prevented the commitment of tanks. Air reconnaissance revealed that the Soviet front between Kholm and Staraya Russa was being fortified. Here alone were the 11th, 27th, and 34th Armies. The 16th Army was, therefore, compelled to give up their initial operational plans and execute an advance to the east.

The attack began on 8/31. The 290th ID, as the left flank division, had to extend its front to a width of 40 kilometers and could no longer cross the Kolpinka. The 30th ID, 3rd Motorized Infantry Division, and SS "Totenkopf" Division tied up the 11th and 34th Armies with flanking attacks to facilitate the advance of the II Army Corps, which was reinforced by the 19th Panzer Division from Army Group Center. The II Army Corps attacked with the 19th Panzer Division in the lead (Lieutenant General von Knobelsdorf) to the northeast.

"As we reached the high ground about 6 kilometers south of Demyansk on 9/7, the 27th Panzer Regiment (Lieutenant Colonel Thomale) was committed to the attack. The 4th Infantry Regiment (Colonel Falley) of the 32nd ID dismounted from their tanks... We next came upon a large forest. About 2 kilometers before Demyansk the lead elements ran into enemy tanks, which were destroyed. At the same time, Russian infantry attacked, so that our infantry regiment had to dismount from the tanks and throw the Russians back. The tank attack continued. Small delays were caused by the blowing of small bridges and road demolition... The objective, for the time being, was the river bridge over the Yavon. Demyansk was quickly taken."[11]

The second division of the LVII Motorized Army Corps — the 20th Panzer Division — also arrived in Demyansk and reinforced the German forces, which immediately attacked to the east. In this manner, a scout troop from the 48th Infantry Regiment (12th ID) became the first German troop of the Wehrmacht to reach the Volga on 9/8 and capture the Volga-Vershove source. The 30th, 32nd ID, and 19th and 20th Panzer Divisions drove the Soviets before them. The 30th ID and 19th Panzer Division encircled a strong enemy group around Molvotitsy. The 12th ID continued the march to the east and reached Lake Seeliger.

Success was achieved: the right flank of the army group was freed, the German front was extended up to and into the western border of the Waldai Hills, and the enemy was forced onto the defense! The combat of the last two weeks resulted in the capture of 35,000 prisoners and the destruction or capture of 117 tanks and 254 guns.

After the conclusion of this battle, the OKH ordered the immediate return of the 19th and 20th Panzer Divisions to Army Group Center on 9/24. The 123rd ID (Major General Rauch) relieved the latter panzer units and widened the friendly front to Ostachkov, the eastern-most and, at the same time, the southern-most frontal position of Army Group North.

From here they had no contact with Army Group Center, only swamp, forest, lakes, and more swamps.

The decisive combat in northwestern Russia was not in the Waldai Hills, but near Leningrad. The Moscow government was willing to hold the city under all circumstances and at any price.

The defensive work was carried out at the end of August/beginning of September just as enthusiastically as before. Lieutenant General Popov, commander of the Leningrad Front, turned over his command to Marshal Voroshilov. He did not have the heart to demand the civilian population to work until their last ounce of strength was spent. Therefore, on 9/11, Moscow dispatched Army General Zhukov to Leningrad and appointed him commander of the Leningrad Front. With Zhukov arrived General Voronov, as the direct representative of the Soviet High Command.

Army General Zhukov arranged the final measures for transforming Leningrad into a fortress. He entrusted Major General Sviridov with the command of all heavy artillery and appointed the commander of the sea defenses, Konteradmiral Sakhvarov, as commandant of Leningrad. He took responsibility for the deployment and commitment of the People's Defense Divisions. By September, six divisions were march-ready. This number was later increased to 20, so that, finally, 300,000 men of all callings and all ages were under arms.

The outer-most defensive line, which ran a distance of 25 kilometers from the edge of the city, was occupied. Leningrad itself was divided into six defensive sectors. The Communist Party functionaries were mobilized to support the Army. The Secretary of the Central Committee of the Communist Party of the Soviet Union, the regional and city committees, Shtykov, Zhdanov, Kuznetsov, Kapustin, and Soloviev were advising members of the front commands.

The home economy and industry worked exclusively for war production. 92 large factories, including the Kirov and Ishora works, were transferred to the interior. The air defense of the city lay in the hands of the II Air defense and VII Fighter Aviation Corps, to which in August were sent four air regiments and in September two air groups. At this point in time, the Soviet air forces were superior to the German.

This made it possible to fly long range bombers to Berlin. The first such sorties occurred during the night of 9 August. Five type DB-3 aircraft of the "Baltic Red Banner Fleet", under the command of Colonel Preobrazhanskiy and Captains Yefremov, Plotkin, Khoklov, and Greshnikov took off in the evening twilight on 8/8 from the Oesel airfield. The aircraft made a wide loop over the sea and approached the capital of the Reich from Stettin, where they dropped their bombs.

At the beginning of September 1941, the Red Army stood in front of Leningrad in the following dispositions, from right to left: 5th Marine Brigade, 125th, 268th Rifle Divisions, 2nd People's Defense Division, 11th, 191st, and 118th Rifle Divisions. These formations occupied the first defensive belt; in the second line were: the 48th and 281st Rifle Divisions, and the 1st and 3rd People's Defense Divisions. The divisions were not in contact with the enemy, because the 42nd Army (Lieutenant General Ivanov) and the 55th Army (Major General Lazarev) were still fighting in front of them.

In the first week of September, Army Group North made the necessary preparations for the concluding phase of the offensive on Leningrad. The 4th Panzer Division was again the main effort. They were organized into three groups. The XXVIII Army Corps (General of Infantry Wiktorin) attacked with the 122nd, 96th, and 121st ID (from right to left) on either side of the Chudovo-Leningrad rail line from the east, where the 122nd ID stood on the right flank on the Neva. The L Army Corps (General of Cavalry Lindemann) came out of the area south of Krasnovardeisk with the 269th ID and the SS Police Division. The XLI Motorized Army Corps (General of Panzer Troops Reinhardt) was deployed southwest of the same city with the 1st and 6th Panzer Divisions and the 36th Motorized Infantry Division. The 18th Army participated in the attack from the west with the XXXVIII Army Corps (General of Infantry von Chappuis). The 291st ID had taken Ropsha, south of the marching 58th and 1st ID.

Again, Luftflotte 1 mobilized all available forces. The I Air Corps (General of Aviation Foerster) commanded Combat Groups 1, 4, 76, and 77, Fighter Group 54, and Pursuit Interceptor Group 26. The combat squadrons took off from Dno, Saborovka, Korove Selo, and Roskopole, and fighters and pursuit interceptors from Sarudine. The VIII Air Corps (General of Aviation Baron von Richthofen) participated in the upcoming commitment with Combat Group 2, Fighter Group 27, 2/210 Combat Group, and 2/2 Training Group from Vereten, Relbitsy, Spasskaya Polisti, Prikhonk, and Lyuban. At the beginning of September, a total of 203 combat aircraft, 60 stukas, 166 fighters, 39 pursuit interceptors, and 13 reconnaissance aircraft were available. Air power of this magnitude would never be seen by the Germans again in the northern sector of the Eastern Front!

The attack began on 9/9 at 0930 hours. The objective was no longer the conquest of, but was now the encirclement of Leningrad. Due to ground fog, there was no air support during the first two hours of the attack. The infantrymen, engineers, wheeled infantrymen, and anti-tankers had to meet the enemy on their own. The stukas and bombers unloaded their murderous cargo at 1100 hours.

The 36th Motorized Infantry Division, which stood in the first line with the 118th Infantry Regiment on the main effort, penetrated into the Soviet fortifications on either side of Bolshie Starokvoritsy and worked their way four kilometers up the slowly rising terrain. The 1st Panzer Division was committed next to the division, in order to complete the breakthrough on the following day. The 1st Panzer Division was attacked by the enemy in the flank, and had to defend on the Krasnovardeisk-Krasnoe Selo road. On the other hand, the 118th Motorized Infantry Regiment (Colonel Casper) captured the Duderhof Barracks after a battle lasting several hours, and assaulted Hill 143 at 2045 hours. Therefore, German soldiers stood on the dominant heights of Duderhof.

The 6th Panzer Division advanced only slowly on the first two days of the attack. They first had to suppress 32 bunkers and two anti-tank defenses before they could even think about advancing. The situation developed similarly in the L Army Corps area of operations. The SS Police Division bogged down on 9/10 in front of Krasnovardeisk. On the other hand, the 269th ID penetrated from the southeast into the city. The Soviet 42nd Army had committed strong forces here. The street battle lasted until noon of 9/13, and then Krasnovardeisk fell.

The attack was more successful and quicker on the left flank of the XLI Motorized Army Corps. The 1st Panzer Division organized a combat group under Major Dr. Eckinger (1/113 Infantry Regiment, 6/1 Panzer Regiment, and 2/73 Artillery Regiment), which captured the town of Duderhof and "Kahle [Bald] Hill" on 9/11. Senior Lieutenant Darius, commander of the 6th Company of the 1st Panzer Regiment, radioed at 1130 hours:

"I see Petersburg and the sea!"

The attack of the 18th Army, which was advancing further to the left, also developed favorably. The 291st, 58th, and 1st ID marched on Krasnoe Selo. On 9/11, the 1st ID reached the military training area in the vicinity of the city. Here, they found the parade field of the former Tsarist gardens — and the inner ring of the second defensive belt of Leningrad. The 58th ID captured Krasnoe Selo on 9/12. The men from North Germany saw Leningrad and the sea from here.

Chapter 3: The Attack

The 58th ID — which was taken over on 9/13 by General Dr. Altrichter — turned northeast toward the coast. The 209th Infantry Regiment marched on Urizk. Senior Lieutenant Sierts, Lieutenant Lembke, and Sergeant Pape of the 2/209 Infantry Regiment were the first to enter the terminal station of the city's trolley car. Here the sign read: "10 kilometers to Leningrad!"

The 1st ID was moving behind the 58th ID and was inserted on the left. The East Prussians won ground to the north and stood on the sea at Strelnya! On 9/20, the Soviet front was broken through! Strong enemy forces lay behind the German front at Peterhof and Oranienbaum! The 291st ID and the 254th ID also penetrated forward and prevented the Soviets from breaking out of Oranienbaum.

The "Oranienbaum Pocket" was established!

1st Panzer Division and 36th Motorized Infantry Division assaulted south of Krasnoe Selo and, in spite of a superior enemy attack supported by tanks, advanced further and reached Pulkovo on 9/15. Leningrad lay directly in front of the soldiers of General Reinhardt.

The rapid advance of the two motorized divisions delineated the attack of the L Army Corps to the northeast, with the 269th ID and the SS Police Division. Pushkin — formerly Tsarskoe Selo, the summer residence of the Tsars — was the objective of these divisions. The 1st Panzer Division detached another combat group on 9/17 to help the 2nd SS Police Regiment during the conquest of the city and the Tsar's palace.

It was the last commitment and the last success of the 4th Panzer Group in front of Leningrad! The 18th Army now arrived south of Leningrad. General Hoepner turned over the sector of his panzer group to General von Kuechler.

In accordance with directive Nr. 35 of 9/5 1941, the 4th Panzer group returned to Army Group North. Hitler explained to the Chief of his General Staff on this day that the mission near Leningrad was fulfilled. The city was now a secondary theater of war. The German Army now had to concentrate on Moscow. Leningrad still had to be encircled in the east and contact had to be made with the Fins on Lake Ladoga.

The VIII Air Corps, which formerly supported the right flank of the German attack groups, also had to give up its airfields and transfer to the middle sector of the Eastern Front. The air corps had to clear the way for

"Group Schmidt" during the attack into the Leningrad defensive positions and to Lake Ladoga.

The XXVIII Army Corps, with its three divisions — from right to left: 121st, 96th, and 122nd ID — advanced along the Chudovo-Leningrad rail line and road and penetrated into the first defensive line between Sluzk and Ivanskoe on the Neva. On 9/15, Sluzk was captured by the 667th Assault Gun Battery (Senior Lieutenant Luetzow). The German soldiers did not make it to Kolpino. Here, the Soviets directed their factory-new tanks — the superior "T-34", against which our anti-tank guns were almost worthless — directly from the assembly line to the battle.

The strength of the XXVIII Army Corps was exhausted.

The complete isolation of Leningrad from the outside world resulted from an attack, which was initiated further to the east. The 20th Motorized Infantry Division (Major General Zorn), which was located in the vicinity of Mga, was reinforced on 9/2 and organized into two attack groups, which were to move to Lake Ladoga. Colonel Count von Schwerin commanded the left group (2/76 Infantry Regiment, 3/30 Infantry Regiment, 1/20 Artillery Regiment, and others), and Lieutenant Colonel Hoppe the right group (424th Infantry Regiment, 1/76 Infantry Regiment, 1/29 Panzer Regiment, and others). One group, under Colonel Thomashi (1/424 Infantry Regiment, 3/3 Infantry Regiment, and 126th Anti-tank Battalion) had to provide flank cover to the east.

The attack of the three groups bogged down on the first day (9/6) after 500 meters. It was impossible, in this forested and shrubbery covered wilderness, to advance any further. Tanks, guns, and trucks became stuck. When all appeared lost, the 11th Company of the 424th Infantry Regiment (Lieutenant Leliveldt) was able to find a gap in the enemy front. The right combat group broke through and captured the railroad intersection north of Mga that evening.

The next day saw the capture of Sinyavino and additional terrain gains on Lake Ladoga. Supply came to a standstill, because during the night Sinyavino was set to flame by exploding ammunition. As the morning sun rose over the horizon on 9/8, Schluesselburg lay in front of the German soldiers.

Chapter 3: The Attack

An advanced scout troop could find no further Soviets. Stukas attacked the city at 0845 hours. Then Lieutenant Colonel Hoppe came to his own decision — contact with the division and the corps was lost long ago — to attack. The battalions of the 424th Infantry Regiment attacked at 0700 hours, and 40 minutes later, Sergeant Wendt (3rd Company of the 424th Infantry Regiment) raised the German flag on the Schluesselburg church tower.

The stukas of the VIII Air Corps already took off. At 0815 hours, Lieutenants Pauli and Fuss, after trying for three quarters of an hour, made contact by radio with a friendly battery near Gorodok. This unit passed the message on by radio to the 20th Motorized Infantry Division, which was able to have the stukas stopped shortly before reaching Schluesselburg.

Leningrad was decisively blocked!

Three Soviet armies were encircled in the city! They were: the 23rd Army (Lieutenant General Tserepanov), which occupied the river bank on the Neva front between Lake Ladoga and Kolpino. Major General Lazarev commanded the 55th Army, which was deployed in the center of the front. The 42nd Army (Lieutenant General Ivanov, after 9/16 Major General Fedyuninskiy) stood in the west with its right flank on the Baltic Sea.

The 8th Army (Major General Cherbakov, after 9/25 Lieutenant General Shebaldin) stood fast in the Oranienbaum bridgehead. The Soviet High Command forbid the surrender of these positions. The bridgehead was seen as protection for the harbors of Kronstadt and Leningrad, when the "Baltic Red Banner Fleet" was again able to operate. At the end of September/beginning of October, the 8th Army had committed, from right to left: 5th, 2nd Marine Brigades, 281st, 48th, 95th, and 91st Rifle Divisions, while the 116th and 80th Rifle Divisions were held in reserve.

After the loss of its Baltic bases, the Soviet fleet withdrew into Kronstadt Bay. The battleship "Marat" was at anchor in Kronstadt harbor. The battleship "October Revolution" was on a dock in Leningrad. The cruisers "Kirov" and "Maxim Gorkiy" were combat ready and in the Neva.

The ships were committed as floating fortresses. The "October Revolution", under naval Captain Moskalenko, was the first unit to fire on the German positions near Peterhof. The ships posed a latent danger to Army Group North, but they could not be ranged from the long range batteries on the land.

The attempts of the Luftwaffe to eliminate the great combat ships in the first stages of the encirclement of Leningrad failed. Stuka Group 2 (Lieutenant Colonel Dinort) of the VIII Air Corps, which was transferred in September to Tyrkovo south of Luga, launched several attacks on the units laying at anchor. The 3/2 Stuka Group (Captain Steen) attacked Kronstadt on 9/21, when Senior Lieutenant Rudel damaged the "Marat" so severely with a 1000 kilogram bomb on the Bug that the battleship later had to be scuttled. An attack conducted on the cruiser "Kirov" two days later was unsuccessful.

At this time, Stalin himself was very concerned about his combat fleet. Only the arrival of People's Commissar Kuznetsov and the Chief of the General Staff Shaposhnikov prevented the scraping of the "Baltic Red Banner Fleet", which provided an invaluable service to the Leningrad Front.

At the end of September, the Soviets believed that the thin German front around Leningrad could be broken after the withdrawal of the 4th Panzer Group and the VIII Air Corps was established. They undertook several landing attempts near Peterhof in order to overrun the German troops stationed there. These operations were coupled with simultaneous counterattacks out of Leningrad in the direction of Urizk.

The defenders were not discouraged and resisted the enemy. The last of the enemy attempts to get a foothold in Peterhof and Urizk by an attack of about 50 combat vehicles failed. The Soviets abandoned a total of 1369 dead and 294 prisoners. 35 tanks, of which the 2/111 Air Defense Battalion (Captain Pizala) destroyed 9, lay as burning wrecks in the streets in front of Urizk.

While the regiments of the 42nd Soviet Army assaulted Urizk, superior formations also attacked Schluesselburg and Kolpino. The enemy searched all over for a week point in the thin front — and everywhere they were repulsed by the tired, bloodied, and emaciated German Landser.

At the end of September/beginning of October, the front exploded between Lake Ladoga and the Baltic Sea. The soldiers had to protect their hides day and night. In the few minutes, when there were no tanks attacking and no fire strikes suppressing the friendly positions, one would grab his shovel and dig into the wet cold ground. The existence of the main combat line around Leningrad ran through high concrete houses and low wooden huts on the outskirts of Leningrad, and through parks and palaces in Pushkin, as well as through the marshes, forests, and river banks.

The army group was no longer strong enough to try to improve the front. The Landser dug in where they stood. By 1/10, Army Group North had lost about 60,000 men, and of them, 25,797 were shipped back to the homeland. Field Marshal Ritter von Leeb only tried to improve the front situation once. He ordered the XXXIX Motorized Army Corps (since 2 October a panzer corps) to expand the thin positions near Mga — the so-called "Flaschenhals [Bottle-neck]" — in the direction of Volkhovstroy.

This attack failed.

The 8th Panzer Division, which was supposed to be the spearhead, could only hold against the enemy counterattack with difficulty. The XXXIX Panzer Corps bogged down.

In view of this dire situation at the end of September, the OKH ordered 20,000 men to be flown immediately to the army group. This was taken care of by the 7th Air (Parachute) Division. The 250th ID — this was the Spanish "Blue Division" — which was deploying to Army Group Center, was immediately stopped and turned back to the north. The 72nd ID loaded up in France with the objective of "Leningrad."

At the beginning of October 1941, the 18th Army was deployed around Leningrad as follows: the XXVI Army Corps was in the west with the 217th and 93rd ID, and the XXXVIII Army Corps was in the eastern portion of the Oranienbaum bridgehead with the 291st and 1st ID. The 374th Infantry Regiment, 563rd Anti-tank Battalion, and 8th Company of the Führer Escort Battalion were responsible for coastal security between Peterhof and Urizk. The L Army Corps controlled the 58th and 269th ID, and the SS Police Division, which had occupied positions between Urizk and Pushkin. The XXVIII Army Corps had committed between Pushkin and Schluesselburg, from left to right: the 121st, 122nd, 96th ID, and 7th Parachute Division. The 212th, 227th, and 254th ID came from the south to reinforce these positions.

The XXXIX Panzer Corps and I Army Corps had, in the meantime, established themselves along the Volkhov front. They received the 250th Spanish Infantry Division and the 2nd SS Infantry Brigade. The mission of the left flank of the 16th Army was no longer "to defend": the XXXIX

Panzer Corps was to prepare for an attack to the northeast in the direction of Tikhvin, in order to make contact with the Finish Army on the Svir.

The right flank of the 16th Army south of Lake Ilmen had to support this attack. The 290th ID on the left had to by-pass Lake Ilmen on the east in order to make contact with the 250th ID, which was located near Novgorod. The majority of the X Army Corps and the II Army Corps were directed to the east into the Waldai Hills to provide flank protection for Army Group Center, which initiated a major attack on Moscow on 10/2.

The preparations went well, because the supply situation improved after the supply routes solidified with the initial frost. The army group had supply distribution points in Luga, Plyussa, Pleskau, Dno, Toropets, Duenaburg, and Riga, which on 10/19 had a total of 14,214 tons of ammunition, 2,172 cubic meters of fuel, and 22,946 tons of rations available. The 16th Army had its own distribution points in Lyuban, Shimsk, Staraya Russa, Kholm, and Loknya, with 5,297 tons of ammunition, 1,355 cubic meters of fuel, and 2,378 tons of rations. The 18th Army possessed, at the same time, 10,655 tons of ammunition, 614 cubic meters of fuel, and 6,223 tons of rations at installations in Krasnovardeisk, Siverskaya, Antashi, and Narva.

The main headquarters of the army group was located in Pleskau, the 16th Army was in Dno, and the 18th Army was in Siverskaya.

Communications between the command posts of the corps and the divisions were provided and maintained by the three communications regiments and the 598th Special Communications Regiment (OKH). During the time period from 29 July to 10/16, 590 kilometers of cable and 8,325 kilometers of wire were laid. Communications with Luftflotte 1 were also secured.

In October, the Luftflotte had the following organization in the following areas:

I Air Corps (Luga) with the 5/122 [Long Range Reconnaissance]
    Combat Group 77 with 1/77 Combat Group (Siverskaya)
    Combat Group 1 with 2/1 Combat Group (Seredka)
    Combat Group 4 with 1/4 Combat Group (Pleskau), 3/1 Combat
Group and 3/77 Combat Group (Dno)

Chapter 3: The Attack

54th Fighter Group with 1st and 3rd Squadrons of the 54th Fighter Group (Siverskaya).

Air Command Baltic Sea (Reval)
125th Reconnaissance Group (Reval)
806th Combat Group (Reval)

I Air Command (Ostrov)
1/172 Special Combat Group [Transport Group] (Riga)
1st Weather Squadron (Ostrov)
54th Communications Squadron (Ostrov)
1st Medical Squadron (Ostrov).

Between 8/30 and 10/21 the Luftflotte had lost a total of 84 aircraft, but, in the same period of time, shot down or destroyed on the ground 589 enemy aircraft. The 54th Fighter Group (Lieutenant Colonel Trautloft) registered, from the beginning of the campaign to 11/6, the destruction of 1130 Soviet aircraft, including 551 bombers.

The reconnaissance squadrons on the Luftflotte lost 35 aircraft from 8/1 to 10/21 and suffered 19 officers and 40 men dead, 13 officers and 18 men wounded. The 20 squadrons committed to the army group operations area logged 2360 sorties of 4903 hours duration while covering an air distance of 1,124,945 kilometers. 13,257 meters of film were taken. The 9th Courier Squadron and the 56th Communications Squadron reported 1,382 sorties with 236,557 air kilometers flown.

Both the 36th and 51st Air Defense Regiments were committed with the majority of their formations in the Leningrad area. The 75th, 291st, and 1/411 Air Defense Battalions were on the Volkhov front; the batteries of the 2/745 and 3/245 were near Staraya Russa. Of the four Army Air Defense Battalions, the 604th and 603rd Army Air Defense Battalions were near Leningrad, and the 272nd and 280th Army Air Defense Battalions were in the Schluesselburg sector. From the beginning of August to the middle of October, the four battalions destroyed 254 aircraft, 93 tanks, and 3 ships.

Army Group North

The deployment of Army Group North in the fall of 1941 was strongly affected by the open sea flank. The Soviet fleet — in opposition to original German assumptions — was very active with its medium and smaller units. Therefore, they had to take early measures to eliminate these "wounds." The Baltic islands, which were important supply bases for the Red Banner Fleet, had to fall.

On 8/27, the Navy dispatched the "Baltic Sea Training Formation" (Naval Captain Rieve) to Riga. In addition to this formation, a German landing corps was selected for transport to the islands. The first landing was undertaken during the night of 9/10 by a battalion of the 389th Infantry Regiment (217th ID), which occupied the island of Worms.

The planning for the occupation of Oesel and Moon — "Operation Beowulf" — was completed by the Army and Navy on 9/13. The commander of the XLII Army Corps (General of Engineers Kuntze) decided to use the 61st ID (Lieutenant General Haenicke) for the operation, considerably reinforced by engineers and artillery. The Luftwaffe established a commitment staff "Air Command B" (Major General von Wuehlisch), to which the units of the Baltic Sea Air Command, in addition to the 1/77 Combat Group, 2/26 Pursuit Interceptor Group, 10th Air Defense Regiment, and 10th Air Communications Regiment were subordinated.

The Navy participated for the first time since the beginning of the campaign with large units. Vice Admiral Schmundt guided the operation at sea. He had available the light cruisers "Leipzig", Emden", "Koeln", the "Baltic Sea Training Formation", the 2nd Torpedo Boat, 1st Mine Sweeper, 11th Submarine Hunter, and 2nd and 3rd Motor Torpedo Boat Flotillas. The Finish Naval Command also deployed the armored ships "Ilmarinen", "Vainamoinen", two ice breakers, and several escorts.

Since June, the Soviets were industriously working on the expansion of their fortifications on the islands. They constructed deeply echeloned trench systems along the coast and increased the number of their coastal batteries. Lieutenant General Yelisseev was in command of the occupation troops. These consisted of the 2nd Rifle Division, 3rd Rifle Brigade, several independent artillery and air defense battalions, as well as naval infantry and engineer battalions. The coastal batteries on the islands of Oesel,

Dago, and Moon were equipped with two 28 cm, eleven 18 cm, nineteen 13 cm, four 15.2 cm, ten 12.2 cm, and four 10.5 cm guns.

The German landing on the islands began on 9/14 at 0400 hours. The 1/151 Infantry Regiment landed on the coast of Moon in assault boats. The battalion established a small bridgehead, but then bogged down under strong opposition. During the course of the day, the 2/151 Infantry Regiment and 3/162 Infantry Regiment succeeded in widening the bridgehead to 6 kilometers.

The landing on Oesel was prepared by a feint by the naval units. The Navy conducted three dummy landings with three formations, by which the Soviets were taken in. As the German ships returned to their departure harbors unmolested, the Finish armored ship "Ilmarinen" was lost after running into a mine. The ship sank in 7 minutes and took 271 men into the depths.

The 61st ID landed additional units on 9/15, including an Estonian volunteer battalion. A day later, the dike on the island of Oesel was reached and captured, and the Soviets withdrew to the south. Arensburg, the largest city on the island, fell into German hands on 9/20.

The Russian defenders entrenched themselves on the Svorbe Peninsula and did not retreat one step further. The 162nd Infantry Regiment fought for the entrance to the peninsula on 9/22 and then established itself in front of the enemy positions. The battle raged all day long. Every meter of land had to be wrestled from the enemy.

The Luftwaffe and Navy supported the courageous commitment of the East Prussian soldiers. On 9/26 and 9/28 the cruisers "Leipzig" and "Emden" attacked with their guns and shot up the coastal batteries on Svorbe. The enemy batteries on Abruku had fired their last shells. As two companies of the 660th Engineer Battalion assaulted the batteries in hand-to-hand combat, the guns were silent.

The battle on Oesel came to an end on 10/5. 4000 Soviet soldiers and sailors were taken prisoner.

The 61st ID had to reorganize and regroup its formations in one week's time. The soldiers of the 176th Infantry Regiment and the 161st Reconnaissance Battalion were landed on Dago on 10/12 at 0530 hours by ferries and assault boats of the "Baltic Sea Training Formation." The cruiser

"Koeln", the 2nd Torpedo Boat, and 1st, 4th, and 5th Mine Sweeper Flotillas rendered the necessary fire support to suppress the enemy coastal batteries.

The two combat groups formed bridgeheads from which they immediately penetrated into the interior of the island. The 151st and 162nd Regiments later crossed to the southern tip of Dago. The enemy resistance crystallized around the coastal batteries. The Soviets slowly moved to the Tahkuna Peninsula and defended there until 10/21, when they surrendered. 3,388 men were taken prisoner.

The battle for the Baltic islands, which cost the German side 2,850 dead, wounded, and missing, was over.

The "Baltic Red Banner Fleet" left the Baltic Sea and withdrew into Kronstadt Bay. At the beginning of December, the Soviets evacuated Hango, their strong point on the Finish coast. During the transport of the defenders, the troop transport "Josef Stalin" (12,000 tons) was severely damaged. It was located by two German patrol boats and towed to a German harbor. The last island in the Baltic Sea — Odensholm — was occupied without a fight by a naval assault troop on 12/5.

The Baltic Sea was now eliminated as a combat zone after the large units of the "Red Banner Fleet", partially damaged, were established in Kronstadt and Leningrad. The Navy had assembled all of the heavy units in the western Baltic Sea in the fall in order to prevent the Soviets from breaking out. After the conquest of the Baltic islands there was no longer such a danger. The German "Baltic Fleet" — including the battleship "Tirpitz" and the armored ship "Admiral Scheer" — was disbanded, and the light cruisers and torpedo boats committed at Oesel were withdrawn and dispatched to the North Sea.

There were no more combat operations and hostile contacts between German and Russian ships in the eastern Baltic Sea. Indeed, a few enemy submarines and mine laying ships were able to break through, but they caused no disruption of German shipping. Only the steamer "Baltenland" was lost to a torpedo hit by a Russian submarine. The remaining losses were caused by mines which, from October to the year's end, included five mine sweepers, one patrol boat, and a submarine hunter.

Chapter 3: The Attack

The Navy took on the responsibility of protecting the entire coast from Memel to Leningrad. The control of all naval units in this sector was placed under the Naval Command East (Vice Admiral Buchardi), whose command post had been established in Reval since August. After mid December, the last torpedo boats and mine ships were recalled home, leaving the following formations in the area of operations of the Naval commander:

Chief of Sea Transport East (Fregattenkapitaen Nicol) with the sea transport sites at Reval, Riga, Libau, Windau, Baltish Port, Pernau;

Senior Dock Staff East (Konteradmiral Goehle) in Reval;

Naval Equipment Point Reval (Naval Captain Graef);

Naval Dock Libau (Konteradmiral Bettenhaeuser);

Coastal Defense Group East (Fregattenkapitaen Schur) in Reval;

Commandant of Sea Defense East (Fregattenkapitaen Terfloth, from December 1941: Naval Captain Joerss);

Harbor Commandant Reval (Korvettenkapitaen Nordmann);

Commandant of Sea Defense Latvia (Naval Captain Kawelmacher);

Harbor Commandant Riga (Korvettenkapitaen Fromme);

Commandant of Sea Defense Leningrad - sector from the Estonian border to the main combat line - (Naval Captain Kopp; from November: Fregattenkapitaen Boehm);

530th and 531st Naval Artillery Battalions (Korvettenkapitaen Schenke and (Fregattenkapitaen von Beckrath);

239th and 711th Naval Air Defense Battalions (Korvettenkapitaen Fuerst zu Leiningen and Korvettenkapitaen Behn);

6th Naval Vehicle Battalion (Korvettenkapitaen Illert);

321st Naval Fortification Engineer Battalion.

The commitment of these units was predominantly in Estonia. The 531st Naval Artillery Battalion was located between Narva and Peterhof, and the 530th Naval Artillery Battalion was around Reval. The 239th Naval Air defense Battalion was also transferred to this area in October, and before that it was stationed in Windau. The 711th Naval Air Defense Battalion was committed directly to the Leningrad combat zone. The 321st Naval

Fortification Engineer Battalion was located in Estonia, while the 6th Naval Vehicle Battalion was transferred to the Narva-Peterhof area.

For "Operation Barbarossa", the Navy formed one additional agency. This was the Senior Dock Directorate under Admiral Feige, which was disbanded in November.

Throughout, the temperature sank in mid October. It became colder. The ground began to freeze. Winter slowly settled in. First light snowflakes fell, which then turned to slush. Later the snow became deeper. The terrain was covered by a white layer, which deepened every day. Men, animals, and guns literally sank into the snow.

A new enemy had come upon the battlefield: the harshest winter in memory had set in.

This enemy was not calculated for in the plans of the German General Staff!

At the end of September, the OKH had sent Army Group North some reinforcements. Therefore, they thought they could master the situation. In Directive Nr. 39, which was issued by Hitler for the conduct of the war, was the sentence:

"...After the arrival of reinforcements, the situation south of Lake Ladoga is to be cleared up ...and contact established with the Finish-Karelian Army!"

After that, the army group had to set out across the Volkhov with strong forces to attack through Tikhvin to Svir and establish contact with the Fins and Germans there. A second group was to attack along the Volkhov to the north in order to throw the Soviets back to Lake Ladoga. When these operations succeeded, Leningrad would be completely isolated and could be — according to Hitler's plans — starved out.

In mid October, the front on the Volkhov ran in a straight line from Novgorod along the western bank to Kirishi. From here, it bowed sharply to the northwest and moved on to Schluesselburg. The plan was to insert an attack wedge from this point of the front to the northeast, while, simultaneously, driving the flanks to the south and east.

Chapter 3: The Attack

The XXXIX Panzer Corps (General of Panzer Troops Schmidt), with the 8th and 12th Panzer Divisions and the 18th and 20th Motorized Infantry Divisions, was selected to be the main effort. However, before the tanks could be set in movement, the infantrymen had to first create a bridgehead.

The East Prussian 11th and 21st ID had this task under control. As the first snowfall began on the morning of 16 October, German artillery fire blazed between Grusino and Kirishi. The 21st ID (Lieutenant General Sponheimer) succeeded, in spite of bitter resistance from the Soviet 267th and 288th Rifle Divisions, in crossing all three regiments over the 300 meter wide Volkhov near Grusino by that evening. The 9/45 Infantry Regiment (Senior Lieutenant Pauls) forced the approaches to the main enemy resistance nests closed.

The ferries were first taken on 10/18. The 21st ID assembled in the north of the bridgehead. The division was ordered to attack directly north on the eastern bank of the Volkhov. The 11th ID, which was moving across the river at the same time near Kirishi, had to join in the attack on the western bank.

On 18 October, the XXXIX Panzer Corps crossed the river near Grusino and organized itself into two attack groups. The corps was ordered to attack to Tikhvin with its four divisions in order to sever the last land connection between northwest and central Russia. The 12th Panzer Division (Major General Harpe) and the 20th Motorized Infantry Division (Major General Zorn) were on the left, while the 8th Panzer Division (Major General Brandenberger) and the 18th Motorized Infantry Division (Major General Herrlein) were deployed on the right. The 126th ID (Lieutenant General Laux) was attached to the southern group to secure the necessary departure base.

The advance of the XXXIX Panzer Corps made it to the river on the third day of the attack and, after the bridgehead was secured, the artillery and motorized units were crossed. Unfortunately, the frosty weather turned to wet weather. Roads, which were indicated on the 1:300,000 map — the German staffs had no better maps than these(!) — were turned into pools of mud within several hours.

The northern group worked slowly to Budogoshch, while the three divisions in the south approached Malaya Vishera. Here, it was planned that the 8th Panzer Division would circle around the back of Tikhvin in a great bow from the south. During another snow storm and drop in the temperature, the Soviets defended bitterly. The bravely fighting 267th Rifle Division withdrew from Malaya Vishera.

The Soviet 52nd Army commander quickly directed the 25th Cavalry Division and 259th Rifle Division to the city, while the 288th Rifle Division, which lost Grusino, occupied new positions near Kolpino. These forces were now superior to the Germans in numbers and equipment. The 8th Panzer Division, therefore, was no longer able to conduct a frontal attack. The division veered to the north in order to eventually outflank Malaya Vishera from there.

Because the enemy resistance increased day by day, and in view of the impending winter, the friendly front could not remain in front of the city, and the army gave the order to attack. Because the 8th Panzer Division already withdrew some elements to support the northern group, only the 126th ID and 18th Motorized Infantry Division remained. The 18th Motorized Infantry Division, however, had to direct its entire force to the south in order to protect the flanks against the fighting formations of the 25th Cavalry Division and the 305th Rifle Division.

The 126th ID (Lieutenant General Laux) prepared to attack, and it began on 10/23. 1st and 2nd Battalions of the 422nd Infantry Regiment, under Major Baron von der Goltz, attacked in the south. The two battalions lost contact with the division, fought on their own, and reached the southern edge of the city at noon. The enemy went to meet these groups and, therefore, left their positions on the western edge of the city. The division took advantage of the opportunity and now attacked from the center and the north. The 426th Infantry Regiment (Lieutenant Colonel Hemmann) penetrated into Malaya Vishera. By evening, the 18,000 inhabitants of the city were in German hands.

The friendly positions were driven somewhat to the east by the Rheinlanders and Westphalians. Nevertheless, the strength of the 126th ID was insufficient to continue the attack. The division was relieved by formations from the XXXIX Panzer Corps and subordinated to the newly formed corps group of General of Infantry von Roques.

Chapter 3: The Attack

General of Infantry von Roques controlled all German formations, which were on the western bank of Lake Ilmen, including the Novgorod bridgehead. The 250th ID — the Spanish "Blue Division" — under General Munoz Grandes, after a 1,000 kilometer foot march, took up positions on the Novgorod front. On 10/18, the division crossed the river with its 269th Infantry Regiment (Colonel Esparza) south of Shevelevo in order to reinforce the positions of the 18th Motorized Infantry Division. In November, the Spanish took over the right sector of this division, which was transferred to Tikhvin.

By the end of October, the attack strength of the southern German group grew weary. The battalions were directed to take up the defense. Combat now was no longer played out on the streets, but around strong points. The troops had to withdraw into the towns in order to be able to shelter themselves from the grim cold, which increased from week to week.

The center attack group — the 12th Panzer Division and 20th Motorized Infantry Division — worked themselves halfway to Tikhvin by the end of October. The 12th Panzer Division continued to advance and occupied Sitomlya on 10/31. The division received additional reinforcement from elements of the 18th Motorized Infantry Division, which were gradually advancing. The 20th Motorized Infantry Division, in the meantime, fought its way into the impassable terrain southeast of Budogoshch and established the flank security with some difficulty.

The Soviet 4th Army commander (Lieutenant General Yakovlev) deployed all of the new formations out of the interior to stop the threat to Tikhvin. The 44th, 65th, and 191st Rifle Divisions, as well as the 27th Cavalry Division and 60th Tank Brigade, were thrown against the two German divisions. After overcoming the marshy terrain on Lake Lebyaske, the 12th Panzer Division broke through to Tikhvin. The advance elements of the 18th Motorized Infantry Division also attacked toward Tikhvin against strong enemy resistance and along a rail line that was not indicated on any German map! During the night of 11/9, both combat groups penetrated into the city. The 51st Infantry Regiment (Lieutenant Colonel Leyser) occupied Tikhvin without firing a shot! The 12th Reconnaissance Battalion veered to the northwest and seized the Zvglevo railroad station. The objective of the XXXIX Panzer Corps was achieved!

The OKW published a special report on the following day:

"In the course of an operation between Lakes Ilmen and Ladoga across the Volkhov during the night of 9 November, infantry and tank formations captured the important communications center of Tikhvin. Many prisoners and much equipment were captured. The staff of the 4th Soviet Army only escaped capture by abandoning their vehicles and important military documents. In the battle on this sector of the front since 10/16, 20,000 prisoners have been captured along with 96 tanks, 179 guns, 1 armored train, and numerous other war materials."

The objective of the third attack group at this time was also directly in front of the German soldiers. The three attacking divisions — the 21st (on the right), 11th (center), and 254th ID (left) — in spite of the poor weather conditions and constantly increasing enemy superiority, fought their way to the north on either side of the Volkhov until the end of October. Losses were very high. In the four weeks since crossing near Grusino until 11/10, the 21st ID lost 79 officers and 2,522 men in dead and wounded!

On 11/14, the attack on Volkhovstroy was ordered!

The Soviets were prepared! The 54th Army commander (Major General Fedyuninskiy) hastily gathered troops, which were not deemed necessary on the Leningrad Front, in order to deploy them toward Volkhovstroy. Ultimately, from right to left, fought: the 122nd Tank Brigade, 285th, 281st, 292nd, 311th, and 310th Rifle Divisions. The 6th Marine Brigade was in heavy contact with the Ladoga Flotilla and took on responsibility for protecting the Volkhov Watercraft Factory.

The deployment of the 11th and the 21st ID weakened. The 254th ID had to gradually turn around to the northwest in order to be able to provide the necessary flank protection. The forward observers of the 11th Artillery Regiment (Colonel von Wrisburg) could see from Bor to Volkhovstroy. The men of the 1/44 Infantry Regiment (Major Sudau) still fought around the ruins of the small town of Bor as the first shells were hurled on the bridges and streets of the city.

The 11th Reconnaissance Battalion broke still further into the depths of the enemy positions and reached the Volkhovstroy-Leningrad road. Then, the strength of the brave East Prussians came to an end. Now, day and night, new enemy formations, well equipped for winter warfare, assaulted the strong point of the 11th Reconnaissance battalion, trying to destroy it. The 21st ID also bogged down in the snow and ice and under the hail of the Soviet guns six kilometers in front of Volkhovstroy. Only two small engineer troops, under Lieutenant Funk and Lieutenant Lessner of the 2/21 Engineer battalion, were able to crawl through the enemy front and advance to the Murmansk rail line north of the city. The engineers blew up a 10 kilometer wide sector of this important rail line.

"Group Boeckmann's" objective was not achieved!

It could no longer be accomplished. The casualties were enormous. The surgeons and medics had less gunshot wounds to bandage than cases of freezing. The temperature fell alarmingly. East of the Volkhov, the thermometer registered minus 30 degrees. Supply came to a standstill. There were no first aid dressings, no ammunition, and no rations that could make it through the snow drifts into the ruins of the strong points and into the sinister forests.

The German offensive petered out.

Army Group North tried to reinforce its two groups around Tikhvin and in front of Volkhovstroy. "Group Boeckmann" received reinforcement from elements of the 223rd ID and the 4th SS Infantry Regiment. These forces were immediately thrown into the combat around the small town, which was constantly under the fire of enemy artillery and bombs of the combat aircraft. The Landser held their strong point in an all round defense, however, they could do no more than hold.

The Tikhvin Group, which was lead by Lieutenant General von Arnim, was, in the meantime, reinforced by elements of the 8th Panzer Division and the 61st ID. The group now had available the 12th Panzer Division, 18th Motorized Infantry Division, 61st ID, and elements of the 8th Panzer Division. The 61st ID, which was transported by air and trucks out of the Baltic area and was in no way equipped for winter warfare, relieved the 12th Panzer Division and, at the end of November, took over responsibility for the defense of Tikhvin. The 18th Motorized Infantry Division moved further to the west, while the front was secured to the southeast and the south only by strong points of the 8th Panzer Division, the 20th Motorized Infantry Division, and the 380th Infantry Regiment (215th ID).

The Soviets took over the initiative. The former commander of the 4th Army was relieved, and Army General Meretskov was entrusted with the command of the army. From his forces, he formed a northern and a southern group in order to concentrate them for a counterattack.

Major General Pavlovich took over the northern group. In addition, there were the 44th Rifle Division, 46th Tank Brigade, 1061st Rifle Regiment, one engineer, and several mortar battalions of the 7th Soviet Army. A central group, under Major General Ivanov, stood east and northeast of Tikhvin. The 191st Rifle Division was reinforced here by additional rifle battalions of reserve units. The third group, under Colonel Devyatov, with the 27th Cavalry Division and the 60th Tank Brigade, assembled south of the city. A fourth group deployed into the Nizhnie Sazhertse and Petrovskoe area. It was the 4th Guards Rifle Division, 65th and 92nd Rifle Divisions, and some motorized battalions under Lieutenant General Yakovlev.

The plan of the Soviet High Command foresaw isolating the forward German pincers near Tikhvin from their withdrawal routes. The 54th Army (Lieutenant General Fedyuninskiy) advanced in the general direction of Kirishi in order to intercept "Group Boeckmann" south of Volkhovstroy. The 4th Army (Army General Meretskov) had to take Tikhvin. The 52nd Army (Lieutenant General Klykov) was to attack directly to the west and retake the Grusino bridgehead. 12/1 was established as the first day of the attack.

The preparatory measures to create a suitable departure position were initiated on 11/15 with partial attacks. The Soviets dispatched their 46th Tank Brigade with brand new "T-34's" against the positions of the 18th Motorized Infantry Division. Infantrymen and anti-tankers were powerless against these camouflaged colossi. The tanks overran the strong point of the 51st Infantry Regiment and did not stop until they reached the battery positions of the 18th Artillery Regiment. The field howitzers of Colonel Berger destroyed 50 enemy tanks during the following days. In [minus] 30 degree cold and in 30 cm deep snow, the division held its front!

The major attack began on 1 December. Reconnaissance, fighter-bomber, and combat aircraft were flown. Fire strikes battered Tikhvin into ruins and rubble. Then, the "Urrahs" of the Russian infantrymen rang out. The Germans defended themselves with the courage of the desperate against the enemy and the cold. The thermometer sank to minus 40 degrees. The machine-guns no longer fired. The bolts of the guns would no longer open. The horses collapsed and, in several seconds, froze solid. The hands of the infantrymen froze to their rifles — and the Soviets attacked.

All contact with the rear was lost. The 30th Infantry Regiment (18th Motorized Infantry Division) had just arrived from Schluesselburg. It was no longer a regiment, as 230 of its soldiers froze on the way. In the meantime, the losses of the 18th Motorized Infantry Division rose to 5000 dead, wounded, and missing. Any further combat around Tikhvin was senseless...

Lieutenant General Haenicke, commander of the 61st ID, decided to give up Tikhvin on 12/8. The 151st Infantry Regiment (Colonel Melzer) formed a blocking position, behind which the division was able to withdraw. The movable guns were taken from the city. The engineer training battalion blew up the supply installations, bridges, and railroad installations. As evening covered the land, the rear guard left Tikhvin. On the next morning, when the Soviets entered the city, they found 42 guns, 46 mortars, 190 machine-guns, and 102 vehicles. These were, without exception, either demolished by grenades or torn to pieces.

During a situation briefing on 12/6 in the OKH, Hitler ordered that the positions around Tikhvin not be given up. As before, they were to try to make contact with the Fins, as the isolation of Leningrad would insure the end of the city of millions. However, what was the value of such an order when the enemy and the frost were dictating events?

Field Marshal Ritter von Leeb came to his own decision on 12/9 to give up the front salient.

The first withdrawal of Army Group North began!

It was a cruel march: the exhausted, fatigued, and bloodied soldiers, which had not had a warm meal in some time and whose blood froze in the smallest wound, trudged back. Russian tanks, mounted Soviet cavalrymen, and enemy guns swarmed around the columns of field gray — winter clothing was still a rarity! Overhead aircraft circled incessantly, stalking the columns like hawks and tearing new gaps into the columns with their onboard weapons.

"Group Boeckmann" broke contact from Volkhovstroy and withdrew on the same route upon which they had previously advanced. To secure the withdrawal, the 3/489 Infantry Regiment, 269th Reconnaissance Battalion, 269th Anti-tank Battalion, and 1/604 Air Defense Battalion were detached. The XXXIX Panzer Corps also plowed through the snow drifts to the Volkhov. The 18th Motorized Infantry Division (which was now commanded by Colonel von Erdmannsdorff) directed the 11th and 12th Companies of the 51st Infantry Regiment, under Senior Lieutenant Grosser, to perform the duties of rear guard. The two companies sacrificed themselves to the last man for their comrades! The southern group also had to withdraw from Malaya Vishera. The 126th ID gave up the important town. The 422nd Infantry Regiment (Lieutenant Colonel von der Goltz) was temporarily encircled, but was able to breakout. The right neighboring elements of the 250th ID — to which there was no contact — evacuated the fiercely fought over strong points of Possad and Otenski. The Spanish 269th Infantry Regiment, which fought here, lost 566 dead in just a few days.

The battered formations withdrew across the Volkhov to the west in mid December 1941.

The recapture of Tikhvin by the 4th Soviet Army portended the ultimate deliverance of Leningrad. The city's economic situation became catastrophic due to the siege in September. At that time, available food supplies in Leningrad were sufficient for at most 30-40 days. On 9/2, the war council of the city established corresponding rations. Accordingly:

Workers: 600g bread daily, 2000g sugar monthly, 1000g fat month
Clerks: 400g bread daily, 1700g sugar monthly, 500g fat month
Dependents: 300g bread daily, 1500g sugar monthly, 300g fat month
Children: 300g bread daily, 1700g sugar monthly, 500g fat month .

Each week the rations were decreased. On 11/20/1941, the first residents of Leningrad died of starvation. At this time, a worker was receiving only 255 grams of bread daily and 600 grams of fat monthly. In December, 52,000 died of starvation. The number increased in January and reached an average of 3,500 daily! (During the blockade, a total of 632,000 men, women, and children died as a result of a lack of nourishment in Leningrad.)

Chapter 3: The Attack

Shortly after the encirclement, the authorities decided to establish a harbor in Osinovets Bay, 55 kilometers north of Leningrad. Now, small and medium sized ships could transport food supplies out of central Russia over Lake Ladoga. The goods, however, were far from being sufficient. In the first months, only 9,800 tons of food were transported by ship, only enough for eight days.

The supply of the city got worse when the communications center of Tikhvin fell. Construction engineers, civilians, and convicts constructed a new, 300 kilometer long supply road, which ran in a large bow from Sabore through Lakhta, Yeremina Gora to Novaya Ladoga. Here, the goods were loaded onto trucks and driven over the ice of Lake Ladoga!

The great lake froze in mid November. Horse-drawn vehicles ventured onto the ice when it was only 1.80 meters thick. On 11/22, the first truck convoy crossed the lake. This showed that the ice was still not thick enough. In eight days, 40 trucks sank through the ice with their cargo! The Soviets began to intensify their utilization of this ice road. Hundreds of trucks crossed the lake every day, without being disrupted by German guns or combat aircraft!

After the recapture of Tikhvin, the truck columns could once again clatter over the roads, and transport trains brought food, bandages, and ammunition. Leningrad was saved!

The Red Army seized the initiative on the entire front between the Baltic Sea and the Waldhai Hills during a point in time when the German Army was thoroughly battered and frantically defending their positions. The following enemy formations were deployed in the Leningrad combat zone in December 1941:

8th Army (from right to left): 5th, 2nd Marine Brigades, 281st, 48th, 85th, 11th Rifle Divisions; 80th Rifle Division in reserve.

42nd Army (from right to left in the first line): 56th, 13th, 70th Rifle Divisions; (in the second line): 44th, 21st, 189th Rifle Divisions, 7th Marine Brigade.

55th Army (from right to left in the first line): 90th, 168th, 125th, 268th Rifle Divisions; (in the second line): 247th, 292nd, 267th, 289th, 261st, 263rd People's Defense Brigades; (on the bank of the Neva):

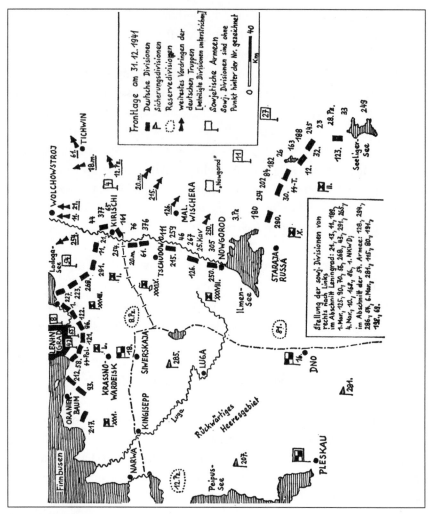

Top Box -
Front Situation on 12/31/1941
German Divisions
Security Divisions
Reserve Divisions
Furthest Advance of the German Troops
[participating divisions underlined]
Soviet Armies
Soviet divisions are indicated without periods (.) behind their numbers

Bottom Box - Positions of the Soviet divisions from right to left. In the Leningrad Sector: 21st, 13th, 41st, 189th, 1st Marine, 125th, 90th, 70th, 56th, 268th, 43rd, 291st, 265th, 4th Marine, 10th, 168th, 86th, 1st NKVD; In the 54th Army Sector: 128th, 294th, 286th, 54th, 6th Marine, 281st, 115th, 80th, 191st, 198th, 69th.

Chapter 3: The Attack

11th People's Defense Brigade, 86th Rifle Division, 4th Marine Brigade, 115th, 5th Rifle Divisions, 1st NKVD Division.

In numbers, the German troops found themselves in the minority. The XXVI Army Corps encircled the Oranienbaum bridgehead with the 217th, 93rd, and 212th ID. The isolation of Leningrad from the south was delegated to the L Army Corps with (from left to right): the 58th ID, SS Police Division, and 121st and 122nd ID. The XXVIII Army Corps, which secured the entire area along the Neva and the so-called "Flaschenhals" [bottleneck] near Mga, had only the 96th and 1st ID available to oppose Leningrad, while the 227th ID stood on Lake Ladoga around Schluesselburg.

The 18th Army operated alone in the northern sector. The army's area of operations was established on 12/3 along a straight north-south line west of Chudovo. By the end of the year, the boundary ran directly south near Kirishi. The army consisted of four corps (I, XXVI, XXVIII, L) and 17 divisions. The adjacent 16th Army also had four corps available (II, X, XXXVIII, and XXXIX). Five divisions were defending the Volkhov front between Kirishi and Novgorod, and six divisions were deployed between Lake Ilmen and Lake Seeliger.

The 28 German divisions fought on a 600 kilometer long front against 75 Soviet divisions, a portion of which were thrown fresh into the battle!

The overwhelming superiority even made an impression on Hitler.

On 12/19/1941, he had taken command of the Army, after having meddled in the operations of the OKH since the beginning of the campaign. On 12/20, Hitler informed his generals and officers, during an address in the OKH, of the irrevocable order which stated that the German Army had to fight where it stood! In addition, he ordered all available formations be transported from the Reich and the West to the Eastern Front!

By the end of December, Army Group North received the following units by rail and ship transport: the 218th ID arrived from Denmark. The division was not transported as a unified formation, but divided into four combat groups, which ended up being committed on different sectors of the front. The 9th SS Regiment came from Finland, the 5th Mountain Division appeared out of Crete, from France came the 81st ID and the "Netherlands Legion", and from Germany elements of the 7th Air Division (Para-troopers).

Lacking "eastern war experience", the units were immediately thrown into the bitterest battles, which raged over the expanse of Russia for weeks.

"The year 1941, full of concerns and crises for the German leader-ship, came to an end. The surge, which the divisions of the Volkhov front produced with their last ounce of strength far across the Volkhov to Tikhvin and the lower course of the river almost to its confluence into Lake Ladoga, ebbed back to the October departure position. All of the sacrifices of men and equipment were for naught. Their strength was borderline exhaustion, but they remained behind their leadership.

It was recognized that the enemy, with highly superior forces, had taken over the initiative. A fifth of the Red Army stood between Lake Ilmen and Karelia.

What they did not know at that moment was that here, in the Volkhov area, they would never again seize the initiative. Any attempts to do so were reserved for other sectors of the front. Their lives began in this bitter cold winter with temperatures of 40 to 50 degrees below zero and icy snow storms..."[12]

NOTES:

[1] *290th Infantry Division. 1940-1945.* Bad Nauheim: Podzun 1960. p. 428.
[2] Stoves, Rolf O.: *1st Panzer Division, 1939-1945.* Bad Nauheim: Podzun 1962. p. 882.
[3] Conze, Werner: *The History of the 291st Infantry Division, 1940-1945.* Bad Nauheim: Podzun 1953. p. 119.
[4] Zydowitz, K. von: *The History of the 58th Infantry Division.* Bad Nauheim: Podzun 1952. p. 159.
[5] Lohse, G.: *History of the Rhenish-Westphalian 126th Infantry Division, 1940-1945.* Bad Nauheim: Podzun 1957. p. 223.
[6] Breithaupt, H.: *The History of the 30th Infantry Division, 1939 to 1945.* Bad Nauheim: Podzun 1955. p. 320.
[7] Zydowitz, K. von: *The History of the 58th Infantry Division.* Bad Nauheim: Podzun 1952. p.159.
[8] Conze, W.: *The History of the 291st Infantry Division.* Bad Nauheim: Podzun 1953. p. 119.
[9] Hubatsch, W.: *61st Infantry Division.* 2nd Edition. Bad Nauheim: Podzun 1961. p. 168.
[10] Lohse, G.: *History of the Rhenish-Westphalian 126th Infantry Division.* Bad Nauheim: Podzun 1957. p. 223.
[11] Knobelsdorff, O. von: *History of the Niedersachsen 19th Panzer Division.* Bad Nauheim: Podzun 1958. p. 311.
[12] Pohlmann, H.: Volkhov. *900 Day Battle of Leningrad.* Bad Nauheim: Podzun 1962. p. 132.

4

THE DEFENSE
Positional War and Combat 1942-1943

"For the time being, the winter was problem number one for the German troops. By mid December, the depth of the snow reached an average of 80 cm. The temperature fell rapidly. At the end of the year, the thermometer registered 42 degrees below zero. The construction of newer soldier shelters, in spite of unspeakable effort, only made slow progress. The companies had to defend from behind snow walls. Heated tents or sheltered huts were the only warm shelters behind the front. The construction of barracks and bunkers posed a problem, because the forests in the marsh region contained only thin trees.

The formations committed on the front suffered from a shortage of winter clothing. The men of the supply troops and artillery gave up their winter overcoats and fur boots to the infantrymen. An almost unsolvable situation developed in the motorized battalions. The antifreeze for fuel, weapons grease, and oil were all useless. The weapons no longer operated, because the bolts froze.

The horses fell by the hundreds from exhaustion and hunger. If they stood outside for a few minutes, they would become covered with a thick layer of ice and snow. The withdrawal of the wounded on stretchers or in ambulances became a race against their freezing to death. Supplies often did not show up for days. The German soldier learned how to live and fight without warm meals, without heated shelters, and without sufficient sleep."[1]

The front of the army group was stretched until it tore. Field Marshal Ritter von Leeb requested to withdraw into the Baltic Provinces because of these conditions. This plan was rooted in the traditional operational thought, that one had to find the time and opportunity to prepare for a new attack. Hitler ordered the contrary; to forbid all withdrawals, to hold the defensive line under all circumstances, and to construct fortresses out of all communications centers and supply bases! A withdrawal of the front to a line of resistance which did not exist was not only a loss of prestige, but would lead to the irreplaceable loss of men and equipment. The uncompromising execution of this "Führer Directive" would avert such a catastrophe.

The Soviets knew this was their chance. They wanted to put an end to Army Group North with fresh and winter-mobile armies. They initiated two large spearheads, which broke through north and south of Lake Ilmen and operated to the northwest, with the long range objective of the Baltic Sea. A third group was prepared south of Lake Ladoga for an attack to relieve Leningrad.

The Russian High Command formed five armies south of Lake Ilmen during the beginning of January. The 11th Army (Lieutenant General Morosov) was on the bank of the lake. The 34th Army (Major General Bersarin) deployed adjacent in the Waldai Hills, while the 53rd Army (Major General Ksenofontov), 22nd Army (Lieutenant General Yushkevits), and 3rd Shock Army were to carry out the breakthrough to Kholm and the encirclement of the 16th Army.

The preparations for this offensive were even felt behind the German front. The Soviets infiltrated partisan units between the strong points. These detachments and groups attacked supply centers and supply installations. One partisan group, which operated in the Staraya Russa area, was able to kill 196 German soldiers, destroy 23 trucks, and blow up three bridges and two ammunition dumps by the end of January.

The major Soviet offensive exploded at three front locations (The question is often raised: Why couldn't one preempt a strike, when the Soviets concentrated their congested forces at one location? However, the war could not be won without knowing where they would concentrate beforehand).

Scouts on skis, which maintained contact between the 30th and 290th ID in the snow covered Neviy marsh, reported unknown tracks in the snow on the first day of the new year. The sentries in the forward trenches heard an increase in engine noise on the enemy side during the following nights. These were indications of an attack.

Darkness covered the winter terrain as the offensive began on 1/8. However, before the guns hurled their shells, strong tank and rifle formations were already located in the rear of the defenders. Transport gliders and transport aircraft had landed on the frozen Lake Ilmen. Tank columns crossed the ice cover and landed shortly before midnight 40 kilometers behind the front of the 290th ID! The formations penetrated to the confluence of the rivers Lovati, Redya, and Polisti. As soon as the day dawned, combat and fighter-bomber aircraft flew in from the east and dropped their bombs and engaged the strong points with their on-board weapons. New columns continued to appear. 19 Soviet rifle divisions, 9 brigades, and several independent tank and ski battalions charged against the front of the X and II Army Corps!

The main effort of the 11th Soviet Army was directed against the front of the 290th ID near Tutilovo. The North Germans defended bitterly, but were overrun. The right flank of the division held for another day, and then it collapsed. The 290th ID was separated from the rest of the front! On the third day of the battle, it had to defend from all sides. The 290th ID withdrew to the west in order to avoid encirclement, and ran into fierce battles around individual towns and strong points.

The Soviet II Guards Corps attacked Parfino. The I Guards Corps pressed across the rail line to the south and out-flanked the division of Lieutenant General Baron von Wrede. Enemy ski companies approached Staraya Russa, which was also bombed by the combat aircraft wearing the red stars. The wooden houses burned like torches, and only the stone buildings of the party and administration installations, the walls of factories, barracks, churches, and monasteries withstood the fire storm. Construction troops, hastily gathered reserves, and airfield companies were thrown against the first Russians. The 51st Infantry Regiment of the 18th Motorized Infantry Division — which was quickly dispatched from Shimsk — defended the Staraya Russa-Kobylkino road.

Many of the German strong points were overrun during these first days of the winter offensive. Only one strong point held: Vsvad on the confluence of the Lovati.

The Soviets surrounded the city on 1/9. The defenders established a circular defense of 2.5 kilometers. Captain Proehl took command of the 290th Anti-tank Battalion, 6th Company of the 1st Air Communications Regiment, elements of the 38th Motorcycle Infantry Battalion of the 18th Motorized Infantry Division, and the 2/615 Guard Battalion. One captain, two senior lieutenants, four lieutenants, two surgeons, and 532 men remained in the town, which within the next two days was reduced to ruins by constant barrage fire and bombing attacks.

The few German defenders repulsed the repeated attacks of the Soviet 140th Rifle Regiment and did not surrender, in spite of the constant urging! The battle raged for thirteen days around the ruins of Lovati. 17 dead and 72 wounded lay under the destroyed houses. Then, a radio message arrived from the OKH: "Evacuate if you must!"

During the night of 1/21, the combat group broke out, taking 62 wounded with them. The men fought through waist deep snow and deadly cold to the frozen Lake Ilmen. They covered 25 kilometers in 14 hours — and as the morning sun rose on the next day, they reached the lake, 7 kilometers east of Uzhin, and ran into German soldiers who spoke Spanish! It was the ski company of the 250th ID (Captain Ordas). The Spaniards were marching across Lake Ilmen diagonally. On this dreadful march, they had lost 150 comrades to freezing.

The battle for Staraya Russa continued without pause. The Soviets attacked past the city from the north and south, cutting the rail line to Shimsk and approaching Dno. The enemy threw new forces into the battle, which advanced selflessly against the defenders. The 290th ID fought for their existence. The rear guard elements defended until their last bullet, as did the 5th Company of the 368th Infantry Regiment of Senior Lieutenant Hinz, which fought to the last man!

The 290th ID was encircled and could only be supplied by air from 1/25. From 1/8-2/13, the division repulsed a total of 146 enemy attacks! Their largest strong point of Tutilovo fell into the hands of the enemy after a five week defense by the 502nd Infantry Regiment.

A breakout from the encirclement failed on 2/12. The attempt on the next day succeeded. The 290th ID withdrew to the south, having to give up the rail line and the town of Pola. The soldiers struggled against the 180th Rifle Division and the 14th, 52nd, and 74th Rifle Brigades. Contact with the 30th ID no longer existed, although the neighboring division supported the 290th ID. The enemy was too strong. For three weeks he fought in the rear of the X Army Corps!

A collapse of the front also appeared to be taking place in the II Army Corps area. Here, the Soviets placed the main effort of their offensive on the seam between Army Groups North and Center. The 3rd and 4th Shock Armies attacked on 1/9 after a two hour fire preparation, with the (from right to left) 357th, 360th, 358th, 249th, 332nd, and 334th Rifle Divisions, as well as several tank and ski battalions, on either side of Ostashkov on Lake Seeliger.

The 123rd ID (Major General Rauch) felt the full weight of the Soviets. Ostashkov was encircled and lost. The 4th Shock Army (Lieutenant General Eremenko) attacked along the railroad, reached Peno on Lake Peno and, therefore, blew apart the fronts of the two German army groups! This paved the way for a catastrophe. The 3rd Shock Army followed, overran the 123rd ID, and marched on Kholm!

The 16th Army had no reserves available. The 81st Silesian Infantry Division (Major General Schopper) just rolled in on the railroad. The first regiment to arrive — 189th Infantry Regiment — was stopped in Toropets and Andreapol, unloaded, and immediately dispatched to the north. The regiment was in no way equipped for winter warfare, having neither winter clothing nor appropriate weapons and equipment.

The 189th Infantry Regiment, 2/181 Artillery Regiment, and 3/181 Engineer Battalion, in spite of these insufficiencies, resisted four fully winter-equipped Soviet divisions between Okhvat and Lauga. The Upper Silesian engineers and infantrymen engaged the enemy tanks with bare hands, defending themselves with shovels, clubs, and bayonets. They held off the attacking divisions all day in minus 46 degree cold and delayed the advance of the 4th Shock Army! Then their strength was exhausted. Colonel Hohmeyer — who was posthumously promoted to Major General — was found dead with 1,100 officers and soldiers of his regiment in the forest near Okhvat. Only 40 artillery men of the 2/181 Artillery Regiment returned. The commander, Lieutenant Colonel Proske, did not!

The valiant struggle of these few regiments was not totally for naught. The German front stabilized near Velikie Luki and prevented an attack into the rear of Army Group Center! However, between Velikie Luki on the one hand and Demyansk on the other yawned a gap. Here lay Kholm on the Lovati, a city of 12,000 population, like a breakwater to the Soviet flood. The 16th Army had to hold the town if it were not to lose its entire front.

Major General Scherer, commander of the 281st Security Division, was named commandant of "Fortress Kholm." He had no unified troop under him. He took what he could get his hands on. On 1/23, the tanks of the 3rd Shock Army appeared and encircled Kholm. "Combat Group Scherer" defended a 1.5 square kilometer area on the Lovati.

At the end of January, contact with neighbors and the interior no longer existed. Kholm had to be supplied from the air. Type "Ju-52" transport aircraft and transport gliders landed on a 70 x 25 meter large provisional airfield and brought equipment, weapons, and men. 27 "Ju-52's" crashed during landing.

"Combat Group Scherer" slowly took shape. At the end of January, 200 men of the 8th Mountain Infantry Command broke through the front and reinforced the groups of the 123rd and 218th ID, the 65th Reserve Police Battalion, and the 10th Machine-gun Battalion. Later, the 553rd Infantry Regiment (329th ID), 386th Infantry Regiment (218th ID), and 3/1 Luftwaffe Field Regiment were flown in on 80 transport gliders. There was no artillery in Kholm. The batteries of the 218th Artillery Regiment and the 536th Heavy Artillery Battalion fired from outside onto the Soviets in the city, directed by forward observers Senior Lieutenant Feist and Lieutenant Dettmann.

The Soviet breakthrough on Lake Seeliger was a threat which the Germans could not prevent. General Busch, commander of the 16th Army, informed Lieutenant General Count von Brockdorff-Ahlefeldt, commander of the II Army Corps, on the evening of 1/9 that the corps could not be given any help.

Chapter 4: The Defense

Field Marshal Ritter von Leeb called the Führer Headquarters on 1/12 and proposed the withdrawal of the armies behind the Lovati. Hitler soundly turned down this proposal! The Field Marshal flew to East Prussia and personally delivered his proposal. He had a memo from his operations officer, Colonel Hermann, which he presented to Hitler.

Hitler again refused. Then, the Field Marshal — as the first commander of a German army group — requested to be relieved! Hitler was in agreement. He relieved Ritter von Leeb along with his Chief of Staff, Lieutenant General Brennecke. General von Kuechler was the new commander of Army Group North; General of Cavalry Lindemann was now commander of the 18th Army.

It was mid January. The southern front of the 16th Army no longer existed! The 123rd ID was eliminated as a combat capable formation. It defended in strong points in the vicinity of Molvotitsy. The 415th and 416th Infantry Regiments were separated from the friendly front. In a ten day battle, the companies fought their way through enemy lines. There were only 900 men left from two regiments!

The 32nd ID (Major General Bohnstedt) and the 123rd ID (Major General Rauch) constructed a temporary southern front. Between the two divisions they had 12,487 men, which had to hold a front 190 kilometers wide.

The II Army Corps was in danger of being encircled. Still newer Soviet divisions attacked, pouring into the 90 kilometer wide gap and forcing the 32nd and 123rd ID further back. The II Army Corps radioed the army:

"When there is a chance to withdraw to the Lovati, we will withdraw immediately..."

The OKH radioed back:

"...Demyansk is to be defended until the last man!"

That was the order for the II Army Corps to defend Demyansk! The corps withdrew all of the battalions, which were under the control of the commander of the SS "Totenkopf" Division, SS Obergruppenfuehrer Eicke, and hastily transported them to the Saluche area, in order to block the front to the west. These jumbled together combat groups immediately occupied a baseline. It was high time. The troops of the 34th Soviet Army and the I Guards Corps met on 2/8 near Ramushevo on the Lovati.

The Demyansk pocket was closed!

Lieutenant General Count von Brockdorff-Ahlefeldt commanded six divisions. The 12th Mecklenburg and the 32nd Pomeranian ID were located east and south of Demyansk. The 123rd Brandenburg ID was fighting in the southwest of the front. The two North German 30th and 290th ID defended north of Demyansk, while the SS "Totenkopf" Division (SS Standartenfuehrer Simon) was in the northeast. The combat groups of SS Obergruppenfuehrer Eicke held positions in the west. The size of the combat area was 3,000 square kilometers. The length of the front totaled 300 kilometers, and the distance between the opposing lines was 50-70 kilometers.

Lieutenant General Brockdorff-Ahlefeldt issued his first order of the day after the encirclement on 2/18:

"...There are 96,000 of us. The German soldier is superior to the Russian; this has been proven! So, let the difficult times come; we are ready!"

The air supply of Demyansk began, and it was the first air bridge in the history of the world! On 2/18, the OKH ordered the re-deployment of the air transport commander (Colonel Morzik) out of the Smolensk area into the area of operations of Luftflotte 1. The transport formations at first took off from Riga, Duenaburg, and Seerappen. An intermediate landing was made in Pleskau and Korove Selo, and later in Dno and Tulebya, to re-fuel. Then, the type "Ju-52", "Ju-96", "Ju-90", and "He-111" aircraft flew deep over enemy lines, dropping their loads or landing at a temporary airfield in Peltsi near Demyansk.

The following combat air groups took part in this months long operation: Special Combat Groups 4, 5, 6, 7, 8, 9, 105, 172, 500, 600, 700, 800, 900, "Oels", "Posen", and the 4/1 Special Combat Group. The groups made 33,086 sorties until the combat zone was evacuated. 265 aircraft crashed somewhere in the forests and marshes between Lovati and the Waldai Hills.

The transport groups brought 64,844 tons of goods to Demyansk in one year and flew 35,400 wounded out.

While the II Army Corps now fought its private war, the Soviet attack flared up against the 16th Army. The X Army Corps (General of Artillery Hansen) was transferred shortly before the encirclement of Demyansk to Staraya Russa and took control of all German troops there. The front solidified at the beginning of February. The 18th Motorized Infantry Division, 81st ID, 53rd Police Regiment, and the 5th Light Infantry Division, which had in the meantime arrived from France, finally stopped the Soviet offensive on 2/19, immediately in front of Staraya Russa — one of the oldest and most dignified cities of the enormous empire.

The XXXIX Panzer Corps was transferred from the army on the right flank to establish a firm main combat line between Kholm and Loknya. At the same time, the XXXIX Panzer Corps was to make preparations to again relieve Kholm.

A similar operation was planned for February by the 16th Army for Demyansk. Lieutenant General von Seydlitz-Kurzbach, commander of the 12th ID, which was outside of the pocket, was entrusted with the formation of a combat group, which was in turn ordered:

"Re-establish the ground contact with the II Army Corps, encircled in Demyansk."

The divisions, which were assigned to Lieutenant General von Seydlitz-Kurzbach's group, assembled in the rear of elements of the 18th Motorized Infantry Division, which were located near Staraya Russa. The deployment of these forces took place at the beginning of March, as the most threatening combat emerged in the pocket. Here, the 1st and 4th Soviet Airborne Brigades were able to infiltrate through the thin German front lines or parachute behind the lines. At the same time, the 2nd and 204th Airborne Brigades attacked from the outside. The II Army Corps had to again strip its already weak front troops to oppose the fanatically fighting and excellently equipped paratroopers, which were already approaching the corps headquarters and holding several supply routes under their control. The combat in the forest and marshes was bitter and finally died out on 4/7.

The German plan for "Operation Brueckenschlag" — the re-establishment of land contact — foresaw two light infantry divisions attacking directly to the east to overtake the Redya, in order to reach the Lovati near Kobylkino. There, they were to establish contact with the forces operating out of the pocket. The operation had to take place before the snow started to melt; an attack at a later time would bog down in the mud.

The following units participated in "Operation Brueckenschlag":

5th Light Infantry Division (Lieutenant General Allmendinger)

8th Light Infantry Division (Major General Hoehne)

18th Motorized Infantry Division (Major General von Erdmannsdorff)

122nd ID (Major General Machholz)

329th ID (Colonel Hippler, later Major General Dr. Mayer)

Security Regiment (Colonel Dr. Mayer, later SS Standartenfuehrer Becker)

additionally, the 1/203 Panzer Regiment, 2/44 Luftwaffe Field Regiment, 132nd Construction Battalion, 659th and 666th Assault Gun Batteries, a platoon each from the 3/745 Air Defense battalion and the 5/31 Air Defense Battalion.

The divisions were organized so that the 18th Motorized Infantry Division was in contact with the defenders of Staraya Russa to provide protection to the north for the main efforts of the 5th and 8th Light Infantry Divisions. The 329th ID protected the right flank. The extremely weak 122nd ID (in actuality only three battalions!) and the 1/203 Panzer Regiment followed in the center as the reserve.

Because "Group Seydlitz" had to operate as close as possible, an enormous gap yawned to the neighbor on the right — the Meindl Luftwaffe Field Brigade (later the 21st Luftwaffe Field Division) — in which several partisan units were reported to be located. Therefore, a security regiment was formed to eliminate this threat. The 290th Anti-tank Battalion, 290th Reconnaissance Squadron, 1/5 Luftwaffe Regiment, 5th Wheeled Battalion, and X Army Corps command group — in all, 20 officers and 964 men — formed the regiment, which in the following weeks would conduct difficult delaying combat in the marshy forests.

"Operation Brueckenschlag" began on 3/21 at 0730 hours with a fire strike. At the same time, Luftflotte 1 attacked with strong forces. Once again, 130 bombers and 80 fighters with the iron cross buzzed over the lines. The Soviets answered immediately with a counterattack by their air squadrons. A thrilling air battle ensued, during which, once again, the maneuverability and fire discipline of the German fighters ruled. (During the air battle over Staraya Russa, the Soviets lost, among others, Lieutenant Frunze, the son of the Bolshevik Army commander in the Civil War.)

The attack of all of the divisions resulted in a decisive success on the first day. the 5th Light Infantry Division forced the crossing of the Porussya near Uchno. Likewise, the 329th ID penetrated deep into the enemy trenches. The 3rd Company of the 203rd Panzer Regiment rolled over the frozen Polisti and came at the enemy in the rear and the flank. The attack went like those in the fall of the previous year. The 18th Motorized Infantry Division took Penna on the northern flank and established a new defensive front. The 5th Light Infantry Division approached Mikhalkino on the Redya, which was an enormous fortification. The division crossed the river. Their 1/75 Light Infantry Regiment (Captain Sachsenheimer) assaulted Yasvy. Therefore, the Russian supply route on the Staraya Russa-Ramushevo road was blocked on 3/25.

The other divisions did not follow. The Silesians of the 8th Light Infantry Division had more difficult terrain to overcome. They had to confront the half-frozen marsh-land, in which there were no towns. The 329th ID — whose commander, Colonel Hippler, fell on the third day of combat — liberated a combat group of the 5th SS Regiment which had been encircled in Podepoche for eight weeks! From here, the division penetrated to the south to the marsh-land near Koslovo. The 1/203 Panzer Regiment (Lieutenant Colonel Baron von Massenbach) blocked the Yasvy-Ramushevo road after beating back a Soviet tank attack.

3/26 brought new snow in big slushy flakes. The weather changed abruptly — and so did the fortunes of war. The senior command of the

Soviet Northwest Front had already ordered a counterattack. The new commander, Lieutenant General Kurotskin, issued an order of the day, which began with the words:

"Not one more step backward!"

Enemy rifle regiments and tank battalions stormed to the west, battering the advanced German assault troops and advance detachments out of the towns and cities. Bitter fighting occurred around Yasvy and Mikhalkino. Instead of reinforcing the main effort to the east, the 122nd ID had to be ordered to the north in order to support the particularly hard hit 5th Light Infantry Division. The division was inserted next to the Wurttembergers and slowly pushed the enemy back. This was not all, however. Stukas battered the Soviet defensive positions. Then, the battalions exploded through waist deep snow into the Russian trenches. The 1/409 Infantry Regiment assaulted Sychevo; not a house or a hut stood at this location any longer! The 2/409 Infantry Regiment established contact with the light infantrymen.

The Soviets did not give up. Their regiments continued to break against the German positions in the Penna bend. It was their plan, to roll over the northern flank of "Group Seydlitz" and simultaneously make it to Staraya Russa. Friend and foe stood in knee high water, fought through impassable escarpment, defended in the shredded forests, and in the mazes of the rifle trenches.

In spite of the thaw, "Group Seydlitz" set out again on 4/5. On this sunny morning, 27 corps batteries (Colonel Guenther) hurled their shells onto the Soviet positions. The division attack bogged down in front of the Russian trenches. The 8th Light Infantry Division succeeded on 4/12 to close a gap and continue on to Ramushevo on the Lovati.

The Silesian light infantrymen accomplished their task. The 1/30 Light Infantry Regiment assaulted Ramushevo, the most important town between Staraya Russa and Demyansk. The commander of the battalion, Captain Steinhart (who was already awarded the Knight's Cross during the Polish Campaign), fell. Simultaneously, with the light infantrymen from Silesia, the Wurttemberger light infantrymen fought for access to the Lovati. Here, the 3/75 Light Infantry Regiment (Captain Kinzelbach) reached Prissmorzhe in a wild attack from Yasvy.

Guns were roaring east of the river. This was the firing of German batteries. The II Army Corps came opposite "Group Seydlitz."

Major General Zorn, commander of the 20th Motorized Infantry Division, was flown into the Demyansk pocket in order to take over the corps group, which was to attack from there to the west. For this mission, which had the cover name "Operation Fallreep [Gangway]", he had available the SS "Totenkopf" Division (SS Obergruppenfuehrer Eicke) and the II Army Corps Assault Regiment (Colonel Ilgen, later Lieutenant Colonel von Borries). The Assault Regiment was composed of a battalion each from the 12th, 30th, and 290th ID, the 5th SS Motorcycle Battalion, and five battalions of the 32nd ID.

Preparations for "Operation Fallreep" were noticed by the Soviets and disrupted by artillery and air strikes. An attack of ten "T-34's" against Kalitkino could only be destroyed by exhausting the last bit of the defenders' strength. The attack of Corps Group Major General Zorn began on 4/14. The enemy anticipated the attack. Their artillery would not let the attackers out of their trenches.

Success was achieved on the following days, as the 5th SS Motorcycle Battalion (SS Sturmbahnfuehrer Kleffner) was able to assault Sakarytino and Byakovo. The attacking regiment, which was taken over by Lieutenant Colonel von Borries on 4/13, penetrated into the front gap and into the enemy positions on the eastern bank of the Lovati on 4/17.

The river was reached on 4/19. The water was high, which made a crossing impossible. The battalions of the SS "Totenkopf" Division stood on the Lovati and occupied the eastern portion of Ramushevo on 4/20. The first sight contact with the lead attack elements of "Group Seydlitz" was established at 1830 hours. SS engineer officers crossed the river in rafts during the night and shook hands with the men of the 5th Light Infantry Division!

The battalions expanded their positions on the bank of the Lovati to the right and left on the following days. The land contact between Staraya Russa and Demyansk was made on 5/1! The land bridge — known as

"Schlauch" for short — ran 12 kilometers long and 4 kilometers wide on either side of the Ramushevo-Vassilevshchina road.

The Demyansk pocket was liberated!

The second pocket in front of the 16th Army — Kholm — was relieved almost on the same day. The defenders of this city held the same positions in May as they held in February! It wasn't that the Soviets had not tried to destroy the 5,000 German defenders. In April, Kholm was besieged by the 33rd Rifle Division, as well as the 26th, 37th, and 38th Independent Rifle Brigades.

The German front had, in the meantime, solidified west of Kholm. The XXXIX Panzer Corps had assigned the 218th ID (Major General Uckermann) the mission of liberating Kholm. On 5/1, the Soviet leadership again intended to capture Kholm. All four large formations attacked, achieved a penetration, and then were repulsed! The enemy had to retreat; the first advance detachment of the 218th ID already stood in their rear.

The lead attack elements approached the fiercely fought over city in the pouring rain. The Soviet battalions withdrew to the east. Again, several groups of "T-34's" attacked. They were destroyed by the guns of the 184th Assault Gun Battalion. They continued further. The 2nd Battery of the 184th Assault Gun Battalion took up the lead. Engineers of the 411th Infantry Regiment (122nd ID) were mounted on the steel colossi. They rode through the night.

As the morning of 5 May dawned, the first assault gun, with the battery commander, Senior Lieutenant Hohenhausen, rattled into the ruined city. It came into contact with the enemy rear guard. Lieutenant Colonel Tromm, commander of the 411th Infantry Regiment, fell. He was the last of 1,550 men to find their final resting place in Kholm.

On 7/1/1941, Hitler established the "Kholm Shield" in memory of the 105 day battle. It was a combat decoration and was worn on the upper left arm of the uniforms of the survivors of "Combat Group Scherer."

In May, the 16th Army established a continuous front, which stretched from Kirishi on the Volkhov to Loknya south of Kholm. the extreme right flank of the army was formed by the XXXIX Panzer Corps (General of Panzer Troops von Arnim). The 218th ID remained in the Kholm sector. A combat group of the 8th Panzer Division, under Colonel Wagner, closed from the south. The last troop unit in Army Group North in the south was the 865th Security Battalion, which secured the rail line on either side of Loknya in loose strong points. Several combat groups of the 8th Panzer Division (Major General Brandenberger) were committed behind these sectors in order to locate partisan detachments and destroy them.

During the winter and spring weeks of the new year, the 16th Army was not alone entangled in the difficult and costly combat south of Lake Ilmen. A situation just as threatening as that near Demyansk emerged north of Lake Ilmen, as strong enemy formations crossed the Volkhov.

On 12/17/1941, the Soviet High Command formed the Volkhov Front out of its Tikhvin armies. The commander of the new army group was the deserving Army General Meretskov. His Chief of Staff was Major General Stelmakh, and the representative from the War Council was Saprozhets. To the Volkhov Front was subordinated: the 4th Army (Major General Ivanov), 26th Army (Lieutenant General Sokolov) — later the 2nd Shock Army — the 52nd Army (Lieutenant General Klykov) and the 59th Army (Major General Galanin). The 52nd Army established a small bridgehead northeast of Chudovo onto the German bank of the Volkhov. This penetration could not be removed due to the lack of combat strength. An additional threatening attack by superior forces occurred at the confluence of the Tigoda on the seam of the 61st and 21st ID. A hastily gathered combat group from the 505th Infantry Regiment (291st ID) and a battalion of the 9th SS Infantry Regiment attacked the enemy in freezing cold and stopped it. Colonel Lohmeyer, commander of the combat group — who was called the "Lion of Libau" — fell in this battle.

The Soviet High Command had bigger plans and was not satisfied with these partial successes. The Army Group Volkhov Front, whose headquarters was located in Malaya Vishera, received considerable reinforcement at year's end. The 2nd Shock Army was formed. Eight rifle divisions and eight assault brigades, each with three battalions, one artilleryl, and one mortar battalion, as well as 10 ski battalions, belonged to this army.

The Volkhov Front was tasked with cutting off the German troops south of Lake Ladoga and relieving Leningrad. In addition, the 2nd Shock and 59th Armies were to advance to the northwest in the direction of Lyuban and meet up with the 54th Army coming out of Leningrad. Some forces were to operate in the Luga direction.

Enemy scout and assault troops put out feelers along the front from 1/7. Gradually, the German soldiers sensed that something was "brewing" in front of them. It could not be determined at which point on the main combat line a possible attack might ensue. The army group established that the Soviet deployment was over by 1/12. The enemy sent a message over the open radio, which was intercepted by the Germans:

"The Volkhov Front is in defensive positions!"

This message was a ploy — then, on the morning of 1/13 at 0800 hours, the enemy guns, "Stalin Organs", and mortars opened fire. A half hour preparation fire suppressed the positions of the 126th ID (Lieutenant General Laux) and the 215th ID (Lieutenant General Knies). Therefore, the attack sector was revealed — it could not have been better located. This was the exact location of the seam between the 18th and 16th Armies, and here also was a division, which had arrived from France, which would experience one of the most unfortunate fates in the Eastern Campaign.

A half hour later, the heavy artillery shifted fire to the rear area. Now white forms advanced in the morning mist in groups and in columns across the frozen river toward the German main combat line. More and more appeared. Their main effort was directed at the inner flanks of the two German divisions.

The few friendly forces, which were located near Yamno and Arefino, were too weak to withstand this tidal wave. In spite of spirited resistance, they were driven back. What could two or three exhausted battalions do against a fresh division? In addition, the uninterrupted commitment of the enemy artillery, mortars, and fighter-bombers could not be resisted.[2]

Soviet ski battalions, in spite of heavy losses, gained a foothold on the western bank of the Volkhov! Two hours after the beginning of the attack, the first bridgehead was established near Gorka, which could not be removed by a counterattack by the men of the 422nd Infantry Regiment (Lieutenant Colonel Baron von der Goltz). The German machine-guns failed to do their duty in the biting cold. The detonations of the defensive fire from the batteries had no effect in the high snow.

There was no break on this day and the following night. New battalions and regiments came across the river. The first anti-tank guns and guns rolled over the ice. As the morning of 1/14 dawned, tanks clattered to the front. The 327th Soviet Rifle Division and the 57th Rifle Division finally broke through the positions on the seam of the 215th and 126th ID. The bravely fighting soldiers of the 426th Infantry Regiment (126th ID) and the 435th Infantry Regiment (215th ID) had to withdraw. Yamno and Arefino fell into Russian hands. The XIII Cavalry Corps entered into the gap and attacked further. By evening, a 6 kilometer wide gap yawned in the German main combat line!

The forward-most strong points were destroyed. Indeed, small platoons and groups held on here and there, giving up only when they ran out of ammunition or there were no more defenders living. Today, no one knows how many German soldiers gave their lives fulfilling their duty in the minus 50 degree cold. Five days passed, then Russian tanks and infantrymen stood on the Novgorod-Kirishi rail line, 8 kilometers on the other side of the Volkhov!

The two battered divisions had to collapse their inner flanks, in order to preserve their regiments. Several strong points remained, but they could not be helped.

The defenders either fought their way through or died.

The 16th Army brought up its reserves, but they could not close the gap. The SS "Flanders" Legion and the "SS Reichsfuehrer's Escort Battalion" arrived in the 126th ID sector, later followed by elements of the 20th Motorized Infantry Division and the 250th Spanish Infantry Division.

By 1/20, the Soviets tore the gap in the front to a width of 30 kilometers!

The troops of the 2nd Shock Army regrouped. They concentrated their cotton-clothed, felt-booted, fur-mittened and ski-equipped formations south of the Orele-Spasskaya Polist road and east of the Krutik-Koptsy road. Two German strong points — Mostki and Lyubino Pole — held further behind the front. The 3/380 Infantry Regiment (Captain Herb) defended

Mostki until 2/4. After the battalion was relieved on this day, it still had one-third of its original combat strength.

On 1/24, the enemy crossed the Novgorod-Kirishi rail line and road between Mostki and Myasnoy Bor. The direction of the Soviet attack formations was now obviously to the northwest. The attack in the tangled forests could not be delayed or stopped by hastily thrown together combat groups. By mid February, motorized formations neared Lyuban. Several days later, they reached the Lyuban-Leningrad rail line not far from Yeglino!

The 2nd Shock Army stood, therefore, 100 kilometers from their departure positions!

Their divisions had traversed half the distance to Leningrad!

The mobile brigades found themselves deep in the rear of the I German Army Corps, which was fighting to the north!

In great haste, the army group pulled battalions of divisions from their "rest areas" and threw them into the Volkhov area. Thus began the "Flickschusterarbeit [Patchwork system of warfare]", or "Armeleutekrieg" in the 18th Army sector. General of Cavalry Lindemann, the new commander of the army, proved to be a master of this type of warfare.

With the first arriving reserves, he formed a thin front line, which he placed in front of the attackers. By the end of January, elements of the 212th and 254th ID and the 8th Wheeled Battalion were north of the Soviet attack wedge. In the west, the 1st Battalion of the 8th Panzer Division's construction regiment and Estonian volunteers established a front against the enemy. In the south, elements of the 20th Motorized Infantry Division were inserted. Several weeks later, the defensive front stabilized.

General of Cavalry Lindemann was able to fetch all non-essential divisions and their units from the long army front and direct them into the combat area west of the Volkhov. By the end of February, the Soviets were beginning to show the effects of supply problems.

The 18th Army commander formed six combat groups, which were placed on all sides of the 2nd Shock Army. The northern front was formed out of the combat groups of the 61st ID (Lieutenant General Haenicke), 254th ID (Lieutenant General Behschnitt), 212th ID (Lieutenant General Endres), and 225th ID (Major General von Basse). In the west were located small groups of construction battalions, security companies, police, and volunteer units. Here was the primeval forest, with no roads or towns, but only forest and frozen marshes. The southern front was also reinforced. There, from left to right, were committed: elements of the 285th Security Division (Colonel Brueckner), elements of the 20th Motorized Infantry Division (Major General Jaschke), and the 126th ID (Lieutenant General Laux), the battalions of the 250th Spanish Infantry Division, and the "Netherlands" and "Flanders" Legions.

The Soviet High Command recognized the danger of their operation petering out. On 2/28, it ordered Army Group Volkhov Front to immediately establish a strong point with the 4th Rifle Division, 4th Rifle Brigade, and the 1st Cavalry Division. This attack group was to continue the attack to the northwest before the German front stabilized here.

Moscow had to order these draconian measures because the relief attack from the north showed no signs of success.

The Soviet 54th Army (Major General Fedyuninskiy) was set out on 1/28 with strong forces near Pogoste (on the Kirishi-Leningrad rail line) in order to attack toward Lyuban. Here, contact was to be made with the 2nd Shock Army. The 269th ID (Major General von Leyser) was hit with their full weight. However, the regiments were able to repulse all of the attacks. Elements of the 11th ID and the 96th ID participated in the defense.

Enemy pressure increased in mid February. The fiercest combat took place around Pogoste, where the 43rd Infantry Regiment of the 1st ID, under Colonel Lasch, played an important role in holding the front. The enemy tank formations achieved a penetration up to Senino. Then their attack momentum slackened.

The second phase of the battle around the so-called Pogoste pocket began on 3/9 and lasted for three fierce weeks. The 54th Army commander sent in fresh divisions in order to widen the penetration. The defenders — these were formations of the 96th and 223rd ID, as well as the 5th Mountain Division, which just arrived from France — could not prevent the loss of terrain. Nevertheless, they stopped the attackers on 3/20 in the Senino-Smerdynya area.

The 11th ID held their front as the right corner-stone, west of Possadnikov-Ostrov. The 269th ID remained as the left cornerstone, directly west of Pogoste. Both divisions and their subordinate combat groups from other units prevented the widening of the penetration area, and the Soviets, in spite of great effort, did not succeed in gaining a better supply route on which their supply columns could ride.

Major General Fedyuninskiy — who was relieved of his command of the 54th Army in April, because of these failures — knew that by the end of March, he would no longer be in a position to break through in the direction of Lyuban in order to advance opposite to the 2nd Shock Army. He, therefore, decided on a smaller solution. The main effort of the new attack was shifted to the southeast. Therefore, he hoped to at least cut off the German salient in the Kirishi vicinity.

On 4/10 the attack won the Soviets 5 kilometers. Dubovik and Lipovik fell into enemy hands. However, after five days, it was evident that the Russian divisions had run out of gas. The 11th ID (Major General Thomaschki), 21st ID (Lieutenant General Sponheimer), 93rd ID (Lieutenant General Tiemann), and 217th ID (Lieutenant General Baltzer (later Lieutenant General Bayer) brought the attack to a halt!

The fate of the 2nd Shock Army was practically sealed.

The Soviet commander, Lieutenant General Klykov, put his all into finally achieving some success. He ordered an attack to the south in the direction of Pobereshe and to the north in the direction of Spasskaya Polist, in hope of finding a weak spot in the defensive front and exploiting it.

However, the front solidified.

The army group removed two trustworthy divisions from the Leningrad and Volkhov front areas and ordered them to the south and western edges of the pocket. These were the 58th and 291st ID.

The Soviets were still superior. However, it showed that the circumspection of the German leadership and the tenacity of their soldiers produced a turn about in the battle. Individual enemy forces, which had penetrated to the rail line west of Lyuban, were cut off and wiped out. The advance units of the 2nd Shock Army began to take up the defensive.

In mid March, the front situation reflected:

GERMAN	SOVIET
[Northern edge of the pocket from right to left]:	
291st ID	259th, 92nd, 53rd, 59th, 25th, 46th, 58th, 327th, 22nd Rifle Brigades, 25th, 87th, 86th Cavalry Divisions, 7th Tank Brigade.
254th ID	191st Rifle Division, 23rd, 57th Rifle Brigades.
Colonel Risse's Brigade	267th, elements of the 372nd Rifle (225th ID) Divisions.
SS Police Division	24th, 4th Guards Divisions, 374th, 259th Rifle Divisions.

[Southern edge of the pocket from left to right]:	
Combat Group of the	382nd Rifle Division, 23rd Rifle
285th Security Division	Brigade.
Combat Group of the 20th	19th, 24th Rifle Brigades.
Motorized Inf Div	
126th ID	305th Rifle Brigade
58th ID	65th, 376th, 305th, 225th Rifle Brigades, 93rd NKVD Battalion.

Combat command and control was set up so that the divisions on the northern edge of the front came under the I Army Corps of the 18th Army. The units which were fighting on the southern edge came under the XXXVIII Army Corps, which was now commanded by Lieutenant General Haenicke, and belonged to the 16th Army. The Soviets subordinated their formations in the south to the 52nd Army commander, while the 2nd Shock Army controlled the north.

In spite of the clear cut enemy superiority, the German leadership was not intimidated. They had earlier planned to cut off the Soviet formations, which were located far to the west of Volkhov, from contact with their rear areas. In addition, two combat capable formations were to attack from the north and the south in order to extend their hands to the Volkhov.

Army Group North

During the days of crises, which broke over Army Group North at the beginning of the new year, Luftflotte 1 supported the armies. The emphasis lay in the 18th Army sector and especially in the Volkhov area. Soviet air forces flew 2439 sorties in January in preparation for the attack of their 2nd Shock Army, and of those 746 sorties were flown over the Demyansk combat zone.

Combat aircraft of Luftflotte 1 reported, for the same time period, 913 sorties in the Volkhov area and 473 over Demyansk. 45 attacks were launched to destroy the Volkhovstroy-Tikhvin rail line and 7 to neutralize the enemy supply traffic on Lake Ladoga. During these sorties in January, a total of 1,414.93 tons of bombs were dropped. The squadrons of the 1st and 4th Combat Groups lost eight aircraft.

The 54th Fighter Group participated exceptionally well in the air war. In January 1942, the squadrons chalked up a total of 1,152 enemy flights, of which 736 were flown over the Volkhov area. Lieutenant Colonel Trautloft developed a special method of attack for his fighters. The "Me-109" circled over the terrain in deep flight on illuminated nights and intercepted Russian bombers in groups. The first nighttime fighter sorties of the Eastern War were flown over the Volkhov! The 54th Fighter Group shot down 99 enemy aircraft, while losing only two aircraft of their own! The 25 year old Captain Phillip, commander of the 1/54 Fighter Group, registered his 100th air victory.

The successes and efforts of Luftflotte 1 for the next three months are listed in the following statistics:

Time Frame	Sorties	Successes	Losses
February	4,600 by 44 combat and 27 stuka aircraft, 2566 by Me-109 288 by Recon	3440 tons bombs, 3279 supp. wagons, 201 shoot downs	9 cbt aft 4 stukas, 5 ftr aft, 2 "Ju-88"
March	9075 by 44 combat and 45 stuka aircraft,	8169 tons of bombs, 3151 supply wagons, 359 shoot downs	12 cbt aft 8 stukas, 11 ftr aft

	3865 by Me-109,		1 "Do-17"
	324 by recon		
April	5859 by 57	4621 tons bombs,	15 cbt aft,
	combat and 50	2764 supp.wagons,	9 stukas,
	stuka aircraft,	261 shoot downs	3 ftr aft,
	2863 by Me-109,		2 "Ju-88"
	325 by recon		

The successes of the latter three months were more remarkable when considering that they were achieved with few losses against the constantly increasing superiority of the Soviet air forces. Russian combat air sorties in February amounted to 6438, in March there were 10,855, and in April there were a total of 14,021 sorties!

Often, Luftflotte 1 could not fulfill the tasks and desires of the army group. The air formations were attached to the Army, however, and they remained subordinate to the OKL [Luftwaffe High Command]. Reichsmarschal Goering directed it by issuing orders to the Luftflotte commands, which reacted more to the results of air reconnaissance then on the proposals of the army group.

The 18th Army dispatched to the I Army Corps the reinforced SS Police Division (SS Brigadefuehrer Wuennenberg) from the north, and to the XXXVIII Army Corps the 58th ID (Major General Dr. Altrichter) from the south.

The order of the day for the commitment of the 58th ID began with the words:

"We have been given a task, which will have a decisive influence on the entire situation in the Leningrad area. Because of the cold and the difficult terrain, it will make extraordinary demands on us!"

The attack began on 3/15, simultaneously from the north and the south. The enemy defended bitterly and made the attacking SS men and the North German infantrymen fight for every meter of ground. SS Brigadefuehrer Wuennenberg led the commitment of his companies west of Spasskaya Polist, standing in the front line. In the meantime, sounds of combat were

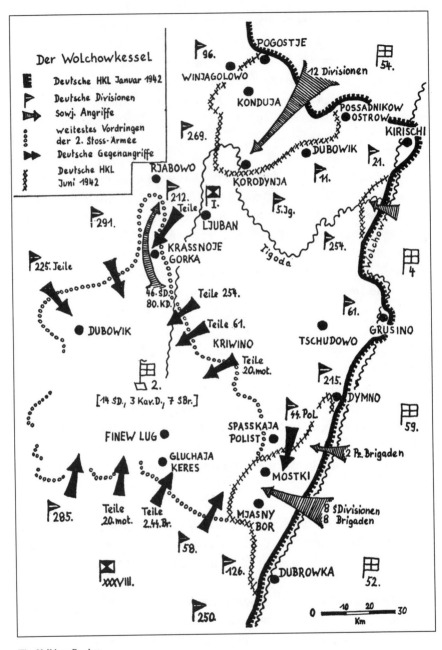

The Volkhov Pocket

also coming out of the south. Here, the 154th Infantry Regiment (Colonel von Pfuhlstein) gained ground north of Semtitsy. The enemy appeared to be ready to withdraw. Major General Dr. Altrichter led the 2/409 Infantry Regiment to this spot. The soldiers attacked on 3/18 in bitter cold, passed through the out posts of the 154th, fought their way through the trench positions in the forest, and then reached the Erika Aisle on the morning of the following day. That was at 1645 hours on 3/19. Then, someone called from the thick bushes. Forms became visible. German soldiers in snow suits emerged.

The northern and southern groups of the 18th Army had met!

The 2nd Soviet Shock Army was separated from the river!

The Volkhov pocket was closed!

Lieutenant General Klykov, the enemy commander, recognized the danger and the threat to his 180,000 soldiers in the forests and the marshes. He ordered the formations, which were located in the northwest, to immediately turn around. The tank and cavalry brigades were inserted to the east in order to crack open the pocket. From 3/22, the riflemen and tankers constantly attacked against the thin security lines of the 58th and 126th ID in the south, and the SS Police Division and Colonel Scheidie's Brigade in the north.

On 3/27, the superior tank formations were able to push the German security back and free the Erika Aisle. The 209th Infantry Regiment (Colonel Kreipe), which was deployed here, was almost completely destroyed. It was similar with Scheidie's Brigade. Here, it was only thanks to the circumspection of the brave commander, who took command of the 61st ID on this day, that there was no catastrophe.

The "Schlauch" [land bridge] to the Volkhov pocket was established. It was only 3 kilometers wide and ran parallel to the Erika Aisle. The Russians fortified the front of this small land bridge since, due to the Soviet superiority and the arrival of bad weather, the Germans could not remove it. The enemy even constructed two field rail lines from the Volkhov to the west, on which the supplies of the 2nd Shock Army were now transported. In places the roads became impassable, covered by mud a meter deep.

The divisions of the 2nd Shock Army were now energetically led. After the closing of the Volkhov pocket, Moscow relieved Lieutenant General Klykov of his command. On 3/21, his replacement was flown into the pocket. It was the most capable army commander Stalin had available: Lieutenant General Vlassov! At the start of the war, the General was the commander of the IV Soviet Mechanized Corps, which fought in eastern Galicia and the Ukraine. Vlassov later defended Kiev with his corps and was the main reason why the German offensive in September 1941 failed in front of Kiev. Therefore, Stalin assigned him command of the 20th Army, which broke the assault of the 4th German Army and 3rd Panzer Army west of Moscow and saved Moscow.

Lieutenant General Vlassov concentrated his 17th Rifle Division and 8th Rifle Brigade. He set up his headquarters in Finev. He planned to hold the 2nd Shock Army in their present positions until the weather improved and they could march again!

The battle around the Volkhov pocket continued with undiminished fierceness. Army Group North placed such importance on the battle that General von Kuechler established a forward command post in Soltsy, southwest of Lake Ilmen. It carried the cover name "Seeadler" and was equidistant from the hot spots of Volkhov and Demyansk.

Weeks of fierce attacks and defensive combat followed. Both sides tried to expand the positions they won. The Soviets attacked the front of the 424th Infantry Regiment (126th ID), under Colonel Hoppe, near Koptsy, with strong tank forces on 4/2. The infantrymen repulsed the attack. In the north, the 61st ID forced the enemy back near Glushitsa and destroyed an encircled group. Colonel Scheidie fell at the head of his men.

As spring set in, the terrain turned into a mud and sea landscape. Movement was only possible on corduroy roads. Positions could no longer be constructed in the ground. The soldiers lived in miserable wooden huts, in tents, or on islands in the middle of this water wasteland. It was the time when Major General Wandel, commander of the 121st ID, first created a sign with an inscription for all of the soldiers of the northern sector:

"Here begins the ass of the world!"

The Soviet soldiers were little disturbed by these natural conditions. They knew how to fight in this miserable terrain. The main objective of their attack was the so-called German "land bridge", which stretched from Tregubovo to the south up to Mostki and was no wider than 3-4 kilometers. The enemy anticipated a threat from here.

The 59th Soviet Army, under Major General Galanin, was to get rid of this "land bridge." He attacked on 4/29 with two tank brigades and seven rifle regiments from the east, while, at the same time, four rifle divisions of the 2nd Shock Army attacked the thin German frontal positions out of the west. The defenders — combat groups of the 61st, 121st, and 215th ID — executed a counterattack through water and marsh, throwing the penetrating enemy forces back. On 5/13, the German front stood exactly where it had on 4/29!

Army General Meretskov, commander of the Volkhov Front, had to realize that the battle was lost.

On the same day, he ordered the evacuation of the Volkhov pocket. Lieutenant General Vlassov, therefore, ordered his main effort corps — the XIII Rifle Corps — to leave the northwestern sector of the pocket and the Lyuban area in order to hold open the land bridge for the deployment of the army. The first heavy batteries and various supply units left the Volkhov area in the following days.

The German 18th Army commander, on the other hand, ordered immediate measures to destroy a good part of the 2nd Soviet [Shock] Army in the pocket. The I Army Corps (General of Cavalry Kleffel) and the XXXVIII Army Corps (General of Infantry Haenicke) had to execute this mission.

The attack began on the entire front promptly on 5/22. The 121st, 61st ID, and elements of the 20th Motorized Infantry Division attacked from the north. The 254th and 291st ID, and elements of the 285th Security Division, worked their way from the west through mud and water. The 2nd SS Infantry Brigade, and 126th and 59th ID came from the south. The front of the 2nd Shock Army collapsed like a balloon that one had let the air out of.

The situation report of Army Group North for the last week of May 1942 noted:

"On the northwest portion of the Volkhov penetration area, an attack began on 5/22 to compress the pocket. By the evening of 5/29, the northwest half of the pocket was cleared by the 291st ID and elements of the SS Police Division, which reached the Cheremna-Vditsko route by attacking along the north-south rail line. The right flank of the 291st ID established contact with elements of the 285th Security Division...

By the evening of 5/29, the 58th ID, elements of the 126th ID, and Group Wandel (20th Motorized Infantry Division and elements of the 1st ID) finally closed the breakthrough position after overcoming great terrain problems. On the morning of 5/30, after good stuka support, the two groups initiated an attack. The attack slowly gained ground against a tenaciously fighting enemy in well constructed and heavily mined positions. During the night of 5/31, through simultaneous attacks from the north and south, the first contact between the XXXVIII and I Army Corps was established and, on 5/31, the block was extended 1.5 kilometers to the west by an attack..."

The Volkhov pocket was closed for a second time!

For the second time, the Soviets attempted to break out of the pocket. However, gradually, the German divisions worked their way in from all sides. They defeated fanatically fighting Russian battalions, overcame wide stretches of marsh land, repulsed tank attacks, constructed new corduroy roads, removed mines, and suffered from a myriad of mosquitoes, marches, and bullets.

In the north, the lead attack elements of the 61st ID (Major General Huehner) and the 254th ID (Major General Koechling) made contact. An enemy group was split and then destroyed. The 291st ID (Lieutenant General Herzog) split off a Soviet force in the west of the pocket. A mixed combat group under Colonel Hoppe (232nd Security Battalion, 3/262 Infantry Regiment, 250th Reconnaissance Battalion, Legion Flanders, 3/126 Artillery Regiment, and a mixed battalion of the 20th Motorized Infantry Division) — units of the 285th Security Division, the 126th and 250th Spanish ID, as well as the 20th Motorized Infantry Division — set out from the south and met with elements of the 291st ID, which was coming from the north. Additional Soviet units were isolated and wiped out.

Lieutenant General Vlassov did not know if the army existed or not. He gathered all of the forces and attacked — with tanks in the lead — the front of the pocket on 21 June! Again his battalions and companies tried to escape to the east.

They were caught by stukas and scattered.

On the following day, combat groups of the 58th ID (Colonel von Graffen) and the 20th Motorized Infantry Division (Major General Jaschke) met and re-established the old front.

Lieutenant General Vlassov gave up the battle!

The Soviet resistance was broken. The pocket was broken into individual parts. The Russian soldiers threw down their weapons and fled into the forests and swamps.

The Wehrmacht High Command reported on 6/28:

"Therefore, the great breakthrough offensive of the enemy across the Volkhov to relieve Leningrad has failed and resulted in a major enemy defeat. The largest burden of this fierce combat was carried by the infantrymen and engineers. According to previous estimates, the enemy lost 32,759 prisoners, 649 guns, 171 tanks, and 2904 machine-guns, mortars, and sub-machine-guns, as well as numerous other war materials. The losses of the enemy increased the number of prisoners many times."

The last remnants of the 2nd Shock Army wandered for weeks through the forests and marshes, hid in abandoned huts, and lived on berries and roots. Many of them died of starvation, while others gave up willingly. The third group was hunted down by German security companies. Only one was missing: Lieutenant General Vlassov.

The German commands distributed flyers with his description. Maybe someone would recognize him among the many prisoners. The Russian buergermeister of a small forest town reported on 7/11 to a German liaison officer that there was a slender Russian staying in a farm.

Captain von Schwerdter, operations officer of the XXXVIII Army Corps, drove off immediately. Shortly afterward, he stood in front of the wooden door of an abandoned house, holding his pistol. The interpreter called into the half-darkness. A form appeared, dressed in the characteristic long tunic of the Red Army soldier, but without any rank insignia. It was a great soldier. His eyes glittered through black horn-rimmed spectacles over his bent nose. The Russian spoke German:

"Don't shoot! I am General Vlassov!"

No one knew then that General Vlassov was beginning a new period of his life that would end on the gallows in Moscow.

The front on the Volkhov stabilized. Nevertheless, the Red Army held on to a small bridgehead near Mostki on the western bank of the 220 kilometer long river. The XXXVIII Army Corps occupied their positions from right to left, with the following divisions: 250th, 126th, and the 58th and 121st ID. Then came the XXVIII Army Corps with the 291st, 215th, 61st, 269th, and 11th ID.

German soldiers now stood on the extreme right and the extreme left flanks on the east bank of the Volkhov. The bridgehead on the Volkhov island east of Novgorod was occupied by the Spaniards. Their most important strong point was the monastery on the hill at the confluence of the Greater and Lesser Volkhov. Here, the 262nd and 263rd Regiments lived under constant enemy artillery fire. The positions, machine-gun firing positions, and observation stands were built into the ancient historical fortification wall, from which one had a wide view of the flat marsh-land.

The 11th East Prussian ID was located near Kirishi on the enemy side of the Volkhov. Contact from the German side to the cut off bridgehead was only possible over a heavily damaged railroad bridge. A smaller footbridge connected both banks. Reserves, supplies, weapons, and wounded could only pass on the bridge at night. During the day, it was always under enemy fire.

This 4 kilometer long and 2 kilometer wide bridgehead was, for the Soviets, the "Door to Leningrad." They did everything they could to attack it. Thus began the sacrificial commitment of the East Prussian division, for whom Kirishi became a second home.

The battle in the Volkhov pocket was still not over when the 11th ID (Major General Thomaschki) first experienced a major Soviet attack. After a preparatory fire like one that had never been experienced before, an attack began on the morning of 6/5 at 0430 hours by two rifle divisions, three rifle brigades, and one tank regiment. On the German side there was only the 23rd Infantry Regiment (Lieutenant Colonel Kolberg), with the 3rd Company of the 2nd Smoke Generation Regiment and the 3/604 Air Defense Battalion, in defensive positions.

Much later, elements of the 11th Reconnaissance Battalion, 11th Engineer Battalion, 3/85 Mountain Light Infantry Regiment, and 3/151 Infantry Regiment came to reinforce the bridgehead.

The Soviet attack was directed on the Kirishi railroad station. The Russians gained ground, but were finally thrown back after a six day bitter battle. The enemy senior command did not give up, and they regrouped their troops. The defenders got only a few weeks rest, which they used to shift some troops.

On 7/20, enemy combat and fighter-bomber aircraft opened the second battle of Kirishi. 13 Soviet artillery battalions fired in the morning out of 100 guns onto the positions of the 44th Infantry Regiment (Colonel Wagner) and the 2/2 Infantry Regiment. The clock struck 0530 hours as the Russians attacked in damp and cloudy weather, with the 44th and 310th Rifle Divisions, 80th Cavalry Division, 24th and 124th Rifle Brigades, and 7th Guards Tank Brigade. On the first day alone, the enemy repeated their attack eleven times and were repulsed eleven times!

The battle of Kirishi raged for six days.

The XXVIII Army Corps (General of Artillery Loch) dispatched reinforcements across the railroad bridge. However, the Soviets also sent the 185th and 195th Tank Brigades to the battlefield. The East Prussians gave no ground without exacting a cost. Only there, where no defenders lived, could the Soviets gain a foothold. This happened in a 800 meter wide strip along a completely shot up forest.

The 11th ID was completely exhausted by this battle and, on 7/31, they were relieved by their sister division — the 21st ID (Lieutenant General Sponheimer). The division dispatched its 3rd Infantry Regiment (Colonel Herrmann) into the bridgehead. The new defenders had no time to settle into their new environment. The major attack began. The Soviets were reinforced and were able to expand their penetration. Colonel Herrmann fell on 8/3, along with many of his soldiers. The 3rd Infantry Regiment was at the end of its strength and was replaced by the 45th Infantry Regiment (Colonel Chill).

On 8/22 another fierce Soviet attack began. The 2/3 Infantry Regiment (Captain Eckstein), which was still in the bridgehead, began its last counterattack, which the enemy defeated. The 6th Company returned with 1 officer, 5 non-commissioned officers, and 14 men! The 45th Infantry Regiment also could not hold out for long. Again, the 3rd Infantry Regiment (Colonel Ziegler) entered the bridgehead. The Soviets did not put up with them for long.

The first three weeks of September were filled with the hurling of bombs, the whistling of shells, the rattling of tanks, and the groaning of German and Russian soldiers. The Soviets widened their penetration, but they could not break into the East Prussian positions. On 9/23, the 3rd Infantry Regiment counterattacked, but it was repulsed. At this time, the 21st Reconnaissance Battalion totaled 2 officers and 26 men, and the 5/3 Infantry Regiment had only 5 soldiers left!

The 21st ID was burned out by the battle — and was relieved.

The battle around the Volkhov continued for another two years.

"Melancholy overcast sky, the little play of light on the shadows of the bunkers and combat positions and in the narrow blockhouses indicated that the day was departing the forests and marshes of the front. The infantrymen had become forest men, learning to light smokeless fires that did not give their positions in the swamp away... The corduroy roads, which branched off of the rail lines, the small track gauge of the field rail line, the trails, the main combat line traces, all connect to the great Moscow-Leningrad highway..."[3]

Leningrad remained the main mission of Army Group North, and this made the fighting on the Volkhov front so bitter.

The commander of Army Group North, Field Marshal von Kuechler (who was promoted after the Volkhov battle), arrived at the OKH headquarters in Rastenburg on 6/30, in order to discuss further plans. There, he received the mission to widen the land bridge to Demyansk, improve the positions in the "Bottle-neck", and reinforce the encirclement front around Leningrad. Hitler stood by his Führer Directive of 4/5/1942:

"...To bring about the fall of Leningrad and establish a ground connection with the Fins."

In spite of the connecting routes from Tikhvin over Lake Ladoga won during the winter, the city of Lenin was not delivered from the crisis of a beleaguered fortress. As before, hunger and epidemics reigned. Therefore, the Defense Committee decided to evacuate the aged, feeble, and incapable. In 1942, a total of 951,000 people were shipped to central and northern Russia.

The west to east traffic was in full swing. The supply of the city also began to pick up. At the end of May 1942, the Ladoga ship route opened. In 1942, the 200 ship Ladoga Flotilla (Naval Captain Cherekov) transported approximately 1 million tons of goods and 250,000 soldiers to Leningrad.

Both the Germans and the Soviets understood the military and the political significance of Leningrad. In the fall of 1942, the OKH planned to translate the Führer Directive "To Bring the Fall of Leningrad" into reality. The 11th Army, (Field Marshal von Manstein), who had assaulted the strongest fortress in the world, Sevastopol, in the spring, had to take Leningrad. Already, the transport trains were rolling from the Crimea, with the 11th Army, including the two corps, the XXX and LIV, and the 24th, 170 ID, and 28th Light Infantry Division.

The "Operation Nordlicht [North Light]" — the assault on Leningrad — was to begin on 9/14 out of the Mga area.

The Soviets expected this offensive!

The Army Groups Leningrad Front (Lieutenant General Govorov) and Volkhov Front (Army General Meretskov) had concentrated strong forces on their flanks. The 8th Rifle Division and 1st Tank Brigade prepared behind the Neva. The 2nd Shock Army (Lieutenant General Klykov) was newly re-built and deployed the 12th Rifle Division, 6th Rifle Brigade, and 4th Tank Brigade south of Lake Ladoga.

The Soviet plan envisioned a simultaneous attack by both spearheads. They were to compress the 20 kilometer deep and 14 kilometer wide "Bottle-neck" between Mga and Lake Ladoga, create a land connection to Leningrad, and destroy the arriving 11th Army as it was deploying.

A daring plan.

The 1st Battle of Ladoga began on 8/24/1942.

After an hours-long fire preparation by continuous bombings, deep air attacks, and barrage fire, the 2nd Shock Army initiated the offensive on a small front between Gaitolovo and Tortolovo. The 223rd ID (Lieutenant General Lueters), which was located here and had been transferred from France to the east during the summer, could not stand up to the superior forces and collapsed.

Enemy tanks and infantrymen crossed the Chernaya and assaulted the dominant heights of Sinyavino. Hastily collected combat groups under determined commanders, supply battalions, and transport companies were thrown against the Russians. The neighboring 96th ID removed a battalion from its front and transported it to the northwest.

Several strong points held for days and weeks and prevented the Soviets from being successful in their sector. The 366th Infantry Regiment (Lieutenant Colonel Wengler) of the 227th ID defended the town of Gontovaya against all attacks. The strong point became known as "Wengler's Nose." It was the only frontal position which was not lost on the Chernaya.

Field Marshal von Manstein, who took up headquarters in Siverskaya, was ordered to do everything possible to "avert a catastrophe." Hitler subordinated the entire frontal sector between the Baltic Sea and Kirishi to him. The 18th Army commander (General Lindemann) now only controlled the Volkhov.

The Field Marshal ordered the 170th ID (Major General Sander), which was arriving in Mga, to counterattack into the flank of the enemy, which was breaking through south of Sinyavino. The soldiers from Holstein and Oldenburg had to deploy directly from the wagons into the battle. The 391st, 399th, and 401st Regiments blocked east of Sinyavino for the time being. The enemy closed on this point and continued to attack. On 9/3, they broke open the blockade and forced their way to Kelkolovo.

The 11th Army was able to parry this attack. Its 24th and 132nd ID reinforced the blocking front in the south. In addition, elements of the 12th Panzer Division came, while the 121st pressed in from the north. The most important points in the combat area, the Sinyavino Heights, Kelkolovo, and Mga, remained in German hands.

The XXX Army Corps (General of Artillery Fretter-Pico) led the divisions on the southern front of the penetration area. The battered 223rd ID secured the front to the east around Voronovo. The XXVI Army Corps (General of Artillery Wodrig) took command of the 28th Light Infantry Division near Kelkolovo, the 5th Mountain Division east of Sinyavino, the 121st, and elements of the 227th ID on the Chernaya.

The divisions prohibited the expansion of the enemy wedge. The Soviet forces had to stop, transition to the defense, and await reinforcement. Field Marshal von Manstein was immediately informed of the threat and ordered the pocket to close to a smaller location.

The most favorable departure point was the salient around Tortolovo, in which, at that very moment, the 24th ID (Lieutenant General von Tettau) and the 132nd ID (Major General Lindemann) stood. Stukas and combat aircraft of the VIII Air Corps, which was again transferred from the middle sector to the north, attacked the positions of the VI Soviet Guards Corps (Major General Gagin) on 9/22. Immediately after the last stuka left, the men of the 132nd ID jumped out of their trenches and attacked.

The Soviets defended bitterly. However, the soldiers slowly fought their way through the forests and marshes to the north. Losses were high. The 132nd ID lost 16 officers and 494 men on the first day of the battle! The attack slowed down. On 9/23, they could only gain 100 meters of ground. Enemy resistance was strong.

Then, luckily, the 3/437th Infantry Regiment (Captain Schmidt) broke through on 9/25. Once again the infantrymen rose up, they overcame the last obstacle, and entered the burning town of Gaitolovo exactly at noon! Here, they stood on the road to Sinyavino and cut the only Soviet rollbahn leading to the pocket!

Tentative contact was finally established with the assault troops of the 121st ID (Major General Wandel), which were coming out of the north. The pocket west of Gaitolovo was closed! The advanced elements of the 3rd Mountain Division (Major General Kreysing) — which came from Finland, unloaded in Reval, and were thrown toward Mga — finally completed the encirclement of the VI Soviet Guards Corps.

It was a repeat of the same situation in the Volkhov pocket. After the enemy was cut off from their rear area and all relief attempts from the east were repulsed by German fire, the resistance collapsed.

By the end of September, the Red Army lost their 94th, 191st, 259th, 294th, and 374th Rifle Divisions, 19th and 24th Guards Divisions, and the 22nd, 23rd, 33rd, 34th, 53rd, and 140th Rifle Brigades in the Gaitolovo pocket. 12,370 Red Army soldiers were captured, while 193 guns and 244 tanks were captured or destroyed.

A great victory was achieved. However, it had required time and sacrifice. As before, the OKH was determined to bring Leningrad to its knees. The attack objective, however, had to be narrowed, because the Finish government informed them that their divisions would not participate in this offensive.

The Germans developed new plans.

Then the Red Army began its major offensive in the southern sector of the Eastern Front!

The 11th Army and the XXX Army Corps were withdrawn. General Lindemann again took over control of the entire front from Volkhov to Oranienbaum. The preparations of the German troops in front of Leningrad were canceled. The first divisions were loaded for transport to the south. One after the next, the northern sector lost: the 3rd Mountain Division, the 12th Panzer Division, the 269th, 93rd, and 291st ID, and the 20th Motorized Infantry Division.

In the fall of 1942, the Leningrad combat zone had become a secondary theater of war!

Army Group North did receive replacements, however, these did not bring it back to its earlier combat strength. The 69th ID (Lieutenant General Ortner) was brought in from southern Norway and occupied positions on the western edge of the Pogoste pocket. The 1st Luftwaffe Field Division (Major General (Luftwaffe) Wilke) relieved the 250th ID near Novgorod. The newly organized 9th Luftwaffe Field Division (Lieutenant General Winter) and 10th Luftwaffe Field Division (Major General von Wedel) were transferred directly from the homeland to the Oranienbaum front without any infantry experience. Here, the III Luftwaffe Field Corps (General of Air Defense Artillery Odebrecht) took control.

Chapter 4: The Defense

In the fall and the beginning of the winter, the 18th Army had to reorganize in order to accomplish its mission. The German front from Urizk on the Gulf of Finland to Schluesselburg was occupied by the following divisions in December 1942: the L Army Corps was deployed on the left flank with the 215th ID, 2nd SS Infantry Brigade, and 250th ID. In the center of the front was the LIV Army Corps with the SS Police Division and 5th Mountain Division. The Neva front and the "Bottle-neck" were defended by the XXVI Army Corps with the 170th, 225th, 1st, 223rd, and 69th ID.

Seven German divisions covered a front sector which was occupied by three Soviet armies! The positions of the Leningrad Front between Urizk and Schluesselburg were secured from right to left by the following:

42nd Army (Major General Nikolaev) with the 109th, 125th, 189th Rifle Divisions, Reserve: 13th, 43rd, 85th Rifle Divisions, 123rd Tank Brigade;

55th Army (Lieutenant General Sviridov) with the 90th, 72nd, 136th Rifle Divisions, Reserve: 220th Tank Brigade;

67th Army (Major General Dukhanov) with the 46th (formerly the 1st NKVD), 56th Rifle Divisions, Reserve: 86th, 268th Rifle Divisions, 45th Guards Division, 11th Rifle Brigade.

The numerical superiority could no longer be made up for by the German 18th Army. From fall of 1942 on, the officers and soldiers knew that they could never again attack. Their mission was: wait and defend!

Around the front of Leningrad, independent artillery duels and scout and assault troop operations took place without having much influence on the front situation. The encirclement front had become so strong that a breakout by the defenders was highly unlikely.

The 303rd Senior Artillery Command had heavy and heavier siege artillery available in order to disrupt or destroy the most important military installations within the fortress of Leningrad. From the winter of 1942/43 on, the army group received reinforcement for its artillery from the super heavy mortars and long barreled guns which had been used in the softening up of Sevastopol. These were guns with calibers of up to 60 cm.

The majority of the siege artillery was concentrated in the western portion of the encirclement front in order to be able to place the harbor and dock facilities, as well as the battleships before Kronstadt, under fire. The batteries were deployed in three groups: the 1st and 2nd Batteries of the 680th Heavy Artillery Battalion, 4th, 5th, and 6th Batteries of the 85th Heavy Artillery Battalion, and the 1st and 2nd Batteries of the 768th Heavy Artillery Battalion, with their 19 tubes, fired on military targets in the city and in front of Leningrad. The eastern group — the 708th Heavy Artillery Battalion — with 12 tubes, engaged enemy battery positions. The southern group consisted of the 686th and 688th Railroad batteries, the 2nd and 3rd batteries of the 768th Heavy Artillery Battalion, and the 503rd Heaviest Battery.

In 1942, Luftflotte 1 also found itself to be numerically inferior. The experienced German pilots were not blind to the fact that the Soviets were a threat in the air. The air formations of the Luftflotte operated, as did the Army, in "combat groups", and had to be committed wherever a threat was forming in the ground war.

After the liberation of the Demyansk combat zone, the secondary effort of the Luftflotte was to oppose front sectors. The Army formations, which were deployed in front of Leningrad, had a legitimate complaint that they had no counter to the fire of the heavy ship-board artillery of the enemy. On 3/28, the Luftflotte decided to order the I Air Corps to destroy the "Baltic Red Banner Fleet"

For "Operation Eisstoss [Ice Attack]", the I Air Corps had available 33 Combat, 62 stukas, and 59 fighter aircraft. The participating units had the following missions:

Stuka Group 1:	All ships;
Combat Group 1:	Battleship "Oktyabranska Revolutsiya" and the cruisers "Maxim Gorkiy"] and "Kirov";
Combat Group 4:	Air Defense positions;
54th Fighter Group:	Fighter cover.

Chapter 4: The Defense

•

The attack of the massed forces began on 4/4. In spite of raging air defense fire, the aircraft dived onto their targets. The defense was so good that no significant success could be expected from this first attack. Therefore, Combat Group 4 was again committed during the following night. A final attack of all the squadrons, during which ninety-three 1000 kilogram bombs were dropped, took place on 4/30.

Throughout all of the attacks, the successes of the German aircraft included four hits on the battleship, seven hits on the cruiser "Maxim Gorkiy", and one hit each on the cruiser "Kirov", the former German cruiser "Luetzow", on the mine cruiser "Marti", training ship "Svir", and a destroyer. They did not succeed in destroying the "Baltic Red Banner Fleet"; however, their heaviest units were not combat capable for months — some forever!

These attacks could not be repeated. The air formations were exhausted throughout the long front. They were flying sorties in the Volkhov pocket, along the Kirishi-Volkhovstroy rail line, in the Pogoste pocket, near Demyansk, over the Kronstadt Bay, Lake Ladoga, and the Sinyavino Heights.

During the summer of 1942, the staff of the I Air Corps was deactivated due to a general reorganization. A staff for a fighter command was formed. All of the front air formations were assigned to this command. The staff was later designated the 3rd Air Division.

The number of committed air formations changed according to the situation. Thus, in May, the 54th Fighter Group had four groups available, and in the fall they had only two squadrons. The 1/54 Fighter Group was transferred to Finland. The fighter squadrons reported 11,328 sorties, during which 2,230 enemy aircraft were shot down and 2,176 aircraft were destroyed in deep attack. Friendly losses totaled 19 dead and 39 missing. The 1st Long Range Reconnaissance Group, which was stationed in Luga, listed the following statistics for their three squadrons for the second half of 1942: they photographed 817,579 square kilometers of terrain during 1,983 flights over enemy territory. Only one aircraft from the 3rd Squadron did not return. Luftflotte 1 lost a total of 267 aircraft!

The air defense artillery — often the most effective artillery help for the trench fighter — received their own independent units. During the spring of 1942, the staffs of the 2nd and 6th Air defense Divisions were deployed. The 2nd Air Defense Division was committed in the 18th Army sector, and the 6th Air Defense Division in the combat area of the 16th Army.

At the end of 1942, Army Group North consisted of one panzer division, two motorized infantry divisions, 31 infantry divisions, three light infantry divisions, one mountain division, and one motorized brigade. These numbers represent considerable combat power, however, when considered in relation to the entire Eastern Front. It showed that the northern sector was not of primary concern at this time. Of the infantry divisions operating in the east, the army group had only 1/4, the motorized divisions only 1/17, and the panzer divisions 1/20.

The army group would no longer start any offensive, so it endeavored to construct its rear area lines of communication and supply centers in such a way that movement and supply would not be broken. The army group established strong points for ammunition, supply, fuel, and food in Luga, Pleskau, Toropets, Riga, and Duenaburg. The 16th Army had similar strong points in Dno, Soltsy, Staraya Russa, Tulebya, Shimsk, and Loknya. The 18th Army had supply bases available in Narva, Volossovo, Krasnovardeisk, Siverskaya, Tossno, Sablino, and Lyuban.

Road conditions were improved by Army construction battalions and the Northern Labor Group. They were able to construct 732 kilometers of corduroy roads — that is equal to the stretch from Hamburg to Vienna — which required 7,328,550 logs. Construction troops and Labor forces constructed 445 bridges in 1942, with a total length of 21.4 kilometers, requiring 93,941 cubic meters of wood and 1.7 million kilograms of iron. The railroad stretches from Shaulen-Riga, Vilna-Pleskau-Krasnovardeisk, and Chudovo-Tossno were converted to double tracks. The important single track stretches for the transport of supplies, i.e. Riga-Reval, Reval-Krasnovardeisk, Novosokolniki-Dno, Pleskau -Staraya Russa, and Luga-Novgorod were kept intact.

The successes of the army group for the year 1942 are expressed in numbers:

Chapter 4: The Defense

Prisoners 84,493

Equipment captured or destroyed: 4,428 tanks, 1,119 guns, 613 anti-tank guns, 62 air defense guns, 6,482 machine-guns.

For individual performance, the members of Combat Group Scherer were awarded the "Kholm Shield." Oak Leaves for the Knight's Cross were received by 14 officers (7 generals, 3 colonels, 1 captain, 2 senior lieutenants, and 1 lieutenant). The Knight's Cross was awarded to 102 officers and 20 non-commissioned officers and men.

Field Marshal von Kuechler issued an order of the day on 12/31, in which he said:

> "Soldiers of the Northern Front!
>
> Another year of difficult and victorious combat has passed...
>
> From the Gulf of Finland far to the south of Lake Ilmen we are holding positions against repeated Bolshevik attacks.
>
> In spite of the heaviest commitment of men and equipment, the enemy's assault on the brave and true German soldiers...has collapsed.
>
> The act of holding and relieving Kholm, the attack to destroy the land bridge in the Demyansk area, the tenacious defense of these combat areas, the battles on the Volkhov and on Lake Ladoga were unrivaled in the pages of German military history and will be forever remembered in the History of this great war.
>
> I give reverent and eternal thanks to our fallen in the Northern Front..."

The new year would pose many difficult questions for the army group, such as those spoken of in the Field Marshal's order of the day.

The Soviet High Command issued the following order on 8/12/1942:

> "The Volkhov Front and the Leningrad Front have to defeat the grouping of the enemy in the Lipka-Gaitolovo-Moskovskaya Bubrovka-Schluesselburg area with united forces and, therefore, lift the siege of Leningrad!"

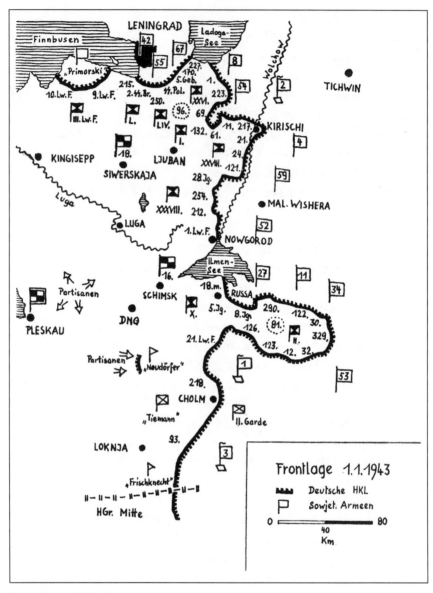

Front Situation 1/1/1943.

Chapter 4: The Defense

From this day on, the two Russian fronts intensively prepared for the offensive, which must bring a change in the fortune of war in the northern sector. The formations assigned as attack groups were gathered behind the front for weeks-long exercises. The staff officers conducted map maneuvers, through which they could discuss all eventualities.

Then the plan was ready.

Army Group Volkhov Front (commander: Army General Meretskov; War Counsel: Lieutenant General Mekhlis; Chief of Staff: Lieutenant General Shakhorin) deployed the attack groups of the 2nd Shock Army, under Lieutenant General Romanovskiy, on the 300 kilometer long front between Lakes Ladoga and Ilmen, directly south of Lake Ladoga. The groups were assigned cooperation with the 14th Air Army (Major General Shurvlov). The massing of the artillery totaled 160 guns per kilometer!

Army Group Leningrad Front (commander: Lieutenant General Govorov; War Counsel: Lieutenant General Zhdanov; Chief of Staff: Lieutenant General Gussev) ordered the 67th Army commander (Major General Dukhanov) to cross the Neva and attack opposite the 2nd Shock Army. The army deployed the 45th Guards Rifle Division (Major General Krasnov), 86th Rifle Division (Colonel Trubachov), and 136th Rifle Division (Major General Simonyak) on the main effort. One independent rifle brigade, moreover, had to provide for the security of the highway (ice road) on Lake Ladoga. 20 artillery and mortar regiments, with 1700 guns, were in support. The 13th Air Army (Major General Rybalchenko) provided air security.

Moscow prepared for the new offensive very thoroughly. Ten partisan detachments were mobilized in the rear of the German front. Transport aircraft dropped 2000 rifles, 660 machine-guns, and 7500 kilograms of explosives to these groups.

During the beginning of January 1943, the Soviet troops occupied their assembly areas. On 1/11, when the deployment of the 8th and 67th Armies between Kolpino and Schluesselburg and the 54th and 2nd Shock Armies between Voronovo and Lipka was complete, they presented the following picture:

The Leningrad Front was deployed on the Neva from right to left with the 46th, 45th, 268th, 136th, and 86th Rifle Divisions in the forward-most positions. Behind them were the 11th Rifle Brigade, 13th Rifle Division, 102nd Rifle Brigade, 123rd Rifle Division, the 142nd, 123rd, and 35th Rifle Brigades, and the 34th Tank Brigade prepared to exploit. The 55th Rifle Brigade occupied positions on the Ladoga ice road. On the eastern front of the German Bottle-neck were located (from right to left): the 128th, 372nd, 256th, 327th, 314th, 376th, 80th, 265th, and 73rd Rifle Divisions, while in the second line were the 12th Tank Brigade, 18th, 239th, 147th, 191st, and 71st Rifle Divisions, as well as the 13th Tank Brigade, 11th, and 364th Rifle Divisions.

On the other hand, the German troops in the same area seemed almost harmless. The XXVI Army Corps (Lieutenant General von Leyser) had the 5th Mountain Division (Lieutenant General Ringel) and the 170th ID (Lieutenant General Sander) on the Neva front, the 227th ID (Lieutenant General von Scotti) around Schluesselburg, and the 1st ID (Lieutenant General Grase) and the 223rd ID (Major General Usinger) at the "Bottle-neck."

During the night of 1/12, the Soviet air forces began to mass attacks against airfields, rail, and traffic centers in the interior. 4500 enemy guns simultaneously opened fire on the German positions in the "Bottle-neck" on the next day at 0930 hours.

The 2nd Shock Army (Lieutenant General Romanovskiy) set the main effort of the attack on Chernayaknie near Gaitolovo. The East Prussians of the 1st ID energetically set themselves against this assault and made the enemy pay for each meter of ground. The neighboring 366th Infantry Regiment (Lieutenant Colonel Wengler) held out in the forest — the so-called "Wengler Nose" — against the 327th Rifle Division (Colonel Polyakov) and the 39th Engineer Brigade all day long. During the night, the Russian 2/1098 Rifle Regiment (Senior Lieutenant Yunyaev) penetrated into the forest. Combat continued. The resistance of one of the German regiments even found expression in the official Soviet History of the war. When the 2nd Shock Army committed the 64th Guards Division, Lieutenant Colonel Wengler had to withdraw his brave infantrymen! The 2nd Shock Army had achieved a 12 kilometer wide penetration, but it was no deeper than 2 kilometers.

The 67th Soviet Army (Major General Dukhanov) arrived at the Neva at the same time. The 136th and 268th Rifle Divisions assaulted onto the ice of the Neva after the last shots of the friendly artillery.

> "Between Marino and Gorodok, on the seam between the 2/401
> Infantry Regiment and the 240th Reconnaissance battalion, both of
> which were defending extremely wide sectors on the right sector of the
> division, the Russians lay their main effort. After the wounding of the
> 401st Infantry Regiment commander, Lieutenant Colonel Dr. Kleinhenz,
> and his adjutant, 10 Russian battalions achieved a breakthrough against
> a combat strength of only 300 men, and that was before the start of the
> preparatory fire. At the same time, three regiments set out from the
> Dubrovka bridgehead to the north and east, and of them, only a small
> portion were able to take the battered trenches and were finally stopped
> in the depth of the main battlefield after very heavy losses. At the same
> time, attacks against the 1/401 Infantry Regiment on the right flank of
> the division, against the wheeled squadron at the hospital, against the
> front of the 399th Infantry Regiment south of the Dubrovka bridge-
> head were all repulsed. Shortly after the commander of the 240th Re-
> connaissance Battalion fell, a thin, strong point-type line was estab-
> lished east of the breakthrough area on either side of the ring road, and
> it was then occupied by a battalion of the 96th ID. The losses suffered
> by the enemy between the power station and the paper factory were
> extraordinarily high...about 3000 dead. Entire rows of fallen Russians
> lay on the Neva ice. ..."[4]

The resistance on the Neva could not be distinguished from that at the
"Bottle-neck." The 45th Soviet Guards Division did not make it across the
ice and the 86th Rifle Division did not reach the bank near Schluesselburg.
The Soviets sacrificed hecotombs of dead — and continued to attack! During the night, the sounds of combat did not fade out. The Russian engineers
of the Leningrad Front built catwalks for heavy vehicles and tanks.

The German leadership ordered countermeasures, as far as the available means would allow. The 61st ID removed one regiment from their
positions north of the Tigoda sector and transported them in trucks to Mga.
The 96th ID, which was in a "rest area" in the Sinyavino area, was alerted.
Elements of the division were immediately directed to Schluesselburg and

Lipki. The rest assembled on the morning of 1/13 to counterattack to the north.

At dawn, the Soviets renewed their attempts to break out. Hard and bitter was the combat on the banks of the Neva. The 45th Guards Division and the 268th Rifle Division were bloodied on this cold January day on the ice of the river. On the other hand, the Russian 136th Rifle Division — later renamed the 63rd Guards Division — and the 61st Tank Brigade, under Major General Simonyak, made it to the east. The heavily battered battalions of the 170th ID no longer had the strength to defend against the tanks and aircraft. The 86th Rifle Division, which was advancing on the left flank of the 67th Army, finally got a foothold on the eastern bank of the river, after repeated attempts, and attacked into the forest south of Schluesselburg. The 227th ID immediately established a blocking position along the Schluesselburg-Lipka road, so that the threat to the city was repulsed.

On 1/14, the 2nd Shock Army committed its reserve. The 18th, 256th, and 372nd Rifle Divisions, and the 98th Tank Brigade entered the hilly terrain north of Sinyavino in minus 28 degree cold and aimed at Poselok 5 (a workers' settlement). Combat increased dramatically. The 284th Infantry Regiment (96th ID), under Colonel Pohlman, in the meantime had arrived at the 170th ID and brought a little relief. The 283rd Infantry Regiment (Colonel Andoys) assaulted the power station at Gorodok and freed the defenders there who had been encircled all day.

The battle continued day and night. There was no rest for the infantrymen, artillerymen, engineers, convoys, nor for the few "Tiger" tanks of the 1/502 Panzer battalion. The Soviets continued to throw new formations into the battle. The 18th Army commander was compelled to transport combat groups and battalions from many divisions to Mga and Sinyavino.

The 96th ID (Major General Noeldechen) shoved the 287th Infantry Regiment (Colonel Dorff) to the north on a mission to make contact. However, the situation did not become any clearer. The thin German front — attacked from the west and the east — ruptured! The 136th Rifle Division and the 61st Tank Brigade, coming from the west, shook hands with the 18th Rifle Division and the 16th Tank Brigade north of Poselok 5! On the same day, 1/15, the 123rd Rifle Brigade and the 372nd Rifle Division attacked past each other near Poselok 1.

The 227th ID, with the 2/287 Infantry Regiment and the 196th Battalion (of the 96th ID), was encircled at Schluesselburg!

The 128th Rifle Division was able to take Lipka on 1/17. The 2/287 Infantry Regiment, under Senior Lieutenant Pawlowski, withdrew to the west. The 12th Soviet Ski Brigade set out across Lake Ladoga and attacked the infantrymen in the rear. At the same time, the 327th Rifle Division and 122nd Tank Brigade encircled Poselok 8, in which elements of the 366th and 374th Infantry Regiments defended until their last cartridge. The attack of the 136th Rifle Division on Poselok 5 failed, due to the resistance of the 374th Infantry Regiment (Colonel von Below). The 227th ID was scattered, after which the 328th Infantry Regiment (Colonel Lamey) had to withdraw to Schluesselburg, where the first street battle occurred.

Then, the 151st and 161st Regiments of the 61st ID, under Major General Huehner, set out from Sinyavino to counterattack. The East Prussian infantrymen unbelievably made it to Schluesselburg! However, behind them, the front immediately closed. Major General Huehner took over the command of Schluesselburg and directed its defense with his combat group.

It was impossible for the 18th Army to establish contact with the strong point on Lake Ladoga. General Lindemann, therefore, ordered them to break out. On the morning of 1/18, the German batteries on the Sinyavino Heights conducted a powerful fire strike on the Russian assembly areas between the Sinyavino Heights and Schluesselburg. Under the protective cover of the fire, the last wounded transport broke out of Schluesselburg.

Then Major General Huehner's combat group broke out!

It was a march of desperation through forest and fire! They had fired the last of their ammunition. Now they wielded shovels, clubs, and hand grenades. The 151st Infantry Regiment (Major Krudzki) took the lead. The East Prussians plodded over the naked terrain, threw themselves onto the strongly defended strong point of Poselok 5, and suppressed the Soviets in man to man combat.

Major Krudzki fell at the head of his regiment. With him died Captain Offer, commander of the 1/162 Infantry Regiment; Senior Lieutenant Kopp, commander of the 6th Company of the 151st Infantry Regiment; Senior

Lieutenant Pawlowski, commander of the 2/287 Infantry Regiment; and many other officers and soldiers. The majority of the combat group got through and reached the Sinyavino Heights!

The bank of Lake Ladoga was lost — the climax of the 2nd Battle of Ladoga was over!

The Soviets regrouped. The 2nd Shock Army took control north of the Sinyavino Heights. On the right stood the 8th, and on the left, the 67th Armies. Lieutenant General Romanovskiy wanted to take the Heights under any circumstances in order to be able to cross through Mga into the rear of the German front near Leningrad and on the Volkhov. Mga, a collection of charred wood huts and destroyed railroad installations, was not only the objective of the Soviets, but the heart of the German defensive front.

The 18th Army commander also adjusted. The important Sinyavino Heights must be held by the army. General of Infantry Hilpert took command of all German divisions that were located between the Neva and Volkhov. From left to right he had: the 5th Mountain Division, 28th Light Infantry Division, and the 21st, 11th, 212th, 1st, and 223rd ID. The 61st, 96th, 170th, and 227th ID were all disbanded due to heavy losses.

The Soviets did not allow a lot of time for regrouping and shifting troops. Fighter-bombers, "Stalin Organs", and batteries of all calibers began the new phase of the 2nd Battle of Ladoga on 1/29. 35 Rifle and tank battalions attacked the Sinyavino Heights on a breadth of 2.5 kilometers! The defenders fought from shell craters and holes in the snow and threw the enemy back from penetrations here and there! On the third day, the resistance strength flagged. Soviet infantrymen assaulted Hill 43.3, attacked the thin front of the 3/390 Infantry Regiment (215th ID), and made it to the Sinyavino church! This was the only building still standing in Sinyavino. All the others were in ruins.

The 11th ID immediately set the 1/44 Infantry Regiment (Major Laebe) to counterattack. The infantrymen fought their way to the Soviets during a heavy snow storm, threw them out of Sinyavino, and back to their departure positions!

The Russian 2nd Shock Army did not give up. They dispatched new regiments into the fire.

Sinyavino had to fall!

Chapter 4: The Defense

The 11th ID (Major General Thomashki), however, was not rattled. They held their positions so well that the Silesian infantrymen of the 28th Light Infantry Division (Lieutenant General Sinnhuber) did not give up one inch. Then, Army General Meretskov suspended the battle. He stopped, but he did not give up. Now, he turned the crank to another location in order to cause the collapse of the Sinyavino front. He ordered the 4th Army (Major General Gusev) and the 54th Army (Major General Sukhomlin) to set out from the Pogoste pocket directly to the west with the objective of Mga. At the same time, the 55th Army (Lieutenant General Sviridov) was to conduct an attack out of Leningrad. This attack was to be directed along the Leningrad-Chudovo rail line. Both armies had to meet between Mga and Lyuban, and a new pocket would be formed in the north of the Eastern Front.

The attack began on 2/10 south of Vinyagolovo. The first day passed without any success for the enemy. On the next day, 20 super heavy tanks penetrated into the German main combat line near Klosterdorf. On the third day, the penetration was expanded to Smyrdynhya. The objective was the road to Lyuban. However, the 96th ID (Major General Noeldechen), 121st ID (Major General Priess), and 132nd ID (Major General Lindemann) would not allow the enemy to get that far. They wrested away from them the territory they won and re-established the old main combat line by 23 February!

The attack, which was initiated by the 55th Army out of Kolpino along the road and railroad to Lyuban, began on the morning of 2/10, with all of the weight on the 250th Spanish Infantry Division (Major General Esteban-Infantes) near Krasniybor. In a few hours the town was a smoldering rubble, in which the 262nd Infantry Regiment (Colonel Sagrado) dug in. The 45th, 63rd, and 72nd Rifle Divisions fought against this one regiment for 48 hours. The men from Andalusia, Castille, and Catalonia would not give up! 2,800 dead lay in Krasniybor on the evening of 2/11, when the Soviets reached the eastern edge of the city.

The L Army Corps (General of Cavalry Kleffel) set elements of the 212th, later the 24th, 58th, and 215th ID — which had come from the Volkhov front — to counterattack on 2/13. The meeting of the Volkhov and Leningrad Fronts south of Mga failed!

Combat on the 18th Army front subsided notably at the beginning of March. The leadership and the troops saw to the construction of positions and traffic routes, the transport of ammunition, and equipment. On 3/10, the combat group of General of Infantry Hilpert was relieved. They had to prepare for new, great days of combat.

The Soviets also worked feverishly on their supply and traffic routes. The City Defense Committee in Leningrad agreed, shortly after the establishment of land contact in January, to construct a rail line along the southern bank of Lake Ladoga. Russian workers, civilians, and prisoners of war erected a 36 kilometer stretch between Polyaniy and Schluesselburg in 14 days. In February, 69 trains traveled on this stretch, in April, 157, and in July, 369.

The third phase of the Ladoga battle had its beginning on 3/19. Enemy preparatory fire battered the positions of the 223rd ID (Major General Usinger) between Voronovo and Lodva for three hours. 10 rifle divisions, 2 rifle, and 5 tank brigades attacked. Melting snow and mud hampered the infantrymen of the 223rd ID in their defense of their bombed and destroyed positions. The superior enemy force cracked the positions and advanced on a 6 kilometer wide front toward Karbussel.

The XXVI Army Corps (Lieutenant General Leyser) committed his corps reserve. The 21st ID took over the threatened sector. The main combat line could not be re-established. Nevertheless, the enemy must be stopped. He did not gain another meter to the west, when finally elements of the 69th, 121st ID, and 5th Mountain Division were thrown into the battle.

The front near Krasniybor again came alive. 6 rifle divisions, 5 tank brigades, and some independent rifle battalions attacked to capture Sablino. The L Army Corps was on guard. The 58th, 170th, and 254th ID held their positions! The 399th Infantry Regiment (170th ID), under Colonel Griesbach, participated in an outstanding manner in this defensive success.

The losses of both friend and foe were high. Soviet losses exceeded those of the 18th Army by far. 270,000 Soviet soldiers died! The combat strength of the Leningrad and Volkhov Fronts were both reduced. The time of mud began, and it covered the clay and sand slopes of the Sinyavino Heights with a layer of mud. The conduct of war was no longer possible.

Chapter 4: The Defense

The 2nd Battle of Ladoga ended at the beginning of April.

"South of Lake Ilmen..."

These three words were repeated every day in the reports of the OKW. They represented a wide combat zone, in which the army group wrote a chapter of its history in spring of 1943.

On 1/29/1943, as the catastrophe at Stalingrad loomed, Hitler was briefed on the situation in the Demyansk combat area. This region projected an arrow to the east. It was sure that, either in the short or long run, the Soviets, with their superiority, would sooner or later remove this salient. The Chief of the General Staff, General Zeitzler, proposed withdrawing the II Army Corps. However, Hitler stuck to his previous point of view, that not one meter of ground be surrendered and that Demyansk must be defended as a fortress!

The 16th Army — without the knowledge of the High Command — worked out plans for the evacuation of the front salient. They initiated "Operation Entruempelung [attic cleaning]." The action required the troops to remove all non-essential equipment. Supply, construction, and engineer units established new routes, on which truck columns transported a total of 8,000 tons of goods by 2/16.

Since the establishment of the land connection, the front in the Demyansk combat area had stabilized. The year 1942 had passed in continuous combat, major attacks, and the respective defensive operations, during which both friend and foe had made exceptional sacrifices. In October 1942, the Soviets had available the 11th, 34th, adn 53rd Armies, as well as the 1st Shock Army, with 2 guards divisions, 19 rifle divisions, 7 rifle brigades, 3 tank brigades, 3 ski brigades, 4 reserve divisions, and 8 independent machine-gun battalions.

The II Army Corps, which, since 11/28/1942, was commanded by General of Infantry Laux, who replaced the ailing General of Infantry Count von Brockdorff-Ahlefeldt, could oppose these superior forces with only the following divisions: the 5th and 8th Light infantry Divisions; the 12th, 30th, 32nd, 58th, 81st, 122nd, 123rd, 126th, 225th, 254th, 290th, and 329th ID; the SS "Totenkopf" Division; and SS Freikorps "Danmark."

In May 1942, the combat area was divided into two operations areas. The II Army Corps was responsible for combat along the pocket front, while the Special Purpose Corps Group was responsible for the land bridge. Here, on this small front, heavy and bitter combat was fought.

At the end of April 1942, the II Army Corps published a report on combat since the beginning of the year. 1,115 enemy attacks and 776 advances were repulsed, 376 counterattacks were made, 3,064 prisoners were taken, 74 tanks, 52 guns, and 81 anti-tank guns were either destroyed or captured. Friendly losses totaled 5,101 dead, 15,323 wounded, 5,866 cases of frostbite, and 2,000 missing. In spite of the thaw, the month of May brought no reduction in the combat. The corps registered 1,407 dead, 4,866 wounded, and 663 missing.

Several formations had to be relieved after their combat strength was completely exhausted. There were many examples of bravery. For example, on 5/1, two officers, 14 non-commissioned officers, and 62 men of the 290th ID defended the Somshino strong point to the last man. The SS Freikorps "Danmark" was battered at the beginning of June during combat around Dubovitsy on the Pola. The 38th Light Infantry Regiment (8th Light Infantry Division) had only 100 men left after bitter combat around the Vassilevshchina center!

The main emphasis of all enemy attacks was directed at the small land bridge. Therefore, the Special Purpose Corps Group, under the leadership of Lieutenant General Knobelsdorff, decided to expand it to the Lovati. The 126th ID, 5th Light Infantry Division, and SS "Totenkopf" Division attacked on 9/27 and, in spite of considerable resistance, were able to achieve the assigned objective by 10/2. The enemy lost approximately 10,000 dead, 3,178 prisoners, and 108 guns. Friendly losses totaled 415 dead and 1,875 wounded.

The widening of the land bridge was important, because, from summer on, the Demyansk combat area could no longer be supplied from the air. The transport groups of the Luftflotte (Colonel Morzik), without exception, had to fly to the southern front. The squadrons had flown 64,844 tons of equipment and 30,500 soldiers into the pocket.

The combat around the land bridge was not over. As the area again sank under snow and ice in November, the Soviets renewed their attack.

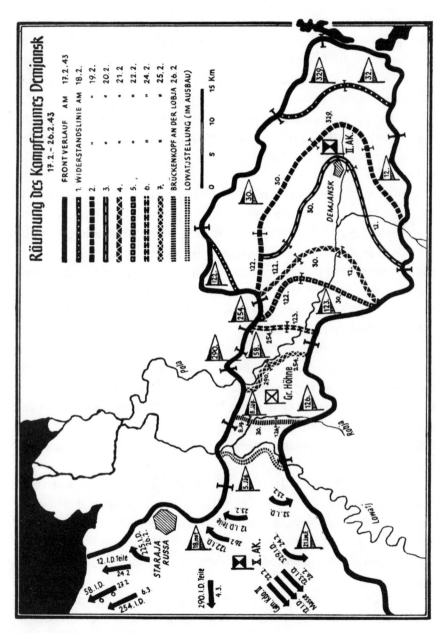

Evacuation of the Demyansk Combat Area 2/17-2/26/43

They wanted to cut off the Demyansk combat area and finally liquidate it. The Special Purpose Corps Group (now under Lieutenant General Hoehne) stood with the 8th Light Infantry Division, and the 290th and 225th ID in the north. These three divisions repulsed all of the attacks by two guards divisions, 5 rifle divisions, 4 rifle, and 2 tank brigades in January 1943. The 123rd and 126th ID defended the southern front against 3 guards divisions, 1 rifle division, 2 rifle, 1 tank brigade, and 1 ski brigade. The losses of the German formations totaled 1,019 dead, 1,032 missing, and 2,271 wounded.

Hitler realized that the combat area could not be held for long. On 2/1/1943, the OKH ordered "All non-essential equipment in the supply region is to be withdrawn west of Staraya Russa and the combat area is to be evacuated in 70 days." The Soviets, who became aware of these measures through agents and intercepted radio communications, multiplied their efforts to intercept the II Army Corps before it withdrew to the west. 12 rifle divisions, with 3 rifle and tank brigades each, attacked the land bridge on 2/15. The German front held!

On 2/17, the code word "Ziethen" arrived at all of the commands in the combat area. It signified: evacuation! Already by late afternoon, the first companies left their shelters for the west. The 32nd and 329th ID (Major General Wegener, Major General Dr. Mayer) left their lake positions on the edge of the Waldai Hills during the night of 2/18. Each division left a rear guard until morning, which deceived the enemy with machine-gun and rifle fire.

The 122nd (Colonel Trowitz), 12th (Lieutenant General Baron von Luetzow), and 30th ID (Major General von Wickede) completed their withdrawal on 2/18. The Soviets immediately pursued the divisions with their ski and cavalry squadrons. The rear guards had to fight their way back with cold steel. The batteries fired from their rear area positions to their last shell!

On 2/19, the Special Purpose Corps Group, 32nd, and 329th ID crossed the Lovati to the west and left the Demyansk combat area! Lieutenant General Hoehne took command of the X Army Corps near Staraya Russa. The former commander, General of Artillery Hansen, became deputy commander of the 16th Army. General of Artillery Hansen took it upon himself to evacuate the combat area in ten days, instead of the 70 required by the OKH. He wanted "to save what could be saved."

The 12th, 30th, and 122nd ID screened the withdrawal around Demyansk on 2/19. The fate of the city was sealed on the next night. In contrast to their orders, withdrawing columns set fire to several houses. The raging night wind spread the fires, so that Demyansk burned like a torch. Only the hospital, with 50 wounded Red Army soldiers and some medical personnel, remained. The Soviets were left with only ashes in their hands.

The II Army Corps and the three divisions reached the fifth resistance line on 2/22. Therefore, the Demyansk combat area was evacuated. The land bridge still held. The Soviets attacked with all their might. Their rifle regiments ran unchecked against the blocking formations of the 30th and 122nd ID. The 12th ID defended the positions on the Pola. A strong attack hit the bridge positions near Kobylkino-Ramushevo. The 8th Light Infantry Division (Major General von Kirchensittenbach), which had already prepared its positions for evacuation, had to concentrate all of its forces in order to repulse this attack.

The attack raged on the following day. Now, the 30th and 122nd ID left the front. The 123rd (Major General Rauch) and 254th ID (Major General Roechling) took up positions and covered the withdrawing formations. The 58th ID (Major General von Graffen) left the front on the next day with the 254th ID and headed west. The 30th, 126th ID, and 8th Light Infantry Division entered the Robya positions. These three old Demyansk divisions held their main combat line until the last rear guards of the 254th and 290th ID withdrew on 2/27/1943.

Therefore, in a short ten days, the combat area and land bridge of Demyansk were stripped bare of German troops! Almost all of the civilians were evacuated; only the old and small children remained. The ground was cratered by thousands of bombs and shells, and towns and cities were deserted. The Soviets occupied terrain on which there were 10,000 wooden crosses on the graves of German soldiers.

On 3/1, General Busch, commander of the 16th Army, issued an order of the day:

"The evacuation of the combat area is over. Here an area was surrendered after the enemy had conducted almost 14 months of uninterrupted attacks. Extreme hardships were suffered. During this time, 1,261 tanks and 416 guns were destroyed, 125 aircraft were shot down. The enemy lost 30,000 prisoners. The Waldai Hills of Lake Seeliger and the Pola Valley with the city of Demyansk had already become our second home. There, many of our comrades rest in the ground. we must now take our leave of these graves, which were guarded in close friendship. However, the spirits of these fallen comrades will follow us west of the Lovati and remain in the divisions of the II Army Corps."

In memory of the combat south of Lake Ilmen, the "Demyansk Shield" was established, which was worn as a combat decoration on the right upper arm of the uniform.

Spring had covered the land. The front had changed little since the evacuation of the Demyansk combat area and the 2nd Battle of Ladoga. The divisions — with the exception of a few dislocations — were located in the same areas. The usual daily positional battles of the scout and assault troops and the fire strikes would flare up on several sectors, when suddenly Soviet companies or battalions would attack. Especially uneasy were positions at the corner-stone of the main combat line and the bridgeheads.

"Throughout the area, displacement, and sometimes even relief, of infantry battalions and mobile battalions was always taking place. This was to give the units the opportunity to rest and refit. Often, battalions were also inserted onto other regimental sectors of the front, especially to relieve those on the "Finger" or "Thumb" sectors — positions on the confluence of the Tigoda and Volkhov. As time passed, the battalions of all three regiments were committed there.

Here it was always the same. The enemy was 80 meters away. The cross-fire came from three sides. Russian assault troops often penetrated and were always repulsed by the 96th ID. They would come with explosives strapped to their bellies, trying to drive us from our bunkers. The 2/284 Infantry Regiment lost 10 dead and 25 wounded in 23 days of their commitment there. When the 2/287 Infantry Regiment (Lieutenant Becvar) was committed here in May, the battalion commander was wounded. The division constantly proposed the evacuation of the "Thumb", which as a position, was just as untenable as the "Merry Louse" near Pogoste."[5]

Once on a May night, the 3/284 Infantry Regiment suddenly had a Russian company in their rear. The Soviets were crossing the river in numerous boats. Lieutenant Colonel Pfuetzner, the regiment commander, immediately set the 2nd Battalion to counterattack. The infantrymen waded in water for four hours until they were able to destroy the enemy.

There was no rest in the Kirishi bridgehead. Here, the 61st ID (Major General Krappe) relieved the 217th ID (Major General Lasch). The 162nd Infantry Regiment took up positions on the enemy side of the Volkhov. The remaining regiments were distributed along a 19 kilometer wide front! This did not allow for the establishment of strong points or a reserve — the infantry groups had shrunk to 5-7 men!

During the dry summer of 1943, the front near Mga also saw no rest. Here, the 11th ID committed all of its forces to construct a deeply echeloned defensive system and for securing the supply route through the marsh-land. After a month's work, they had constructed trenches, combat positions, obstacles, and mine fields, firing positions, and corduroy roads.

The combat area along the Leningrad front was also active. The Soviets were trying to improve their positions. The Spanish held their positions before Pushkin tenaciously, as did the soldiers of the 170th and 215th ID in the ruins of Staro Panovo and Urizk.

In July 1943, the 18th Army was on a unified stable front. The XXXVIII Army Corps was on the right flank with the 1st Luftwaffe Field Division, 217th ID, and the Latvian SS Brigade. Their left neighbor was the I Army Corps, with the 13th Luftwaffe Field Division and 227th ID. The XXVIII Army Corps defended the front around the Kirishi bridgehead and the Pogoste pocket, with the 96th, 61st, and 81st ID, the 12th Luftwaffe Field Division, and the 225th and 132nd ID (from right to left). The XXVI Army Corps controlled the "Bottle-neck" as before. They had available the 212th and 69th ID, 5th Mountain Division, and the 1st, 290th, 11th, and 23rd ID. The LVI Army Corps closed along the Neva to Krasniybor, with the 21st

ID, SS Police Division, 24th, 58th, and 254th ID. The L Army Corps was deployed from there to the Gulf of Finland, with the 250th, 170th, and 215th ID. The III Luftwaffe Field Corps held the Oranienbaum bridgehead in Shakh as before, with the 9th and 10th Luftwaffe Field Divisions.

The 16th Army — which mastered the difficult withdrawal from Demyansk — again was hit by a major Soviet attack. Army Group Northwest Front, which was commanded by Marshal Timoshenko since March 1943, was not satisfied by the withdrawal from Demyansk. The Northwest Front wanted more. They wanted Staraya Russa, the most important city between Lake Ilmen and Vitebsk!

The 34th, 27th, 11th, and 53rd Armies and the 1st Shock Army deployed from north to south at the beginning of March to shake up the front of the 16th German Army.

The army of General Busch stood there in positions with the X Army Corps and the old Demyansk divisions. The 30th, 32nd, 122nd, 329th ID, and the 5th and 8th Light Infantry Divisions lay like a ring around Staraya Russa. They had contact with the right neighboring 21st Luftwaffe Field Division on the Redya.

Marshal Timoshenko wanted to capture Staraya Russa before the German troops were able to fortify it. In March 1943, Staraya Russa was no longer the splendid center of the region south of Lake Ilmen. The civilian population was evacuated. The outskirts of the city were torn by bomb and shell craters. Entire sections of the city were obliterated. Only the stone buildings of the government, the party, warehouses, barracks, and factories stood. And one could still see the towers of St. Georges, St. Nicholas, Mary of Sacrifice, All Lakes, St. Dimitriy, St. Mina, St. Johannes, the Monastery Church, the Parfino Church, the Preobrazhenskiy Monastery, and the landmark of the city: the Resurrection Cathedral.

These ancient church walls resisted all shells. They shined splendidly in the spring sun. On the obelisk, which commemorated the Russo-Japanese War, the Tsar's eagle still spread his wings. The churches and cupolas were the last evidence of Staraya Russa's eternal history.

...until on 3/14 at 0545 hours, Soviet artillery fire erupted, covering the land and the city in smoke, fire, and blood for two hours. New fires broke out in Staraya Russa. The Parfino Church was torn to shreds by the bombardment of "Stalin Organs." As the smoke settled on the landscape and the noise of combat died out, tank engines began to roar.

The Fourth Battle of Staraya Russa had begun.

The full weight of the attack hit the 30th ID (Major General von Wickede). The men from Schleswig-Holstein held their positions. In the afternoon, the "T-34's" and "Kv-I's" evoked a crises in the neighboring 14th Luftwaffe Field Regiment area, nevertheless, this was also mastered. The enemy repeated his attack on the next day and directed it against the 17th SS Police Regiment, which was broken through.

> "The only reserve available to the division was the staff of the 30th Wheeled Battalion and the 3rd Squadron, which was reconstituting in the Staraya Russa School, it consisted of its commander, Senior Lieutenant Adloff, and 10 men. The order to commit was accompanied by the commander's reply: 'Well, this time I can bring my troop to the front in a Volkswagen!' However, there were no infantry forces available to the division, the engineer companies were already committed as "corset rods." However, three assault guns and a mortar detachment of the 70th Smoke Generation regiment were made available by Major Jass, and the entire 30th Artillery Regiment ... was preparing to concentrate fire on this sector."[6]

The situation was further clarified, but not until the evening. Then, the Soviets had to withdraw for a second time. The soldiers of the 30th ID and their attached forces from the 18th Motorized Infantry Division had just begun to re-group, when the artillery fire started up again. On 3/17, the soldiers saw no sunshine, only shells. The Soviet batteries fired without pause for the entire morning.

The weather limited visibility for both friend and foe. In spite of this, the tanks rolled on, followed by countless rifle battalions. Fierce hand to hand combat broke out on the entire front, while the artillery from both sides dueled. There was no rest that day or the following night.

Russian losses were high. They wanted to take a breather. On 3/19, the Soviets suspended their attack on Staraya Russa! The defenders also took a breather. The 30th ID, with the attached 14th Luftwaffe Field Regiment, had lost 1000 men in five days. From the 2/94 Infantry Regiment (32nd ID), there were now only 2 officers and 99 soldiers combat capable.

A deeper enemy penetration was only achieved south of Staraya Russa on the road between Penna and Mikhalkino. The X Army Corps decided to lance this boil. The 5th Light Infantry Division (Major General Thumm) was assigned the mission. The division prepared two attack groups, which occupied their departure positions on 3/29.

The attack began on the morning of 3/30 at 0515 hours, with a fire preparation from 34 batteries. As the clock struck the sixth hour, the men of the 56th Light Infantry Regiment, 75th Light Infantry Regiment, 426th Infantry Regiment, 3/411 Infantry Regiment, 5th Engineer Battalion, and elements of the 5th Anti-tank Battalion rose from their trenches.

"The 56th Light Infantry Regiment was soon hit by strong flanking fire from the right and the left. They stopped. The 75th Light Infantry Regiment (Colonel Baron von Muehlen), which had prepared in the area approximately 2 kilometers north of Penna, gained ground to the southeast with their 1st and 3rd Battalions, opposite the 56th Light Infantry Regiment. While penetrating into fortified positions, the 1/75 Light Infantry Regiment (Captain Maier) captured numerous Russians. By noon, the 2/75 Light Infantry Regiment (Major Sachsenheimer) was also committed. In spite of having to wade through the muddy forest ground and in spite of an enemy counterattack, supported by tanks, they fought their way through to the Penna road east of Penna and established contact with the 56th Light Infantry Regiment after 1700 hours...

For the subsequent mission they advanced in the afternoon of 3/31 through the forest in a concentrated attack to the northeast in order to take the old Russian defensive positions as the new main combat line. They were supported by strong, but cautious, artillery fire. The operation was broken off in the evening, because the attack ran into a strongly constructed enemy defensive position in the swampy forest and suffered heavy losses."[7]

Chapter 4: The Defense

Combat along the Redya and Porussya ebbed at the end of March. Spring slowly set in with a thaw. The walls of snow melted away and had to be replaced with earth trenches. The unfortified roads turned to mud. Torrents now flowed in the streams. The war came to a halt.

The Special Purpose Corps Group, which fought its last battle under the X Army Corps, was disbanded. The VIII Army Corps (General of Infantry Hoehne) was created from it. The corps took over the 21st Luftwaffe Field Division, 329th, 32nd, and later the 122nd ID. These divisions protected the front south of Staraya Russa.

The German Landser fought feverishly at their positions. The entire situation of the Eastern War required that they still hold on. The main emphasis of the combat obviously lay in the south and, later, from July on, in the center of the front. The divisions of the 16th and 18th Armies had to transition to the defensive. The once magnificent city of Staraya Russa was turned into a fortress in the summer of 1943.

The X Army Corps (General of Artillery Hansen) anticipated the 5th Battle of Staraya Russa at the beginning of August. The 30th ID (Major General Wickede) and the 8th Light Infantry Division (Major General Volckamer von Kirchensittenbach) were tasked with the defense of the important city south of Lake Ilmen. The few available Luftwaffe reconnaissance assets reported troop movements, artillery positions and lively railroad traffic. The army decided to remove the 122nd ID (Major General Chill) from the front and hold it in reserve.

Then 8/18 arrived. Hundreds of Soviet batteries thundered their steel greetings into the positions of the North German, Silesian, and Pomeranian soldiers. Then they came: hoards of tanks with mounted infantry, behind them were rifle battalions on a wide front, engineer units, anti-tankers, and then again more "T-34's" and "Kv-I's."

The battle was fierce. As evening fell, 40 combat vehicles lay burning and destroyed in the positions before Staraya Russa. Indeed, at several positions, they were able to penetrate into the forward-most trenches of the 30th ID.

On 8/19, the frontal attack was repeated and repulsed. The third attack on 8/21 hit the seam between the 30th ID and the 8th Light Infantry Division. The third attack also bogged down under heavy losses. The OKW reported:

"All Soviet attacks near Staraya Russa have collapsed under heavy losses. According to the enemy attack plan, this city was to have been captured five days ago. ...All enemy breakthrough attempts have failed. Infantrymen and anti-tankers, engineers, and artillerymen have all participated in this defensive success. The positions remain firmly in the hands of our soldiers!"

The Fifth Battle of Staraya Russa was defeated!

The Soviets gave up south of Lake Ilmen. They could not break through the front of the 16th Army. Therefore, they tried to repeat their offensive in the north against the Sinyavino Heights. German Army Groups South and Center were already battered and had to withdraw.

On 7/22, the sun had still not risen over the eastern horizon when the sky between the Neva and Chernaya began to turn a blood red color. Preparatory fire from countless batteries began promptly at 0300 hours. Shells of all calibers tore into the ground anew, shredded the last corduroy roads, and destroyed bunkers, huts, and farm houses. Squadrons of fighter-bombers and deep strike aircraft stalked the terrified with their on-board weapons.

The Third Battle of Ladoga began.

The objective of the Soviet leadership was to finally capture the vital Kirishi-Leningrad rail line. Therefore, they first had to overwhelm the German front on the Sinyavino Heights. The positions of two armies were to be reinforced in the forests on the Chernaya and near the railroad intersection. This time the attack had to succeed. Between Mustolovo and Gaitolovo stood only the 23rd (Colonel von Mellenthin), 11th (Major General Thomashki), and 290th ID (Major General Heinrichs).

The 67th Army (Major General Dukhanov) attacked through the trenches against the Sinyavino Heights, with the 63rd, 64th, and 45th Guards Divisions, as well as the 11th and 43rd Rifle Division. From the east, on both sides of Gaitolovo, assaulted the 8th Army (Major General Stanikov), with the 128th, 314th, 372nd, 18th, 378th, 256th, and 364th Rifle Division.

Chapter 4: The Defense

The follow-on 30th Soviet Tank Brigade was able to penetrate into the positions of the Brandenburgers at the railroad junction near Poselok 6. The 23rd ID defended in desperation, but still had to give up ground. The 1/9 Infantry Regiment began to withdraw. Therefore, contact was lost with the neighboring 11th ID, which was also involved in heavy defensive combat. The enemy had achieved several deep penetrations here and had broken through to the regimental command posts. The enemy won a 2 kilometer wide and 2 kilometer deep penetration. Since the East Prussians did not withdraw and their left flank was open, the Soviets began to assault here. The men of the 3/44 Infantry Regiment did not give up one square meter of ground without exacting a price. They conducted energetic counterattacks and forced the enemy to take up hasty defensive positions around Poselok 6 in the afternoon!

The battle continued with undiminished fierceness. Hoards of tanks and rifle battalions tried to find a weak position in the front. The East Prussians and Brandenburgers held on. They forced the enemy to take a combat break. The 67th Army regrouped and initiated a new attack on 7/26, again directed at the seam between the two divisions. It did not help. The Soviet soldiers bogged down in the first German trenches.

Day and night the artillery fire rolled and the super heavy bombs thudded. Every meter of ground on the Sinyavino Heights was plowed up. In the meantime, the 11th ID received its first reinforcements. The 561st Special Purpose Infantry Battalion, 1/70 Mortar Regiment, and 912th Assault Gun Brigade had arrived just in time. At 0800 hours, after a powerful preparatory fire, a tank attack of unexpected strength was unleashed. The 11th Light Infantry Battalion (Captain Berger) and the 1/47 Artillery Regiment (Major Radecker), 2nd and 3rd Batteries of the 912th Assault Gun Brigade (Senior Lieutenant Hartl-Kusmenek, Senior Lieutenant Schoenmann), shattered the attack. The batteries of the 1/47 Artillery Regiment fired their 100,000th shell since the beginning of the campaign.

After three bitter days, the Soviets were again stopped. The Sinyavino Heights remained firmly in German hands. The OKW reported:

"The East Prussians of the 11th Infantry Division distinguished themselves south of Lake Ladoga. In bitter combat, they destroyed penetrating enemy units that were conducting strong attacks."

The 18th Army commander committed the first reserves to the threat-ened front at the end of July. The 121st ID (Lieutenant General Priess) was moved into positions to the east, and the 28th Light Infantry Division (Ma-jor General Schultz) to the west of the Sinyavino Heights. Combat intensi-fied. The enemy 67th Army commander was forced to suspend the break-through west of the Heights.

At the beginning of August, the Soviet leadership transferred their main emphasis of their major attack to the east. They planned on hitting the Ger-man divisions on the Chernaya in order to roll over the Heights from the rear. 19 rifle and tank battalions rolled onto the positions of the 290th ID and the right neighboring 1st ID (Major General von Krosigk) on 8/4.

The combat was no less fierce than on the Sinyavino Heights, and the enemy superiority was just as evident as before. The soldiers had to con-tend with the inflexibility of the terrain. It was treeless and flat, with thin shrubs and muddy ground. It was no terrain on which to fight a positional war. There was no material from which bunkers could be built.

The defensive will of the East Prussian and North German Landser finally forced the enemy to halt on this sector of the front. The 18th Army commander took advantage of the situation. He removed the 58th ID (Ma-jor General von Graffen) from the Leningrad front and inserted it to rein-force west of the Sinyavino Heights. The 26th ID (Lieutenant General Hoppe) came from the 16th Army. They took up the positions of the heavily battered 28th Light Infantry Division.

The 67th Army did not give up their chance to again assault the Sinyavino Heights. The 58th ID ran into the new attack on 8/4. It was one of the heaviest combat days for the division. Defense was followed by counterattack and vice verse. Hand to hand combat raged around individual pools of water and tree stumps near Poselok 6, on the railroad intersection, or on the "Burma Road."

The Red Army poured new forces into the battle. On 8/12, seven rifle divisions renewed the assault against the Sinyavino Heights from the north and east. The few divisions, which had been in combat since the first days of the battle, simply could go on no longer. The Landser had no sleep in the forward trenches. The strengths of the companies, at best, were at a handful of men.

The 18th Army commander directed the 21st (Major General Matzky), 61st (Major General Krappe), 215th (Lieutenant General Frankewitz), and 254th ID (Major General Thielmann) to relieve the weakened divisions on the Sinyavino front. Among the formations being taken from the front was the 11th ID, which, in a 20 day battle, stood alone against 7 enemy divisions and defended against 86 attacks. The 126th ID, which had registered more than 300 dead in the two weeks of August between the Heights and Poselok 6, gave up its main combat line just as they had taken it up. The enemy did not penetrate it.

The fierceness of the battle continued through the second half of August. There was no end to the bloodshed. Since their frontal attack did not produce any results, the Soviet leadership now tried to penetrate some positions or cut off frontal assailants by numerous small, concentrated attacks. Again there was bitter fighting in the trenches, bunkers, bushes, and hillocks. The enemy was only able to gain some ground northwest of Voronovo, for elsewhere the front held.

XXVI Army Corps losses were heavy. The 290th ID alone lost 1/3 of its personnel strength!

The losses of the Soviets were higher.

They gave up!

The Third Battle of Ladoga finally fizzled out at the end of September. The XXVI Army Corps (General of Infantry Hilpert) had halted two Russian armies.

In the fall of 1943, the front of Army Group North was in the same position as it had been in the spring. The two armies of the northern sector lost nothing to the Soviets in these battles, although they had to rely on the means they had available. The sectors of the German front in the center and south of Russia, during the same period of time, suffered from considerable withdrawal. Therefore, after the end of the 3rd Battle of Ladoga, the OKH shifted one division after the other to crisis points. The 5th Mountain Division — the only division of its type in the army group — was transferred to Italy.

Army Group North

The fate of the Spanish 250th ID was particularly interesting. The government of Madrid was pressured by the Allies (the USA and Great Britain threatened the Spanish with bombing!) to withdraw their division. The soldiers from the land beyond the Pyrenees had, since November 1941, bravely struggled on the side of their German comrades. They left 4000 graves behind them in Russia. Major General Esteban-Infantes formed the "Spanish Legion" out of volunteers, which was committed in the 121st ID area until March 1944. Then, this legion was also forced to return home.

Army Group North intensively tried to continue the defense of its front with fewer divisions. It was a noble effort in a lost cause. The hotly contested Kirishi bridgehead and the so-called "Sektpfopfen [Champagne Cork]" were evacuated.

The 81st, 96th, and 132nd ID, therefore, gave up positions which were the objectives of enemy attacks since 1941, all of which had been repulsed by the divisions of the army group. All supplies and unneeded ammunition were shipped out of the bridgehead to the west on 9/14.

The 132nd ID (Major General Wagner) left the bridgehead during the night of 10/2. The railroad bridge over the Volkhov, the landmark of Kirishi, was blown during the following night!

The withdrawing divisions, which were not hindered by the enemy, occupied the new Kussinka positions, which were established by eight construction battalions from the army group, with a length of 14.5 kilometers and with 192 shelters. The positions ran from a bend at the mouth of the Tigoda up to the eastern edge of the Pogoste pocket.

The Soviets now took notice of the withdrawals. They fired hours-long barrages on the positions and assaulted them. When the leadership sensed a weakness, they advanced their rifle divisions to the attack. The 96th ID (Lieutenant General Wirtz) had to fend off heavy attacks near Lessno for ten days, during which time the 287th Infantry Regiment (Major Lorenz) distinguished itself. As the combat around Lessno came to an end, the division was removed and transferred to the northern sector.

Additional combat, assault troop operations, and fire strikes occurred on the southern edge of the Pogoste pocket, on Lazarettberg near Lyuban, and between Sinyavino and the Neva. Here, a backup position was established. This "Mga Position" was 74 kilometers long and had 1,872 combat positions. There was another position being constructed north of Chudovo.

Army Group North was fortifying its interior.

Luftflotte 1 supported the ground troops during the battles of the last weeks and months, as far as their strength allowed them. At the beginning of 1943, the Luftflotte had available the following air units:

3rd Air Division (command post Ropti near Luga)

> 53rd Combat Group, with 3/53 Combat Group, 3/1 Combat Group, 14th company of the 1st Combat Group (Dno), L Special Group (Pleskau), 4/1 Combat Group (Schaulen);
> 1st Stuka Group (Gorodets);
> 54 Fighter Group, with 1/54 Fighter Group (Kransonvardeisk), 2/54 Fighter Group (Relbitsy), 54th Night Fighter Squadron (Dno);
> 1st Harassment Combat Group (Siverskaya);
> 8th Reconnaissance Group (Siverskaya);
> 11th Reconnaissance Group (Soltsy);
> 1st Long Range Reconnaissance Group (Grosstkino);
> The Lake Reconnaissance Squadron (Laksberg near Reval);
> 2nd Courier Squadron (Dno), 9th (Pleskau), 12th (Siverskaya);
> 2/7 Communications Squadron (Duenaburg), 6/7 (Ukmiste), 51st (Spilve near Riga);
> 1st Medical Squadron (Spilve near Riga).

During the course of the year, the formations were not always committed in the northern sector. The situation in 1943 reflected a considerable air superiority by the enemy, therefore, combat and fighter groups were committed wherever the main emphasis of a battle appeared to be. In July, the Luftflotte — as the initiative was once again returned to the German side during "Operation Citadel" — only had the 2/101 Combat Group available.

The first half of the year for the 3rd Air Division reflected the following:

Combat aircraft sorties: 8,227 in the 18th, 5,167 in the 16th Army area;
Fighter aircraft sorties: 7,915 in the 18th, 2,879 in the 16th Army area;
Reconnaissance flights: 1,113 in the 18th, 1,088 in the 16 Army area;
Long Range Reconnaissance flights: 1,512 in the entire operations area.

The month of May was the most difficult month of combat. In the 18th
Army sector alone the combat air groups registered 2,769 enemy flights.
During the evacuation of Demyansk and the heavy combat around Staraya
Russa, 2,706 sorties of combat and stuka aircraft were flown in the same
month.

Bombs were not the only things dropped from German aircraft onto
Soviet positions. Psychological warfare had also taken to the air. The
Luftflotte had to drop leaflets during some sorties. Thus, floating to the
ground were

in the month of March	4,412,650 leaflets,
in the month of June	30,236,420 leaflets,
in the month of August	33,159,700 leaflets.

The Soviet superiority was evidenced by the commitments of their 6th,
7th, 13th, 14th, and 15th Air Armies. The five air armies, during the same
period of time, flew 16,825 attacks against the 18th Army and 9,673 against
the 16th Army!

The combat of the 54th Fighter Group over the region between Lake
Ilmen and the Gulf of Finland provides an example of the air war at this
time. The fighter group, at the beginning of 1943, had only 23 operational
aircraft. The 1/54 Fighter Group was equipped with the new aircraft of
type "FW-190" in January. Between 12/15/1942 and 1/20/1943, German
fighters registered a total of 260 shoot downs. The 1st and 2nd Groups
alone participated in these successes. The 3/54 Fighter Group was transferred to the west.

The German Luftwaffe leadership planned to transport squadrons from
the western theater of war since the beginning of the campaign. The 26th
Fighter Group was to be exchanged. The 1/26 Fighter Group (Major Seifert)
arrived from the Channel coast at the end of January to the Relbitsy airfield

near Shimsk. The 1/26 Fighter Group became the 3rd Group of the 54th. Additionally, the 7/26 Fighter Group was exchanged for the 4/54 Fighter Group.

It was soon obvious that the pilots of the 26th Fighter Group ("Schlageter") were not accustomed to the peculiar conditions of the eastern Front. It was the same for the 54th Fighter Group ("Gruenherz") in the west. In June 1943, the 1/26 Fighter Group was recalled. During the six months of their eastern commitment, the group had shot down 127 enemy aircraft and lost 9.

In the second half of the year, the 54th Fighter Group seldom flew over the front of the army group. A staff and two groups were transferred to the central sector. Here, on 12/17, the second commodore of a squadron, Major von Bonin, died. The 54th Fighter Group took the lead over all other German fighter formations with its shoot down successes. The commander of the 1/54 Fighter Group, Captain Novotny, with his 210th victory, was the ace of the German Luftwaffe on 9/5. After his 250th victory on 10/20/1943, the young officer was the first soldier in the northern sector to receive the highest German award for bravery!

The two air defense divisions — the 2nd (Major General von Rantzau, from September: Lieutenant General Luczny) and the 6th (Lieutenant General Anton) — participated in the successes of the Luftflotte. In February and March, they registered 178 shoot downs, the destruction of 110 tanks, 34 guns, and 1 ammunition train. Their successes from 4/1-6/30 included shooting down 81 enemy aircraft. By the end of September, another 239 Soviet aircraft were brought down by air defense fire.

The heaviest commitments for the men of the Luftwaffe still stood before them.

The southern portion of the front would necessitate these commitments. In the fall of 1943, the army group stood as the only major formation in front of the "Panther Positions!" Since their positions during the past months were stable, the OKH ordered a weakening of the northern front. Thus, in the second half of the year, 13 divisions had to leave the army group area! Two additional divisions followed in December and January 1944.

Field Marshal von Kuechler had a longer front than previously to defend with the remaining formations. The southern boundary of his sector was extended 50 kilometers to the south in September. The XLIII Army Corps (General of Infantry von Oven), which was in charge of this area, came to the army group with three divisions (from right to left: 263rd, 83rd, and 205th ID). Contact was established with the 331st ID — the former flanking division.

The army group command, which, from October 1943 to February 1944 was located at Snyatnaya Gora near Pleskau, established an increase in the massing of enemy forces in front of the right flank in October. A report from the OKH related the following dispositions of forces in the east (81/ 43 gKdos from 10/14/1943):

	Divisions	Soldiers	Tanks	Guns
Army Group	44 Inf Divs	601,000	146	2,389
Soviets	94 Rif Divs	959,000	650	3,680
	25 Tank Divs			.

At the beginning of October, the XLIII Army Corps stood with its divisions on a 80 kilometer wide front and was — according to air reconnaissance — to defend against two enemy armies! The army group commander effected the surrender of Kirishi and the "Champagne Cork" in order to be able to transfer the formations thereby freed up to the southern flank. The 58th ID arrived first and was directed behind the 263rd ID (Lieutenant General Richter), the flanking division, as a reserve on 10/5.

The Soviet deployment, which was not established by air reconnaissance due to poor weather, was already finished. The 3rd and 4th Russian Shock Armies deployed their attack groups — the 47th, 357th, and 360th Rifle Divisions, and the 143rd and 236th Tank Brigades — in front of the seam between Army Group Center and Army Group North.

The Kalinin Front (Army General Eremenko) attacked on the early morning of 10/6 on a 12 kilometer wide front on the seam of the 16th Army and 3rd Panzer Army. The main effort lay in the left flank of the 3rd panzer Army. The II Luftwaffe Field Corps was thrown back during the course of the morning. The Soviets immediately shoved their 21st Guards Division and 78th Tank Brigade into the resulting gap, which now advanced against the deep right flank of the 16th Army. 30 tanks and infantry mounted on trucks suddenly assaulted into the vacated city of Nevel at noon! Combat groups assembled from the 58th ID stopped the Russian attack, for the time being, 3 kilometers north of the important communications city.

A gap 5 kilometers wide yawned between Army Groups North and Center!

The 547th Infantry Regiment (Colonel Colli) of the 83rd ID, which was located here, could not stem the influx of the enemy. The 3rd Battalion fought bitterly in the ruins of Bardino. The 2/547 Infantry Regiment fought their way through with elements of the 2nd Luftwaffe Field Division.

"The fate of the 1st Battalion was still not known. What was going on there? The battalion could not hold on the seam of the pocket as the attack erupted against their positions. Several machine-gun points were immediately destroyed. Contact between battalion and companies, companies and platoons no longer was available. The main combat line cracked. The Russians were already on the right of the rollbahn in the depth of the battlefield. Near the battalion command post, stragglers from withdrawing units were able to assemble for a brief defense under the cover of a still intact heavy machine-gun platoon. There was not enough time to collect the rest of the battalion. On the right, the Russians were advancing further... Individual groups of 20 to 30 men left their positions and withdrew to cover..."[8]

The army group command and the 16th Army commander recognized the seriousness of the situation and did not await the usual order from the OKH: "Contact with Army Group Center must be re-established!" Field Marshal von Kuechler ordered Nevel to be re-captured. He also removed the 122nd ID from south of Staraya Russa in order to dispatch them with the 502nd "Tiger" Battalion and the 368th Infantry regiment (285th Security Division) to the threatened front.

The counterattack planned for 10/7 had to be postponed, because the artillery was not ready. In the meantime, the 58th ID established a security line north of Nevel. The 263rd ID, who's right flank was hanging in the breeze, withdrew to the east to the northeastern tip of Lake Vorotno. The

58th ID (Colonel Siewert) advanced on 10/8, in spite of insufficient preparation, on the Nevel. The division was thrown back to their departure positions!

The Soviets immediately recognized their chance.

They shoved new forces into the front gap and, on 10/8, attacked the already hard-pressed 263rd ID (Lieutenant General Richter) repeatedly. Therefore, the army group ordered the retreat to the un-threatened Voronino-Lake Ivan line. The 263rd ID withdrew on a muddy route and was immediately set upon by pursuing enemy forces. The 46th Guards Division, 28th and 357th Rifle Divisions, as well as the 34th Guards Tank Brigade threw themselves on the last three battalions of the German division!

The XLIII Army Corps was able to prevent the further breakthrough of the enemy to the north, but the front gap to Army Group Center could not be closed with the battered divisions and security regiments. Therefore, the army group commander requested — for the first time since the beginning of the war — the Wehrmacht Commander of the East (General of Cavalry Braemer) to screen the former Latvian border to the east. All available police and partisan search units were assembled under SS Gruppenfuehrer von dem Bach-Zelewski and thrown into the gap.

The army group had taken the I Army Corps (Lieutenant General Grase) from the Volkhov sector and tasked it with conducting combat in the Nevel area. The 58th, 263rd, 122nd, and later the 69th ID came under the corps control.

The Soviets utilized the time between 9 and 10/15 to refill their formations. The 3rd Shock Army (Major General Galitzkiy) arrived at this time with 13 rifle divisions, 2 tank, 1 artillery, 3 rifle brigades, and 6 independent machine-gun battalions to attack to the north on either side of Lake Ivan. The 28th Rifle Division and 100th Rifle Brigade burst open the lake passage between Lakes Karatai and Ivan. The 69th ID (Lieutenant General Ortner) defended desperately. They transitioned to a counterattack and re-established the old positions! The enemy lost 1,850 dead and 120 prisoners.

The 3rd Shock Army did not give in. Five rifle divisions and one tank brigade again attacked the front of the 69th ID on 10/17. They achieved a small penetration near Putily — but no more than that! Finally, the Soviets gave up. Their losses were high — so were those of the 69th and the 263rd ID. The front calmed down.

The I Army Corps planned to improve its front to the IX Army Corps of Army Group Center, with which they had no contact, during the next few days. The corps formed Combat Group Colonel von Below (Group Nevel, 16th Assault Battalion, 374th Infantry Regiment) and transferred it to the extreme right flank.

The 3rd Shock Army transitioned to the defense on Lake Ivan. Major General Galitskiy concentrated his main effort southwest of the Nevel. From here, he wanted to get into the rear of the German front, capture the Nevel-Polozk rail line, establish contact with the strong partisan formations in the Rossono area, and outflank the I Army Corps from the southwest. In addition, the army received reinforcements from central Russia.

The army group commander looked upon these deployment preparations with concern. On 10/31, General of Artillery Loch (former commander of the XXVIII Army Corps) was tasked with the leadership of all of the German formations, which were subordinate to the I and XLIII Army Corps.

Since 10/27, air reconnaissance had been reporting strong concentrations of enemy forces in the gaps between the two army groups and in front of the I Army Corps. The last reserves of Army Group North were set to march to this threatened sector. There were no more reserves. Only the 290th ID, a regiment of the 218th ID, and assembled battalions from various troop units, which were being partially held up by partisans, were slowly arriving into the forest and lake region near Nevel.

At the beginning of November, winter fog lay over the land. German reconnaissance was paralyzed. Then the 3rd and 4th Shock Armies initiated their offensives. The 46th Guards Division, 28th and 146th Rifle Divisions, 34th Guards Tank Brigade, and 184th Tank Brigade set out north of Lake Ivan to outflank the I Army Corps. Simultaneously, the 31st and 326th Rifle Brigades assaulted the front of the 122nd ID on either side of Nevel.

The I Army Corps was in the defense, when an additional Soviet deployment was noticed in the Novosokolniki area, which was directed against the northern flank of Corps Group Loch. Therefore, it was apparent that the enemy wanted to take the entire corps group into the pincers. The 16th Army commander — since 10/11 General of Artillery Hansen — and the army group commander removed still further battalions from the remaining fronts and directed them to the heavily threatened corps group.

The 11th Rifle Division and 3rd Tank Brigade were fighting against the I Army Corps on 11/6. The bravery of the soldiers of the 122nd (Major General Thielmann), 290th ID (Lieutenant General Heinrichs), and the 502nd Panzer Battalion (Major Jaehde) fiercely repulsed all attacks. The Soviet leadership was compelled to cut it short.

New re-grouping and committing of additional forces occurred in the following days. The 2nd Baltic Front (Army General Popov), which arose from out of the Kalinin Front, took over the Nevel combat area. The 3rd Shock Army, 6th Guards Army, and 16th Army made preparations south of Nevel. There, they had to outflank the right flank of Army Group North and create the prerequisites for the Red Army's main attack, which would break out in the Leningrad area in January 1944!

The outflanking of the I Army Corps was realized on 11/7. At this time, there was no longer a unified front! Lieutenant General Thumm took over command of the troops west of the Ushcha, while Lieutenant General Usinger, 315th Senior Artillery Commander, defended the pass between Lakes Nevendro and Orleya with his weak combat group. The crisis came to a head in the next three days. The friendly formations withdrew from the unthreatened positions in order to stop enemy elements that were already in their rear.

In view of this outflanking movement, the army group ordered the removal of the 81st ID from the 18th Army and the 329th ID from the 16th Army in order to direct both divisions to Corps Group Loch. In the meantime, the 6th Guards Army attempted to break through the front of the 58th ID in order to meet up with the 3rd Shock Army, which was approaching from the northeast. Therefore, the chance to attack to close the gap between the 16th Army and the 3rd German Panzer Army was lost. The army now had to commit the last battalions to the defense of the threatened encirclement of the I Army Corps!

The Soviets were not content with encircling the southern flank of the 16th Army. They simultaneously attacked with strong forces directly to the west where there were only weak security forces. SS Obergruppenfuehrer Jeckeln conducted a hopeless battle against the tank troops of the 2nd Baltic Front, with 19 battalions and 2 artillery detachments of German, Latvian, and Estonian police. The 128th Tank Brigade, as well as the 115th, 146th, and 245th Rifle Divisions were shoved between the combat groups of SS Gruppenfuehere von dem Bach and Lieutenant General Thumm. The army group ordered the immediate transfer by air transport of one battalion each from the 81st, 132nd, and 329th ID into the threatened Idritsa area.

The situation became even more critical. On 11/13, the enemy reached the road between Pustoshka and Sabele — where they found a large ammunition dump — and, therefore, stood on the Novosokolniki Heights. The I Army Corps already appeared to be encircled. Only with the utmost effort were the Upper Silesian infantrymen of the 81st ID and the Westphalian 329th ID able to stop the Soviets.

The commander of the VIII Army Corps (General of Infantry Hoehne) took over the combat groups of SS Obergruppenfuehrer Jeckeln and Lieutenant General Thumm on 11/19, in order to provide a unified control over the threatened Pustoshka-Idritsa area. Fierce combat occurred on Lakes Zhadro, Beresno, Rudo, and Ushcho against the 18th Guards Division, 119th Guards Division, 115th Rifle Division, and the 78th Tank Brigade. The 329th ID (Lieutenant General Dr. Mayer) was even able to reclaim the lost pass between Lakes Rudo and Ushcho!

The separation of the two flanks of Army Groups Center and North, meanwhile, represented an enormous threat to the entire Eastern Front. The OKH required the two army groups to close this gap with their own assets. Accordingly, Army Group North planned an attack out of the area south of Novosokolniki to the south. They ordered the 18th Army to remove the 23rd and 132nd ID and transfer the 32nd ID into the 16th Army area into this assembly area.

An attack would only be successful if the enemy 3rd Shock Army was destroyed near Pustoshka. This "Operation Bekassine" did not succeed, in spite of the commitment of all of the participating combat groups, as well as the newly arrived 12th ID. The Luftwaffe supported the ground troops, particularly with the 5th Fighter-Bomber Group and the 11th Harassment Combat Group. The 81st ID (Lieutenant General Schopper) attacked directly to the south on 11/22. The Silesians threw back the 115th Rifle Division and 18th Guards Division behind Lake Beresno. The attack did gain some ground, as all of the Soviet counterattacks were repulsed. On 11/25, the 81st ID was halted south of the lake.

The I Army Corps, in the meantime, prepared a second attack, which was to be conducted by the 23rd and 32nd ID to Lake Jasno. The group of SS Obergruppenfuehrer Jeckeln was to work opposite them from the west, along with the subordinate 16th Panzer Division. The 16th Panzer Division was not able to be committed, and it was immediately detoured to Army Group Center. On 12/1, the two infantry divisions met and drove a 5 kilometer deep wedge to the west. The Soviets quickly reacted. They threw back the 23rd ID (Major General Gurran), while the 32nd ID (Lieutenant General Boeckh-Behrens) held their newly won positions.

Combat continued along the entire front. The 3rd Shock Army bitterly defended themselves. The friendly troops were still inferior, advancing through the muddy terrain without tanks, assault guns, or artillery.

The corps group gap disintegrated. The 18th Army commander redeployed his staff to Opochka and directly commanded his three southern corps. General of Artillery Hansen knew that the continuation of the attack against this enemy, which became stronger every day, would not succeed.

On 12/8, the German attack was suspended. The I Army Corps, which was still hanging in the breeze, withdrew to the "Luchs Position" — an unthreatened line running from west to east between the left flank of the VIII Army Corps and Novosokolniki.

The Soviets attacked from the south against the "Luchs Position" on 12/16. The 2nd Baltic Front advanced with far superior forces — the 21st, 51st, 52nd, and 67th Guards Divisions, along with the 71st, 115th, 150th, 282nd, 370th, 379th Rifle Divisions, and also the 27th, 29th, 38th Guards Tank Brigades, 32nd, 118th Tank Brigades, and the 27th Artillery Division — against three German divisions (32nd, 122nd, and 290th ID)! The enemy achieved a penetration 2 kilometers deep and cut off two battalions of the 290th ID, which were, nevertheless, able to fight their way through during the night. The friendly main combat line was withdrawn to the eastern bank of the Ushcha.

The few combat and fighter-bomber formations joined the battle on 12/17. The 58th and 122nd ID fell victim to all of the rest of the Soviet

A short fire strike from all weapons initiated hostilities with the Soviet Union on the morning of 6/22/1942 at 0305 hours.

By evening, the army group had reached its assigned daily objectives. What would the following days bring?

On 6/24, troops of the II Army Corps enter Kovno and are joyously greeted by the population.

In spite of intensive bridge demolition by the Soviets, the Duena is crossed on a wide front by the end of June.

In August, East Prussian troops cut the Moscow-Leningrad rail line near Chudovo.

The 291st ID entered Narva at the same time. The infantrymen pass by the Hermann Fortress.

In autumn 1941 the army group approached Leningrad

. . . the first infantry elements view the city.

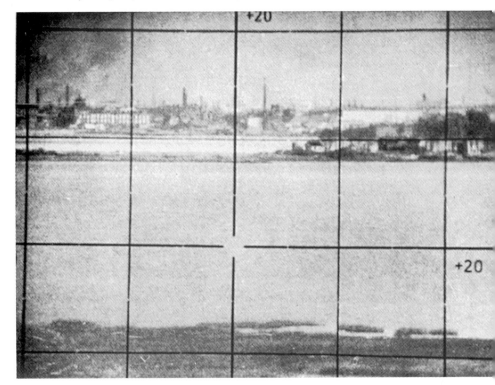

German observers view the cathedral, palace and industrial works of the ancient residence of the Tsars through their telescopes. In the severe winter of 1941/42, it was supplied only by truck transports, which made their way over the ice on Lake Ladoga.

Field Marshal Ritter von Leeb, commander of the army group (May 1941-February 1942).

Field Marshal von Kuechler, the second commander of the army group, with General Lindemann, at that time commander of the 18th Army.

General Model took command during the crises rich period of January 1944. He was only able to order its retreat.

General Schoerner lead the army group back to Kurland.

Marshal Voroshilov, commander of Northwest Front (7/10-8/30/1941) and the Leningrad Front (9/5-9/12/1941); later President of the USSR.

Marshal (here still general) Govorov, commander of the Leningrad Front from 6/9/1942 up to its dissolution.

Army General Meretskov, commander of the Volkhov Front (12/17-2/5/1944), the liberator of Leningrad.

Admiral Tribuc, the prominent commander of the Baltic Red Banner Fleet.

German troops have reached the Volkhov. In the fall of 1941, they stood on the Svanka Hills.

The attack of the XXXIX Panzer Corps on Tikhvin in late fall 1941 bogged down in mud and later snow and ice. The maneuver war had come to an end.

In winter of 1941/42, the II and elements of the X Army Corps were encircled in Demyansk. In spite of strong defenses, "Ju-52's" bring weapons, ammunition, and food into the pocket. This is the first "air bridge" in history!

The bell tower of Klein-Blaehingen near Demyansk. Here for a time was the command post of General Count von Brockdorff-Ahlefeldt.

The combat group of General von Seydlitz-Kurtzbach established contact with the troops encircled at Demyansk in April 1942. Combat was constantly fierce and conducted under inhumane conditions in marsh and forest.

To maintain the Demyansk pocket, the construction of supply lines was vital. Engineers, construction soldiers, volunteers, and prisoners constructing a field rail line in the pocket.

The front on the Volkhov with its primeval forests, swamps, and river courses made the most difficult demands on the German soldier. Here, not only was the enemy merciless, but so was nature.

The three Battles of Ladoga raged from summer 1942 to fall 1943 in and around the "Bottle-neck". The Soviets wanted to fight their way to Leningrad under any circumstances. The German Landser could not rest day or night in this "Inferno". (Above) A battalion command post of the 126th ID in Tetkingrund. (Below) From the routine of the Ladoga fighters: A severely wounded soldier is recovered in the swamp. A prisoner (the second from left) volunteers assistance.

Staraya Russa, the ancient princely city with the magnificent facade, is the center of a heavy Soviet attack in summer 1943.

In November and December 1943, the Soviets were able to penetrate the German front near Nevel. There was heavy combat throughout, during which many Soviet tanks were destroyed.

The Navy and Luftwaffe support the Army in the heavy defensive battles, but, due to their material inferiority, they were in no position to have an effect on the operations. The commitment of the Navy was limited to smaller units. An artillery barge secures a transport en route to Libau.

The 54th Fighter Squadron (the "Green Heart Squadron) often provided air support for the ground troops. The fighters took off against enemy flights in the worst weather and terrain conditions.

In autumn 1944, the Soviets continued their offensive. The army group had to withdraw to Kurland. In the winter of 1944/45, the German Landser had no more illusions. He knew, however, that his holding on in Kurland would give the homeland a breather. Reserves prepare to counterattack near Frauenburg.

In spite of all of the technology on both sides, in the end, the war was conducted and mastered by the individual fighter.

General Hilpert, the last commander of Army Group North. On 8 May 1945, he was taken prisoner, along with his soldiers, by the Soviets, from which he, like hundreds of thousands of others, never returned.

In the last days, the army group tried to rescue the men. Still on 8 May, men of all branches of arms waited in the harbors of Libau and Windau to be embarked and taken to the homeland. Infantrymen are loaded onto a mine sweeper, while light air defense guns secure against attacking Soviet aircraft.

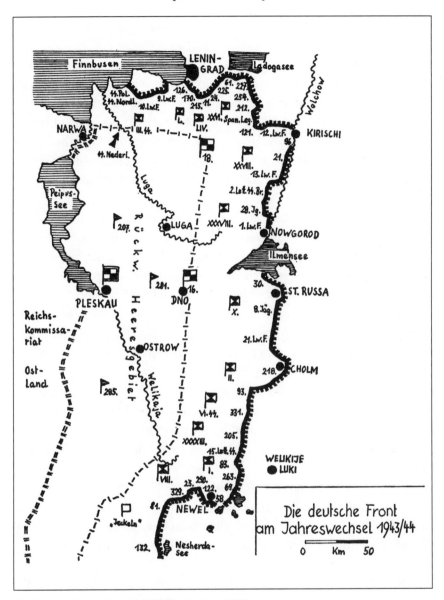

The German Front at the end of 1943/beginning of 1944

attacks. Losses on both sides were enormous. In three days, the enemy lost 106 tanks.

The German divisions were battered!

The 3rd Soviet Shock Army gave up the encirclement of the I Army Corps. Their former commander was relieved of his post and replaced by General Chibisov. The 2nd Baltic Front withdrew its forces north of Nevel and shoved them to the west. Here, in the meantime, the 1st Baltic Front was able to overrun the left flank of Army Group Center and achieve a penetration 80 kilometers wide and 30 kilometers deep. The Vitebsk-Polozk rail line was cut.

The army group inserted the 132nd ID (Major General Wagner) on its extreme right flank, which took over the thin security line established by the police and SS forces. The weak battalions were to look for the possibility of establishing contact with additional SS formations (partisan hunter commands), which were located between the two army groups.

The 16th Army had indeed achieved a defensive success, but was no longer in a position to withstand new enemy attacks. The army was weakened further. The 12th ID went to Army Group Center. Therefore, General of Artillery Hansen ordered the withdrawal of the I and XLIII Army Corps. During the night of 12/30, the 32nd and 122nd ID withdrew into the intermediate positions. The Soviets pursued them in spite of considerable snow fall, and had to be bitterly repulsed by the rear guard. The 32nd ID was, nevertheless, removed and directed to the right flank of the VIII Army Corps.

The new year was arriving. The 58th, 69th, 122nd, and 290th ID evacuated their positions on 1/2. The enemy closely pursued. Movement was very difficult due to road obstacles. The troops were exhausted. The 290th ID was taken from the front and transferred to the reserve in the Lake Ilmen area.

On 1/5, the I Army Corps reached the terminal line. The 23rd, 69th, and 83rd ID occupied these positions under the leadership of the XLIII Army Corps. The I Army Corps continued further to the south with the 58th, 122nd, and 263rd ID. On 1/10/1944, the boundary with Army Group Center was again shoved another 65 kilometers to the south! The I Army

Corps had to secure this new combat zone from the VIII Army Corps to northeast of Polozk.

A difficult year for Army Group North was coming to an end. Its front on the extreme left and right flanks was battered. The tenaciousness of the divisions did not allow the enemy to win any large areas. It was clear, however, that the army group would quickly collapse under the weight of a new Soviet offensive.

The losses of the army group were considerable. The losses of dead, wounded, and missing were increased even more when the many sick and frostbite cases were added. The number of sick totaled 600,018, of which 337,020, or 56%, would recover and return to their units. A distribution of hospital beds revealed the following statistics:

	1/1	1/4	1/9
Number of Hospital beds	44,400	51,300	55,600
In the Army Areas	44%	41%	35%
In the Army Group Area	46%	48%	50%
In the Area of Reichskommissar Ostland	10%	11%	15%

An important task for the commanders — Field Marshal von Kuechler, General Lindemann, General of Artillery Hansen, and General of Aviation Pflugbeil, who had replaced General of Aviation Korten as commander of Luftflotte 1 on 8/24/1943 — was the securing of the interior. The army group ordered the rear area services to construct several positions with army construction battalions, labor groups, labor units, prisoners of war, and civilian workers. As a result, from December 1942 various defensive positions appeared in the area between Leningrad and Nevel.

Circular defensive positions constructed in the area of the 16th Army:

near Dno - construction began in May; labor force: 450 soldiers, 210 civilian workers

Porkhov - construction began in June; labor force: 280 soldiers, 60 civilian workers

Soltsy - construction began in May; labor force: 220 soldiers, 180 civilian workers

Novosokolniki - construction began in April; labor force: 620 soldiers, 450 civilian workers

The following positions were constructed in the 18th Army area:

Mga positions - construction began in September; labor force: 1,800 soldiers, 500 civilian workers

Krasnibor - Grusino rollbahn position - construction began in September; labor force: 4,800 soldiers, 0300 civilian workers

The Tannen positions near Chudovo - construction began in December 1942; labor force: 1,700 soldiers, 1,700 civilian workers

Positions near Novgorod - Construction began in May; labor force: 7,000 soldiers, 600 civilian workers.

The four positions, which were constructed up to the end of 1943, consisted of 122 kilometers of trenches, 27.6 kilometers of anti-tank ditches, 151.3 kilometers of wire obstacles, and 4,828 combat positions. Four additional positions — Glint, Rand, Alexander, and the 2nd Volkhov positions — were still in construction, as were the four strong point positions near Krasnovardeisk, Luga, Novgorod, and Narva.

The most important backup line for the army group was the "Panther Position", the construction of which was hastened after September. The position ran from the confluence of the Narva into the Gulf of Finland up to the northeast tip of Lake Peipus, and from the southeastern exit of the lake it ran in a bow east of Pleskau to the southeast up to Lake Ale, and from there to Lake Ivan northeast of Nevel.

In December 1943, 15,000 soldiers from the construction and engineer battalions, 7,500 men from the labor force, and 24,000 civilians were utilized during the construction of the "Panther Position." Up to this point in time they had completed 39.9 kilometers of anti-tank ditches, 38.9 kilometers of trenches, 251.1 kilometers of wire obstacles, and 1,346 combat positions.

Chapter 4: The Defense

NOTES:

[1] Haupt, W.: *Demyansk. A Bulwark in the East.* 2nd Edition. Bad Nauheim: Podzun 1963. 230 pages.

[2] Lohse, G.: *History of the Rhennish-Westphalian 126th Infantry Division.* Bad Nauheim: Podzun 1957. 223 pages.

[3] Pohlmann, H.: Volkhov. *900 Days of Combat Around Leningrad.* Bad Nauheim: Podzun 1962.

[4] Kardel, H.: *The History of the 170th Infantry Division.* Bad Nauheim: Podzun 1953. 88 pages.

[5] Pohlmann, H.: *History of the 96th Infantry Division.* Bad Nauheim: Podzun 1959. 495 pages.

[6] Breithaupt, H.: *The History of the 30th Infantry Division.* Bad Nauheim: Podzun 1953. 320 pages.

[7] Reinicke, A.: *The 5th Light Infantry Division.* Bad Nauheim: Podzun 1962. 428 pages.

[8] Tiemann, R.: *History of the 83rd Infantry Division.* Bad Nauheim: Podzun 1960. 378 pages.

5

THE RETREAT
The Soviet Offensive 1944

The front situation at the beginning of 1944 showed the army group to be in positions as follows (from left to right):

The Oranienbaum bridgehead was surrounded by the newly arrived III SS Panzer Corps. Here, they had available: SS Police Division, SS "Nordland" Division, and the 10th and 9th Luftwaffe Field Divisions. The SS "Niederlande" Division was in transport to the corps.

The southern ring around Leningrad, which ran in a half circle from Urizk through Pushkin to the Neva, was formed by the L Army Corps (126th, 170th, and 215th ID) and LVI Army Corps (11th, 24th, and 225th ID).

The front of the Sinyavino Heights and Pogoste pocket was seen to by the XXVI Army Corps, with the 61st, 227th, 254th, and 212th ID, the Spanish Legion, 121st ID, and the 12th Luftwaffe Field Division.

The Volkhov front from Kirishi to Novgorod was held by the XXVIII Army Corps (96th, 21st ID, and 13th Luftwaffe Field Division) and the XXXVIII Army Corps (2nd Latvian SS Brigade, 28th Light Infantry Division, and 1st Luftwaffe Field Division).

These four large sectors belonged to the 18th Army. The area south of Lake Ilmen to Army Group Center was occupied by the 16th Army. Between Lake Ilmen and Kholm was the X Army Corps, with the 30th ID, 8th Light Infantry Division, and 21st Luftwaffe Field Division. From Kholm to the Novosokolniki Heights were the II Army Corps (218th and 93rd ID) and VI SS Corps (331st and 205th ID).

The hotly contested Nevel area was occupied at year's end by the XLIII Army Corps (15th Latvian SS Division, 83rd, 263rd ID) and I Army Corps (69th, 58th, 122nd, 290th, and 23rd ID). The adjacent security positions from Pustoshka to Lake Nezherda were defended by the VIII Army Corps, with the 329th, 81st ID, Combat Group Jeckeln, and 132nd ID.

The entire front between Nevel and Army Group Center began the new year in heavy combat, which was conducted day and night in biting cold and snow storms. The Red Army had already achieved its assigned objective here. They now turned to the extreme left flank of the army group.

The main Soviet strike against the army group was to occur where the October Revolution had its start: Leningrad. The High Command in Moscow believed that the time had arrived to strike the death blow against the northern front.

The Leningrad, Volkhov, and 2nd Baltic Fronts were ordered in January 1944, in cooperation with the "Baltic Red Banner Fleet", to destroy the German 18th Army, liberate Leningrad, reach the Narva-Pleskau -Velikaya sector, and lay the foundation for the conquest of the Baltic Provinces.

The commander of the Leningrad Front set out to accomplish these tasks by taking the 2nd Shock Army out of the Oranienbaum bridgehead and the 42nd Army from the Pulkovo area. Both armies had to move to Ropsha (halfway between Leningrad and Oranienbaum) to encircle elements of the 18th Army near Strelnya and Peterhof and conduct a joint attack on Kingisepp. The 67th Army was, in the meantime, to initiate a secondary operation on Mga.

The Volkhov Front planned attacking on either side of Novgorod with the 59th Army and directing the offensive on Pleskau. The 8th and 54th Armies had to advance against Tossno, Lyuban, and Chudovo. The 2nd Baltic Front had to expand their success near Nevel in order to reach the middle Duena, if possible.

The Russian offensive began at the Oranienbaum bridgehead.

Soviet batteries of the 2nd Shock Army and the heavy guns of the battleship "Oktyabraska Revolutsiya", the unfinished cruiser "Luetzow", and the half-sunk battleship "Marat" opened a 65 minute fire preparation onto

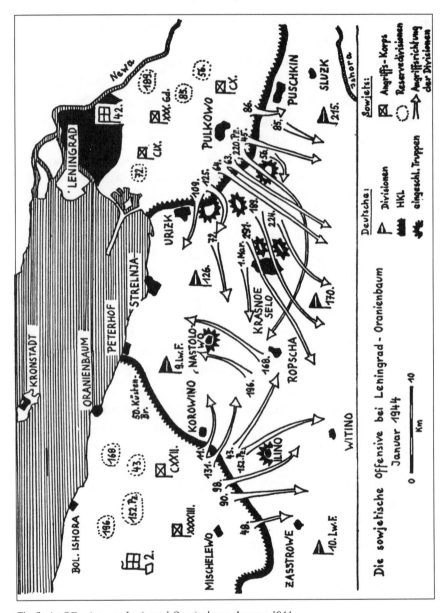

The Soviet Offensive near Leningrad-Oranienbaum, January 1944

the positions of the III SS Panzer Corps (SS Obergruppenfuehrer Steiner). 100,000 shells of all calibers fell onto the trenches and bunkers of the SS and Luftwaffe soldiers. As the last shells and bombs were still falling, the 2nd Shock Army attacked.

Lieutenant General Fedyuninskiy, the commander, committed the XLIII Rifle Corps, along with the 48th, 90th, and 98th Rifle Divisions and 43rd Tank Brigade on the right; and on the left, the CXXII Rifle Corps, with the 131st, 11th Rifle Divisions, and the 122nd Tank Brigade. Directly behind them followed the 43rd, 168th, 186th Rifle Divisions, and 152nd Tank Brigade. The German soldiers opposed the superior enemy force in their trenches and shelters with their last intact machine-guns and anti-tank guns. They could not prevent the Soviet divisions from achieving a 4 kilometer deep penetration by that evening.

The main strike occurred the next day in front of Leningrad. On 1/15 at 0710 hours, hundreds of batteries fired 220,000 shells within 1.5 hours onto the main combat line of the L and LVI Army Corps.

"Mortar and artillery impacts could not be distinguished from the explosions of the bombs, the noise of the Stalin Organs, and the guns from the ships at Kronstadt. At 0820 hours, the fire jumped into the rear, and the Russian companies and battalions marched through the trenches, which were flattened by the fire. From the 391st Infantry Regiment, which was now lead by Colonel Arndt, the battalion commanders Captain Moeller and Captain Meyer fell in the battle on the main combat line. The few combat capable soldiers remaining in the main combat line did their best. They held their places with machine-guns and hand weapons as the new waves came in upon them, even though the fire of friendly heavy weapons was landing on the friendly main combat line and in the anti-tank ditches behind it. ...Although the remnants of the infantry companies, which were fighting forward in the old main combat line, were ordered to withdraw and fight their way through, the enemy was already in the hills on line with the regimental command posts."[1]

The 42nd Soviet Army (General Masslenikov) in the first assault bit into the trenches of the defenders. Command posts, intersections, and towns were bitterly contested. The fierce combat wavered all day. During the evening, the XXX Guards Corps (Major General Simonyak) achieved a 2.6 kilometer breakthrough.

The 18th Army Commander realized the threat. As in the past two years, he could only operate with battalions and combat groups to eventually fill the gaps in the front. During the night, the first regiments were removed from their posts and inserted behind the L Army Corps and the III SS Panzer Corps. The cities of Krassnoe Selo, Duderhof, and Pushkin were turned into soot and ash after 500 attacks by enemy air forces.

The German front still held on 1/16. Then, the enemy changed their direction of attack. Hastily combat groups were thrown into the Ropsha and Krassnoe Selo area. The sluices near Duderhof were opened. The watercourses of the icy streams turned into wide water ways and blocked the Russian companies.

In spite of unheard of losses, the enemy tanks and guns continued to attack. On 1/18, they stood on the Duderhof Heights! Before them lay the wide flat land. The 170th ID (Lieutenant General Krause), which was fighting here, consisted of only a handful of men which were assembled by resolute officers. Oak Leaf recipient Colonel Griesbach collected the remnants of the 399th Infantry Regiment, 240th Anti-tank Battalion, and the 18th Army Assault Battalion. With this band, he fought back to Krasnovardeisk. He was joined by elements of the 2nd Infantry Regiment (Lieutenant Colonel Ramser) of the 11th ID. The combat group set up a hasty defense in the ruins of the city and defended here until 1/26. The Soviets repeatedly attempted to get into the city. The East Prussian and North German infantrymen were not shaken, not even when mined dogs were set after them. On 1/26, Combat group Griesbach broke out.

The battle before Leningrad raged further.

The situation was untenable!

The 18th Army commander ordered the withdrawal of the L and LVI Army Corps during the night of 1/19.

The Soviets attacked without pause. The 2nd Shock Army penetrated into the Ropsha area, with the CVIII Rifle Corps, while elements of the

42nd Army occupied Krassnoe Selo. The pincers appeared to be closing around the 126th ID and the 9th Luftwaffe Field Division. The fire from the ship-board artillery and the 101st Soviet Railroad Artillery Brigade hammered the German positions.

"At 2000 hours, it was observed from Kotselovo that the battle had ignited along the Krassnoe Selo-Kipen road. Numerous tanks were rolling to the west, droning loudly and firing heavily. Tracer ammunition indicted their route from the east to the lead attack elements in the west and made it clear they had closed the ring around the divisions. ...Colonel Fischer (Commander of the 126th ID) decided to quickly regroup the division and break out of the encirclement. ...All who were to breakout to Telesi stood ready south of Kotselovo at midnight. The 424th Infantry Regiment was now at the head of the division. On both sides, the attack wedge was supported by assault guns. ...Tracer rounds and the flames of Telesi illuminated the battlefield. Nobody who had experienced this would ever forget it. ..."[2]

The majority of the 126th ID, the 9th Luftwaffe Field Division, and the 530th Naval Artillery Battalion made it through. The heavy weapons, almost all of the horses, and all baggage was left behind. On the morning of 1/20, the ring closed around the last strong point. The 43rd Rifle Division of the 2nd Shock Army and the 189th Rifle Division of the 42nd Army shook hands northwest of Ropsha! 1,000 prisoners and 265 guns, including 85 of the heaviest, fell into their hands.

The first objective of the offensive was achieved. The left flank of the 18th Army was destroyed!

The right flank of the army was also involved in heavy combat.

The Volkhov Front (Army General Meretskov), with the 59th Army (Lieutenant General Korovnikov), attacked the German positions north of Novgorod between Myasno Bor and Shendorf on 1/14 after a three hour artillery preparation. The army's objective was to bring the front here to collapse and cut off Novgorod from the west. Therefore, the right flank of the 18th Army would be shaken. Then, the remaining armies could continue the offensive across the Volkhov.

The VI and XIV Rifle Corps were deployed for this attack (from right to left) with: 310th, 239th, 378th, 191st, and 225th Rifle Divisions, and the 58th Rifle Brigade. The VII Rifle Corps followed with the 256th, 372nd, and 382nd Rifle Divisions, as well as the 122nd and 7th Tank Brigades. On the other hand, in the same sector on the German side was only the XXXVIII Army Corps (General of Artillery Herzog), with the 1st Luftwaffe Field Division (Major General [Luftwaffe] Petrauschke) near Novgorod and the 28th Light Infantry Division (Lieutenant General Speth) between Teremets and Slutka on the Volkhov.

The first Soviet assault out of the bridgehead positions near Teremets and across the Volkhov ice collapsed under the fire of the Silesians. The 59th Army was bloodied and had to withdraw back to its departure position. A second and third attack gained no ground. Then, the 58th Rifle Brigade (Major General Sviklin) made it across the ice on Lake Ilmen and achieved a penetration into the positions of the Luftwaffe soldiers south of Novgorod.

Lieutenant General Korovnikov saw his chance and knew what he had to do. He immediately shoved the 225th and 372nd Rifle Divisions to Lake Ilmen and drove them into the bridgehead. Now the German resistance stiffened, after the army's first reserves — including elements of the 290th ID — were brought forward. The Soviets bogged down. They brought forward the CXII Rifle Corps, which systematically forced the defenders back and into the city.

The men of the 503rd Infantry Regiment, the 2/290 Artillery Regiment (290th ID), and several formations of the 1st Luftwaffe Field Division took up defenses in the ruins of the venerable city. In the meantime, the Soviets were arriving from the south, north, and east, and had already blocked the only road to the west. The combat groups held for two days, then they received the order to break out. During the night of 1/19, the last intact ammunition and supply installations in Novgorod were blown. The companies and platoons fought their way through individually. Not many returned. From the 503rd Infantry Regiment there were only 3 officers and 100 men. The regiments of the 290th ID no longer existed from this day on!

Chapter 5: The Retreat

Field Marshal von Kuechler recognized the threat of his army group being outflanked.

He wanted to order a retreat.

The OKH refused! Therefore, on 1/22, the Field Marshal flew to East Prussia and the Führer Headquarters. He proposed withdrawing the armies to prepared positions on the Luga. Hitler brusquely turned down the proposal and demanded that the army group remain where it was. He would make one panzer division available!

Field Marshal von Kuechler was relieved of his post.

General Model, the former commander of the 9th Army in the central sector, was the new commander of the army group. As the wiry and energetic General looked upon the map and situation at his headquarters near Pleskau, he could only approve the orders of his predecessor.

General Model ordered — without getting approval from the Führer Headquarters — the withdrawal of Army Group North to the "Luga Positions!"

The battered and dispersed divisions of the III SS Panzer Corps, which were near Oranienbaum, withdrew in heavy combat to Narva. The corps, which formerly stood in front of Leningrad, withdrew to the southwest in the direction of Pleskau.

The entire front of the 18th Army found itself in withdrawal. Its two corner-stones — Oranienbaum and Novgorod — had collapsed. At the same time, strong Soviet formations were attacking near Mga and Lyuban from the front.

The interior was also in movement. Partisan brigades in strengths of up to 40,000 men were mobilized and organized. In January (according to Russian figures) they destroyed 58,000 tracks, blew 300 bridges, and derailed 133 trains.

The flanks of the 18th Army were widely separated. The Soviet divisions exploited this immediately with well equipped tank and ski formations, not giving the German soldiers a chance to catch their breath. The attack on the positions between the Sinyavino Heights and the Volkhov could no longer be stopped. The army broke contact with the enemy on the entire front!

"Often the troops remained for days in the icy cold without warm food, with wet winter clothing that would freeze stiff, with merely crumbs of frozen bread to eat and frozen tea in their canteens to drink. They would catch a few minutes of sleep when they could. ..."[3]

On 1/21, Soviet troops occupied Mga. A day later, they penetrated into Pushkin. On 1/26, Russian soldiers raised their flags over the ruins of Krassnovardeisk, Tossno, and Chudovo!

The 27th of January was celebrated in Leningrad as the day of liberation. The city on the Baltic was finally free!

During the past 900 days, Leningrad had not only suffered privations, which were expressed by the number of civilians who had starved and frozen to death, but the city also showed heavy wounds caused by 150,000 German shells, 100,000 incendiary, and 4,600 high explosive bombs. 1,400 residents were killed by shelling in 1943, while during the same period of time 4,600 people were wounded.

After the end of the blockade, Moscow created a war decoration "For the Defenders of Leningrad." This order, suspended from a light green ribbon, is a bronze medal showing members of the Army, Navy, and Peoples' defense in front of an obelisk with a five pointed star. The award was given to 1.5 million soldiers, men, and women. Moscow applied such importance to the liberation of Leningrad that 12 officers and non-commissioned officers were conferred with the title "Hero of the Soviet Union." The President of the USA sent a congratulatory message to the residents of the city.

The battle between Narva and lake Ilmen continued.

Formations of the 13th (Major General Rybalchenko) and 14th Air Armies (Major General Yuralev) joined in the ground battle. In January and February, the Soviet squadrons flew 12,855 sorties, and the combat groups of the "Baltic Red Banner Fleet" reported 4,404 enemy flights.

The III SS Panzer Corps (SS Obergruppenfuehrer Steiner) withdrew into intermediate positions on the Narva until 1/26. The SS "Nordland" Armored Infantry Division (SS Brigadefuehrer von Scholz) and the dwindled 10th Luftwaffe Field Division (Major General von Wedel) dug themselves into the ground around Kingisepp and, for the time being, prevented the 2nd Shock Army from gaining any more ground.

Chapter 5: The Retreat

The corps, to which later came the SS "Niederlande" Armored Infantry Division (SS Brigadefuehrer Wagner), after five days of combat, shifted into the Narva bridgehead. The two SS divisions occupied the positions east of Narva. The river bank up to its mouth was protected by the combat group of the 227th ID (Lieutenant General Berlin), as well as alert and naval units, while south of the city a police battalion and a Norwegian volunteer battalion established defenses.

The Soviet troops marched on the Narva front, which was slowly being fortified by the Germans, at the beginning of February.

The weather changed, and it became warmer. The snow began to melt. The Russian tanks got stuck in the mud caused by the melting snow. However, this weather was also a problem for the hungry, exhausted, and withdrawing German soldiers.

The Soviets struggled through Siverskaya — which fell into their hands on 1/30 — to the Luga. Surprisingly, on the next day, they were able to cross the frozen Velikaya directly south of Lake Peipus and threaten the German withdrawal. General Model, who spent most of his time forward with the fighting troops, personally lead the attack reserve forward and saved the situation once more.

On 2/4, the bank of Lake Peipus was entirely in Russian hands, after the last strong point — Gdov — was assaulted by partisan units on this day. The 42nd Soviet Army (General Masslenikov) had reached its first great operational objective!

The 67th Army (Lieutenant General Sviridov) pushed on the Luga positions with all its might. Since the lead attack elements of the Volkhov Front were already approaching this line, the German defenders were trying to hold on just as long as it would take the last formation to cross over from the north.

The combat continued with undiminished ferocity. The 18th Army commander operated only with division combat groups. General Lindemann understood how to utilize the minimal assets available. At the beginning of February, he succeeded in not only halting the lead Soviet attack elements on the Plyussa, with assembled forces of the 12th Panzer Division (Major General Baron von Bodenhausen), 121st ID (Lieutenant General Priess), and 285th Security Division (Major General von Auffenberg-Komorow), but even encircled them near Oklyuzhe. The 256th Rifle Division, elements of the 372nd Rifle Division, and the 5th Partisan Brigade sat in the pocket. Unfortunately, the pocket could not be systematically reduced, because the front was exploding everywhere and the few motorized units of the 12th Panzer Division were needed at many locations to extinguish fires.

Therefore, General Model ordered the evacuation of Luga. The 69th Soviet Army entered the city on 2/12. The commander tasked the 18th Army with the defense forward of Pleskau. Hitler gave his permission to withdraw the entire army group into the "Panther Positions" on 2/17.

Hitler was forced to make a decision after the news arrived from Finland that the government in Helsinki put out peace feelers to Moscow. Therefore, the political issue, to which they had stuck with since the beginning of "Operation Barbarossa", was adhered to!

The retreat of the 18th Army, naturally, had to affect the 16th Army. The Soviets did not stop with the capture of Novgorod. They advanced rifle formations along Lake Ilmen to the south in order to come into the rear of the X Army Corps.

A German defense crystallized on the southwestern stretch of the lake in the Shimsk area. Here, there were formerly only convoy units, which, naturally, could not offer the Soviets much resistance. The 30th ID, which was located near Staraya Russa, was tasked with the control of operations in that sector. They formed a combat group under Colonel Kossmala, in which they placed their most combat effective units. Elements of the 8th Light Infantry Division were inserted on the bank of the lake east of here.

The 2nd Baltic Front (Army General Popov; War Counsel was the later President of the USSR, Lieutenant General Bulganin) went over to the offensive on 2/17 after a strong artillery preparation. The Russian tanks rolled against the defenders as the heavy shells were still plowing up the trenches. The German soldiers defended bitterly. Alone, the 1/46 Infantry Regiment, which was located north of Mshaga and defended the confluence of the Mshaga and Shelon, destroyed 17 "T-34's" and "Kv-I's" in close combat on the first day of the battle.

The army group commander had to realize that it was no longer possible to close the gaps between the 30th ID, which was the left flanking division of the 16th Army, and the 290th ID, which was the right flanking division of the 18th Army. The X Army Corps was ordered to withdraw during the night of 2/19. The withdrawal out of the Mshaga-Shimsk bridgehead was accomplished in two sectors.

Staraya Russa, the ancient city of princes south of Lake Ilmen, fell into the hands of the Soviets on 2/18. It was a dead city. The civilian population, which had not already been evacuated, followed the withdrawing German columns with all of their property and cattle.

The withdrawal of the 16th Army between Lake Ilmen and the chain of lakes north of Nevel was conducted systematically and without haste. The enemy pursued. The rear guard troops of the divisions had to defend energetically to prevent the outflanking of the columns. In addition, there was the danger of partisans, which had established themselves in the forested areas west of the Lovati. The army, ignoring their right flank, turned to the southwest toward the "Panther Positions." Kholm was given up on 2/21. Dno, the great communications center and long-time headquarters of the 16th Army commander, was held for two more days before the railroad installations and supply warehouses were blown into the air. On 2/24, Soviet troops entered the city. Porkhov was evacuated on 2/26.

Then, the "Panther Positions" were reached. The left flank of the army had to complete a march of 300 kilometers. The troops established a defense. The divisions recalled their combat groups. Combat sectors were assigned. The artillery occupied positions — and everywhere the Soviet attack was repulsed.

The Soviet High Command ordered a halt!

Supply problems became noticeable. The formations of the 2nd Baltic Front and the Volkhov Front needed a combat pause. The Soviets had achieved their initial offensive objectives. 7,200 prisoners, 275 armored vehicles, 1,962 guns, 3,642 machine-guns, 4,278 trucks, and 42,000 rifles was their booty.

The senior command of the Volkhov Front was disbanded in mid February.

The Red Army again regrouped. They stood in front of the "Panther Positions."

General Lindemann, commander of the 18th Army, who succeeded in withdrawing his divisions to the "Panther Positions", in spite of equipment and personnel shortages and the overwhelming superiority of the enemy, issued an order of the day on 3/1, in which he said:

"Now we have reached the line in which we will establish a decisive defense in prepared defensive positions. Our slogan now is not one step backward! The enemy will try to overrun our lines. I bid you to do your duty. ...We are in the advanced guard of the homeland. Each step backward brings the war closer to Germany!"

The front of the 18th Army lay on either side of Lake Peipus. The sector between its northern tip and the Gulf of Finland was controlled by the newly formed Army Detachment Narva, under the command of General of Infantry Friessner, Chief of Staff Colonel Reichelt, since 2/4. Available to the Army Detachment, from right to left, was the XXVI Army Corps (Lieutenant General Grasser) and the III SS Panzer Corps (SS Obergruppenfuehrer Steiner).

The III SS Panzer Corps, whose southern boundary ran directly south of the city of Narva, had to fend off a heavy enemy attack in February. The Soviets, from right to left, deployed the 47th Army, 2nd Shock Army, and 8th Army. These three armies tried, during the next few weeks, to improve their positions in relation to the German positions on either side of Narva, throw the III SS Panzer Corps into the sea, and create a free route for themselves to Estonia.

The battle for Narva began while they were still withdrawing into the "Panther Positions." The 8th Soviet Army (Major General Sukhomlin, and from 3/1, Major General Stanikov) attacked across the river southwest of Narva near Krivasao. In the neighborhood were only alert units of the 227th ID (Lieutenant General Berlin) and the attritted 170th ID (Colonel Griesbach). The few defenders were simply overrun. the Soviets were able to establish a deep bridgehead and approach the railroad in the vicinity of Vaivara.

The III SS Panzer Corps threw everything they had against the enemy. This included the newly organized "Feldherrnhalle" Armored Infantry Division, the remnants of the 61st ID, and a combat group of the Führer Escort battalion. The combat groups were thrown directly from the railroad cars, which stopped at the Vaivara railroad station, into the battle. The OKH ordered the 214th ID from Norway. However, until the combat inexperienced division arrived, the III SS Panzer Corps had to help itself.

The Soviets wanted to bring Narva down with all their might. On 2/13, they landed twelve boats of 500 volunteers — including women — on the coast near Hungerburg in the German rear. The individual Soviet fighters waded through ice cold water to the land, where they all met their end in the defensive fire of the defenders.

The army recognized the significance of Narva as security for Estonia and brought up three of their best divisions there. The 61st ID was reconstituted and relieved by the 214th ID. The Russians attacked straight away. They attacked during the relief operation and assaulted up to the fire positions of the 2/61 Artillery Regiment (Captain von Kleist-Retzow). Here, they bogged down.

The 214th ID lost its foothold. Then, the first elements of the 58th ID arrived. The 209th Infantry Regiment (Lieutenant Colonel Eggemann) appeared in the lead and held their positions south of the Lauka marsh. The regiment was encircled but did not give up, therefore, the frontal gap did not get any wider. The 58th ID (Major General Siewert) dispatched the 158th Reconnaissance Battalion (Major von Cramm) to assist. The 158th Reconnaissance Battalion itself was encircled near Putki before it could reach its objective. They took up a defense and repulsed all attacks.

Then, the 11th ID (Lieutenant General Burdach) arrived. The 23rd and 44th Regiments attacked from the move. In bitter hand to hand combat they were finally able to advance to the encircled units and free them in the first days of March.

The East Prussians established contact with the SS "Nordland" Division (SS Brigadefuehrer von Scholz). Therefore, the situation quieted somewhat in the enemy bridgehead near Krivasao. Since the Soviets realized that they could not advance between Putki marsh and the Vivikonna trenches and that the German front was reinforced in this area, they suspended their attack.

The III SS Panzer Corps received the 20th SS Division (SS Brigadefuehrer Augsberger) in the second half of February. It was an Estonian division, which formerly fought near Nevel and was now hastily being transferred through Pleskau to the homeland. The Estonians moved to the coast, inserting themselves to the left of the 225th ID (Major General Risse). The 45th SS Regiment (SS Obersturmbannfuehrer Vent) attacked the Soviet bridgehead near Sivertsi, directly north of Narva, in the beginning of March. In fierce hand to hand combat, the Estonians forced the Soviets across the river and, therefore, across the national border!

The 8th Army still held a bridgehead southwest of Narva. They were designated by the names "East-" and "Westsack." Both wedges led directly to the rail lines on either side of Vaivara. The Army Detachment Narva had to remove these bridgeheads. They organized their divisions, which had been completely dispersed during the defensive combat in February. These maneuvers took time, because the mild weather had made the roads completely impassable. The terrain became a swamp and offered no cover from the enemy shells and bombs.

The first attack of the XLIII Army Corps (Lieutenant General Boege) removed the so-called "Westsack." In addition, the Army Detachment Narva had deployed from right to left: the 170th, 11th, and 227th ID. The 11th ID was reinforced by a panzer formation, which was named after its commander, Colonel Count Strachwitz.

On 3/26 at 0555 hours, German batteries initiated the operation with a ten minute fire strike. The 502nd Panzer Battalion lead the way, closely followed by the men of the 23rd and 44th Infantry Regiments. The enemy bitterly defended in the thick swamp forest. They protected their positions with stockades as high as a man. The East Prussian Landser had to clamber up these stockades in order to get into the Russian trenches. The attack objective was achieved by evening. The 2/502 Panzer Battalion (Senior Lieutenant von Schiller) particularly distinguished themselves. Communications to the individual regiments was completely broken.

The Soviets did not give in. They seized the initiative on the following days. However, the Germans also did not retreat. The battle see-sawed for three days. Then, the enemy began to withdraw and evacuate the "Westsack."

On 3/31, the OKW reported:

"The Majority of several Russian divisions were encircled and destroyed in a several day offensive operation in the trackless forests and marsh region southwest of Narva, with effective support from artillery, rocket launchers, tanks, and fighter-bombers. Repeated enemy relief attacks failed. In this battle, the enemy lost over 6,000 dead, several hundred prisoners, and 59 guns, as well as numerous other weapons and war material of all types."

The second frontal tumor — the "Eastsack" was to be removed by the 61st ID and Panzer Formation Strachwitz. Colonel Count Strachwitz was the senior panzer leader in the army group. He was committed, from time to time, with his few panzer and armored infantry companies, to the main effort of local limited operations.

The spring had made its entrance. The last snow melted. Therefore, rivers, swamps, and lakes were swollen and set most of the terrain under water. It was impossible to maintain regular vehicular traffic.

The destruction of the remaining Narva bridgeheads was planned. The Army Detachment assembled a combat group on Easter 1944, which was to take part in this operation. The 502nd Panzer Battalion was again to be the battering ram. The attack began on the morning of 4/19 at 0435 hours. The combat groups of the 61st, 122nd, 170th ID, and "Feldherrnhalle" attacked out of their trenches and worked their way through the forests and mud to the Russian positions.

It was pouring rain. The corduroy roads swam in the marshes. Sand hills merged with bunkers in the thinly forested terrain. The soldiers inched their way through to the enemy trenches. The 401st Infantry Regiment (170th ID) and 151st Infantry Regiment (61st ID) penetrated into the Soviet positions.

Combat was fierce. The enemy did not withdraw. The wounded drowned when they sank into the wet ground in the trenches. The 2nd and 3rd Companies of the 401st Infantry Regiment reached the first line of bunkers and captured them. Then, the infantrymen had to withdraw. The Soviets continued to close behind them. The 1/399 Infantry Regiment tried to follow the advanced companies, but they could not. The battalion only totaled 69 men!

Finally, the companies of the "Feldherrnhalle" Division had more luck when they caught hold of a reasonably dry road. Count Strachwitz immediately committed his heavy "Tiger" tanks here, and the enemy was thrown back. The tanks advanced 800 meters further, and then they were hit by Soviet artillery. It was impossible to continue the attack. The enemy fire was so strong that the partially immobilized "Tigers" could not be towed away and, therefore, had to be destroyed.

On 4/20, the Army and Luftwaffe still hoped to seize the initiative. The 3rd Fighter-Bomber Group (Lieutenant Colonel Kuhlmey) joined in the battle with his two groups (Major Nordmann and Captain van Bergen). The aircraft recklessly dived onto the known enemy positions. Since January, the squadrons had flown 7,600 sorties. However, the bravery of the pilots and infantrymen did not help. The enemy was stronger.

On 4/24, the Army Detachment Narva ordered the suspension of the attack. Colonel Count Strachwitz was the second soldier in the northern sector of the Eastern Front to receive the Diamonds to the Oak Leaves with the Swords of the Knight's Cross, for his circumspect leadership of the combat group and his personal bravery.

The Russian bridgehead southwest of Narva stood. The front ran tightly to the north from the confluence of the Piata into the Narva south of Auvare and bowed back approximately 16 kilometers to the south, ran through the Lauka marsh toward Omati, and here ran back to the east bank of the Narva.

The Army Detachment Narva established a defense on the line they achieved at the end of April. On the left flank stood the III SS Panzer Corps, with the "Nordland" Division, the "Niederlande" Division, and the 20th Estonian SS Division. The XLIII Army Corps, with the 122nd, 11th, and 58th ID, was located in the center of the front. To the right closed the XXVI Army Corps, with the 225th, 170th, and 227th ID. The "Feldherrnhalle" Division and Panzer Formation Count Strachwitz were pulled from the front and transferred.

The Army Detachment Narva formed from the staff of the battered 13th Luftwaffe Field Division and the staff of the 300th Special Purpose Division. The division was formed from the 1st to the 4th Estonian Border Guard Regiments. These pure Estonian troop units, with German commands, were placed on the northern coast of Lake Peipus and took over flank protection there. The division remained directly subordinate to the Army Detachment.

Chapter 5: The Retreat

The front quieted down somewhat in the following months. The divisions began to construct positions. Slowly, the battered formations re-constituted.

The Soviets in this sector also transitioned to the defense, since they were not able to shake the German front. They shifted the main emphasis of their attacks to the south. In March, the conduct of bombing attacks by Russian combat formations noticeably slackened. Reval suffered particular damage. On 3/9 an attack occurred here, during which the Nikolai Church, Weight House, Antonius Chapel, and City Hall received considerable damage.

During the previous years, Army Group North not only had to operate according to military factors, but also had to play a political role. Back in 1941 it was ordered to establish contact with the Fins. Therefore, at one time the front ran from the Black Sea to the Arctic Ocean and the Finish Army was included in the overall concept of the Eastern War.

After the successful Soviet offensive in January/February 1944, Finland was suddenly isolated. The hoped-for contact with the German Wehrmacht had now become an illusion. Finland now had to fight alone on its own territory.

Field Marshal Keitel, Chief of the OKW, wrote to Field Marshal von Mannerheim on 1/31/1941 that the retreat by Army Group North was no grounds for the Finish People to worry. Field Marshal von Mannerheim in reply made known his feelings, after the surrender of the Gulf of Finland: Now the road is open to the Red Army, not only to Estonia, but also to Finland.

The German government tried, with all military and economic means, to hold on to Finland. At the beginning of February, it became known in diplomatic circles that Finland was prepared to negotiate with the USSR and abandon Karelia. The political discussions between Germany and Finland then began in earnest.

The military leadership of Helsinki was completely neutral. An officers' delegation, under the leadership of the Chief of the Operations Department of the Finish General Staff, Colonel Nihtila, visited the Army Detachment Narva between 4/7 and 4/14.

The OKW had Luftflotte 1 transfer a strong combat group to Finland in June. This was in recognition of the achievements of their brotherhood in arms and an attempt to delineate German strength. The air units were tasked to remain in Finland "as long as Army Group North exists!"

Lieutenant Colonel Kuhlmey led the combat group, which consisted of the staff of the 3rd Fighter-Bomber Group, with the 1/3 Fighter-Bomber Group and 1st Company of the 5th Fighter-Bomber Group, 2/54 Fighter Group, and 1st Company of the 54th Fighter Group, as well as elements of the 1st Company of the 5th Reconnaissance Group. There were a total of 70 aircraft. It represented a powerful drain on the Luftflotte, which, in June had only 137 aircraft of all types available!

After the Soviet winter offensive ran its course, the front of Army Group North became quiet. It allowed the armies, corps, and divisions to form new units and re-constitute. The front divisions were established in the "Panther Positions." It is necessary to note that the Soviets also needed a breather to improve their supply and communications routes and strengthen their weakened formations for a new attack.

General Model, commander of the army group, was promoted to Field Marshal after the conclusion of the winter battle. He left the northern sector in order to take command of the retreating Army Group North Ukraine in the south of the Eastern Front. General Lindemann was his successor. General of Artillery Loch led the 18th Army.

Obviously, there were no completely quiet days on the long front between Lake Peipus and the hills near Nevel and Polozk. There was particularly fierce combat in April in the sector between Pleskau and Ostrov. Here, the Red Army wanted to achieve favorable departure positions for the planned summer offensive.

The OKW reported these events as follows:

> 3 April:
> "The Bolsheviks again attacked south of Pleskau with fresh divisions, supported by numerous tanks and fighter-bombers. They were repulsed with very heavy losses and, additionally, lost 57 tanks..."

Chapter 5: The Retreat

4 April:

"The Soviets continued their breakthrough attempts south of Pleskau, after deploying additional forces. After difficult combat, our troops achieved another complete defensive success and destroyed 24 tanks. Therefore, the Bolsheviks have lost 172 tanks in this sector during the past three days..."

6 April:

"Southeast of Ostrov and south of Pleskau our troops held their positions against the continuous breakthrough attempts of the Bolsheviks and destroyed 48 enemy tanks. Renewed enemy assembly areas were destroyed by artillery and mortar batteries. From 3 to 5 April, the Soviets lost 117 aircraft in air combat and through air defense artillery..."

11 April:

"Southeast of Ostrov, after deploying new forces, the Bolsheviks again fruitlessly assaulted our positions. ...The Soviets also could not gain any ground south of Pleskau yesterday. Since 3/31, the German troops here, under the command of General of Artillery Loch (18th Army) and under the leadership of Lieutenant General Matzky (commander XXVIII Army), have frustrated the breakthrough attempts of far superior enemy infantry and tank formations and inflicted high personnel and equipment losses on the enemy. At least 306 enemy tanks and assault guns, as well as 121 aircraft, have been destroyed. In these battles, the Upper Silesians of the 8th Light Infantry Division (Lieutenant General Volckamer von Kirchensittenbach), as well as assault gun units, under Major Schmidt, were particularly successful. The Luftflotte of General of Aviation Pflugbeil had also played an important role in the success of the defensive battle. Air formations, under the leadership of Colonel Kuehl and an air defense regiment (164th Air Defense Regiment), under Lieutenant Colonel Bulla, have distinguished themselves."

Army Group North

The army group, which changed command on 3/31/1944 to the deserving commander of the 18th Army, General Lindemann, knew that the "Panther Positions" would not hold. The preparations of the Soviets for new deployments had become more obvious since May.

General Lindemann, the Chief of Staff Lieutenant General Kinzel, the army commanders General of Artillery Loch, and General of Artillery Hansen and General of Infantry Friessner did all they could to stabilize the front. During these weeks, the divisions remained somewhat unified. They were only broken up into combat groups when a strong enemy force had to be blocked.

When, in the beginning of June, the Soviet Air Force flew reconnaissance into the interior, the German commanders knew that there would be an attack soon. In the first half of 1944, the Red Army had been reinforced with considerable amounts of British and North American equipment.

The USA sent the following weapons and equipment to the Soviet Union between 6/22/1941 and 4/30/1944:

6,430 aircraft	10 mine sweepers
3,734 tanks	12 artillery boats
210,000 trucks	82 escort ships
3,000 heavy air def guns	991 million cartridges
1,100 light air def guns	22 million shells
17,000 motorcycles	218,000 tons of gun powder

The shipments from Great Britain and from the other Allies during the same period of time totaled:

5,800 aircraft	12 mine sweepers
4,292 tanks	103,000 tons of rubber

Weapons shipments increased considerably after the beginning of the Soviet summer offensive. In addition to the above named materials, the Red Army received another 13,000 tanks, 2,000 guns, and 35,000 motorcycles.

Chapter 5: The Retreat

During the beginning of June the Allies landed in Normandy. Therefore, the "Second Front", long requested by Stalin, was now a reality. The German Army now had to defend to the west and the east against far superior and better equipped enemy forces.

The Red Army gathered itself for its last combat efforts, which the Moscow regime hoped would bring the war to an end. On 6/9, Generalissimo Stalin wrote Prime Minister Churchill:

> "The preparations for the summer offensive by the Soviet armed forces are almost completed. On the morning of 6/10 will begin the first phase of the summer offensive on the Leningrad Front."

By this time the German leadership was aware of the deployment of the enemy armies, which appeared to be concentrated particularly in the central sector. The commander of Army Group North issued a warning to the OKH on 6/16. In it he noted that, day by day, there were more indications of the assembly of strong Soviet formations on the right flank. Prisoner statements and agents confirmed that several armies were assembling on either side of Vitebsk for an offensive directed at Polozk.

The Soviets deployed two army groups — the 1st Baltic Front and the 3rd Belorussian Front — into this region. The senior command of the Red Army dispatched Marshal Vassilevskiy to coordinate the operations of the two fronts. Additional reinforcements from all parts of the country were sent to the main effort of the anticipated summer offensive. In this manner, the 2nd Guards Army and 51st Army were transported from the Crimea to northwestern Russia.

The 1st Baltic Front stood in front of the right flank of Army Group North. The front — Commander: Army General Bagramyan; War Counsel: Lieutenant General Leonov; and Chief of Staff: Lieutenant General Kurassov — received the following mission:

> "Attack through the German main combat line west of Gorodok, northwest of Vitebsk, on a 25 kilometer wide front, force a crossing over the western Duena and, in cooperation with the 3rd Belorussian Front, encircle the German troops near Vitebsk."

Subordinated to the 1st Baltic Front for this major offensive were the 6th Guards Army (Lieutenant General Chistyakov), the 43rd Army (Lieutenant General Beloborodov), and the I Panzer Corps. The 3rd Air Army (Lieutenant General Papivin) was assigned to cooperate. The troops on the right of the 1st Baltic Front were also newly grouped. Here stood the 2nd Baltic Front (Army General Eremenko) and the 3rd Baltic Front (Army General Masslenikov). The three Baltic Fronts had over 2000 combat vehicles available by mid June. The positions up to the Baltic Sea were held by the Leningrad Front, whose commander, Govorov, was promoted to Marshal on 6/18.

June 1944 was hot compared to previous summers. The blazing sun sent its beams of light across the wide, slightly hilly land, which was slowly preparing for the harvest. However, the harvest in the land between Vitebsk and the Duena this summer would be of the dead!

The 22nd of June arrived.

The German officers inspected the readiness of their soldiers in their positions during their nighttime rounds. Indications had increased that the Red Army would attack on the 3rd anniversary of the deployment of the Wehrmacht.

The first indications occurred while the morning fog still roamed through the forests and marshes. The indications changed to a staccato of thunder, lightening, fire, and smoke. The Soviet artillery preparation began. Hundreds of guns of all calibers sent their steel greetings onto the positions of the I Army Corps northwest of Velikie Luki. Simultaneously, the volleys of the "Stalin Organs" took flight and the shells of the mortars roared. Dozens of combat positions were blown into the air. Fighter-bombers hammered the trenches, shelters, corduroy roads, and rollbahns with their on-board weapons.

The fire lasted 1.5 hours.

It was 0445 hours — then the tanks rolled, and through the smoke and the morning fog a thousand voices rang out with "Urrah!"

The Soviets came!

"There, wherever the enemy penetrated into the positions, because of their unheard of superiority, they were thrown back by counterattack. Also, when individual strong points were surrounded, they were relieved by counterattack. It was still hoped that the majority of the positions would hold. The main combat line appeared to be penetrated at several locations, but it was still not torn apart."[4]

The right flank of Army Group North was covered by heavy fire on this morning. The 205th ID (Major General von Mellenthin) was located in the forests on the Obol, northeast of Polozk. The soldiers from Baden-Wuerttemberg resisted the rolling steel colossi out of desperation. However, what good is bravery when the other side employs "T-34's", "Stalin Organs", and bombers?

It was 1800 hours on 6/22: Contact between the 205th ID and the left flank division of Army Group Center, the 252nd ID, was broken. The XXII Guards Corps (Major General Ruchkin) of the 6th Guards Army broke through the former main combat line. The remnants of the 252nd ID withdrew to the south on the Polozk-Vitebsk rail line.

The German leadership knew, during the first hours of the day, that much depended on maintaining contact with the neighboring army group. The 24th ID was providently made available by the OKH at 1200 hours. At the same time, the 290th ID, which was still in positions near Shvary, was relieved by elements of the 281st Security Division. The division was loaded up for transport to the threatened area of Polozk.

General Lindemann made telephone contact with the OKH at 1835 hours and requested that the 24th ID be placed on the seam between the army groups.

Contrary to expectations, the OKH reacted quickly, and 1/2 hour later ordered the 24th ID and the 909th Assault Gun Brigade, which was located in an assembly area near Polozk, to be transported by rail into the Obol area.

During the night, German officers tried to assemble and organize their battered formations. The Soviets constantly fed new troops into the gap. The I Soviet Tank Corps moved in. The night was illuminated from the burning forests, from the crack of exploding tanks and ammunition, and from the boom of artillery. The moaning of the wounded and the cursing of those marching intermingled.

Army Group North

The transport of the Saxon 24th ID (Lieutenant General Versock) rolled on. The 24th Anti-tank Battalion took over the protection of the important town of Obol. The 24th Engineer Battalion was the first unit to oppose the enemy, which had crossed the only connecting road between the 205th and 252nd ID. The following 24th Fusilier Battalion attacked to the north to relieve the 472nd Infantry Regiment (252nd ID), which was encircled in the vicinity of Grebentsy. The counterattack was launched with shouts of "Hurra", but the old main combat line could no longer be reached. The arrival of the 31st Infantry Regiment did not bring any help for the two battalions. The regiment had to cross the Obol immediately to the south in order to prevent enemy tank forces from crossing the river there. The 909th Assault Gun Brigade and the "Hornissen" (self-propelled anti-tank guns) of the 519th Anti-tank Battalion arrived on the following day and were immediately thrown into the battle north of the Obol.

The 24th ID was subordinated to the IX Army Corps of the 3rd Panzer Army. General Reinhardt, the commander, visited the division command post on 6/23. He was informed that the Soviets had broken through on either side of Vitebsk and he could not expect to receive any more forces from the 24th ID.

On this day, the 2nd Baltic Front attacked the positions of the 18th Army on the Velikaya. Therefore, the Red Army had extended its offensive to the Pleskau area! Hundreds of combat and fighter-bomber aircraft continued to fly and bomb, thousands of tanks continued to drive over the cratered landscape, and hundreds of thousands of Red Army soldiers continued to assault the main combat line of the German soldiers.

During the afternoon, the 18th Army was in combat on a wide front with waves of enemy attackers. The positions could be held with small penetrations. The greatest Soviet success was that achieved near the 121st ID, but the division maintained its unity.

While the situation was being controlled here, the situation on the right flank was reaching a crisis. Field Marshal Busch, commander of Army Group Center, talked with General Lindemann at 2155 hours. The Field Marshal was informed of the threatening situation. Several minutes later, General Lindemann submitted a proposal to the OKH to insert the 290th ID into the frontal gap near Obol and transfer the 212th ID to Polozk. During the night, the army group commander issued an additional order to remove the 81st ID.

On 6/24, the enemy continued his attack with the same pressure as the previous two days. The left flank of Army Group Center collapsed! The Soviet breakthrough was complete. The German front had a 90 kilometer wide and 30 kilometer deep gap torn in it! Soviet infantrymen and tanks stood on the Duena west of Vitebsk. The 1st Baltic and 3rd Belorussian Fronts met!

The Soviets extended their attack further. The 205th and 83rd ID (Major General Heun) held on only with their last ounce of strength. The 24th ID, which had no contact on the right or the left, was now subordinated to the I Army Corps. The flanking corps of Army Group Center, the IX Army Corps, was no longer in the position, on 6/24, to control a division located north of the Obol.

The army group commander ordered the commitment of the 290th ID. The 503rd Infantry Regiment, 2/502 Infantry Regiment, and 3/290 Artillery Regiment arrived in the Ulla area during the night. The 1/502 Infantry Regiment, the 501st Infantry Regiment, 2/814 Heavy Artillery Battalion, 2nd Battery of the 912th Assault Gun Brigade, and 751st Heavy Anti-tank Battalion followed. Additional formations could not be freed up.

In view of the catastrophe which threatened to break over his army group, Field Marshal Bush, during the morning, received the Chief of the General Staff of the OKH, General Zeitzler, and the operations officer of Army Group North, Colonel von Gersdorff, in his headquarters in Minsk. The essential thing to come out of this meeting was the commitment of reserves to Army Group Center. Colonel von Gersdorff could only reply:

"...we have nothing to give to Center!"

The three flanking divisions of the army group — 290th, 24th, and 205th ID — were heavily pressured by the enemy during the night. The 24th ID withdrew to Obol as ordered. The brave Saxons held on for another full day. Then they had to evacuate the city. Another fortification had come to an end, then the Russian tanks rolled on the right and left to the west.

On 6/25 at 1700 hours, Field Marshal Busch called the northern head-quarters and asked for help! The 6th Guards Army was marching on Polozk with the 29th, 47th, and 119th Rifle Divisions!

In view of this situation, which was also a threat to them, Army Group North decided to order the 16th Army to prepare to move behind the Duena. Only the 81st Upper Silesian ID was to remain south of the Duena near Polozk.

The OKH agreed. During the night, they ordered the immediate transfer of the 12th Panzer Division, 212th ID, and the 277th and 909th Assault Gun Brigades to Army Group Center. Not only was the army group weakened by these losses, but, on 6/26, they had to extend their front!

The OKH ordered that Polozk be held and defended as a "fortress!"

General of Infantry Hilpert, commander of the I Army Corps, was named commandant. At that moment, the General had no combat effective units at his disposal. His 205th, 290th, and 24th ID were still in bitter combat against enemy forces southeast of the city. Contact between the individual regiments and battalions was still broken. The front of the I Army Corps was 100 kilometers long at this time! The corps was folded back to the west, south of the Duena. Here, they were threatened with encirclement by the 29th, 47th, 51st, 360th and Rifle Divisions, 90th Guards Rifle Division, and 65th Tank Battalion of the 4th Soviet Shock Army and 6th Guards Army! The objective of these formations was obviously Polozk!

The German battalions, which were being transported by truck or rail, came under strong enemy air attack. The 7 heavy, 4 medium, and 3 light air defense batteries that were stationed near Polozk had no rest during these days and nights. The friendly air formations were much too weak to be able to oppose the Soviet air forces. Luftflotte 1 had petitioned the OKL for combat and fighter squadrons since the beginning of the offensive. On 6/27, the Luftflotte was promised the 4th Fighter-Bomber Group and the 3/3 Fighter-Bomber group. The transfer of the groups was not conducted satisfactorily. The 4th Fighter-Bomber Group made it to Duenaburg — then ran out of fuel!

On 6/27, Field Marshal Model took command of Army Group Center.

He knew Army Group North and its commander, General Lindemann, very well. The two senior commanders cooperated well in the following days. Field Marshal Model supported every proposal General Lindemann made to the OKH. However, the Field Marshal also knew that both army groups had to insure that a catastrophe, such as that at Stalingrad, did not befall the German Eastern Army.

The I Army Corps was involved in a bitter struggle with all of its divisions east and southeast of Polozk. The front gap to the IX Army Corps was widened another 40 kilometers on 6/27. Day by day, the enemy directed new divisions into this gap. On 6/27 at 1200 hours, the OKH ordered:

"The army group is to attack the enemy from the north!"

It was an impossible demand.

The army group established a combat group under the command of the 401st Senior Artillery Command (artillery commander of the I Army Corps), Lieutenant General Usinger, which was to carry out the order. He only had available the 161st Infantry Regiment (81st ID), 1/187 Infantry Regiment (87th ID), elements of the 181st Anti-tank Battalion (81st ID), and elements of the 909th Assault Gun Battalion. These weak units moved up to Lake Suya south of Polozk during the evening and prepared to attack.

It was 0200 hours as the motors of the tracked vehicles started up. The advance detachment of Combat Group Usinger set out. The 2/161 Infantry Regiment (Major Sulzer), with attached anti-tankers, began the march with doubts. They had no maps. The forest loomed on both sides of the sandy rollbahn like a black silhouette. Lieutenant Haupt had to search for the route at the head of the column with a flashlight. After an hour it was light. The forest was left behind. The plain opened up. The anti-tankers rattled downhill.

Suddenly, soldiers in field gray appeared. They were stragglers, and they called:

"Behind us is Ivan!"

Lieutenant Haupt called a halt and moved his guns into position. Soon the trucks with the first infantry companies arrived. Major Sulzer immediately deployed the companies on the hills before Prudok. The second company was redirected. The area was quiet.

At 0400 hours, gun fire rattled, machine-guns pinged, and rounds from mortars roared. The Soviets were coming! Battalion after battalion of the 90th Guards Rifle Division advanced. The 2/161 Infantry regiment could not hold. It had to withdraw into the hills of the anti-tank gunners. Another hour passed.

Then, the first Soviet regiment attacked. Just like on the parade field the rows of infantrymen crossed over the hills. When they approached to within 400 meters of the friendly positions, Lieutenant Haupt gave the order to fire. The three still operable 7.5 cm anti-tank guns fired more than 100 rounds in five minutes! The attack bogged down 100 meters in front of the guns! Friend and foe transitioned into the defense.

The morning passed quietly. A friendly attack of 4 assault guns from the 1181st Assault Gun Battery (Lieutenant Zahn) was frustrated by enemy artillery. The enemy gradually reinforced. His batteries engaged the German battalion at close range. Every shot was a hit. Losses increased. The anti-tank guns were knocked out one after the other. There was no friendly artillery.

The German soldiers lay in the burning heat of 6/28, like on a platter, on the plain in front of Prudok south of Polozk. At 1700 hours the order came over the radio: "Withdraw!" It was not an ordered retreat. It was more like: "Everyone for themselves!" Soviet tanks and infantrymen were attacking past the battalion on the right and left. Only remnants reached Lake Suya during the night. They no longer had guns or vehicles.

The attack of Combat Group Lieutenant General Usinger was defeated!

On the morning of 6/28, General Lindemann knew of the futility of the attack of Combat Group Lieutenant General Usinger. He himself went to Polozk and met with General of Artillery Hansen, commander of the 16th Army, and General of Infantry Hilpert, commander of the I Army Corps. The generals did not stop the attack of the combat group, but halted the majority of the 81st ID, which had, in the meantime, arrived in Polozk. The Silesian battalions established a temporary defensive position south of Polozk.

Chapter 5: The Retreat

The army group ordered the removal of the 170th ID from the Narva front and hurriedly transferred it to the right flank of the 16th Army. The army was being engaged on its entire front by enemy forces and could not free up one more company. Only the 132nd ID was set in a round-about march to Polozk. The 18th Army commander had to form a blocking formation (44th Engineer Battalion, 18th Army Assault Battalion, and a mixed anti-tank battalion) and dispatch it to Drissa. Therefore, the right flank was eventually covered.

The combat diary of the army group noted on 6/28 at 1115 hours:

"The right flank of the army group is hanging in the breeze!"

Major General Geiger from the Special Engineer Staff of the OKH was tasked with constructing a defensive position along the Duena with elements of the Wehrmacht's Eastern Command. The 3rd Latvian Police Regiment, 3rd Border Guard Regiment, 605th Security Regiment, and the 210th and 2901st Security Battalions were first directed to the river to build such positions.

The commander of the II Army Corps took control of the Duena sector. He had no troop units under him. The corps broke contact with the closely following Soviets from the combat zone west of Nevel. The II Army Corps was able to construct a solid front by month's end. The 132nd ID (Major General Wagner), along with the 3/322 Infantry Regiment (207th ID), 2/368 Infantry Regiment (290th ID), and 1/751 Anti-tank Battalion, arrived at the end of June. The 132nd ID formerly fought in the Slobodka area northwest of Nevel and now took over the extreme right flank of the army group. Later the 290th ID (Major General Henke) followed, which, in the past few days, had distinguished itself and been named in several OKW reports. The 226th Assault Gun Brigade and the 3/666 Heavy Anti-tank Battalion were the first battalions in the Duena positions with heavy weapons.

Now Polozk was threatened! Enemy tank and infantry forces moved 27 kilometers south of the city. Here, as the last bulwark on Lake Suya, stood only the few forces of Combat Group Lieutenant General Usinger. They consisted of: the 161st Infantry Regiment, 174th Infantry Regiment,

181st Engineer Battalion, 1181st Assault Gun Battery, one platoon of the 181st Anti-tank Battalion (all from the 81st ID), and the 656th Army Engineer Battalion.

At 2235 hours, the commander of the army group requested "Freedom of Operation!" from the OKH. The OKH refused!

On 6/29, the Soviet offensive continued in the same strength and at the same momentum. During the night, it was established that the extreme right was outflanked by the enemy! Now there were only security battalions, supply companies, and police units between Polozk and Duenaburg.

The civilian population left their dwellings in disorder. Men, women, and children followed the withdrawing columns of field gray with bag and baggage. Above circled fighter-bombers with the red stars, and they dived down upon those fleeing. The artillery hammered the roads and towns, the bridges, and railroad tracks. Towns and forests on both sides of the Duena were in flames.

On 6/29 at 2400 hours, in view of this catastrophe, the army group issued the following situation report to the OKH:

> "The development of the situation in the Army Group Center area of operations has decisively changed the situation of Army Group North. The right flank of the army group hangs in the breeze. South of here, the enemy has achieved operational freedom on a wide front and can quickly advance strong forces to the west. The chance of re-establishing the former contact with Army Group Center does not exist!"

Field Marshal Model endorsed the proposals of General Lindemann and, eight hours later, proposed withdrawing the right flank of Army Group North. However, the OKH again said "no." Hitler, against all opposition, ordered Army Group North to attack to the south in order to cut off the lead Soviet tank elements.

This irrevocable "Führer Directive" hit the army group like a bomb. General Lindemann passed this order on to the 16th Army commander with a heavy heart and bid him to do what he could with it. He personally disagreed with this attack. On 6/30 at 1700, the General entered the following grave sentence in the army group commander's combat diary:

Chapter 5: The Retreat

"With this attack order, we send people to a sure death!"

At this point in time, General of Infantry Hilpert had no combat effective troops available that could conduct such an attack to the south. The 81st Upper Silesian ID (Lieutenant General Luebbe) stood alone in and around Polozk. The Saxon 24th (Lieutenant General Versock) and the Thueringian 87th ID (Major General Baron von Strachwitz) were approaching. They had to form the lead attack elements. The remaining two divisions — the 205th ID (Major General von Mellenthin) and the 389th ID (Lieutenant General Hahm) — were still fighting east of the city and could not disengage from the enemy.

The commander of the 16th Army, General of Artillery Hansen, therefore, judged the situation as hopeless. To strengthen this view, strong Soviet air formations attacked the Polozk railroad station during the night of 7/1. On this night, 900 tons of ammunition were blown into the air!

General Lindemann spoke on the telephone with his superior commander for an hour. However, Hitler would not give in. He categorically demanded the flank attack south of Polozk! General Lindemann recommended, as an alternative, an attack further to the west near Dissna, in order to eventually close the gap to the 3rd Panzer Army. Hitler turned down this proposal.

At 0300 hours, the army group commander gave the order to the 16th Army commander:

"The Führer has ordered an attack out of the Polozk area with all available forces in the direction of Plissa...in order to cut off the enemy forces, which are attacking Dissna! ..."

Now things were overcome by events. The I Army Corps tried to assemble its few forces around Polozk and transport ammunition and equipment forward. The commanders again strived to gain operational freedom. General of Artillery Hansen was refused all responsibility. General Lindemann again complained to the OKH and begged them to withdraw the "Führer Directive." He got in contact once more with Hitler that night at 2300 hours:

"I don't believe that we can execute the ordered attack."

Then Hitler returned:

"The attack is to be executed with all means and with utmost energy!"

"Do you believe, mein Führer, that an attack against the 6th Guards Army with only two divisions will have any effect?"

"Yes, of course! Thank you!"

7/2 arrived. Polozk burned like a torch.

The 81st ID was directed to the Belchitsa Heights to secure and hold the assembly area for the 24th and 87th ID. The sun stood high in the sky. It was a hot day.

As the clock struck 1000 hours, the call sounded: "Tanks!"

However, these were not "Tiger" or "P-IV" tanks whose motors were heard. "T-34's" and Kv-I's" rolled on, penetrating into the forward positions of the infantrymen, and approaching Belchitsa. Already the steel colossi were rattling on the road to Polozk. Here there were 7.5 cm anti-tank guns of the 1/181 Anti-tank Battalion. The guns of Lieutenant Haupt stopped the first attack of the tank battalion of the 51st Soviet Guards Division after four 46 ton tanks lay burning.

The hours passed. The enemy reinforced.

As elements of the 24th ID launched a counterattack with assault guns, both friend and foe dug in their heels.

At 1255 hours, General of Infantry Hilpert reported:

"The ordered attack is not moving. It is simply suicide!"

At 1315 hours, General Lindemann, without consulting the OKH, ordered the suspension of the attack!

Six hours later, the commander reported to his superiors that not only did he cancel the attack of the I Army Corps, but he also ordered the evacuation of Polozk!

Chapter 5: The Retreat

Hitler was dumbstruck. At midnight, he subsequently gave his permission!

During these hours, the first companies of the 24th, 87th, and 389th ID withdrew over the temporary bridge across the Duena toward Polozk. The large "Kurhessen Bridge" over the deep river valley no longer existed. It collapsed under the bombing of Soviet aircraft.

The 81st ID held on for another day in the shrinking bridgehead. As the engineers blew the last temporary bridge and promptly withdrew through Polozk to the west, there were only ruins remaining for the battalions of the 51st Guards Division (Major General Chernikov).

The Soviet 6th Guards Army (Lieutenant General Chistyakov) attacked toward Duenaburg, south of the Duena, almost without opposition!

On the morning of 7/4, Army Group North defended, with its 19 divisions, a 350 kilometer front against 180 Soviet divisions. Including the Eastern troops, the army group now totaled 965,543 men.

The right flank of the 16th Army hung completely in the breeze on 7/4. The 16th Army (commander: General of Artillery Hansen; Chief of Staff: Major General Hermann; and operations officer: Lieutenant Colonel Hartmann) redeployed its command post to Stolpi in order to be closer to the threatened area. The II Army Corps (Assistant commander: Lieutenant General Hasse; Chief of Staff: Colonel Huhs; and operations officer: Major Weise), which was responsible for the right sector, was ordered to defend Duenaburg. Lieutenant General Pflugbeil, commander of the Northern Field Construction Detachment, was named commandant.

The 215th ID stood on the extreme right flank. The 435th Infantry Regiment, 393rd Assault Gun Brigade, and 1/10 Mortar Battalion formed a thin screen through the forests and marshes to re-establish contact with the 3rd Panzer Army wherever that may be possible. The combat group could not achieve its mission. Two days later, they were encircled in the vicinity of Vydziai. The closest German formations were 15 kilometers to the north and 20 kilometers to the south.

One combat group of the Senior Eastern Territory SS and Police (SS Obergruppenfuehrer Jeckeln) was organized in order to close this gap with police and border guard units. An additional blocking formation (two infantry, one alert battalion, one each assault gun battery, and a heavy anti-tank company), under Major General Pamberg, was quickly shifted to Duenaburg.

Several minutes after midnight on 7/4, the telephone rang in the headquarters of the army group in Segewold. Lieutenant General Schmundt, Hitler's chief adjutant, identified himself. He bluntly informed General Lindemann that he had been relieved of his post and that General of Infantry Friessner was now the new commander of the army group!

General Friessner, who turned over the Army Detachment Narva to General of Infantry Grasser, arrived in Segewold in the afternoon. His first order of the day ran:

"To Army Group North! All of our assets must be gathered. Every available man must avert this threat!"

General of Infantry Friessner, who was willing to execute Hitler's attack order unconditionally, realized after his first map briefing and discussion with Field Marshal Model that he had been misled. The new commander stuck to the plan to withdraw the southern flank of the army group!

The Soviet tank and rifle formations reached the old Russian border! The first Latvian and Lithuanian towns were overrun. At the beginning of July, between here and the Baltic Sea, there were no combat effective German formations.

On 7/5, General of Infantry Friessner visited the command posts of the 16th Army and II Army Corps. He had to establish that the greatest threat was to the Duenaburg area. From here, the enemy could attack to the north at any time in order to fall on the rear of the army group. The gap to Army Group Center was again widened. Vilna, the next strong point, was already encircled!

From 8/6 to 8/7, the II Army Corps regrouped with the 205th, 225th, and 263rd ID west of lake Dissna. The corps was to again try to attack from here to the south into the flank of the 6th Guards Army, in order to eventually establish contact with the 3rd Panzer Army.

The attack surprised the enemy. They quickly recovered, throwing new forces into the battle. The Soviets brought the attack of the II Army Corps, which had begun with so much momentum, to a halt near Ignalino. The divisions had to return to their departure positions.

In addition, on the next day, the I Army Corps ran into trouble. The 6th Guards Army, after the capture of Polozk, made new preparations and attacked the withdrawing 24th, 81st, 87th, and 290th ID. General of Infantry Friessner decided to withdraw the southern flank of the 16th Army to the provisional "Latvian Positions."

Hitler refused the corresponding request rigorously with the stereotypical answer, that they had to remain where they were located. He ordered that the army group immediately free up four divisions from its inactive eastern front. The 69th and 93rd ID had to be sent by the most direct route to Army Group Center!

The enemy offensive continued.

On 7/9, eight large formations — the 21st Guards Division, 26th, 28th, 119th, 200th, 332nd, 360th, and 378th Rifle Divisions — attacked north of the Duena to the west, while, simultaneously, mobile forces of the 6th Guards Army penetrated deeper into Latvia. Hitler seized on this as a reason to replace the commander of the 16th Army with General of Infantry Laux. The army group quickly transferred three field construction battalions (2/639, 3/640, and 391st) into the Mitau-Shaulen area. These combat inexperienced battalions were to stop an army!

At midnight on 7/9, the commander of the army group issued an order of the day. The pompous sentences read:

> "The Führer has again, in a combat directive, ordered that Army Group North will hold its present positions! ...I order: ...any thought of further withdrawal to the west is criminal. We will fight to the last breath and the last drop of blood in our assigned positions! ..."

The Soviets wiped these sentences away...

The next day, 7/10, at 2235 hours, General of Infantry Friessner had to inform Hitler that Army Group North was in no position to establish contact with the 3rd Panzer Army!

At this time, the Russian summer offensive was entering its second phase.

The 2nd Baltic Front (Army General Eremenko) attacked on a 150 kilometer front against the left flank of the 16th Army near Novosokolniki. The resistance of the divisions of the X Army Corps and the VI SS Corps was bitter and hard. From left to right fought the 93rd ID, 19th, and 15th SS Divisions, the 23rd, 329th ID, and 281st Security Division, as well as the 263rd ID. A combat group under Major General Sieckenius (commander of the 263rd ID) maintained contact with the I Army Corps with much difficulty.

The front did not tear apart.

According to Soviet accounts, the soldiers offered the Soviets significantly more resistance than the formations of Army Group Center on 6/22 had. Here the 912th Assault Gun Battalion distinguished itself, as Captain Engelmann (commander of the 1st Battery) destroyed 17 enemy tanks in one day! Army General Eremenko threw division after division into the battle. He succeeded in capturing the communications center of Idriza. Therefore, contact between Pleskau and Duena was broken!

The first attack effort of the 2nd Baltic Front was now exhausted. The Soviets had to re-group.

The 3rd Baltic Front (Army General Masslenikov) was on plan on 7/14. The attack was directed against the right flank of the 18th Army, with the objective of separating the two German armies from one another in order to hasten the collapse of the army group.

The L Army Corps (General of Infantry Wegener) fought bitterly in the trackless forest and marsh-land in front of Ludsen. However, all of the bravery came to naught. Russian tank forces broke through the front of the two neighboring Latvian SS divisions. The two armies collapsed! The 18th Army commander immediately ordered the 126th ID, which was in reserve near Pleskau, into the gap. However, before the division could arrive, it was too late.

The Soviet tank and rifle formations forced the left flank of the X Army Corps ever backward. The 93rd ID gave ground without notifying its neighbor. In this manner, the Soviets were able to break through and reach Opochka on 7/16. The defenders of the city resisted as no soldiers had before!

Chapter 5: The Retreat

The 18th Army did not have one more battalion that they could throw into the front gap. The great attack of the 3rd Baltic Front not only tied up the L Army Corps, but expanded to include the left neighboring XXXVIII Army Corps (General of Artillery Herzog). The corps still held on forward of the Velikaya with its divisions — the 83rd ID, 21st Luftwaffe Field Division, and 32nd ID.

The enemy did not take a pause for breath. New tank formations rolled forward. They attacked through the main combat line of the 21st Luftwaffe Field Division (Major General Licht). The corps had to fold back its flank. A small bridgehead east of Ostrov was still held by the 32nd (Lieutenant General Boeckh-Behrens) and 121st ID (Lieutenant General Busse).

"Actually, the front of the 21st Luftwaffe Field Division cracked under strong enemy pressure during the evening of 7/20. As the advanced elements of the 32nd ID arrived in the Utroya sector early on 7/21, they found it occupied by enemy forces. The crossings were either destroyed or in the hands of the enemy. The regiments crossed the river under difficult conditions, fighting their way through enemy troops and occupying a position between Utroya and Kukhva, in which they continued to fight bitterly with the enemy. ...The 21st Luftwaffe Field Division was completely exhausted, there was also an insurmountable gap on the right flank. To the left of the division there was only spotty contact with the 121st ID, which was also in heavy combat."[5]

The XXXVIII Army Corps evacuated Ostrov on 7/21 in order to avoid being encircled by the enemy.

The breakthrough was complete! 15 enemy rifle divisions and 5 tank brigades tore the 16th and 18th Armies asunder between Karsava and Ostrov!

Combat continued without pause. The troops marched, fought, and fired. The atmosphere was reported by a diary keeper in the 290th ID:

"We are exhausted. One cannot recognize another; over the tanned, dusty faces are sweat encrusted furrows. Stubbly beards are pasted with sweat and dirt. The wide open field shirts are covered in a layer of yellowish-brown powder. Thus we plod through ankle deep sand, one behind the other. ...We haven't slept for days, the dust burns in our throats. Our tongue and gums are like wood. No one speaks..."

In this atmosphere came the news of the assassination attempt on Hitler. The troops could not believe this report. The combat around them was more important than events in Berlin. The commander's order of the day for 20 July — "The army group now fights for the right!" — was not forwarded from the division command posts.

The Soviets had penetrated and broken through the majority of the "Panther Positions." Even the XXVIII Army Corps (General of Infantry Gollnick) could no longer hold out south of Lake Peipus. The order to withdraw was given.

"The major fire fight in Pleskau gave the impression of a ghost-like background on the first night of the withdrawal. The Velikaya bridge, which was in the 24th Infantry Regiment sector, held out until the last minute, then was blown by infantrymen and engineers as the enemy stood on the opposite bank. The initial withdrawal out of the "Panther Positions" went as planned. However, when strong enemy forces achieved a breakthrough further to the south on the seam between the XXXVIII Army Corps and the XXVIII Army Corps, elements of the division had to transition to the defense at several locations. The closing of the gap was the job of the 21st ID (Lieutenant General Foertsch)."[6]

Army Group North, with the exception of Army Detachment Narva, was in retreat into the Baltic Provinces. From 6/22 their losses totaled:

16th Army:	33,020 dead, wounded, missing,
18th Army:	12,158 dead, wounded, missing,
Army Detachment Narva:	4,320 dead, wounded, missing.

The battle for the Baltic Provinces began.

Chapter 5: The Retreat

On 7/12, the commander of the army group had already proposed to the OKH a retreat of his armies in the direction of Kovno-Riga. Army Detachment Narva would be transported by sea to Memel.

General of Infantry Friessner explained his proposal:

> "This is the last attempt to avoid having the army group encircled and destroyed!"

Hitler obviously did not agree with this plan. On 7/14 he ordered the commanders and chiefs of Army Groups Center and North to his headquarters. In this manner, General of Infantry Friessner received the unambiguous order to stay put. The Baltic Provinces had to be defended under all circumstances! The unrest of the Latvian and Lithuanian civilian population, which was fleeing to the west, had to be silenced. From now on, control of the army rear areas had to be exercised by the commanders. The German civilian administration in the Baltic region had to submit to military authority. In addition, the Wehrmacht Eastern Command was ordered to construct a bridgehead position around Riga.

The army group organized still another combat group to secure the open right flank. General of Cavalry Kleffel, with the 61st, 225th ID, and 11th SS Reconnaissance Battalion, was to attempt to establish contact with the 3rd Panzer Army. On 7/14, the combat group set out and reached formations of the neighboring corps with assault troops. The connection was again broken.

As before, Soviet troops were in the gap between the two army groups. The 1st Baltic Front operated in open terrain. They even received additional reinforcements. The 2nd Guards Army (Lieutenant General Chanchibadse) and the 51st Army (Lieutenant General Kreiser) were directed into the Lithuanian area. The 2nd Baltic Front penetrated to the Duena.

The army group could not match these forces. On 7/18, General of Infantry Friessner made an estimation of the individual divisions, the results follow:

16th Army: 2 divisions fully combat effective (61st, 225th ID),
        7 divisions worn out,

4 divisions partially combat effective,
1 division combat ineffective (23rd ID);

18th Army: 5 divisions fully combat effective (30th, 32nd, 121st, 126th
ID, 12th Luftwaffe Field Division),
2 divisions worn out (218th ID, 21st Luftwaffe
Field Division),
1 division partially combat effective (93rd ID),
1 division combat ineffective (83rd ID).

On 7/18, this inferior combat effectiveness was put to the test. Field
Marshal Model requested that the army group close the front gap from
Lithuania. Hitler called the commanders to a meeting. Reichsmarshall
Goering favored the withdrawal of the army group to the Duena. Hitler
brusquely turned this down. There was to be no withdrawal! He even went
so far as to order the army group to strip the Narva front bare. The XLIII
Army Corps, with the 58th ID, 11th SS Reconnaissance Battalion, 202nd
and 261st Assault Gun Brigades, and 2/62 Army Artillery Battalion had to
conduct the attack through Lithuania.

Then, the Leningrad Front (Marshal Govorov) attacked the Army Detachment Narva, while, at the same time, the 2nd Baltic Front initiated an
offensive against Duenaburg!

Shortly before the beginning of the battle for Vitebsk, the army group
requested the support of Luftflotte 1 for the ground troops. The few remaining air formations could only be committed on the main effort. On 7/
16, General of infantry Friessner spoke on the telephone with General of
Aviation Pflugbeil and asked him to commit all of his forces to maintain
the connection between the 16th and 18th Armies.

Moreover, the OKL had ordered Luftflotte 1 to manage their ground
personnel and supply troops without their non-essential officers and men.
These were made available to the army group for security tasks. On 7/14
the Luftflotte surrendered the first 200 soldiers, and two weeks later another 1500 followed. By the end of September, the Luftflotte had made a
total of 5,000 available to the Army. These soldiers, with only limited com-

bat experience, were not utilized in their own units, but distributed as replacements to infantry units.

The combat around Duenaburg — the gateway to the Baltic Provinces — began on 7/19. 5 rifle divisions, 1 tank, and 1 mechanized brigade launched a concentrated attack on the city after an infernal artillery and air preparation. Entire blocks of houses, including the citadel, burned and illuminated the new 16th Army battlefield with their flames.

The 81st ID (Colonel von Bentivegni), the 132nd ID (Lieutenant General Wagner), the 393rd Assault Gun Brigade (Captain Pelikan), and the 502nd Panzer Battalion were on the main effort of the day-long battle in front of Duenaburg. Neither side gave any leeway. The 437th Infantry Regiment (132nd ID) would not be thrown from their positions. The few "Tigers" of the 502nd Panzer Battalion attacked the superior "Stalin" tanks (these were committed for the first time in the army group sector!) without regard to their own safety. The 1st and 3rd Companies of the 502nd Panzer Battalion (Senior Lieutenant Boelter and Senior Lieutenant Carius) destroyed 17 "Stalin" tanks and 5 "T-34's" on the first day.

The battle for Duenaburg raged day and night. The German defenders still held as, on 7/25, the city was threatened with encirclement. These were only the remnants of the 81st and 215th ID. The 502nd Panzer Battalion perished while fighting near Duenaburg! The 393rd Assault Gun Brigade lost the majority of its guns.

On 7/26, the army group ordered the evacuation of Duenaburg. Holding the city was pointless.

The army group Chief of Staff, Lieutenant General Kinzel, who was called to the Führer Headquarters after the 20 July assassination attempt, reported to the new Chief of the General Staff of the OKH, General Guderian. Word-for-word, the Lieutenant General said:

"Before long, the army group will be destroyed! Therefore, the Führer will not only lose two armies, but the entire East!"

With sharp words, General Guderian refused to approve each additional withdrawal. He took Hitler's "fortress" slogan to heart and ordered the army group to fight where they stood. On 7/24, a corresponding order from Hitler arrived at the army group command in Segewold. According to this, the 16th Army even had to close the gap to Army Group Center!

With the "Führer Directive" arrived the new commander of the army group, General Schoerner, and the new Chief of Staff, Major General von Natzmer.

A Führer order of the same day gave the commander absolute authority"

"I am naming General Schoerner as commander of Army Group North and transfer to him the authority, in his entire area of operations, over all available combat forces and means of the Wehrmacht units and Waffen SS, the organization of the Wehrmacht, the Party and civilian agencies, to defend against the enemy attack and hold the Eastern Territory...

The entire area of operations of the army group is the operations area. In every instance, the Wehrmacht Eastern Command is subordinate to the commander of Army Group North.

The civilian administration in the operations area ... will maintain its former organization.

I authorize the Reichskommissar of the Eastern Territories in the civilian area and the commander of Army Group North in the military area to take whatever repatriation and evacuation measures they deem necessary. ..."

The new commander did not find a favorable situation.

On 7/24, the divisions of the army group were classified as the following:

Combat ineffective: 23rd ID, 15th and 19th Latvian SS Divisions;
Exhausted: 24th, 32nd, 81st, 83rd, 87th, 93rd, 121st, 132nd, 205th, 218th, 215th, 290th, 329th ID, 281st Security Division;
Partially combat effective: 126th, 225th, 263rd, 389th ID, 20th Estonian SS Division, 21st Luftwaffe Field Division;
Fully combat effective: 11th, 21st, 30th, 58th, 61st, 227th ID, 12th Luftwaffe Field Division.

Chapter 5: The Retreat

Meanwhile, a dangerous situation had developed on the seam of the 18th and 16th Armies. Here, the combat group of General of Infantry Wegener (L Army Corps, with the 83rd, 218th ID, XXVIII Army Corps, with the 21st, 32nd, and 227th ID) was committed, in order to prevent the further separation of the flanks of the two armies. However, the large frontal gap — the so-called "Baltic Gap" — still existed as before between the 16th Army and the 3rd Panzer Army. The group of General of Cavalry Kleffel, which was fighting here, was not in a position to attack through to the south.

The Soviets pressed further to the west and found themselves deep in Lithuania with their tank formations. On the morning of 7/26 Shaulen was reached by the advance detachment of the III Guards Mechanized Corps. The city commandant, Lieutenant General Pflugbeil, had only guard and security companies, which became engaged in heavy combat. A combat group under Colonel Maeder arrived and held up the enemy for a full day and a full night. Shaulen burned on 7/27. On the night of 7/28 the army group ordered the breakout of Combat Group Colonel Maeder to Libau.

The situation became more critical not only day by day, but hour by hour.

The senior command of the 2nd Baltic Front was ordered on 7/28 to immediately attack toward Riga with all of their forces and separate Army Group North from East Prussia!

Enemy tanks were already rolling on either side of Shaulen. Mitau was threatened. No supply vehicles could now travel from north to south or from south to north. The army group was practically cut off. On 7/28, the bread ration for the soldiers of the 16th Army had to be cut to 200 grams. There were only 40 tons of ammunition in the entire area!

General Schoerner ordered the withdrawal of the 16th Army and the right flank of the 18th Army to the so-called "Marienburg Positions." The OKH raised an objection. Major General von Natzmer could only laconically reply:

"We can't change it, the troops are already occupying the positions!"

Army Group North

The "Marienburg Positions" tied the Duena with Lake Peipus. In the past weeks, 99 kilometers of trenches, with 358 anti-tank obstacles, 3,061 combat positions, and 130 mine obstacles were emplaced.

The OKH was not in agreement with these measures. It still anticipated the main effort of the enemy attack toward the west. However, the army group commander had recognized the advance direction of the 2nd Baltic Front (Army General Eremenko)! He ordered the Wehrmacht Eastern Command to evacuate Riga as quickly as possible and defend the bridgehead positions with their troops.

The morning of 7/28 arrived. The first reconnaissance results, which were initiated at dawn, gave a frightful picture:

"About 900 vehicles, including tanks, are rolling from Mitau to the northeast toward Tuckum!"

Army Group North quickly shoved two companies of the 58th and 61st ID to Schlock in order to block the pass there. Before this, there were only weak forces of the Army Group Weapons School, without any heavy weapons. General Schoerner reported the threatening situation to the OKH. General Guderian answered at 1230 hours by telephone:

"...at this moment, there is nothing I can do for the army group!"

General Schoerner's order of the day was issued at 1415 hours:

"1) Enemy tank forces, with motorized infantry, in previously unknown strengths, have outflanked the western flank of the army group and are attacking in the Mitau area. Additional enemy forces are advancing on Riga from the Baltic Gap.

2) Army Group North prevents further enemy advance from the Shaulen area to the north and attacks the enemy forces, advancing out of Mitau, in the eastern flank. Another option is to close the gap between the 3rd Panzer Army and the army group by attacking in cooperation with the 3rd Panzer Army.

3) New organization on 7/28. ...

4) Missions:

       a) Wehrmacht Eastern Command holds the Riga bridgehead against all attacks. The holding of the advanced positions in Mitau, including the bridges, will be given special attention.

       b) 16th Army attacks on 7/28, with weak forces from Bauske in the direction of Eleja, in order to prevent the further advance of the enemy between the rollbahn and Bauske. ...Defend the achieved line with the left flank....

       c) 18th Army and Army Detachment Narva defend on their present lines."

The order of the day was overtaken by events. The army group ordered the organization of two combat groups, which had to be placed on the front immediately against the advancing tank elements. Lieutenant General Ortner, with formations from his 281st Security Division, took up positions along the Libau-Mitau road and the Mitau-Tuckum road. Colonel Maeder held along the west side of the Shaulen-Mitau road, with mixed companies, and there repulsed the initial enemy attack in the direction of Libau.

The heavily battered 93rd ID (Colonel Hermann) was transported to Riga in trucks. The arriving battalions were directed to the west in order to block the pass near Schlock. The Wehrmacht Eastern Command had committed all available guard and security formations to protect Riga.

General Schoerner ordered the immediate departure of the Wehrmacht female retinue. 1,500 communication assistants and employees of the military administration were removed by ship from the Latvian capital. The commander had been underway for hours to personally manage the communications and supply agencies.

Then, on 7/29, Hitler's order to immediately attack the 16th Army in the direction of Ponevish arrived.

It was too late!

The III Guards Mechanized Corps (Lieutenant General Obukhov) entered Mitau on 7/30 with tanks and infantry! The 8th Guards Mechanized Brigade, under Colonel Kremer, advanced on Tuckum on the same day! Soviet tanks reached the sea near Klapkalnice!

Army group North was encircled!

The extreme left flank of the army group in the bend in the Narva was also in a bitter struggle for its existence at this time.

The Leningrad Front (Marshal Govorov), with the 2nd Shock and 8th Armies, had been at parade rest until mid July. Then, they finished their deployment. On 7/24 at 0449 hours, Soviet guns opened a one hour preparation on the positions of the III SS Panzer Corps (SS Obergruppenfuehrer Steiner) southwest of Narva. Then tanks, infantry, and aircraft attacked.

The 11th East Prussian ID (Lieutenant General Reymann) and the 20th Estonian SS Division (SS Brigadefuehrer Augsberger) were the targets of the major enemy attack. The battle on either side of Auwere lasted 12 hours. Then the Soviets gave up. They had not gained one meter of ground! The Narva front held!

It was predicted that the Leningrad Front would renew its attack. Therefore, the army group commander ordered the III SS Panzer Corps to give up the bridgehead and the river positions in order to spare forces. The corps was already weakened from giving up units to the 16th Army. On 7/26 at 2230 hours, both SS Divisions "Nordland" (SS Gruppenfuehrer von Scholz) and "Niederlande" (SS Brigadefuehrer Baron Wagner) evacuated the city and the Narva bridgehead. Both divisions moved into the prepared "Tannenberg Positions." Only the rear guard regiment of the SS "Niederlande" Division — 48th SS Armored Infantry Regiment — could not withdraw from the river bank promptly. It ran into strong Soviet forces north of Auwere and was wiped out.

Russian tanks immediately attacked into the gap, which could not be closed in time. Fierce combat developed on either side of Vaivara. The battle was bitter. Each meter of ground, each bunker, and each shell crater had to be wrestled for. There was no difference between the battle for Vaivara and the battle of Verdun in the 1st World War.

Chapter 5: The Retreat

The Flemish "Langemarck" Assault Brigade, which had just arrived on the battlefield from their far away homeland, was bloodied after three days. The "Danmark" Regiment fought without a break around the Blauberg and did not retreat one step. The 1/45 SS Infantry Regiment (Estonian) sacrificed itself to cover the withdrawal of heavy guns. As the battle died out on 7/27, the III SS Panzer Corps had not lost one square meter of ground! Nevertheless, the losses were enormous. One division commander (SS Gruppenfuehrer von Scholz) and three regiment commanders (SS Standartenfuehrer Count zu Westphalen, SS Obersturmbannfuehrer Collani, and SS Sturmbannfuehrer Stoffers) had fallen along with many Estonian, Danish, Norwegian, Finish, and Belgian volunteers.

There was no rest between Lake Peipus and the Gulf of Finland. On 7/28, the Leningrad Front repeated its major attack. The attack involved all four divisions of the corps. The SS "Niederlande" Division and the "Nordland" Division were in heavy combat west of Narva. The right neighboring 11th ID also held its positions, as did the 20th Estonian SS Division and the 300th Special Purpose Division on Lake Peipus, along with the 227th Naval Infantry Battalion and the 111th Security Regiment.

The volunteers from northern, eastern, and western Europe defended bitterly. They fought no worse than the combat experienced East Prussians of the 11th ID. The Estonians knew this was their homeland. Not one SS volunteer left his unit during this time. Only where there were border guard and police units, which had never before fought with the Soviets, were there several desertions. From the Estonian 4th and 6th Border Guard Regiments alone, 6 officers and 923 men crossed over to the enemy by month's end!

Several times the army group commander proposed evacuating Estonia. Hitler resisted these requests. He wanted to hold the land under all circumstances. In this matter, he thought less of Finish and Estonian friendship than he did about the economic necessity of the Baltic oil works in northern Estonia. However, the front situation compelled them to remove three air defense batteries from these works at the end of July and transfer them to the Narva front. Additionally, 5,000 workers from the oil works had to build new intercept and reserve positions.

The front held north of lake Peipus...until it had to be given up as the result of further events.

By the beginning of the month of August, the army group was separated from the rest of the front. The separation from the homeland was complete! Telephone communication between the army group commander and the OKH in Berlin-Zossen was only possible over the civilian Segewold-Helsinki-Oslo-Zossen line!

Supply and replacements were obtained by ship to Riga. In the first two days after the encirclement, the following transports arrived in Riga:

"Robert Moehring"	with	441st March Battalion = 594 men,
	with	1/434 March Battalion = 165 men,
"Brake"	with	434th March Battalion = 589 men,
	with	437th March Battalion = 525 men,
"Wartheland"	with	435th March Battalion = 426 men,
	with	436th march Battalion = 493 men,
	with	439th March Battalion = 504 men,
	with	451st March Battalion = 496 men,
	with	45 tons of ammunition,
"Gothenland"	with	450th March battalion = 504 men,
	with	453rd March Battalion = 486 men,
	with	454th March Battalion = 472 men,
	with	3rd Naval March Bn = 650 men,

	with	45 tons of ammunition,
"Las Palmas"	with	435 tons of Lt Field How am.,
	with	15 tons of machine-gun am.
	with	390 bazookas
	with	50 tank alarms.

The army group was still bound by the Führer order to establish contact with the 3rd Panzer Army, which was 120 kilometers distant! The 16th Army initiated attacks in the Bauske area and east of Mitau. They both bogged down in the fire of multiple rocket launchers and artillery of the enemy. The 81st, 215th, and 290th ID (from right to left) attacked Birsen. Contact was not made. The regiments advanced well to the south. The 390th Infantry Regiment (215th ID) made it to the outskirts of Birsen on 8/5[sic?]. The Soviets counterattacked on the following day and pushed the three divisions back to their departure areas. Therefore, on 8/2, General Schoerner ordered the suspension of all operations. The OKH confirmed this instruction with a new Führer Directive, which arrived at army group headquarters on 8/3 at 1010 hours:

"The attack of Army Group Center to re-establish contact cannot be executed at this time, Army group North will attack to maintain combat strength, for the time being!"

The staff of the Wehrmacht Eastern Command and the 394th and 395th Senior Comandanturas, which were still in the Eastern Territories Reichskommissariate, were disbanded on 8/4. Their former areas of operations were immediately subordinated to the commander of the army rear areas. The Eastern Territories Reichskommissariate was defined as an operations area!

The army group and the 16th Army commander, for the time being, set everything available to repulse the threat to Riga. Additionally, the 93rd ID (Colonel Hermann) was to try to take Mitau in order to separate the Soviet tank formations, which were located near Tuckum, from their lifeline. The attack of the Brandenburger Division succeeded. The 273rd Infantry Regiment, 1/272 Infantry Regiment, and 93rd Fusilier Battalion took Mitau by assault and established a bridgehead.

This success confirmed what air reconnaissance had reported in the Tuckum area at the beginning of the withdrawal operation. Therefore, two additional combat groups were formed on the western flank of the 16th Army, which were to try to make their way through to Tuckum and Doblen. The strongest combat group consisted of motorized SS formations under the leadership of Obersturmbannfuehrer Gross.

Before the situation changed on this front sector, the army group had to place all of its attention on the main effort in front of the 16th and 18th Armies. The 2nd and 3rd Baltic Fronts re-grouped at the beginning of August and again attacked on 8/5 with great ferocity between Lake Peipus and Duena.

The entire front of the 18th Army was in desperate defense. The 24th, 126th, and 218th ID struggled against superior forces in front of Ludsen. The 426th Infantry Regiment (126th ID) was encircled near Licagals, but later fought their way through. The 83rd ID fought south of Marienburg.

> "At noon, the enemy fired on the positions with all heavy weapons. We crawled into the holes in the earth. There were great losses until evening. The left neighbor had to leave his positions several times, the right neighbor likewise. ...The right flank was open! This is a great danger! Ivan crept into our rear. ...The 2/257 Infantry Regiment lost all of its officers. Its combat strength: 1 non-commissioned officer and 30 men!"[7]

The VI SS Corps (SS Obergruppenfuehrer Krueger) fought in the forests and marshes. The divisions no longer existed, only individual combat groups, which marched, fought, and died in isolation. The Soviets split the seam between the VI SS Corps and X Army Corps. Therefore, the two German armies were again separated. A counterattack was immediately executed by elements available from the 24th, 32nd, and 122nd ID, which just arrived from Finland, but they could not get through.

Chapter 5: The Retreat

The 2nd Baltic Front intended to throw back the left flank of the 16th Army further near Birsen to prevent the eventual uniting of the two armies. The attack hit the 81st ID with its full weight. The division was at most equal in strength to a weak regiment; artillery, anti-tank, and engineers consisted of smaller and smaller groups. The Upper Silesians did not waver or withdraw. They faced up to the 10 rifle divisions and I and XIX Soviet Tank Corps!

The army group commander ordered the withdrawal of the inner flanks of the 16th and 18th Armies to the Bauske-Memele-Trentelburg line. The evening report from the OKH on 8/6 ran:

"125 tanks were destroyed in the area of the army group, of them, 87 tanks were destroyed in the I Army Corps area. The total number of tanks destroyed by the army group since 6/22 = 1325. During the attack and defensive battle in the Birsen area, the 81st ID, under the leadership of Colonel von Bentivegni, distinguished itself by the fierceness of its attack and the steadfastness of its defense. ...The ferocious combat of the division, which inflicted considerable casualties, is to be thanked for the failure of the operational attack of the enemy in the direction of Riga. ...The 912th Assault Gun Brigade also excelled in the same area, destroying 53 tanks. ..."

The combat on the right flank of the 16th Army, on the other hand, quieted considerably. The Corps Group General of Cavalry Kleffel established contact with Combat Group SS Obersturmbannfuehrer Gross. The SS Group advanced on 8/8 against only marginal enemy resistance from the northwest toward Tuckum.

The 3rd Baltic Front (Army General Masslenikov) initiated the second phase of their offensive against the left flank of the 18th Army on 8/10. Bomber squadron after bomber squadron flew against the positions of the XXVIII Army Corps, which were, simultaneously, covered by an hours-long fire preparation by Soviet artillery. Then the Russian divisions assaulted. The XXVIII Army Corps (General of Infantry Gollnik) could not resist the superior forces. Against the front of the 30th ID alone attacked 1 tank division, 1 mechanized brigade, and 4 rifle divisions.

"In a short time, a desperate battle erupted on the main combat line involving the defenders in the trenches, meanwhile, the lead attack elements were already behind the battalion command posts. The enemy had also used smoke in some places, which blinded the artillery observers, therefore, in some places, tanks simply appeared in front of the batteries, while they were preparing to fire blocking fires. This is a big crisis..."(8)

The Soviets threw back (from right to left) the 121st, 30th ID, 21st Luftwaffe Field Division, and 21st ID, and penetrated into Petseri. By evening of this "Black 10th of August", they stood 20 kilometers east of Werro!

The way for the Red Army into Estonia was free!

General Schoerner ordered the positions to be held, because otherwise the Eastern Territories were lost! The operational air squadrons of the Luftflotte took off on 8/11, in spite of bad weather, in order to assist the XXVIII Army Corps.

The Army Detachment Narva had to give up combat groups. First they dispatched the SS "Niederlande" Division from their right flank and the newly arrived "Wallonie" Assault Battalion (SS Sturmbannfuehrer Degrelle). The 16th Army also requested the transport of formations, but without success. On 8/12 at 0915 hours, the combat diary of the army group noted: "16th Army is fighting by hook or by crook, perhaps more by crook, around Riga!"

The OKH dispatched help. This was the newly created 31st ID (Major General Stolzmann). The division was flown in 86 "Ju-52's" from East Prussia to Latvia in the following days. The 82nd Infantry Regiment was the first to arrive in Laatre, 15 kilometers northeast of Walk, on 8/13.

It was about time.

On 8/12, the Soviets broke through the "Modohn Positions", 45 kilometers west of Pleskau. The tank and rifle formations of the CXVI, CXXIII Rifle Corps, and XIV Guards Corps attacked through to the west. The XXVIII Army Corps was no longer in a position to offer resistance. On the evening of 8/13, Werro was lost. There were no more German troops between here and Lake Pleskau!

Chapter 5: The Retreat

The army group assigned the block between Lakes Peipus and Wirz to the Army Detachment Narva. The 18th Army (commander: General of Artillery Loch; Chief of Staff: Major General Foertsch; and operations officer: Colonel Starke) took over the threat to the left flank themselves. On the right flank was formed the Army Group General of Infantry Wegener, with the L, X Army Corps, and the VI SS Army Corps. The II Army Corps (General of Infantry Hasse), which was formerly committed in the 16th Army area of operations, was inserted between the XXVIII and XXXVIII Army Corps. This was handled, for the time being, by Combat Group Colonel von Below, which was located here, and the deploying 31st ID. Later, the 87th ID would also be transferred to this combat area.

The widening of the Soviet breakthrough was prevented until 8/16 by the commitment of all available formations and means, including the 3/2 Fighter-bomber Group (Major Rudel). The 30 divisions of the 3rd Baltic Front stopped! They turned a portion of their force to the north, in order to gain the western bank of Lake Peipus. Here, the German front stabilized on either side of Dorpat after elements of the Army Detachment Narva were committed.

SS Brigadefuehrer Baron Wagner formed a combat group, which took over the protection of the right flank of Army Detachment Narva, because the 207th Security Division withdrew. The 23rd Infantry Regiment (11th ID), the SS "Wallonie" Battalion, 11th SS Armored Reconnaissance Battalion, 3/3 Mortar Regiment, and the 2/58 Artillery Regiment repulsed the first enemy attack against Dorpat. Then, on 8/16, the Soviets suddenly landed on the western bank of Lake Peipus near Hehikoorma, with the 25th Inland Waterway Brigade. An immediate counterattack by Combat Group Wagner did not succeed!

The army group was not in a position to begin the attack to the south that was constantly demanded by the OKH. Their entire force was engaged in the north and the south.

On 8/15, the 2nd Baltic Front again attacked with strong troop formations near Bauske. The I Army Corps, which had been fighting incessantly for weeks, was not able to withstand the first assault. 50 heavy Soviet tanks threw back the exhausted Upper Silesians and Lower Germans of the 81st and 290th ID five kilometers. The two brave divisions fought against the

6th Guards Army. With the support of the 912th Assault Gun Brigade, they destroyed 40 enemy tanks on the first day of the battle!

The Soviets would allow no rest. On 8/16 at 1015 hours, an hour-long preparation fire initiated the second part of the battle for Bauske. Again the 81st ID stood on the main enemy effort — and again the men from Oppeln, Gleiwitz, Ratibor, Hindenburg, and Breslau held their positions. However, it was evident that the strength of the division must slacken. The 16th Army commander, therefore, brought forward the 438th Infantry Regiment and 132nd Fusilier Battalion (132nd ID) during the course of the day.

The 6th Guards Army wanted to get through the front of the I Army Corps to Riga. They continued to dispatch the infantrymen and tanks from the 46th, 67th, 71st, and 90th Guards Divisions, as well as the 51st, 166th Rifle Divisions, 202 Tank, and 26th Motorized Brigades forward!

For two more days, the bloodied combat groups of the I Army Corps held on. However, when the Soviet attack waves again crashed against the infantry trenches under the cover of the early morning fog on 8/19, the strength of the corps was at an end. The Bauske bridgehead was lost.

The army group order for this day ran:

"1. The enemy is through on the left flank of the X Army Corps up to Lake Kalu moving to the west and northwest...

2. The army group prevents further enemy advance through the seam between the 16th and 18th Armies on Riga and withdraws the left flank of the 18th Army and the southern flank of Army Detachment Narva into the Walk - Lake Wirz - Embach Positions and holds these positions....

3. 16th Army holds its present main combat line. ...

4. The 18th Army holds the present main combat line on the northern flank of the X Army Corps...and withdraws the left flank gradually into the Walk Positions.

Chapter 5: The Retreat

5. Army Detachment Narva withdraws in a gradual delaying battle, in close cooperation with the 18th Army, into the Embach Positions...."

The collapse of Army Group Center and the resulting isolation of Army Group North compelled the OKH to take decisive countermeasures at the beginning of July. The 7th Panzer Division, which was reconstituting in Rumania, was put on rail transport to East Prussia. Several weeks later, the "Grossdeutschland" Armored Infantry Division followed.

At the beginning of August, the divisions ran into the withdrawing 3rd Panzer Army in East Prussia. There was no longer an organized front. The troops were dispersed. No officer knew anything about the situation. Every attempt to halt failed.

In spite of this, the 3rd Panzer Army commander (General Raus) was able to form two combat effective panzer corps in mid August, which were to establish contact with the 16th Army in Lithuania. The attack, which was executed under the cover name "Operation Doppelkopf", began on 8/16.

The XXXIX Panzer Corps operated out of the Libau area with the 4th, 5th, and 12th Panzer Divisions, and the Panzer Formation Count Strachwitz (SS Gross Brigade and the 101st Panzer Brigade). The XL Panzer Corps assembled around Tauroggen with the 1st ID, 7th and 14th Panzer Divisions, and the "Grossdeutschland" Armored Infantry Division.

The advance of the XL Panzer Corps reached the Venta. The advanced 1/26 Panzer Regiment (Captain Count Rothkirch) bored through the enemy front directly to the west of Shaulen. However, they could not go any further. "Grossdeutschland" stopped, as did the neighboring 7th Panzer Division, which could not cross the Venta.

The attack of the XL Panzer Corps against 10 rifle divisions, 3 artillery divisions, 1 mechanized brigade, and 4 anti-tank brigades was condemned to failure. The Soviets had the overwhelming advantage and transitioned to the counterattack. The corps had to regroup in order to repulse the enemy.

The attack of the XXXIX Panzer Corps was luckier. Panzer Formation Major General Count Strachwitz, which was on the extreme left flank, initiated the attack on Tuckum in the morning of 8/19. The formation was able to break the Soviet resistance. The enemy slowly retreated. The night of 8/20 they took a short pause. In the morning they continued. At 0715 hours, the panzer formation captured the Dzukste railroad station. Major General Count Strachwitz re-grouped for the last time and ordered: "Attack Tuckum!"

From the lake roared ships' guns. 20.3 cm shells bored into the street, houses, and barricades of Tuckum. A naval formation under Vice Admiral Thiels — consisting of the heavy cruiser "Prinz Eugen" and destroyers — had traversed the Irben route from Oesel during the night and stood 25 kilometers from the coast. It was exactly 0700 hours when the first salvo of eight 20.3 cm guns from the "Prinz Eugen" thundered over the land. On this day, the naval combat group fired a total of 284 rounds of heavy artillery. The two destroyers "Z-25" and "Z-28" participated with 168 rounds.

Major General Count Strachwitz made use of the naval support. His formation continued to roll. Major General Count Strachwitz rode at the head of his unit. It was exactly 1200 hours on 8/20 when the first security was emplaced near Kemmern. Contact with Army Group North was finally established!

Two hours later, Major General Count Strachwitz rolled into Tuckum with his lead panzer elements! The Soviets had fled the city and abandoned guns, vehicles, hand weapons, equipment caches, and horses. The last enemy rear guard defended until 1700 hours. Tuckum was firmly in German hands!

The army group immediately ordered Major General Pawel to hold the land connection open. Only military columns were allowed to pass through the narrow passage. At the same time, General of Cavalry Kleffel was instructed to advance to Tuckum with his corps group. The lead elements of the corps group were able to make it to the Tuckum-Mitau road by evening.

The Panzer Formation Count Strachwitz was transferred to the army group area. Elements of the 52nd Security Division, which had followed them, remained in Tuckum and were subordinated to the 16th Army. On 8/21, the 2/272 Infantry Regiment (93rd ID) attacked from the east toward Kemmern. Therefore, a solid contact was secured between the 16th Army and 3rd Panzer Army! 23 guns, 10 tanks, 11 anti-tank guns, 7 machineguns, and 47 trucks were the booty of Soviet weapons on the Baltic Sea coast.

Chapter 5: The Retreat

Against the will of the OKH, the army group commander moved the Panzer Formation Count Strachwitz, which was supported by the 153rd Army Artillery Battalion and the 1/44 Engineer Battalion, to Estonia...

The battle for Estonia erupted on 8/21.

The 3rd Baltic Front (Army General Masslenikov) committed the 54th and 67th Armies and the 1st Shock Army between Dorpat and Walk to attack to the north in order to make contact with the Leningrad Front forward of Reval.

The battle on the Em took shape on the first day. The battle on the eastern bank of Lake Wirz was just as bitter. It was clear: the Soviets wanted to capture Dorpat and, therefore, gain free reign to the interior. The II Army Corps slowly withdrew. Soviet tanks of the 67th Army approached to within 7 kilometers south of Dorpat!

The Panzer Formation Count Strachwitz — supported by the Army Detachment Narva — was to remove the enemy penetration in the 87th ID sector between Modohn and Werro. The Panzer Formation arrived in Elva on 8/23 and prepared for the attack during the night. Major General Count Strachwitz had an accident during a reconnaissance trip and was severely injured.

The panzer formation was leaderless for its decisive mission. The commander of the 12th Luftwaffe Field Division, Lieutenant General Weber, took over the attack preparations, but refused to lead the unknown formation. The army group tasked Lieutenant General Chales de Beaulieu, commander of the 23rd ID, with the leadership of the panzer formation. The attack was executed. Colonel von Lauchert later led the formation.

The 101st Panzer Brigade and the Gross Panzer Brigade set out, as instructed, on 8/24 toward Elva and Loo. The 11th SS Armored Reconnaissance Battalion entered Tamsa 1.5 hours later. Here, their strength was at an end. The Soviets proved to be the stronger. They forced our formations into the defense. By evening, Panzer Formation Strachwitz had 3 operational tanks and 100 men!

The Russians seized the initiative. They broke through the thin German lines. The 10th Rifle Division and 5th Tank Brigade attacked. On 8/24 they stood on the southern tip of Lake Wirz. Therefore, the 18th Army and

Army Detachment Narva were separated! The attack wedge aimed toward Pernau, which defined the operations area.

The battle for Dorpat began on the following day. The II Army Corps had committed elements of the 11th ID, among others. During the morning, heavy Russian artillery covered the city and surrounding area. Fighter-bombers and combat aircraft attacked. The German soldiers could not show themselves. The Soviets advanced.

Street battles raged. The East Prussian soldiers engaged the "T-34's" with bazookas. Bitter fighting occurred around the blocks of houses and the harbor, the installations of which were blown during the afternoon. The 1/23 Infantry Regiment defended the Estonian National Museum. The battalion was the last group of infantrymen to give way, and they were forced to by flame throwers. The 1st Battery of the 393rd Assault Gun Brigade suppressed one wave of tanks after another, but they finally had to withdraw.

Soviet infantrymen raised the red flag over Dorpat at 1800 hours!

The last defenders were evacuated by 4 artillery barges, 2 customs boats, and 7 smaller boats of the Navy. The enemy immediately pursued, occupied the airfield, and reached the Dorpat-Taps rail line. Then the 67th Soviet Army also took a breather. They suspended further advance!

Estonia had become a combat zone.

On 8/23, the army group had already ordered the alerting of the national security agencies. General Schoerner summoned to his headquarters the representatives of the local national government, the Reichs, and General Commissariates to conduct extensive discussion of possible countermeasures. The head of the Estonian government, General Dankers, promised his full support in the fight for the freedom of his country. (Nevertheless, he could not prevent the increasing numbers of Estonian soldiers, including entire police units, from defecting to the enemy!)

The 2nd Baltic Front (Army General Eremenko) did not give up on its idea of overrunning the left flank of the 16th Army and advancing on the Latvian capital at the end of August. A new main effort was formed near Ergli, from where they were to break through to the Duena.

The 16th Army organized an army group, under General of Infantry Boege in the same area in order to secure unity of command and control.

Chapter 5: The Retreat

The members of the group included:

Corps Group Lt. General Risse, with the 58th, 205th, 225th ID;
The independent 389th ID;
The X Army Corps, with the 24th ID;
Corps Group Lieutenant General Wagner, with the 121st and 329th ID.

At this critical time, the 16th Army was dealt a heavy blow. The commander, General of Infantry Laux, was shot down during a reconnaissance flight over the front on 8/29. The General suffered severe burns, from which he later died in a hospital in Riga. His operations officer, Colonel Hartmann, also died. The commander of the I Army Corps, General of Infantry Hilpert, took command of the 16th Army. Lieutenant General Busse (formerly the commander of the 121st ID) took over the I Army Corps.

The new commander had to turn his attention to the army's right flank. There were indications of a considerable reinforcement of enemy forces in the Mitau area. Corps Group General of Cavalry Kleffel zealously improved their positions. The right flanking division — the 81st ID — was able to establish contact with elements of the "Grossdeutschland" Armored Infantry Division near Ammenieku.

The OKH wanted to subordinate Group Kleffel to the 3rd Panzer Army. General Schoerner vigorously protested against this idea. He claimed Kurland as his army group's rear area!

The battle for Riga appeared to be approaching. On 8/31, the army group commander ordered the Reichs Commissar to evacuate 100,000 civilians from the city in four weeks and see to the construction of defenses! The female support forces of the Wehrmacht, SS police, and the civilian agencies had to be transported back to Germany by the beginning of September. The Reichs Minister for the occupied Eastern Region was to arrange for the central control of supply installations for the Wehrmacht and the local population.

The army group prepared itself for the Soviet attack on Riga. At the end of August, the 14th Panzer Division was deployed behind the seam between the 16th and 18th Armies as a reserve. In addition, the 731st Army Anti-tank Battalion arrived and was sent to the 16th Army. Three battalions of the 563rd ID and the 10th Special Purpose Luftwaffe Fighter Battalion were flown in by air transport. They were assigned to protect the military harbor at Pernau.

At the end of August, the army group defended its 700 kilometer long front with the 32nd ID, 3rd Security Division, 1st Panzer Division, 1st Panzer Brigade, and 1st SS Panzer Brigade. The 23rd ID defended the Baltic islands. 1,960 officers and 68,606 men had died, were wounded, or were missing in August. On 9/1, the actual strength of the army group was 571, 579 soldiers and 42,833 volunteers.

The Chief of the General Staff of the OKH, General Guderian, during a briefing at the Führer's Headquarters on 9/5, informed the Chief of Staff of the army group, Major General von Natzmer, that he was concerned about the entire Eastern front — and then the General continued:

> "...to prevent the general evacuation of the Eastern Territories, we would soon need the formations of the army group to secure other threatened areas of the Eastern Front!"

The withdrawal of the army group could not occur.

The Red Army saw to that.

At the beginning of September, the Soviets were organizing themselves between the Gulf of Finland and Riga. 125 rifle divisions, 5 tank corps, 1 mechanized corps, and 7 fortifications brigades, with 900,000 men, 17,480 guns, 3,080 tanks, and 2,640 aircraft stood ready for the offensive!

The Leningrad Front (commander: Marshal Govorov, Chief of Staff: General Popov) was deployed with the 2nd Shock and 8th Armies from the Gulf of Finland to Lake Peipus. Southwest of the lake stood the 3rd Baltic Front (commander: Army General Masslenikov; Chief of Staff: Lieutenant General Vaskevich) with the 67th Army, 1st Shock, and 54th Armies. The 2nd Baltic Front (commander: Army General Eremenko; Chief of Staff: General Sandalov) deployed the 10th Guards, 42nd Armies, 3rd Shock, and 22nd Armies to the north. The 1st Baltic Front (commander: Army General Bagramyan; Chief of Staff: General Kurassov) assembled the 4th Shock, 43rd, 51st, and 6th Armies, and the 2nd Guards and 5th Guards

Chapter 5: The Retreat

Tank Armies south of Riga. For air support, the individual fronts were supported by, from north to south, the 13th, 14th, 15th, and 3rd Air Armies.

A special staff of the Red Army High Command, under Marshal Vassilevskiy, coordinated the three Baltic fronts, while the Leningrad Front was to operate separately. The objective of the Baltic fronts was simple: Riga!

The 14th of September arrived.

At exactly 0400 hours, a 1 1/2 preparation fire was initiated between Lake Peipus and Shaulen. Hundreds of fighter-bombers, fighters, and combat aircraft hung in the air and dived with motors roaring onto the German positions. Even before the last columns of smoke and dirt from the exploding bombs and shells settled, the three Baltic fronts attacked!

The German blocking fire exploded without effecting this colossal superior force. The commitment of the death-defying pilots of the 54th Fighter Group did not hinder the enemy air superiority, despite shooting down 76 aircraft on the first day of the battle.

The main effort of the Soviet 1st Shock Army was directly south of Lake Wirz. 13 rifle divisions assaulted the main combat line of the XXVIII Army Corps. The enemy established bridgeheads, into which tanks were soon shoved. The first penetrations into the main combat line were repulsed. The combat strength of the defenders wilted from hour to hour. During the evening, the 30th ID and 12th Luftwaffe Field Division were separated. The 31st and 227th ID withdrew into the 2nd and 3rd blocking positions. Only the 21st ID held its front before Walk and frustrated all enemy attacks!

The second enemy main effort was in front of the 18th Army on either side of Ergli, west of Modohn. The X Army Corps bitterly defended with the 24th, 132nd, 121st, 329th, and 126th ID (from right to left). The corps held its positions and only surrendered its first trench line during the evening. The 2nd Baltic Front could not penetrate anywhere!

The decisive attack was to be made by the 1st Baltic Front in the Bauske area. 18 rifle divisions and 2 tank brigades conducted the first blow against the I Army Corps, which, with four divisions — the 58th, 215th, 290th ID, and 281st Security Division (from left to right) — was clearly out-manned. The first attack of the 4th Shock (Lieutenant General Malyshev) and 43rd

Armies (Lieutenant General Beloborodov) solidified in front of the main combat line.

Then the enemy batteries conducted a second bombardment on the positions of the 215th and 290th ID during the morning. Groups of up to 60 fighter-bombers dived onto the individual German positions. Then the waves of tanks rolled between Memele and Musa. The Wuerttembergers of the 215th and the North Germans of the 290th ID no longer had any defensive weapons. The 21 cm mortars of the 636th Army Artillery Battalion and the heavy field howitzers of the 814th Army Artillery Battalion lay bombed and damaged, and the artillerymen were dead.

The weight of the attack hit the 215th and 290th ID. The resistance of the divisions collapsed. Soviet tanks penetrated into the main combat line and captured Bauske! The 16th Army commander committed his reserve — 101st Panzer Brigade (Colonel von Lauchert) — to Bauske. As the German tanks attacked at 1500 hours, they hit the enemy III Guards Mechanized Corps and fought bitterly.

During the night, General Schoerner telephoned the Führer Headquarters and reported on the new situation. He requested to immediately evacuate Estonia in order to break out to the west. The commander said:

> "We are now fighting for our lives! ...This is our last chance to get away!"

The OKH refused.

On 9/15, the army group commander developed plans to fortify the front. All available guard and security battalions, as well as the last 1,500 men of the Reichs Labor Detachment, were ordered to take up positions in the defenses around Riga. The music corps of all units were disbanded. Convoy and supply troops were instructed to attack the penetrating tanks and not surrender any strong points. Hastily, the 3rd Senior Engineer Commander, Major General Geiger, began construction on positions at Aa and Tuckum to defend Kurland.

On 9/15 the army group committed its last reserve. They could not prevent the 12th Luftwaffe Field Division, after defending against 13 enemy attacks, from collapsing under the 14th. The 14th Panzer Division advanced to block the Soviet penetration near Ergli.

"Although only a stretch of 40 kilometers had to be covered, the deployment was time consuming and difficult. The Red Air Force bombed the rollbahn without pause, while the enemy artillery blocked the north-south roads behind the front with the fire from their heavy caliber weapons..."[9]

9/16 developed dramatically. The 18th Army, on the whole, maintained its unity. The catastrophe occurred in the I Army Corps area. The I Soviet Rifle Corps (Lieutenant General Vassilev) broke out from Bauske. Tanks with mounted infantry attacked through the last German positions, by-passing the artillery positions, to advance on the "Mitau-East Positions" between Jecava and Friedrichstadt. The far advanced 145th Rifle Division (Major General Dibrova) took Baldone, 25 kilometers southeast of Riga!

In the morning, General Schoerner flew to the Führer Headquarters in East Prussia to personally obtain permission to evacuate Estonia. He described to Hitler, in the presence of Reichsmarshall Goering, Grand Admiral Doenitz, General Guderian, Lieutenant Generals Wenck, and Kreipe, as well as Vice Admiral Voss, the situation in the Baltic Provinces. 15 minutes after the discussion, Hitler, against expectations, ordered the execution of "Operation Aster."

"Operation Aster" signified the evacuation of Estonia.

It had a long and interesting history.

Shortly before the beginning of the Soviet summer offensive, Finland reflected a general war weariness, so that, sooner or later, they were expected to remove themselves from the armed conflict. Therefore, it was necessary to make timely preparations to deal with the possibility of an exposed left flank of the army group and, accordingly, of the entire Eastern Army.

Even as late as the beginning of July, Hitler had prohibited thoughts about surrendering Estonia. He pointed out the importance of the oil region for the conduct of the war. Therefore, the OKH and OKM had to provide for the protection of the Estonian coastal area.

Army Group North

The "Baltic Red Banner Fleet" had not only occupied the southern coast of the Gulf of Finland up to the mouth of the Narva, but also the islands of Koivisto, Tiurinassaari, Piisari, Narvi, Lavansari, and Seiskari as strong points. Only the two islands of Tytaersaari and Hogland in the Gulf of Finland between Narva and Wilborg were still in the hands of the Finish Navy.

German mine fields protected the waters between the Estonian coast and the northern island of Hogland.

If Finland were to remove itself from the war, then these two islands would be occupied by the " Baltic Red Banner Fleet" without a fight, representing a latent threat to the German flank.

On 6/18/1944 — already before the summer offensive — Army Group North transferred the 209th Infantry regiment of the 58th ID as "Training Brigade North" to Reval to exercise landings on the Finish islands. On 7/4, the OKH was excluded from the planning to conquer these islands, because the army formations had to be committed on the front.

The OKM began to independently prepare for "Operation Tanne-Ost." On 7/9, in a discussion with the Führer, Grand Admiral Doenitz again hinted at the decisive importance for the war of the Estonian coast as the front line of security for the construction of submarines. He instructed the Admiralty of the Eastern Baltic sea to take decisive measures.

On 9/2, as Finland surprisingly negotiated a truce with the Soviet Union, Hitler ordered the immediate execution of the operation. The army group had to prepare landing battalions. Elements of the 68th Fusilier Regiment of the 23rd ID were assigned the task.

A German naval formation, under Naval Captain Mecke, set out on 9/14, with the 3rd, 25th Mine Sweeper, 13th, 21st, 22nd Landing, 7th Artillery, and 1st and 5th Motor Torpedo Flotillas. The 68th Fusilier Regiment and the 531st Naval Artillery Battalion were embarked. The Fins refused to give up the island of Hogland — being faithful to their truce with the Soviet Union. At 2300 hours, as the German ships approached land, the Finish batteries, under Lieutenant Colonel Miettinnen, opened a heavy defensive fire. In spite of this, the S boats pressed on and landed the fusiliers on the coast. The men worked their way forward, under constant attack from Soviet fighter-bombers and the counterattacks of the fanatically fighting

Fins. The landing troops were encircled. Radio contact could not be established between the landing troops and the "Admiralty of the Eastern Baltic Sea" and the naval formations under Vice Admiral Thiele. Naval Captain Mecke requested a truce with the Finish commander on 9/15 at 1700 hours.

"Operation Tanne-Ost" was a lamentable failure. 400 dead and 1,056 prisoners were left on the island. They were later handed over to the Soviets. 2 landing boats and 3 barges were sunk. The most senseless German operation of the year 1944 was over!

The flank cover for the army group was lost.

Ten days before this hapless operation, General Guderian — without Hitler's knowledge — verbally ordered the army group commander to make preparations for the withdrawal from the Narva positions. On 9/9, the army group commander, together with the commander and the Chief of Staff of Army Detachment Narva, worked out the plans for "Koenigsberg" at the headquarters in Segewold. The cover name was changed to "Aster" on the next day.

After receiving Hitler's permission, the staff of Army Detachment Narva was dissolved. General of Infantry Grasser was named to the Wehrmacht Eastern Command with command of all three Wehrmacht elements, the civil administration, the police, the SS, and the Reichs Labor Detachment.

On 9/18, the army group ordered "Operation Aster":

"1) At dawn on 9/18, III SS Panzer Corps withdraws to the west along a line toward Pernau. The last elements leave Wesenberg during the evening of 9/19...

2) II Army Corps holds its present line ... then, on 9/19, quickly withdraws...

3) Group Gerok ... defeats the advance of the enemy on Reval with its combat effective elements, defends Reval and the Baltic port until the end of the embarkation.

4) The Admiralty of the Eastern Baltic Sea terminates evacuation approximately 9/22 and transports Group Gerok to the Baltic islands."

This tight and precise plan would be changed over the course of several days. However, the withdrawal of Army Detachment Narva would occur exactly as ordered. The troops of the Army, Waffen SS, and Luftwaffe would conduct an orderly withdrawal, without being threatened by the enemy. The Soviets did not recognize the German retreat in time and, therefore, were not prepared to harass the withdrawal.

The evacuation of the Narva front and Estonia was conducted exactly as that from Demyansk.

The question remains: What would have happened if the entire army group had withdrawn into the Reich? An organized retreat was possible in September 1944. However, with "what if" there is no comparison — after every losing battle each officer asks "what if ..."

In September 1944 only the military facts speak!

The 2nd Shock Army (Lieutenant General Fedyuninskiy), which had taken over in the Dorpat area days ago, continued its breakthrough attempt on either side of the city on 9/18. The Russian tanks were able to penetrate into the seam between the 87th ID and 207th Security Division. The II Army Corps (General of Infantry Hasse), however, was in no position to intercept them.

It was on the next day of the enemy attack that the corps withdrew. The immediate pursuit by mobile forces was so disorganized, however, that the corps was not torn apart. The VIII Estonian Rifle Corps (Lieutenant General Pern) — a unit organized by the Soviets — set out west of Lake Peipus. It was here that Estonians in Russian uniforms shot Estonians in German uniforms!

The Navy had to transport the III SS Panzer Corps to Reval in 24 transport steamers and 45 coastal motor craft. Here began the embarkation of the first German troops, civil agencies, and Estonians. The population of the Estonian capital became restless. Isolated revolts flared up. Partisan groups occupied the transmitter. German units recaptured the transmitter on 9/21.

The III SS Panzer Corps (SS Obergruppenfuehrer Steiner) evacuated its positions. The troops that were not motorized, including the horse-drawn convoys and artillery of the 11th ID, were already in march to the west. The last German ships on Lake Peipus — 2 naval artillery barges and 24 patrol boats — were blown up. The III SS Panzer Corps moved all of its front troops along the Oberphalen-Reval road in good order and quickly, withdrawing in haste toward Pernau, without being bothered by the Soviets. Only some Estonian border guards and coastal defense forces lost contact and were captured.

On 9/17 at 1800 hours, the Navy began embarking German formations in Reval. The naval formations of the "Admiralty of the Eastern Baltic Sea" (Admiral Burchardi), up to the end of the evacuation, transported a total of 37,831 soldiers, 13,049 wounded, 20,418 civilians, and 931 prisoners of war.

The security of this embarkation and the defense of Reval was provided by Major General Gerok. He had available naval formations, Estonian national battalions, one army artillery battalion, anti-tanker combat groups of the III Panzer Corps, motorized elements of the 11th ID, and the 20th Estonian SS Division. On 9/19, these mixed combat groups took up positions in Reval.

The first enemy armored scout troops appeared on 9/21, but they were repulsed. The embarkation of the last formations waiting in Reval was hastened. On 9/22, the companies and combat groups of Major General Gerok withdrew from the harbor. The last German ships left Reval on 9/22. The steamers "Eberhard Essberger", "Peter Wessel", "Tanga", "Aletta Noot", hospital ship "Oberhausen", the torpedo boats "T-13", "T-17", "T-19", and "T-20" had 9,000 men on board. The large torpedo boats "T-23" and "T-28" formed the rear guard and, during the departure, destroyed the first Soviet tanks entering the city.

The 72nd Soviet Rifle Division reached Reval. The 14th Rifle Division occupied the city hall. The red flag waved over the Estonian capital!

The staff of Army Detachment Narva was subordinated to the 18th Army for the time being. The III SS Panzer Corps quickly withdrew through Pernau to the south and was absorbed by the 16th Army. The infantry elements of the 11th ID withdrew 125 kilometers! On 9/23, Soviet troops occupied Pernau and, on 9/24, Hapsal. At the same time, the 1st S boat Brigade (Naval Captain Olenik) landed on the island of Tytaesaari. The last German escort ship withdrew from the Gulf of Finland.

The battle of Estonia was over!

The combat on the southern flank of the army group was still going strong. Soviet rifle and tank formations were attacking in the Baldone area since 9/19. The 205th ID (Major General von Mellenthin) was encircled between Misa and Kecava. The combat group fought its way through to Vecmuiza and made contact with the 215th ID.

The I Army Corps established a bridgehead near Kecava on the Duena. The 389th, 225th, 58th, 215th, and 205th ID (from left to right) repulsed the crashing waves of enemy forces. For the time period 9/14-18, the corps reported the following losses: 15 officers and 496 men dead, 21,818 wounded, and 432 missing. The battle ultimately extended through the entire front of the 16th Army. The divisions of the III SS Panzer Corps, which were coming from Narva, were quickly thrown onto the threatened positions — then, the army had no more reserves.

The III SS Panzer Corps was committed on the right of Corps Group Kleffel and established contact with the XXXIX Panzer Corps. The latter of the three corps was included in the Army Detachment General of Infantry Grasser on 9/25. Army Detachment Grasser had to secure contact with the 3rd Panzer Division. General of Cavalry Count von Rothkirch took control of all convoys and rear area services of the 3rd Panzer, 16th and 18th Armies, and Army Detachment Grasser, which were still located in Kurland. In a few days, field railroad and railroad engineers constructed a rail line directly behind the front, which ran through the middle of the battery positions of the 81st ID. Therefore, it was possible to secure all of the hospital trains from the army group area and an additional 200 intact locomotives by 9/20.

The 18th Army, as before, was in unequal combat with pursuing formations of the 3rd Baltic Front. The divisions left their main combat line between Pernau-Walk-Schwanenburg on 9/18. The XXVIII Army Corps resisted the enemy flood near Walk with the 30th and 61st ID. The L Army Corps could not resist the assault of the X Soviet Panzer Corps. 40 super heavy combat vehicles tore a gap between the 21st and 31st ID and rattled toward Wolmar. The 31st ID defended the city for hours, then had to withdraw. The 21st ID was destroyed. They now consisted only of remnants. Among the fallen this day was the 32 year old commander of the 45th

Infantry Regiment, Colonel Schwender, who was awarded the Swords with Oak Leaves after his death. The 218th ID was down to regiment strength and one machine-gun!

The commander of the L Army Corps, General of Infantry Wegener, was found among the dead in the front lines.

Communications between the divisions and the corps had been out for some time! Also, the X Army Corps and VI SS Corps, which were fighting in the south, had lost their cohesiveness. The 18th Army stood on the verge of collapse. Their command post reported:

> "In the defensive battle since 9/14, the army stood against almost 70 Russian divisions, 2 tank corps, and numerous independent tank formations. During the battle, 622 enemy tanks were destroyed. ...Because of heavy losses, 10 of the 18 divisions of the army are now fighting as combat groups!"

The army group commander, who moved his command post from Segewold to the Pelci Palace near Goldingen in Kurland on 9/24, issued the following instructions for the further conduct of combat:

> "1. Hold the present line near the 3rd Panzer and 16th Armies and withdraw the northern flank of the army group to the "Segewold Positions.""

> 2. 3rd Panzer Army holds its present positions and detaches a strong combat group west of Dzukste. ...

> 3. 16th Army holds their present positions, prevents a breakthrough to the Tuckum land bridge and Riga. Withdraw the left flank on line with the withdrawal of the 18th Army. Secure an orderly withdrawal of the troops from the north through Riga to Kurland. After the withdrawal into the "Segewold Positions", the army takes over the entire front north of the Duena.

4. 18th Army withdraws into the "Segewold Positions." These and the Baltic islands are to be defended. After occupying the "Segewold Positions", the army is to move into the Frauenburg -Telsche area. ..."

The withdrawal of the 18th Army into the "Segewold Positions" began on 9/26. The new positions ran from the Gulf of Riga directly north of Riga east in the direction of Segewold and turned from here to the southwest through Baldone in the direction of Mitau. The marches of the divisions and combat groups were constantly harassed by enemy deep air strikes and advanced groups of tanks, but they could not be prevented from reaching the positions.

On the evening of 9/26, the army group commander reported to the OKH that the "Segewold Positions" were occupied as ordered! The following divisions had already left the front and were being transported to Kurland to the new blocking area of the army group: 11th, 21st, 30th, 31st, 218th ID, SS "Nordland", and "Niederlande" Divisions.

On the same day, General Schoerner ordered the inconspicuous evacuation of the Latvian capital. The senior quartermaster of the army group (Major General Rauser) had to see to it that 100,000 tons of equipment, which was in Riga, made it to Kurland as quickly as possible. The Senior SS and Police Command of the Eastern Territories issued a proclamation to the civilian population to evacuate the city. This proclamation was disapproved of by the army group, because it only increased the unrest of the Latvians.

"In these days, Riga itself presented the picture of a dying city. The means of transportation were paralyzed, offices and businesses were closed. The population either prepared to flee or awaited their fate with apathy. Houses and churches burned. Starving cattle perished in the streets. ...At the end of September/beginning of October, a stream of convoys of the withdrawing army, intermixed with fleeing Estonians and Latvians, flowed through the city. Over the great Duena bridge rolled horse-drawn wagons and trucks, men, women, and children, and grunting cattle. It was pouring rain and very windy..."[10]

Chapter 5: The Retreat

Since the middle of September, the developments on the lower course of the Duena could not be stopped. So they would not loose their cohesion, the army group had to withdraw to Riga. It no longer involved political or economic prestige — the immediate evacuation of the Baltic oil works was ordered on 9/18 — but existence itself!

In a telephone conversation with General Guderian on 9/17, General Schoerner pointed out: "It's do or die now. It is a false picture when we rely on the bravery of our soldiers alone. This does not always work..."

The sectors the Germans evacuated were, of course, known to the Soviet leadership. The 2nd Baltic Front took measures to attack into the rear of the 18th Army near Riga. The 18th Army was to be intercepted. However, before doing this, the front of the 16th Army near Baldone had to be broken through south of Riga.

The I Army Corps, which was located here, committed their last supply companies, in order to confront the assault of the 2nd Baltic Front. There was no Luftwaffe support possible. The weather had worsened for days. Continuous rainfall had turned the streets and roads to mud. Severe autumn storms lashed trees, shrubs, horses, and guard posts.

The army group only had the 14th Panzer Division, at this time commanded by Colonel Munzel, available for reserve. A counterattack made it through to Baldone. The armored infantrymen under Colonel Mummert and Colonel Goecke again pushed the Russians back, however, two days later, they themselves had to withdraw back over the Duena to avoid encirclement. The Soviets immediately pursued and recaptured Baldone on 9/22.

On 9/21, the 3rd Panzer Army was subordinated to the army group. During the last five days, under the leadership of General Raus, the army had been able to improve its front south of Dzukste. The XXXIX Panzer Corps (General of Panzer Troops von Saucken) destroyed 62 tanks, 29 assault guns, 147 anti-tank guns, and 37 guns during this time. After this battle, the corps detached a combat group west of Dzukste. This consisted of: the 25th Panzer Regiment (7th Panzer Division), I/2 Armored Artillery Regiment (12th Panzer Division), 3/32 Engineer Battalion (12th Panzer Division), 2/461 Infantry Regiment (252nd ID), and the 510th Panzer Battalion.

With the absorption of the operations area of the 3rd Panzer Army, the army group operations area was extended up to Memel! The right flank of the army group was reorganized. Army Detachment Grasser defended the main combat line from Aa northwest of Mitau to the hills east of Moscheiken. In addition, from left to right were deployed: Corps Group General of Cavalry Kleffel, with the 93rd and 81st ID; III SS Panzer Corps, with the SS "Nordland" and "Niederlande" Divisions; and the XXXIX Panzer Corps, with the "Grossdeutschland" Armored Infantry Division and the 4th and 12th Panzer Divisions. The 5th Panzer Division was maintained as reserve in the Autz area.

The 3rd Panzer Army was deployed from south of Autz to Memel east of Christmemel in a thin security front, which, with a frontal indentation near Kurseni, ran straight to the south toward Windau.

The 175 kilometer long front south of Riga was secured on the left flank by the XXVIII Army Corps (General of Infantry Gollnick) with the 7th Panzer Division, 201st Security Division, and 551st Fortification Division. The XL Panzer Corps (General of Panzer Troops von Knobelsdorff) was in the center of the front and, at that time, held the western bank of the Dubyssa with only security forces. The IX Army Corps (General of Artillery Wuthmann) was on the army's right flank up to Memel with the 548th Fortification Division and the 96th and 69th ID.

The subordination of the 3rd Panzer Army to Army Group North was maintained until 10/11.

At the end of September, the Soviets stopped their attack against the 16th Army. Air reconnaissance and scouts established re-grouping operations. The majority of the enemy tank and rifle formations disappeared from the front south of Riga. They were transferred further to the south. The new deployment was in the sector of the 3rd Panzer Army. On 9/29, the army group ordered Panzer Formation Colonel Lauchert, 303rd Assault Gun Brigade, SS Panzer Brigade Gross, 25th Panzer Regiment, and the 2/6 Armored Infantry Regiment into the XL Panzer Corps area.

The Soviet main effort was in the 1st Baltic Front (Army General Bagramyan) area. The 4th Shock Army, 43rd and 51st Armies, and the 5th Guards Tank Army were detected in the Shaulen area. Marshal Govorov —

whose Leningrad Front staff was dissolved — took command of the 2nd and 3rd Baltic Fronts. The High Command in Moscow tasked the 1st Baltic Front with the breakthrough to the Baltic Sea and the cutting off of Army Group North, which was to be the target of concentrated attacks by the two other Baltic fronts.

On 9/29, Stalin wrote to the British Prime Minister Churchill:

"At this time, the Soviet armies are destroying the German Baltic Army Group, which threatens our right flank. Without the destruction of this army group, it is impossible to strike deep into eastern Germany!"

The army group commander prepared for the withdrawal of the 18th Army from the "Segewold Positions" into the "Riga-East Positions." Here the army was deployed in a half-circle, which began directly north of Lilaste on the Gulf Of Riga, stretched to the north of Segewold, and from there in a circular line to the Duena 20 kilometers west of Friedrichstadt.

The organization of the 18th Army at the beginning of October reflected the following, from left to right:

II Army Corps with the 87th, 563rd ID, 12th Luftwaffe Field Division, (30th ID in reserve);
XXXVIII Army Corps with the 61st, 227th ID, 21st Luftwaffe Field Division, 83rd ID;
VI SS Corps with the 19th SS, 126th, 122nd, 31st ID;
X Army Corps with the 132nd, 32nd and 24th ID.

The army group commander directed all rear area units to Kurland and moved the Estonian formations into the Reich. The 22,500 prisoners of war, with 3,440 civilians, were transported to the Baltic islands.

The preparations for the evacuation of the last positions forward of Riga were completed on 10/4. The order for "Operation Donner" was signed by the Chief of Staff of Army Group North, Major General von Natzmer, on this day. It read:

Army Group North

"1. On the evening of 10/5, the army group begins "Donner" by withdrawing the left flanks of the 16th Army and the 18th Army to the Riga - East Positions, which will be reached on the morning of 13/10.

2. The Riga-East Positions are occupied by the 16th Army, with one division, and the 18th Army, with six divisions.

3. These movements will free up four divisions of the 16th Army and two corps and nine divisions of the 18th Army, their re-deployment is foreseen as follows:

a) The freed up corps and divisions, according to special orders of the army group, will move through the Riga-Schlock pass to the west on 10/7, presumably two divisions per day. ..."

Luftflotte 1 had to join in the movement of the army group. In autumn, the Luftflotte consisted of a total of 48,000 officers, non-commissioned officers, and men. This number represented 60 percent of the personnel strength of June 1941.

The few air formations were again almost filled in September 1944, although they were still not in the position to guarantee the necessary air cover for the ground troops. With the incorporation of the 3rd Panzer Army in the operations area, the 4th Air Division was assigned to cooperate with Luftflotte 1. The division, as before, remained subordinate to Luftflotte 6. This "hybrid", of course, lead to various problems.

During the summer, the Luftflotte had to form two more staffs, which were now dissolved. It now operated with the "Estonian" Luftwaffe Legion, with the 11th Night Combat Group, the 1/127 Lake Reconnaissance Squadron, the Estonian Ground-Air Group, the 1/101 Shipyard Battalion, the 617th Air Defense Battalion, the 12th Special Purpose Air Courier Battalion, and the "Latvian" Luftwaffe Legion with the 12th Night Combat Group and Latvian Ground-Air Group. The Estonian and Latvian pilots had fought with bravery, but by the end of September were unwilling to fight. Some Estonian crews deserted with their aircraft to Sweden. Because of this, they were prohibited from taking off and, finally, on 10/7, the dissolution of the Legion was ordered.

On 10/3, Luftflotte 1 had 267 aircraft available, of which: 80 were fighter-bombers, 73 night combat aircraft, 19 long range reconnaissance aircraft, 32 close reconnaissance aircraft, and 63 fighters. There were no bomber formations in the north of the Eastern Front!

The sorties, successes, and losses of two units can give a picture of the combat in the air over Riga:

The 3/4 Fighter-bomber Squadron reported in the time period 7/4 -10/ 27/44 the following numbers: 76 days of commitment with 363 sorties; 709.45 tons of bombs were dropped, 10 enemy aircraft were shot down in the air, 7 were destroyed on the ground; destroyed: 16 tanks, 36 tracked vehicles, 1889 vehicles, 238 horse-drawn vehicles, 54 guns and 10 bridges.

The 54th Fighter Squadron, which was not active completely in the Luftflotte 1 area, but participated in all of the crises of the battle, shot down 2,613 enemy aircraft and lost 310 in the year. The squadron, therefore, achieved its 8,502nd shoot down in the east. It had destroyed 9,141 enemy aircraft and was the 2nd most successful of all German fighter squadrons.

The withdrawal of the army group to Riga had still not started, because of the Soviets.

The 1st Baltic Front (Army General Bagramyan) attacked on 10/5, after an hour-long artillery preparation, with three armies west of Shaulen on a 90 kilometer wide front. Soviet rifle and tank groups were running over the German positions since 0830 hours.

The 43rd Army (Lieutenant General Chistyakov) hit the combat inexperienced 551st Fortification Division (Major General Verhein) with its full weight. The division held for three hours in the bombarded positions. Then they were overrun and scattered.

One tank corps, 8 tank brigades, and 29 rifle divisions attacked into the gaps! By evening, there was a 90 kilometer gap torn into the German front! The 43rd Army had penetrated 17 kilometers deep into the interior of the XXVIII Army Corps! The 2nd Guards Army (Lieutenant General Chanchibadse) stood 7 kilometers behind the main combat line of the XL Panzer Corps!

The army group commander, who still did not agree with the OKH belief in an offensive with the objective of East Prussia, quickly shoved his available reserves to the front of the 3rd Panzer Army. The "Grossdeutschland" Armored Infantry Division was set in march to the XXVIII Army Corps, the 5th Panzer Division to the XL Panzer Corps, and the 21st ID to the IX Army Corps. Removed from their former positions and ordered transported to the south were: the 14th Panzer Division, the 502nd Panzer Battalion, the 752nd and 753rd Anti-tank Battalions, the 3rd Mortar Regiment, the 768th Heavy Artillery Battalion, and the 1/818 Artillery Battalion.

No unified command and control was possible that night. The officers and non-commissioned officers collected the remnants of their units, held their strong points for a little while, and then tried to fight their way to the west. The front of the 3rd Panzer Army collapsed on the first day of the battle!

The front cracked even further on the following day.

The Soviets shoved the 5th Guards Army between the 2nd Guards and 43rd Armies. At the same time, the 2nd Guards Army was reinforced by the I Tank Corps, while the XIX Tank Corps went to the 6th Guards Army. Four well equipped armies marched with strong tank formations without stopping to the west. There was nothing left to oppose them!

On 10/7, the Soviets deployed two new armies into the field. The 4th Shock Army was inserted near Papile across the Windau and took up flank protection for the 1st Baltic Front to the north. The 51st Army was inserted on a main effort between the 6th Guards and 43rd Armies. The XXIX Tank Corps (Major General Malakhov) moved without resistance and, on the evening of 10/7, stood on the East Prussian border!

Here, the 3rd Panzer Army had no active troops! Only the II Field Light Infantry Command, under General of Infantry von Oven, took up the necessary protection against the advancing enemy tanks. At the same time, they had the task of stopping individual deserters and directing them back to their troop units.

The army group commander recognized the threat represented by the breakthrough of the Soviets to East Prussia. The 18th Army commander relinquished command of the troops east of the Duena on 10/7 to the commander of the 16th Army. General Schoerner ordered the freed army to prevent the advance of the 1st Baltic Front to the northwest and the west. A counterattack was initiated from the Moscheiken area to Telsche.

General of Infantry Boege, who had commanded the 18th Army since 9/5, had available: the X Army Corps (General of Infantry Foertsch), with the 11th, 30th, and 61st ID; and the XXXIX Panzer Corps (General of Panzer Troops von Saucken), with the 4th, 12th, and 14th Panzer Divisions.

These divisions tried to establish a block between Moscheiken and Skuodas to stop the 4th enemy Shock Army from breaking through.

"In this situation, the 11th ID hastily conducted a motor march, partially assisted by old omnibuses from Riga, through Goldingen-Grobin on the road to Memel to the south. ...However, the road was already blocked. The division was greeted by haggard construction battalions and other rear area services and committed to block southeast of Libau. The 44th Infantry Regiment crossed over the bridge near Kesteri and blocked the shortest route to Libau on either side of Ozolmezi. ...During the attack of the regiments from the move against the reinforced enemy, a rifle platoon of Staff Sergeant Schureit developed momentum, just like in the days of 1941, and attacked furthest to the south. ..."[11]

The battle continued.

The 51st Army (Lieutenant General Kreyser) reached the Baltic Sea near Polangen north of Memel on 10/10/1944!

Army Group North was cut off from the homeland for the second time — this time it was forever!

No counterattack could remove the enemy's front wedge!

The XXVIII Army Corps (General of Infantry Gollnick), directly subordinate to the 18th Army, was encircled with the 58th ID, "Grossdeutschland" Armored Infantry Division, and the 7th Panzer Division around Memel!

The 3rd Panzer Army was re-subordinated to Army Group Center on 10/11.

Army Group North

The splintered front units located north of the Telsche-Polangen line remained with the 18th Army.

Army Group North had to risk holding the vital harbors of Windau and Libau. Both cities were declared fortresses.

"In great haste a temporary security line was constructed south of the city of Libau out of alert units (particularly from the Navy) and from blocking formations of the 83rd and 122nd ID, as well as the 327th and 667th Engineer Battalions, the 3rd and 4th Battalions of the 158th Artillery Regiment (which division made to Memel unmolested) and several panzer units, which was under the command of the 519th Engineer Regiment staff (Lieutenant Colonel Kuhn). Here, directly on the coast, the staff of the 126th ID (Lieutenant General Fischer) was to take over, in order to establish a solid and defensible front after the arrival of friendly troops during the next few days."[12]

With the breakthrough of the Soviets to the sea, the fate of Riga was sealed.

The "Operation Donner" withdrawal began on 10/5. The East Prussian 61st ID was the first division of the 18th Army to cross the Duena. Later followed the XXXVIII Army Corps, 30th ID, 21st Luftwaffe Field Division, and the 32nd, 11th, and 225th ID. In view of the Soviet breakthrough in the 3rd Panzer Army area, these divisions were immediately set in march to the south.

Army and construction engineers had erected an additional temporary bridge next to the two existing bridges in Riga to hasten the movement of the columns. Additionally, 40 naval and army engineer ferries were provided to cross the marching formations, while the bridges were reserved for the motorized units.

A traffic control staff was formed from the army group that organized the channeling of the formations through Riga and monitored it. Lieutenant General Frankewitz, commander of the 215th ID, was responsible, with his staff, from Riga to about 8 kilometers east of Dzukste. From there to the Vadukse crossing the division staff of the 329th ID (Lieutenant General Dr. Mayer) provided for the smooth development of the withdrawal.

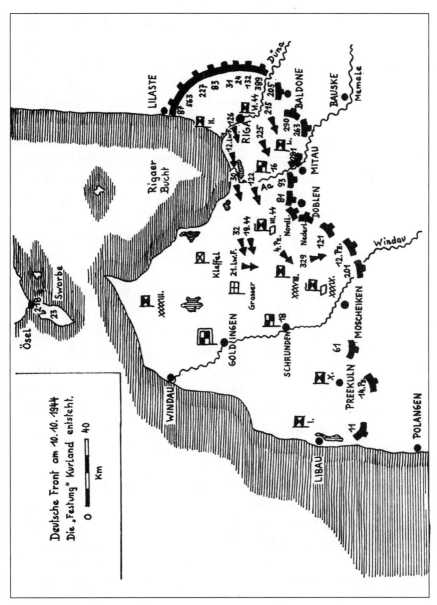

German Front on 10/10/1944
The Development of "Fortress" Kurland.

Troop transport required, in Riga East alone, 3000 railroad cars loaded with equipment, while another 40 fully laden trains were standing on a side stretch between Riga and Schlock. The OKH directed transport steamers to Riga until 10/11, by which they were able to unload the material from the trains onto the ships. This was accomplished under the fire of enemy artillery!

The security of the withdrawal was guarded by the 6th Air Defense Division (Lieutenant General Anton). The division had formed four strong points, at which its operational guns were emplaced. Thus, in the Riga area stood 16 heavy, 14 light, 3 Air defense of the Homeland, 3 searchlight, 2 heavy, and 2 light railroad air defense batteries. The mouth of the Duena was protected by 8 heavy and 12 light air defense batteries. The Schlock pass had 9 heavy and 11 light batteries, and around Tuckum were deployed 12 heavy and 9 light batteries.

The situation was untenable, as on 10/10 the 2nd Baltic Front began to attack Riga. The OKH reported that Hitler had categorically prohibited the withdrawal from Riga! General Schoerner ignored the "Führer Directive." He ordered the immediate withdrawal from the Latvian capital!

The Soviets followed directly on the heels of the withdrawing troops. The 87th, 132nd, 205th, 227th, and 563rd ID had to fight for their lives before they made it to the Duena. The 227th ID (Major General Wengler) was the last German division in front of Riga. They still held out on the enemy bank and held the two bridgeheads in order to cover the retreat of the remaining formations!

The army group transferred the freed up divisions into the threatened area. The 11th, 30th, 61st, 126th, 225th ID, and 14th Panzer Division were subordinated to the 18th Army. The 21st Luftwaffe Field Division, 19th SS Division, 32nd, 122nd, and 29th ID went to Army Detachment Grasser. The 12th Luftwaffe Field Division and 83rd ID took over the protection of the coast in northern Kurland, along with Combat Group Major General Gerok, which came out of Reval.

The army group command recognized the futility of holding the 16th Army forward of the Kurland Aa. The OKH brusquely prohibited the withdrawal of this army. General Schoerner, therefore, flew to the Führer Headquarters on 10/11. He described the situation of his army group with brutal openness. Hitler gave in! He permitted the withdrawal of the 16th Army into the "Tuckum Positions" and re-subordinated the XXVIII Army Corps, which was encircled in Memel, to Army Group Center!

10/12/1944 was the last day the German soldiers marched through Riga. The 227th ID gave up their bridgehead and withdrew. The 393rd Assault Gun Battalion (Captain Barths) was the last unit to roll across the Duena bridge. The temporary bridge was already scuttled. After the last assault gun crossed, an engineer officer lit the fuse. It was exactly 0144 hours on 10/13/1944 when the Riga railroad bridge dived into the rushing water with a thunderous roar.

The first Soviet battalions entered the Latvian capital. The 245th Rifle Division (Major General Rodinov) assaulted from the north, while the 212th Rifle Division (Colonel Kuchinev) came from the east.

Riga was Russian!

The 87th ID (Major General Baron von Strachwitz) still stood on the enemy bank of the Duena. The division was charged with protecting the flank of the troops moving through Riga to the north. They also protected the mouth of the Duena with one combat group.

Now their mission was completed. Engineer and naval ferries crossed the 5000 men, 132 vehicles, 160 trucks, 3 assault guns, 20 infantry guns, and 462 guns over the river during the night and the morning of 10/13. The last two rear guard companies crossed in assault boats at 0505 hours.

Still, the withdrawal of the army group behind the "Tuckum Positions" was not finished. On 10/16, all units had crossed the 45 kilometer long and 6 kilometer wide "land bridge" near Schlock. Three armies, 20 divisions, 1 brigade, 68 army engineer and police battalions, 120 air defense batteries, 200 tons of equipment, 13 army tank battalions and assault gun brigades, 28 army artillery battalions, and 111,007 vehicles of all types were moved from the Riga area to Kurland between 9/23 and 10/16.

The "Tuckum Positions" between Klapkalnice on the sea and Dzukste were occupied by Corps Group General of Cavalry Kleffel, with the 205th, 227th ID, and 281st Security Division. Adjacent to Petseri stood the VI SS Corps (SS Obergruppenfuehrer Krueger) with the 290th ID and 19th SS Division.

Army Group North

The majority of Army Group North was located behind these positions in their last operational area — Kurland.

NOTES:

[1] Kardel, H.: *The History of the 170th Infantry Division*. Bad Nauheim: Podzun 1953. 88 pages.

[2] Lohse, G.: *History of the Rhenish-Westphalian 126th Infantry Division*. Bad Nauheim: Podzun. 223 pages.

[3] Buxa, W.: *Route and Fate of the 11th Infantry Division*. 2nd Edition. Bad Nauheim: Podzun 1963. 163 pages.

[4] Melzer, W.: *History of the 252nd Infantry Division*. Bad Nauheim: Podzun 1960. 364 pages.

[5] Schroeder, J.: and Schultz-Naumann, J.: *The History of the Pomeranian 32nd Infantry Division*. Bad Nauheim: Podzun 1956. 229 pages.

[6] Podzun, H.-H.: *Route and fate of the 21st Infantry Division Kiel*: Podzun 1951. 40 pages.

[7] Tiemann, R.: *History of the 83rd Infantry Division*. Bad Nauheim: Podzun 1960. 378 pages.

[8] Breithaupt, H.: *The History of the 30th Infantry Division*. Bad Nauheim: Podzun 1955. 320 pages.

[9] Grams, R.: *The 14th Panzer Division*. Bad Nauheim: Podzun 1957. 359 pages.

[10] Haupt, W.: Kurland. *The Last Front*. 4th Edition. Bad Nauheim: Podzun 1964. 134 pages.

[11] Buxa, W.: *Route and Fate of the 11th Infantry Division*. 2nd Edition. Bad Nauheim: Podzun 1963. 163 pages.

[12] Lohse, G.: *History of the Rhenish-Westphalian 126th Infantry Division*. Bad Nauheim: Podzun 1957. 223 pages.

6

THE SEA

The Battle on the Flanks to the Sea

Since the beginning of the campaign, Army Group North had to conduct its operations with an open left flank. The Baltic Sea did not form a front boundary, but the uncertain extension of it. It was known that the "Baltic Red Banner Fleet" included the strongest formations of the Soviet Navy. The ships could at any time be committed in an offensive against the flank of the Eastern Army. The strength of the naval formations of the "Baltic Red Banner Fleet" in comparison to other Russian formations in June 1941 reflected:

	The entire Soviet Fleet	Committed in the Baltic
Battleships	3	2
Modern cruisers	4	2
Old cruisers	5	1
Escorts	7	2
Modern destroyers	41	18
Old destroyers	17	7
U-Boats	241	93

The strength of the "Baltic Red Banner Fleet" was considerable in comparison to the entire Navy when considering that the other formations of the Soviet Navy were committed in the Black Sea, the North Sea, the Pacific, and the Caspian Sea (here there were only 10 small U-Boats).

The strength of the naval formations in the Baltic sea influenced the planning for "Operation Barbarossa", especially, of course, for the German Naval operations, which, therefore, ordered their units to take a defensive posture. Nevertheless, in the first weeks, it turned out that the Soviet leadership also viewed the Baltic Sea war as a defensive one, so that the superiority of the "Baltic Red Banner Fleet" did not come into play. The German Navy held its heavy units back in the first months, although they stood ready for an offensive commitment in the Baltic Sea!

The naval war in the Baltic sea was conducted primarily by small and medium units from both fleets.

The initial operations of these formations was described in the chapter "The Attack." The following information about the sea war only takes into consideration the actions affecting the flanks of Army Group North. The commitment of the German, Finish, and Soviet Navies has been described in various publications (see annex) today.

In the autumn of 1941, the war to the sea appeared to enter a new phase. The 18th Army and the 4th Panzer Group stood directly before the approaches of Leningrad. The Baltic islands were being fought over. The "Baltic Red Banner Fleet" had withdrawn into Kronstadt Bay.

The German leadership — OKW and OKM — at this time raised suspicions that the Soviet fleet would be able to either break out of this encirclement into the middle Baltic Sea or fight its way to Sweden. Hitler ordered the OKM to prevent such a breakout with all available means!

On 9/20/1941, Naval Operations ordered the construction of the so-called "Baltic Fleet." The commander, Vice Admiral Schmundt, received the battleship "Tirpitz", the armored ship "Admiral Scheer", the light cruisers "Nuernberg", "Koeln", "Leipzig", and "Emden", the destroyers "Z-25", "Z-26", "Z-27", the 2nd Torpedo Boat Flotilla, and S-Boats.

The Majority of the "Baltic Fleet" was shifted to the Aalands Sea, While the "Leipzig", "Emden", and several S-Boats were commandeered to Libau. The fleet assembled in Swinemuende. In preparation for the deployment of these strong formations, the route between Swinemuende and the Aalands Sea was cleared of Soviet mines by mine sweepers. The mine ships "Kaiser", "Cobra", and "Koenigin Luise" reinforced the Juminda blockade with 400 mines to secure the deployment. The "Air Command Baltic sea" received long range reconnaissance aircraft of type "Ju-88" for sea observation.

Both combat groups of the "Baltic Fleet" arrived at Swinemuende on 9/23. They reached their destination without any enemy action.

The reconnaissance aircraft reported on 9/24 that the heavy Soviet units were damaged by bombs at their docks in Kronstadt and in the Neva. Therefore, the eventual breakout of the Soviet fleet was an illusion. Naval Operations ordered the return of the "Tirpitz" and "Admiral Scheer" to the homeland during the evening. The "Nuernburg" and "Koeln" continued on to the Aalands Sea with the destroyers. The southern group, which was in Libau, was reinforced with a torpedo boat flotilla.

The commitment of strong German naval formations in the Eastern Campaign was over on 9/29. They would never repeat this concentration for the rest of the war.

With the surrender of Reval and the encirclement of Leningrad, the "Baltic Red Banner Fleet" was decisively dislodged from the combat area. The still operational large combat ships were now subordinated as artillery systems to the land front, under the commander of the coastal artillery, Konteradmiral Gren. The battleships, cruisers (including the former German cruiser "Luetzow", which was re-christened the "Petropavlovsk"), escorts, and destroyers were established in Kronstadt and on the Neva as floating batteries.

The small and medium units of the "Baltic Red Banner Fleet" were united into squadrons under Vice Admiral Drozd. These formations were not committed operationally with the evacuation of Hango at the end of November/beginning of December.

The crews and personnel of the surface ships that were not needed for work on the artillery ships were formed into marine infantry brigades. In the first two years of the war, the Navy organized a total of 9 naval brigades with 130,000 men. These brigades were chiefly utilized in the Oranienbaum bridgehead and on the Neva front.

The sea war was left to the mine ships, S-Boats, and U-Boats.

After the reinforcement of the "Juminda blockade" at the end of September, the German side did without emplacing additional minefields to secure the "Baltic Fleet", because the breakout of the Soviet fleet appeared unlikely. Mine sweepers and R- and S-Boats, nevertheless, established a vigilant watch, because Soviet motor torpedo boats were always trying to run the blockades and attack German convoys. In the course of the year, there were several small engagements with enemy motor torpedo boats, in which losses were equal on both sides.

Most losses occurred from mines. Thus, from September 1941 to the year's end, the German side lost from mines: the mine ship "Koenigin Luise", the tender "Mosel", one sub chaser, one patrol boat, and four mine sweepers. In convoys between German, Baltic, and Finish harbors, in the last quarter of 1941, were lost eight steamers, and one each floating crane, tug, and coast guard ship. Damages were also received by one steamer. From September to December, through direct enemy action, there was not one military or cargo ship lost!

The German losses in 1941 totaled 25 military and 18 commercial ships; damaged were 24 military and 7 commercial ships. Soviet losses, on account of German naval formations, totaled 8 destroyers, 3 torpedo boats, 9 mine sweepers, 6 submarines, 5 motor torpedo boats, 5 escorts, 2 troop transports, and 40 freighters.

The strength of the Soviet submarine arm, which alone conducted naval warfare operations in the Gulf of Finland or in the Baltic sea, was not known. On 10/23, the German steamer "Baltenland" was torpedoed northwest of Oeland and, on the next day, the steamer "Hohenhoern" was unsuccessfully attacked by a Russian submarine between Reval and Helsinki.

The Soviet submarine force had sustained losses by the end of the year. 27 submarines were lost, of which 15 were sank from running into mines, 6 were scuttled by their own crews, 3 were destroyed by German U-Boats, 2 from S-Boats, and one was lost from a direct hit by a bomb.

The icy winter of 1941/42 froze Kronstadt Bay and the Gulf of Finland from December on. The submarine war was over.

The resumption of the naval war in 1942 occurred much later. As before, both fleets were confined to defensive operations. Finish and German landing troops occupied the two islands of Hogland and Tytaersaari in the spring. Therefore, the inner Gulf of Finland between Reval and Wiborg was closed off. However, the sea could not be made impervious to penetration.

The F.d.M. (Commander of Mine Sweeper Forces) East, Naval Captain (from 2/1/1943 Konteradmiral) Boehmer, had to strengthen the security of the Gulf of Finland by laying additional mines with his mine sweeper flotillas. In 1942, the German ships laid eight mine fields with 12,873 mines.

As before, the Soviet fleet leadership emphasized the artillery support of the Leningrad Front. Only the submarines conducted offensive operations in the second half of the year.

The Russian submarine "S-303" (Korvettenkapitaen Travkin) was the first Soviet ship to break through the mine field on 6/13 and make it to the open sea! "S-317" (Kapitaenleutnant Mokhov) and "S-406" (Kapitaenleutnant Ossipov) followed later.

Additional submarines also made it to the Baltic Sea in the following months and repeatedly attacked German convoys and individual shipping. German commercial shipping losses totaled 23 steamers at 52,000 tons for 1942.

This number, which appears high, pales in comparison to that in the eastern Baltic sea. The convoy traffic between German, Finish, and Baltic harbors in 1942 ran at high speed. A total of 203 war ships, 75 hospital ships, and 1868 commercial ships with a total tonnage of 5,592,189 tons took part in convoys here. The ships transported 405,459 soldiers, 15,454 horses, 12,866 vehicles, and 377,856 tons of goods. These convoys were attacked by enemy U-Boats 17 times, whereby only 7 steamers were lost.

Control of the commitment of German naval forces lay with Naval Command Eastern Territories (Vice Admiral Burchardi, Chief of Staff: Naval Captain Engelhardt), who had established his headquarters in Reval. His area of operations stretched from the German-Lithuanian border to the main combat line in front of Leningrad and Oranienbaum.

The following units were directly subordinated:

Sea Transport Chief East, with the Sea Transport sites of Riga, Libau, Windau, Baltischport, Pernau, Reval, Hango and Abo;

Senior Dock Staff Eastern Territories;
Harbor Commandant Riga;
Island Commandant Tytaersaari;
531st Naval Artillery Battalion;
311th and 321st Naval Fortification Engineer Battalions;
6th and 9th Naval Vehicle Battalions;
Naval Commitment Battalion Eastern Territories (since 1/15/1943).

The only floating formation was the Coast Guard Flotilla Eastern Territories. In September 1941, this was transferred to Libau as the Coast Guard Group Eastern Territories and, on 5/21/1942, received the new designation. The flotilla was committed along the Baltic coast on a security mission.

The Eastern Territories Command was organized into two Sea defensive areas. The Latvian area ran from the German-Lithuanian border to the Latvian-Estonian, including Riga and the lower course of the Duena. The Commandant (Naval Captain Dr. Kawelmacher, from January 1942 Naval Captain Karstens) had his seat in Libau. The harbor captains of Libau and Windau, the 712th Naval Air Defense Battalion (Libau), the 7th Replacement Naval Artillery Battalion, and the Libau Naval Dock were subordinate to him.

The Commandant Eastern Territories (Fregattenkapitaen Terfloth, Naval Captain Joerss, Naval Captain von Dresky, and Naval Captain Mulsow) was superior to the Harbor Commandant Reval, 530th and 532nd Naval Artillery Battalion, 239th and 711th Naval Air Defense Battalion, and the Naval Artillery Arsenal in Reval. Their authority stretched from the Estonian-Latvian border to the main combat line and across to the Baltic islands.

The control of naval operations in the eastern Baltic lay in the hands of the F.d.M. East, Konteradmiral Boehmer. He was subordinate to the Naval Group Command North. His task was to conduct all operations at sea, for which purpose he had subordinate destroyers and torpedo boats. The F.d.M. East was located on fleet tender "F-3" with his staff (1st Admiral Staff Officer: Korvettenkapitaen Forstmann), and sometimes they were stationed in Helsinki or Reval.

Chapter 6: The Sea

The subordination of mine sweepers, blockade breakers, patrol boats, escorts, sub chasers, convoy, and harbor escorts, as well as motor torpedo boats, changed according to the situation in the theater of war. Thus, from spring 1942 on, deployed in the eastern Baltic Sea were: 1st Mine Sweeper, 18th, 31st, 34th Mine Sweeper, 12th Sub Chaser, 3rd Patrol Boat, 27th Landing Flotillas, the 11th and 12th Mine Sweepers, the mine ships "Kaiser" and "Roland", and 32 coastal motor boats.

As before, the Soviet fleet was still superior. However, due to the reinforcement of the mine field belt, they were condemned to defend in the Gulf of Finland. In 1943, the 33 submarines and 29 torpedo boats available to the "Baltic Red Banner Fleet" did not venture to run the blockade.

Therefore, the air activity increased from month to month. the reinforcement of the Soviet air forces made itself disagreeably noticed. The German ships had less to worry about from the naval units than the constant threat from the air. German ship and personnel losses were almost exclusively as a result of bombing attacks. The security forces of the F.d.M. East lost 139 officers and men dead and 100 wounded from the attacks of Soviet aircraft, of which 26 were shot down.

The most significant nautical achievement of 1943 was the laying of a submarine net in the Gulf of Finland. The "Blockade Net Formation" (Chief: Naval Captain Tschirch) laid it in April 1943 with 141 ships (net layers, net tenders, and tugs), and Blocking Net Flotilla Center (Korvettenkapitaen Becker) laid a double net 60 meters deep that was almost 60 kilometers long. This net was emplaced between Naissaari and Porkkala.

By the beginning of May, mine ships expanded the already existing mine blockades by another 9,834 additional mines. Therefore, the breakout of Soviet submarines was unlikely. No enemy submarines appeared in the eastern Baltic sea in 1943!

The Soviet conduct of naval warfare had its consequences. They reorganized their submarine force. The boats were organized into a brigade with four divisions. Each division consisted of up to 25 submarines. Intensive construction was occurring in Kronstadt Bay. The Russian submarines were to return to the offensive in 1944.

The German successes of 1943 were documented in the number of convoys supplying Army Group North. 148 cargo and 139 hospital ships with a tonnage of 1,085,000 tons passed between German and Baltic harbors. In the twelve months, the convoys repulsed 318 air attacks, during which 30 enemy aircraft were shot down, while 6 cargo ships and 11 small warships were lost in the same period of time.

The war of the floating formations was now not confined to the eastern Baltic sea. The great Russian inland lakes were taken into consideration in the overall plan of the conduct of the war. All along, the Soviets had stationed small security, patrol, and police boats on these lakes, which, from the German point of view, had to be destroyed to establish the front on these lakes.

The flotilla of about 20 boats on the 3500 square kilometer Lake Peipus was destroyed in summer 1941 by German air attack. When the troops of the 18th Army reached the lake, they found no serviceable ships. Only on the eastern bank of the lake did they discover 2 tugs and 5 barges, which were immediately put to use for supply and wounded transport. Later, these boats were protected by motorboats equipped with machine-guns and anti-tank guns and, in the first month, transported 4,300 tons of equipment, 500 wounded, and 600 prisoners. Naval and landing engineers took up the security of the lakes in the autumn from Dorpat. Police patrol boats, with mounted 3.7 cm anti-tank guns, finally relieved the Wehrmacht.

With the first withdrawal of the Army from Leningrad, the naval forces of Lake Peipus were calculated into the operations plan. The 4th Artillery Flotilla (Korvettenkapitaen Wasmuth) was transported over land and committed on the Lake. The flotilla consisted of 24 artillery barges, 30 transport, 4 coastal motor, 4 commando boats, and an armed steamer. The Army had stationed: the 4th Field Water Battalion with 12 steamers, 10 tugs, and 7 barges, and the 772 Engineer Landing Battalion with 12 landing boats and 27 assault boats.

After reaching the eastern coast of the lake, the Soviets immediately committed motor torpedo boats and flat artillery boats. The German flotilla was confined to patrolling. The first combat occurred on 6/12/1944 between 4 German coastal motor boats and small Soviet ships, during which the "KM-8" was lost.

In August, the German ships were transferred to Dorpat, because the coastal strong points were not secured from partisans. By the end of the month, all of the ships but 4 coastal motor boats were lost from air attacks or scuttling. These last vehicles were taken apart and shipped by rail through Dorpat before the Soviets assaulted the railroad station.

The second large inland lake, on which ships battled, was the 18,700 square kilometer Lake Ladoga. Contact was made between Finish boats and the Soviet Ladoga Flotilla. Combat activity gave way to the winter of 1941/42.

On 7/7/1942, German ships entered the lake when Army Group North planned the conquest of Leningrad with the 11th Army. The boats of the 31st Mine Sweeper Flotilla (Fregattenkapitaen von Ramm) operated from Finish harbors. Because the boats had technical shortcomings, they were recalled in October. More successful was the 12th Italian MAS Flotilla, which was active in the same region at the same time. They were likewise recalled in October.

The backbone of the Lake Ladoga force was formed by the "Siebelfaehren." These ships belonged to the Luftwaffe! They were air defense barges and, for the most part, were manned by personnel who had no nautical experience. Nevertheless, Colonel Siebel lead his flotilla so cleverly, that, with their 8.8 cm air defense guns, they were superior to the Soviet artillery boats. The ferries were committed on the lake from August 1942 on.

The only large battle — which was unfortunate for both sides — took place on 10/22-23/1942. 16 German ferries, 7 boats, and an Italian MAS Boat attacked the coastal battery on the island of Suho during the night of 10/23. While the ferries fired at the battery, four engineer assault troops were landed. The operation had to be broken off in 10 minutes, because two ferries ran aground and one was destroyed by a direct hit! When the Soviet battery finally quieted after three hours of firing, the German formation retreated. Soviet aircraft attacked without letting up, and the "Me-109's" from a unit of the 54th Fighter Squadron became involved in the battle. The coming of winter storms prevented further commitment of the German and Soviet ships.

1943 brought no major events. After the Soviets established the land bridge to Leningrad, a blockade of the city from the sea was senseless. The German forces gradually withdrew. The "Siebelfaehren" had performed so well, that, henceforth, they were utilized as escorts or transports in the eastern Baltic Sea.

In spring 1944, the Soviet forces were very active on Lake Ladoga. They initiated landing operations and, by September, drove out the last Finish boat. Lake Ladoga was again Russian territory.

The year 1944 dawned. It was not only a fateful year for German troops on the land, but also for the naval units in the eastern Baltic Sea. The F.d.M. East, Konteradmiral Boehmer, had available:

1st, 3rd and 25th Mine Sweeper (Minensuch) Flotillas (20 boats);
1st Mine Sweeper (Raeumboot) Flotilla (15 boats);
13th, 21st and 24th Landing Flotillas (40 ferries);
7th Artillery Barge Flotilla (17 ferries);
3rd, 14th Security Flotillas and
3rd, 9th and 17th Patrol Boat Flotillas (120 steamers).

These few forces were, naturally, in no position to oppose the expected breakout of Soviet flotillas from the Kronstadt Bay in summer 1944. The OKM, therefore, transferred the 6th Destroyer Flotilla, with "Z-25", "Z-28", "Z-35", "Z-36", and the torpedo boat "T-30" to Baltischport and Reval after the enemy offensive to the Narva.

It was the mission of these forces to secure the left flank of the army near Narva. This could best be accomplished by strengthening and expanding the mine blockades. The mine ships "Linz", "Roland", and "Brummer" began laying the first blockades on 3/13 north of Hungerburg at the mouth of the Narva. Soviet aircraft were constantly in the air, observing the ships and their activities.

In March alone, the enemy air forces attacked the ships in Narva Bay 137 times, dropping 7000 bombs! 29 aircraft were shot down by naval air defense and fighters. Losses were insignificant.

The first heavy losses suffered by the Navy occurred during the night of 4/21, when the mine ship "Roland" ran into a mine and quickly sank.

The second loss was the torpedo boat "T-31", which had just arrived in the area of the Finish group. The ship was cruising with "T-30" in the area of the island of Narvi and, during the night of 6/20, ran into a pack of

Soviet motor torpedo boats. Unfortunately, "T-31" was hit by a torpedo. It sank in its first commitment.

The increased activity of the enemy's naval forces, which was particularly noticeable during the offensive in the Finish Group, required corresponding measures by the Navy. The F.d.M. East was re-designated the 9th Security Division. Konteradmiral Boehmer was reinforced by torpedo boats "T-8" and "T-10", the 10th S-Boat Flotilla, and the U-Boats "U-481", "U-748", and "U-1193."

The enemy's best weapons against ships were not the daring attacks of the Soviet motor torpedo boats, but their aircraft. Every day the type "Il-2" fighter-bombers buzzed overhead, diving on the boats, dropping bombs, or firing their on-board canon.

On 7/16, 130 aircraft with the red star attacked the air defense ship "Niobe" in the Finnish Group and sank it. Four days later, "M-20" sank after being hit by bombs, as did "M-13" 24 hours later. Two naval ferries (237 and 498) and the patrol boat "V-1707" were likewise lost in July.

The combat diary of the 3rd Mine Sweeper Flotilla (Korvettenkapitaen Kieffer), which was deployed in Narva Bay, registered the following:

"7/30: Three battles, each with 30-40 Il-2 with fighter cover. 6 shot down. Friendly losses: 1 dead, 26 wounded. ...7/31: Major attack by about 70 aircraft. 2 shot down, 7 dead, 30 wounded, lead boat "M-15" overwhelmed by heavy bomb hits. ...8/1 : five battles with 85 enemy aircraft. 6 shot down. ..."

In spite of these constant attacks from the air, the German flotillas were not disheartened. They continued to lay mines, clear the coast, repulse aircraft and motor torpedo boats, as well as escort convoys, which brought much needed equipment to Army Group North or transported wounded and refugees back to the homeland. Alone in the month of August, 414 steamers, with a total tonnage of 2,390,970 tons, traveled between German and Baltic harbors without losing one ship!

The 9th Naval Security Division received more help in July. The 6th Torpedo Boat Flotilla (Korvettenkapitaen Koppenhagen), with "T-22", "T-23", "T-30", "T-32", and "T-33" was deployed in its well camouflaged hiding places near Kotka in the Finish Group. From here, the boats undertook mine and reconnaissance trips into the Gulf of Finland and up to the Estonian coast.

The three U-Boats were reinforced with additional boats, which were stationed in Norway as training or commitment boats. The new U-Boats were not originally equipped with the "Snorkel." Because they were committed as guards of the mine fields, they always had to surface to fire their batteries. The boats "U-250", "475", and "1001" were committed in the first half of July. A little later followed "U-242", "U-348", "U-370", "U-479", and "U-679." In August, another six boats arrived — 286, 290, 717, 745, 958, and 1165 — and in October "U-676" and the mine boat "U-218."

The commitment of the U-Boats was led by the commitment leader of the Admiralty of the Eastern Baltic Sea, Fregattenkapitaen Brandi (from January 1945 Kapitaenleutnant Gehlhaus). The first success was registered by "U-475" (Kapitaenleutnant Stoeffler) on 7/28, when a Soviet mine sweeper was sunk. Two days later, "U-481" and "U-370" dispatched another mine sweeper to the deep. On the same day, "U-250" was detected and destroyed by the Soviet sub chaser "MO-105" and a second sub chaser "MO-103."

The strongest force in the Baltic Sea was the 2nd Naval Combat Group, under Vice Admiral Thiele. The heavy cruiser "Prinz Eugen", destroyers "Z-25", "Z-28", "Z-35" and "Z-36", and the torpedo boats "T-23" and "T-28" had stood combat ready in Gothenhafen since 7/30. On 8/20 they directed the ships to Tuckum, where their well placed artillery fire facilitated the breakthrough of the Panzer Formation Count Strachwitz and, therefore, the contact with Army Group North.

Nevertheless, the success was overshadowed by a tragic misfortune which occurred several days before in Narva Bay near Valaste.

On 8/17, the four large torpedo boats "T-22", "T-23", "T-30", and "T-32" left their hiding places near Kotka. Only "T-30" was considered an "old timer" in the eastern Baltic Sea. The other boats were new to this combat area. Korvettenkapitaen Koppenhagen, chief of the 6th Torpedo Boat Flotilla, had a mine laying mission. The boats approached the assigned point in the vicinity of the Estonian coast at high speed. The night was clear, so the flotilla soon reached the dock area. The assigned mine field had already been expanded.

They reached the blockade area. The lead boat — "T-30", on which the flotilla chief was located — turned 90 degrees. At this moment, the boat received a jolt. An explosion occurred. "T-32" was likewise hit with an explosion. Its bow was torn open.

"Torpedo strikes!" "Motor torpedo boat attack!"

Thus signaled the radio operator into the night. The two remaining boats withdrew with extreme care. Too late! "T-22" exploded and split apart like a stone. In as little as one half hour, three large German torpedo boats sank, torn apart by their own mines! The 6th Flotilla had run into the old mine blockade and had come to their end!

Those that lay shipwrecked in the water were attacked on the following day by Soviet aircraft, which fired on the defenseless men with their on-board weapons! A German sea rescue aircraft "Do-24" appeared and landed among the swimmers. The crew of 12 took 91 sailors on board! 420 found their death beneath the waves!

On 9/2, the commitment of German ships in the northern portion of the Gulf of Finland came to an end when Finland concluded a truce with the USSR. The former German-Finish comradeship ended with a bang.

On 9/6, German formations evacuated their strong point at Kotka, as well as the observation positions on the island. At the same time, steamers transported the 164th ID, 303rd Assault Gun Brigade, and other elements from various harbors. Now the 20th Mountain Army, which was located in northern Finland, was removed. The heavy cruisers "Luetzow" and "Prinz Eugen" and the 3rd Torpedo Boat Flotilla cruised between the Aalands islands on 9/15 to secure the convoy. They were evacuating 4,049 soldiers, 3,336 wounded, 746 vehicles, and 42,144 tons of equipment. Unfortunately, 13,064 tons of equipment was lost, because the Finish steamers ran to neutral harbors. Because of the lack of time, 100,000 tons of equipment could not be loaded and had to be destroyed on land!

The Finish government and the Finish Navy reacted sharply to the mining of Kotka by the last German mine ships and the 9/14 landing on Hogland.

This unfortunate operation for both sides (see Chapter 5) suddenly turned the comrades into enemies. During the battle on the island, 155 German and 37 Finish soldiers died! 175 Germans and 79 Fins were wounded!

Therefore, there was "de facto" war between Germany and Finland!

In the following weeks there were repeated attacks by German U-Boats against Finish convoys, which were headed for the Soviet Union. In mid October, the first three Finish coastal vessels were sunk by the gun fire of U-Boats near Odensholm. However, the operation of German ships in the northern and eastern portions of the Gulf of Finland did not achieve any more success to speak of.

When Army Group North withdrew from Estonia, and the last naval strong point in the Gulf of Finland was lost. After the evacuation of Reval and Baltischport (see Chapter 5) another six mine blockades were laid by the mine ships "Linz", "Brummer", the torpedo boat "T-28", the 1st, 2nd, and 3rd Mine Sweeper [Minensuch], 1st Mine Sweeper [Raeumboots], 24th Landing, 5th S-Boat Flotillas, "U-242", and "U-1001." Because the blockades could no longer be watched over, the Soviets were able to quickly remove them.

Soviet submarines were operating in the eastern and middle Baltic Sea as early as the beginning of October!

The main mission of the 9th Security Division, which was taken over by Fregattenkapitaen Blanc on 10/1 (Konteradmiral Boehmer was shot by partisans on this day) was, as before, the protection of convoys, which brought additional men and material into the Baltic Provinces and, later, to Kurland.

The U-Boats, which operated from Libau, Memel, and Danzig, were used more for surveillance than for tactical operations. Their successes in October and November against Soviet shipping included the sinking of two escorts by "U-679" and "U-745", one mine sweeper by "U-1165", one artillery boat by "U-370", one sub chaser by "U-475", one survey ship by "U-242", one barge by "U-481", one tug by "U-745", and four Finish yachts by "U-481" and "U-958." "U-242" laid an additional mine blockade on 10/8.

The success of Soviet boats against German convoys was likewise negligible. In October, 587 German steamers transported 881,000 tons of goods and equipment to Army Group North. Only 6 ships were lost. In November, there were 764 ships with 1,577,000 tons, of which 2 were lost. In December, one steamer was sunk, while 575 ships with 1,112,000 tons of weapons, ammunition, rations, etc., reached their goal.

The offensive of the German naval leadership against the Soviets came to an end in 1944. The 2nd and 5th S-Boat Flotillas conducted operations involving several attacks in the Gulf of Finland without running into any Russian ships. The last operations of the Navy ended in a fiasco.

Medium forces were to reinforce the mine blockade near Reval on request of Army Group North. The 6th Destroyer Flotilla under Naval Captain Koth left Pillau on 12/11 with the destroyers "Z-35", "Z-36", "Z-43", and the torpedo boats "T-23" and "T-28." When, at midnight, they started to receive light fire from Baltischport, the ships headed for the docks.

Then "Z-35" hit a mine and went down. Shortly thereafter, a column of fire rose up from "Z-36." The destroyer went under in a few minutes after an ammunition explosion. "Z-35" ran into a second mine. The ship was so heavily damaged that it could not be salvaged. The remaining ships were ordered to withdraw and leave the night of misfortune. Naval Captain Koth and 600 officers and men lost their lives. Only 67 sailors were taken prisoner by Finish and Russian ships the next day.

The year 1944 ended with a German misfortune at sea.

The great German strong point in the eastern Baltic Sea — the Baltic islands — were also lost.

After the evacuation of Estonia, the islands became terribly important for covering the left flank of the army group and for protecting the convoy traffic to Riga. On 9/9, the army group transferred elements of the 23rd ID, 202nd Assault Gun Brigade, the staff of the 1006th Army Coastal Artillery Regiment, the 289th and 810th Army Artillery Battalions, 530th Naval Artillery Battalion, and the 239th Naval Air Defense Battalion to Oesel. The Estonian Naval Commandant (Naval Captain Mulsow) was the Naval Commandant of the Baltic islands. Lieutenant General Schirmer, commander of the 23rd ID, was assigned Wehrmacht Commander. The German civil administration was subordinated to the commander on 9/20.

The defenders from Worms evacuated the island on 9/25 without a fight.

On the next day, Soviet artillery began firing from Virtsu (Werder). On 9/29, enemy aircraft attacked the capital Arensburg. At the same time, Russian assault troops landed on Moon, which was not defended.

The battle for the Baltic islands had begun.

On 10/1, the army group ordered the staff of the 218th ID (Major General Lang), with the 1/323 Infantry Regiment and 1/386 Infantry Regiment, to Oesel. Later followed the remaining infantry battalions, elements of the 218th Artillery Regiment, 218th Communications Battalion, and the 218th Engineer Battalion. The 531st and 532nd Naval Artillery Battalions were also dispatched to Oesel.

On 10/2 the Soviets crossed to Dago with deep air support. The elements of the 23rd Fusilier Regiment, which were located here, in addition to a few batteries, could not offer the enemy any realistic resistance and evacuated the island the next day with the support of landing engineers.

The Soviet assault on Oesel occurred on 10/5 with the VIII Estonian Rifle Corps, which was shortly followed by the CIX Rifle Corps. Both corps landed at locations where the German leadership had not expected. Early morning fog also favored the landing boats, which landed the infantrymen on a 20 kilometer wide front at six locations on the coast between Keksvere and Jaani in the northeast of the island. The widely dispersed landing tied up so many German forces in the first hours that they could not organize a strong counterattack. Elements of the Naval Commitment Battalion Eastern Territories were encircled and could only break out with heavy losses. The first tangible resistance was offered by Colonel Count zu Eulenburg, commander of the 67th Infantry Regiment, with the Naval Commitment Battalion, 532nd Naval Artillery Battalion, elements of the 67th Infantry Regiment, and the 2/323 Infantry Regiment.

The strength of the enemy forced Lieutenant General Schirmer to give up the north and center of the island and withdraw toward Sworbe. Russian tanks attacked over the Moon-Oesel Dam and immediately broke through to the Southwest. The next day, the German formations fought back to a line 20 kilometers north of Arensburg. All agencies were evacuated from the city during the evening and it was surrendered on the next day.

The 218th ID, in the meantime, occupied a blocking position in the Salme bridgehead in front of Sworbe. However, two days later, enemy tanks appeared and penetrated at two locations. The German combat groups withdrew to the narrowest location on the peninsula between Ranna-Kristi and defended the Ariste blocking position. Here stood the 67th Infantry Regiment (Colonel Count zu Eulenburg) and the 23rd Artillery Regiment.

Major General Henke, Senior Landing Engineer Commander, was responsible, along with his battalions, for the supply of the Baltic islands and the evacuation of convoys, wounded, etc. Due to enemy air superiority, these transports could only be conducted at night. For his operations, he had available 20 naval barges, 17 engineer landing ferries, 23 landing, and 15 heavy assault boats.

The Soviets tried — after they could not break through the Ariste blocking position on the first attempt — to land behind the German front near the Loeu lighthouse. The attempt was beaten back by the infantrymen of Colonel Count zu Eulenburg. A second landing of the Soviet 300th Rifle Regiment on 10/12 was also stopped by the 386th Infantry Regiment, 218th Engineer Battalion, and 531st Naval Artillery Battalion. The Germans captured 215 prisoners.

The staff of the 218th ID and elements of the division loaded for Windau on 10/13. Elements of the 12th Luftwaffe Field Division (Major General Weber) then arrived on the island.

The command planned an evacuation of the Baltic islands, because, in view of the Russian superiority, a defense of Sworbe appeared pointless. However, the army group insisted that Oesel be held in order to tie up additional Soviet forces. The XLIII Army Corps (General of Mountain Troops Versock), which was responsible for the defense of northern Kurland, took command of all of the German formations committed to Sworbe.

The Soviets — that is, the VIII Estonian and XXX Guards Corps — took a break between 10/13 and 10/17. They regrouped, so that, by 10/17, the first scout troops were dispatched against the Ariste blocking position.

Strong barrage fire initiated the battle for Sworbe in the afternoon of 10/19. Fighters and combat aircraft dived onto the German trenches and forced the defenders to take cover, while the enemy infantry assaulted. German losses were high. Only small combat groups now existed, which defended behind the tattered wire defenses. 50% of the officers fell on this day. Lieutenant General Schirmer and his operations officer, Colonel

Niepold, stood on the front line. Colonel Reuter, commander of the 386th Infantry Regiment, attacked the penetrating combat vehicles, along with a few soldiers armed only with a bazooka.

The Ariste blocking position had to be given up.

A counterattack was conducted. Elements of the 239th Naval Air Defense Battalion (Korvettenkapitaen Schulz) penetrated far into the enemy front, however, they could not prevent the retreat from the Ranna and later the Leo blocking positions. On the German side, the combat strength totaled 4,620 men, of which only 2,740 were infantry qualified (the head count of all Wehrmacht elements totaled 7,177 soldiers).

On 10/23, the defenders still held the Leo blocking position. The reinforcements of the 12th Luftwaffe Field Division, which, due to rough seas, could only make the crossing in mine sweepers, were immediately ordered to the front. Then the enemy came! He attacked the Leo blocking position on 10/24 and was repulsed!

The 2nd Naval Combat Group, under Vice Admiral Thiele ended the first phase of the battle of Sworbe. The formation stood in front of Sworbe with the heavy cruiser "Luetzow", the destroyers "Z-28", "Z-35", and the torpedo boats "T-19", "T-21", "T-23", "T-28", and "T-31." On this day, the ships fired 1,100 shells. The effect of the fire was that the Soviets suspended their attack against the Leo blocking position.

Combat subsided somewhat. Naturally, there was no out and out pause, because the enemy was constantly trying to achieve a penetration at some new position in the German main combat line. The OKH, in a directive to the army group on 10/22, demanded that Sworbe be held under all circumstances!

The Soviets reinforced at the end of October. Alone on 10/29, they tried to break through the Leo blocking position at five locations. 236 enemy bombers, which could be opposed only by the 3/54 Fighter Group on the German side, bombarded the trenches, shelters, and lines of contact without pause. The 23rd Luftwaffe Light Infantry Regiment, under Colonel Jordan (12th Luftwaffe Field Division) and the 323rd Infantry Regiment (Colonel von Vietinghoff) of the 218th ID stood at the center of the battle at this time. A battery of the 202nd Assault Gun Brigade, under Lieutenant Colonel Brandt, destroyed 54 tanks at this time! All attacks were repulsed!

The enemy suspended his breakthrough attempts and transitioned to positional warfare. For two weeks a "calm" lay over the battlefield, only occasionally broken by fire strikes, bombing attacks, scouts, and assault troops.

During these weeks, smaller Soviet and German ships tried to fire on the enemy forces on the coasts. In this manner, Russian motor torpedo boats were able to surprise the German guards several times and avoid pursuit by S-Boats through the use of smoke screens. Because the weather became increasingly worse, operations on the sea front slackened.

Then came 18 November.

Strong artillery fire and constant bombing attacks initiated the final phase of the battle for the Baltic islands. The CIX Soviet Rifle Corps attacked with the 109th and 131st Rifle Divisions into the front of the main combat line now held by only four German battalions (1st and 2nd Battalions of the 67th Infantry Regiment, 23rd Fusilier Battalion, and 1/397 Infantry Regiment)! The second Russian wave followed close behind. Here operated the 64th Guards and 249th Rifle Divisions, as well as the 27th and 47th Tank Regiments.

The attackers were not stopped. The Leo blocking position was broken through on the west of the front at three locations. The 23rd ID immediately committed its available reserves. The 1/239 Infantry Regiment, 531st Naval Artillery Battalion, and the 23rd and 141st Engineer Battalions launched a concentrated attack that penetrated 5 kilometers deep into the rifle and tank formations. It did not stop the enemy from attacking further. The friendly forces were too weak. They were only able to establish a unified defensive front during the night.

The naval combat group, under Vice Admiral Thiele, was alerted. The armored ship "Admiral Scheer" and four ships of the 2nd Torpedo Boat Flotilla — "T-5", "T-9", "T-13", and "T-16" — joined in the land battle with their guns at 0730 hours. The ships moved in and around the coast until 1440 hours, firing their shells at the attacking Soviets.

The Russian Air Force answered promptly. At midday, 30 bombers attacked the German combat formation again, after several squadrons had already dropped bombs during the morning. Three mine sweepers — "M-15", "M-204", and "M-328" — took direct hits during the morning, while the armored ship was hit during the afternoon attack. Damage was light.

On the early morning of 11/19, the Soviets resumed their breakthrough attempt. The main effort again lay on the right flank. The 23rd ID committed all available forces between Kulli on the coast and Loupollu. They had no more reserves! The right German flank was covered by the 386th Infantry Regiment (Colonel Reuter) south of Teesso. This group was pushed a good distance away from the bulk of the defenders and was in danger of being encircled.

Lieutenant General Schirmer organized his troops with much difficulty during the night. It was clear to him that he could not defend any longer. The exhausted German soldiers could effectively hold out for one more day. During the night of 11/21, the 23rd ID ordered the withdrawal to the Torkenhof blocking position. When the Soviet regiments attacked this blocking position in the morning, they bogged down in the defensive fire.

The 22nd of November passed similarly.

Then 11/23 dawned. Again the destructive fire of the deployed Soviet artillery broke over the defenders. Four divisions attacked with tank support! The main combat line held until 1100 hours. Then the enemy tanks achieved their first penetration. The 64th Guards Division penetrated into the center of the front. At the same time, the Soviets were able to gain ground on the east coast. After the most bitter defense by the 1/435 Infantry Regiment, they occupied the road intersection near Torkenhof on the western portion of the peninsula.

At 1100 hours, Lieutenant General Schirmer requested permission to evacuate.

General Schoerner, who had personally satisfied himself with the state of the defensive battle of the 23rd ID in Sworbe, did not pass on this request to the OKH! At 1205 hours, he ordered:

"The 23rd ID withdraws to the narrow bridgehead north of Zerel. During the coming night, all is withdrawn that is not needed to conduct battle. The remainder will be collected on the following night."

Chapter 6: The Sea

Major General Henke, Senior Landing Engineer Commander, believed that a withdrawal over two nights would not be possible. He requested permission to evacuate the peninsula in one night! General Schoerner issued an order several minutes later:

"Evacuate Sworbe tonight in one trip!"

Major General Henke had the following units available for this operation:

128th Landing Engineer Battalion (Major Schaefer),
772nd Landing Engineer Battalion (Captain Banning),
772nd Landing Engineer Company,
128th, 772nd, 774th Landing Engineer Transportation Companies,
128th, 903rd Engineer Assault Boat Companies.

The boats left Windau under the protection of elements of the 9th Security Division at 1500 hours. Major General Henke was on board patrol boat "V-317" with Fregattenkapitaen von Blanc, to personally lead the evacuation of the troops.

On this day, the combat groups held their positions against heavy enemy attacks. At twilight, they began to withdraw toward Zerel as ordered. One combat group, under Colonel Reuter, screened this withdrawal until 0315 hours.

The embarkation began at 1900 hours. The wounded were first loaded on the ferries and landing boats. Congestion formed when the boats did not arrive on time. The troops maintained extraordinary discipline. The Soviets did not disturb the embarkation, although burning vehicles illuminated the embarkation point. They were even able to load several guns and vehicles. Shortly before the embarkation of the covering force (Colonel Reuter), the staff of the 23rd ID went on board a ferry to await the loading of the last elements. The majority of the troops were loaded by 0540 hours.

Then it was morning. The first enemy assault and scout troops showed up. Now the enemy realized what was going on! Immediately Soviet machine-guns and anti-tank guns were put into position and fired at the boats.

Major Schaefer, commander of the 128th Landing Engineer Battalion, was the last to embark. His ferry pushed off a few meters. Then the ferry of Senior Lieutenant Buchholtz was still noted on the shore. They wanted to collect the last stragglers. Thanks to God a thick cloud cover hung over the sea, so that no aircraft appeared. The Russian machine-gun bullets pinged — however, the landing engineers held out. Senior Lieutenant Buchholtz withdrew his ferry at 0615 hours.

The Baltic islands were in Russian hands.

On the island, for the enemy, there remained only destroyed material or equipment blown during the last night: 205 trucks, 105 smaller vehicles, 30 motorcycles, 1 captured "T-34", 63 machine-guns, 44 mortars, 12 infantry guns, 7 anti-tank guns, 21 light field howitzers, 9 heavy field howitzers, and 1,403 horses.

The landing craft, assault boats, and ferries withdrew in stormy seas to Windau on 11/24. The last ferry arrived in the secure harbor at 1810 hours. The landing engineers brought 4,696 men, 7 guns, 3 air defense guns, 18 vehicles, 1 caisson, and 18 tons of equipment back with them. No wounded were left on the island.

The 23rd ID had fought bravely. They were battered. They consisted of only 81 officers and 4,246 men, of which only 842 were infantrymen! The division had to be sent back to the homeland to reconstitute.

General of Mountain Troops Versock, commander of the XLIII Army Corps, issued an order of the day to the defenders of Sworbe:

"... the combat spirit of all Wehrmacht elements on Sworbe proved the best and had achieved significant defensive success in the last days. Alone, 42 tanks were destroyed in six days. During the battle for Sworbe, the support of the 9th Naval Security Division and the landing engineers was exceptional, those who in brotherly solidarity, against storms and waves, provided us supplies, secured our flank to the sea and now brought us back to solid ground. ..."

7

THE INTERIOR
Military and Civilian Administration - Partisan Warfare

The preparation for "Operation Barbarossa" led necessarily to considerations as to how best to militarily protect the expansive regions of the occupied land, administer it politically, and utilize it economically. In January 1941, the OKH drew up the initial plans for a military administration. The occupied area was to be administered by field and local commandanturas and stretch from the front to a depth of 200 kilometers behind it. Each army had in their interior 3 to 4 field commandanturas, which were subordinate to the Commander of the Army Rear. The commandants received their instructions from the Commander of the Army Rear of the army group, who had far reaching independence, but was bound by the technical instructions of the Quartermaster General of the OKH.

On 3/31/1941, Hitler issued the "Special Principles for Directive Nr. 21." Paragraphs 2 and 3 of the principles read:

"2. In the course of an operation to occupy Russian territory, as soon as the termination of combat operations allows, a friendly government is established according to these special principles. From this occurs:

a) That with the advance of the Army across the border of the Reich
... operations areas are formed ... the depth of which are confined to the
extent possible. ...

b) In the operations area of the Army, the Reichsfuehrer SS has the
special mission of preparing for the political administration ...

c) As soon as the operations area has reached sufficient depth, it
becomes the rear boundary. The newly occupied area to the rear of the
operations area establishes a friendly political administration. It will
be divided according to the elements of the nationalities and its prox-
imity to the boundaries of the army groups. In these regions, the political administration transitions to the Reichs Commissar ...

3. For the execution of all military missions in the political administration areas ... the Wehrmacht commander is utilized ... The
Wehrmacht commander is the senior representative of the Wehrmacht
... and exercises the rights of the military. He has the mission of a territorial commander and the authority of an army commander. ..."

The principles far surpassed the suggestions of the OKH. The occupied region was to have priority as a political administration. The Wehrmacht
had only to be concerned with the administration of its immediate rear
area. The majority of the occupied region — in the Army Group North area
of operations this was the three Baltic republics of Lithuania, Latvia, and
Estonia — was withheld from the military and subordinated to the political
organs. Only a Wehrmacht commander would look after the interests of the
Army.

These interests were outlined in the above named principles as follows:

"a) Close cooperation with the Reichs Commissar, in order to support him in his political task,

b) The utilization of the land and the securing of economic valuables for the benefit of the German economy,

c) Utilization of the land for the supply of troops according to the
requirements of the OKH,

d) Military security of the entire region ...,

e) Regulation of road traffic,

f) Regulation of shelters for the Wehrmacht, police, and organizations for prisoners of war ..."

These principles remained unchanged, even after the start of the Eastern Campaign on 22 June 1941.

The Baltic people welcomed the advance of the German troops. The local inhabitants were immediately ready to cooperate. The local commanders supported their wishes. Civilian life suffered little interruption; only where extended combat was taking place was there any impairment.

A Lithuanian central administration was organized shortly after the troops entered Kovno. Its independence was maintained as the Commander of the Army Rear, Lieutenant General von Roques, established his headquarters in the Lithuanian capital. The harmony was quickly disturbed by the arrival of the SS, which, on the basis of the "Führer Principles", wanted to dominate the central administration. Lieutenant General von Roques was able to prevent this outrage. Nevertheless, he had to urge the central administration to avoid independent operations.

The first differences between the military and the later civilian administration appeared before the latter was legally established!

Lieutenant General von Roques exercised his authority after 7/1, once the rear of the frontal area was established on a line Libau-Shaulen-Jonava. Six days later, the boundary was shifted forward to the line Schlock-Bauske-Birsen-southwest Duenaburg. A third re-deployment occurred on 7/14 to a line halfway between Riga and Pernau-Wolmar-Wenden-Rositten-east of Duenaburg.

The 207th (Lieutenant General von Tiedemann), 281st (Lieutenant General Bayer) and 285th Security Divisions (Major General Edler Herr von Plotho) were responsible for the security of this region. The 207th Security Division was in the Shaulen area in mid July. The 281st Security Division was committed in and around Kovno. The 285th Security Division moved out of Kovno further to the east. Lieutenant General von Roques emigrated with his staff to Riga on 7/17.

The security divisions formed combat groups, which were deployed directly behind the front troops in order to track down and destroy Soviet formations that had been cut off in their areas. Moreover, roads and rail lines were maintained in order by construction engineers, Reichs Labor Detachments and OT (Organisation Todt) [Death Organization] groups. An additional mission was the securing of economic valuables and their corresponding protection. Finally, Wehrmacht shelters had to be secured. The 207th Security Division immediately took over responsibility for the mouth of the Duena.

The Wehrmacht helped the local administration — in mid July, Hitler refused to turn over the occupied area to the newly formed "Reichs Minister for the Occupied Eastern Territories" — construct their economic lives. With the goal of quickly normalizing conditions, lines of communication were repaired and improved throughout.

The construction of lines of communication was necessary in order to properly supply the armies in the shortest amount of time possible. The bridge construction battalion under Colonel Bruns constructed 35 bridges in the 18th Army sector, 15 in the 16th Army sector, and 26 in the 4th Panzer Group sector, including two 35 ton and ten 24 ton bridges, by 7/16! Railroad traffic was in full swing. The railroad stations at Shaulen, Riga, Schwanenburg, Kovno, Duenaburg, Rositten, Ostrov, and Sebezh were under German administration by mid July. 323 trains transported a total of 145,000 tons of Wehrmacht goods by 7/19. The tracks were still on the Russian gauge, only the Memel-Libau and Tauroggen-Shaulen lines were modified to the German gauge.

An administrative distribution of the occupied territories was conducted on 7/25. The Duena became the boundary between the region of the Commander of the Army Rear and the newly authorized "Wehrmacht Eastern Command." The area south and west of the Duena was subordinated to the Wehrmacht Command, Lieutenant General Braemer.

As the front advanced further to the east, the larger the area became over which the Wehrmacht Eastern Command exercised authority. The army rear area also expanded. The boundary was shifted on 8/14 to a line half-way between Riga and Pernau to the center of Lakes Wirz and Peipus. On

9/8, it was extended to the northern tip of Lake Peipus. Lieutenant General von Roques' staff was now located in Werro.

The 207th Security Division was responsible for the security of the Republic of Estonia, as well as an area to a depth of 30 kilometers east of Lake Peipus including the city of Pleskau. This area was administered by six field commandanturas, with 14 local commandanturas. The garrisons of the staffs were:

> Field Commandantura Pleskau (Major General Hofmann), with Local Commandantura Pleskau;
> Field Commandantura Gdov (Colonel Lieser), with Local Commandanturas Jamm, Slantsy;
> Field Commandantura Dorpat (Major Gosebruch), with Local Commandanturas Petseri, Walk, Werro, Dorpat;
> Field Commandantura Wesenberg (Major General Aschenbrandt), with Local Commandantura Joehvi;
> Field Commandantura Reval (Colonel Scultetus), with Local Commandanturas Noemme, Baltischport;
> Field Commandantura Pernau , with Local Commandanturas Fellin, Arensburg.

The remaining two security divisions had left the Baltic region and were now in northwestern Russia. The 285th Security Division was behind the 18th Army in the area south of the Gulf of Finland. The 281st Security Division protected the area east and southeast of Lake Peipus.

With the crossing of the old Russian border, the security formations were tasked with a new mission: partisans! Only once in the Baltic area did they come into conflict with these groups, when 140 partisans parachuted into Hungerburg. This group was suppressed by Estonian police, who only needed nine days to destroy the partisans.

On 11/9, the three security divisions reported their success in combat against the stragglers of regular Red Army formations and partisans:

> Prisoners: 283 officers, 4,457 men;
> Killed in combat: 1,767 partisans;

Executed by court-marshal: 1,813 partisans;

Civilian prisoners: 5,677, of which 648 were turned over to the organs of the senior SS and police commands.

Security for the supply of the army group was intensively expanded. The 4th Field Railroad Command ran the following trains from 7/20 to 10/21:

1,658 supply trains with 746,100 tons for the army group;

500 supply trains with 225,000 tons for Luftflotte 1;

531 troop transport trains;

360 trains for the field railroad command.

During the same period of time, German, local national railroad workers, and engineer battalions from the army had operated 6,710 kilometers of broad gauge track and 503 kilometers of narrow gauge track, while laying 6,050 kilometers of track and constructing 186 railroad bridges.

On 10/15, the army rear area boundary was shifted to the northeast and east. The forward boundary ran: Pernau-Reval-coast west of Narva-Slantsy-Luga and then bent sharply to the south.

As autumn fell over the land, it became certain that the Eastern Campaign would not obtain the hoped for success and that they must contend with a campaign of longer duration. The security troops made plans to spend the winter. The forward boundary of their area of commitment was again shifted at year's end. The line extended from Narva — to the east to include Siverskaya — and from there sharply to the south in an almost straight line through Dno — on to the boundary with the army rear area of Army Group Center. This line remained constant until the Soviet summer offensive of 1944.

In the meantime, the rear boundary met the newly established Reichs Commissar of the Eastern Territories. The responsibilities of the two military staffs — Commander of the Army Rear and the Wehrmacht Eastern Command — were equally divided between them.

The activities of the Wehrmacht Eastern Command and its agencies now had to be coordinated with the situation in the new Reichs

Commissariate. The Commander of the Army Rear, who received authority over the security troops in 1942, directed his activities according to events on the front.

His three security divisions were responsible for the protection of all rear area communications. The 207th Security Division was committed east of Lake Peipus. The 285th Security Division covered the area between Siverskaya and Dno. The 281st Security Division held the watch in the great forest and marsh-land between Dno and Nevel. The combat situation was such that all three divisions, at one time or another, had to commit their assigned regiments and combat groups to the front. Thus, officers and men of the security divisions fought in the Volkhov pocket, in Kholm, near Novgorod and Nevel, as well as in other places.

As before, the main task of the Commander of the Army Rear was the security and construction of supply routes and lines of communication. To illustrate the immensity of this task, the following three statistics may help:

Railroad transport from the rear area to the front in 1942:

> 3,238 supply trains,
> 1,291 ammunition trains,
> 563 fuel trains,
> 2,895 trains with other materials.

Vehicle columns in 1943 traveled a total of 11,045,262 kilometers and transported 1,475,067 tons of goods. The quantity of goods were distributed as follows:

> 358,540 tons of ammunition,
> 69,251 tons of fuel,
> 163,336 tons of rations,
> 883,940 tons of other material.

The commitment of the 4th Field Water Route Battalion, whose staff was located in Pleskau, for 1943 reflected:

Army Group North

Body of Water	Persons Transported	Cattle	Wood	Goods
Lake Peipus	114,850	62,000	78,510 tn	15,520 tn
Narva	305,450	—	43,390 tn	7,580 tn
Luga	5,300	—	1,276 tn	3,744 tn
Upper Duena	6,150	—	—	9,300 tn

Body of Water	Committed Vehicles		Local Assets
	Steamers	Barges	
Lake Peipus	18	39	190
Narva	11	17	90
Luga	7	6	35
Upper Duena	3	4	20

The third task, next to security of the rear area and protection of the lines of communication, was the economic utilization of the land. This obligation had to be carried out on the basis of the "Special Principles for Directive Nr. 21 from 3/13/1941" by the Wehrmacht economic inspector. The inspector received his authority not from the commander of the army group, but from the Defense Economic Bureau of the OKW.

During the beginning of the Eastern Campaign, an Eastern Economic Staff (Lieutenant General (Luftwaffe) Dr. Schubert, from 1942 General of Infantry Stapf) was formed, which was subordinate to the Economic Inspectorate of the army group, as well as that of the Wehrmacht Command in the Reichs Commissariate. In summer of 1941, Army Group North received the Economic Inspectorate North (Colonel (Luftwaffe) Becker).

The mission of the economic inspectorate was to take over the existing industries in the army area and construct new ones. Moreover, the army group had priority over the agricultural yield. In addition, local labor was needed for commitment for local industry and for working in the Reich.

The Economic Inspectorate North, with its seat in Pleskau, organized Economic Commands in Pleskau, Dno, Opochka, Ostrov, Gdov, Narva, Luga, and Krasnovardeisk. These commands supervised workers' bureaus in Pleskau, Dno, Utorgozh, Soltsy, Porkhov, Sushchevo, Loknya, Opochka, Idritsa, Ostrov, Gdov, Narva, Kingisepp, Luga, Krasnovardeisk, Krassnoe Selo, Volossovo, Siverskaya, Tossno, Lyuban, and Oredezh.

The responsibilities for heavy industry in the army rear area was divided up into four groups, which were administered by the Economic Inspectorate. They handled 13 electric power stations, 8 mineral oil, 19 peat, and 11 brick making factories.

The influence of the Economic Inspectorate crossed the boundary of the army rear area to the front.

The security of the regions behind the front was the direct responsibility of the army commanders. Field commandanturas and local commandanturas administered military and civilian concerns. The two rear area army regions of the army group were mutually divided. A Commandant of the Army Rear — for short called Korueck — was the representative for the army commander to all commandanturas and security troops.

On 10/31/1943, the army rear areas were divided as follows:

16th Army
584th Korueck

Field Commandantura	607 Porkhov, with
Local Commandanturas	862 Porkhov, 633 Dno,
	526 Soltsy, 565 Shimsk,
	865 Volot, 360 Staraya Russa,
	912 Dedovichi, 311 Pazhevitsy.
Field Commandantura	820 Bezhanitsy, with
Local Commandanturas	321 Bezhanitsy, 257 Dulova,
	329 Loknya.

18th Army
583rd Korueck

Field Commandantura	819 Narva, with
Local Commandanturas	852 Narva, 371 Kingisepp,
	362 Koly.
Field Commandantura	583 Volossovo, with

Local Commandanturas	574 Volossovo, 315 Yashchera, 351 Vyritsa, 299 Lyuban, 331 Chudovo.
Field Commandantura	312 Krasnovardeisk, with
Local Commandanturas	305 Krasnovardeisk, 322 Krassnoe Selo, 255 Tossno, 341 Siverskaya.
Field Commandantura	605 Batetskaya, with
Local Commandanturas	276 Ordezh, 361 Batetskaya, 864 Utorgozh.

The year 1944 brought multiple missions for the rear area services in order to make the withdrawal of the front troops as smooth as possible. In spring 1944, the 18th Army commander began with the establishment of local national workers' detachments. These were to help with four problems, one of which was to keep in check the political and moral administration of youth. Additionally, the forming of workers groups prevented the desertion of young men to the partisans and bandit detachments. Thirdly, youth of military service age were denied the enemy. It had been established that the Soviets immediately armed the male population of newly occupied towns and dispatched them against the withdrawing Germans. The fourth and most important point was the commitment of these worker units to construct rear area positions.

The Soviet offensive did not allow for the development of this plan. The 18th Army commander and all of his subordinate units had enough to deal with in spring and summer of 1944. When the front finally stabilized on the Velikaya, the formation of these units was too late!

"Too late!" These words describe all measures of German Eastern Politics!

The bravery of the soldiers and their relations with the civilian population could not be shaken. The soldier strived to maintain this relationship, however, when it was in contrast with the political leadership.

The memorandum, which was issued by the Commander of the Army Rear in October 1943, sported the following sentences:

"Each German soldier is to take it upon himself to behave properly in reference to the local national populations, particularly with the women. He must be aware that his actions are a reflection on the German Wehrmacht and the German people. ..."

The war plans for the east did not only involve the military preparations, battles, and end objectives, but were interwoven with the necessary economic politics. Therefore, on 4/20/1941, Hitler charged Reichsleiter Rosenberg to create plans for a political order in Eastern Europe. The first instructions for the reorganization of the north Russian area — in this case, excluding the Baltic Provinces — were laid down on 5/8/1941. The concept of "Ostland" was coined, which would ultimately encompass the former Baltic republics and Belorussia.

The political leadership viewed — in contrast to the Wehrmacht — the populations in the occupied regions not as partners in combat against Bolshevism, but as economic-political "objects." The "Decree of the Führer on the Utilization of the Newly Occupied Eastern Territories of 7/17/1941" published the first regulations on civil administration.

An additional decree from the same day dealt specifically with the region that was occupied by Army Group North during the first weeks of the campaign. This decree ordained:

"...The region of the former free states of Lithuania, Latvia and Estonia, as well as Belorussia, will be transferred over to the civil administration of the Reichs Minister for the Occupied Eastern Territories. This entire region forms a Reichs Commissariate ... and receives the title "Ostland." ...Gauleiter and Senior President Hinrich Lohse is assigned as Reichs Commissar for Ostland. He has his seat in Riga."

On 7/27, the Reichs Commissar arrived in Kovno. Here, he took over from the Commander of the Army Rear the administration of the entire area south of the Duena. On the following day, Lohse issued his first proclamation to the population, which was rife with National Socialist propaganda that was not understood by the Lithuanians.

At the end of August, the civil administration set up "house keeping" after the military administration gave up the Latvian area on 8/20. The General Commissariate of Lithuania was now located in Kovno, and the General Commissariate of Latvia was in Riga. With the general commissariates were created regional, main, and county commissariates. German bureaucrats, clerks, and party functionaries took them over. (In Latvia alone there were 25,000 bureaucrats and clerks active!)

The local population participated in the administration and — with the exception of Riga — were appointed area chiefs, mayors, and local superintendents. The Baltic self-governing organizations — the General Commissariate of Belorussia was no longer considered, because it belonged to the operations area of Army Group Center! — were directed to cooperate with the German authorities, however, they could not make any independent decisions. The clear subordination of the Baltic authorities to the General Commissar was made particularly evident during the 3/7/1942 reorganization of the administration.

The General District of Lithuania was organized into an agency designated the General Council, whereby the General Council was the representative of the people to the General Commissar. The General District of Latvia was led by a General Director, who, internally, was considered the "first among equals." The authority of the General District of Estonia, first established on 12/5/1941, was vested in the Director. The First Territorial Director functioned as Administrative Chief.

Agricultural administration was completely under the Reichs Commissariate. The Reichs Commissariate was organized into three main departments (1st Personnel and Organization, 2nd Political and Administration, and 3rd Economic). The Reichs Commissariate further instructed the General Commissariate.

Next to the Reichs Commissar, two German agencies had unlimited power in the execution of their work. These were those in charge of the Four Year Plan and the Einsatzkommandos of the Reichsfuehrer SS and Chief of the German Police.

Additional special administrations of various Reichs ministers directed bureaus and agencies. Here, one would find the Reichs Ministers for Weapons and Munitions; the Technical Central Bureau; the General Inspectorate for Roads, Railroads; as well as the Reichs Post, Reichs Labor Department, etc.

The Reichs Commissar was to administer Ostland according to the principles of National Socialist nationality politics. Drastic measures were, therefore, taken in the economic sector. On 8/19, a "Disposition on the Securing of the Assets of the USSR" was issued, as well as a decree on the seizure of Jewish property. Additional orders issued in 1941 included:

9/11 - Prices and Wages;
9/13 - Removal of Bolshevik Economic Measures;
9/17 - Re-organization of Small Industries;
10/24 - Establishment of a Custodial Administration.

The most important decree followed on 11/29 and concerned agriculture. This order went against the grain of all former principles in the Baltic republics. It made it impossible for local industrial merchants to acquire businesses and firms. Therefore, this policy was practically the same as under the Soviets! The newly founded "Ostland-GmbH" seized all industrial operations. Because the agricultural economy was centrally regulated, it remained as it was under the Soviets!

The Baltic population, above all the intelligentsia, was excluded from all private initiative! Lithuanians, Latvians, and Estonians became second class citizens!

The NSDAP [National Socialist German Workers Party] required their doctrine be carried out in the new land. On 4/7/1942, Hitler issued an order creating the regional leadership of the NSDAP Ostland. The party was officially founded on 5/16/1942. With its existence soon followed the Hitler Youth, Women's Movement, etc. German bureaucrats were searched out for their party membership and corresponding party political work and dispatched to Ostland.

The Senior SS and Police Commander Ostland was responsible for the security of the Reichs Commissariate. For this, he had the Police Regiment North available. The first police battalions, the 11th, 33rd, 69th, and 105th, were deployed with the Army in June 1941, for security measures. An additional three battalions followed and were stationed as unified groups.

The latter three battalions were marked for commitment against bandits and partisans.

The organization of the German police force in the area of the Senior SS and Police Commander Ostland and North Russia reflected the following in July 1942:

9th Police Regiment (Home station Saarbruecken, Metz), with the 6th, 112th, 132nd Police Battalions;

15th Police Regiment (Home station Hamburg, Kiel, Bremen), with the 305th, 306th, 310th Police Battalions;

16th Police Regiment (Home station Stuttgart, Karlesruhe), with the 56th, 102nd, 121st Police Battalions;

17th Police Regiment (Home station Frankfurt/Main), with the 42nd, 74th, 69th Police Battalions.

Independent Police Battalions:

44th (Leipzig), 61st (Dortmund), 84th (Gleiwitz), 105th (Bremen), 319th (Koeln) and 321st (Breslau).

The 11th and 33rd Police Battalions, which had been committed in the northern sector since June 1941, had, in the meantime, left the operations area. The 11th Police Battalion was sent back to Koenigsberg, while the 33rd Police Battalion was transferred to the Ukraine. The 105th Police Battalion went to Holland in July 1942. During the summer and fall, the 84th Police Battalion stood in the front before Leningrad and suffered such heavy losses in October 1942 that it was disbanded. The 44th, 319th, and 321st Police Battalions formed the 27th Police Regiment in March 1943, which then went to Norway.

The commander of the security police was concerned with internal order. Detachments of the security police were established in the three area capitals. Additional home stations were Libau, Duenaburg, Pleskau, Dorpat, and Vilna. Moreover, gendarme corps were located in Riga, Mitau, Wolmar, Libau, Duenaburg, Pleskau, and Dorpat.

The personnel of the German police, apart from the battalions, were thought of as only cadre personnel. Therefore, support forces were brought forward to assist them. With the decree of the Reichsfuehrer SS and Chief of German Police of 11/6/1941, local national police battalions — the so-called constabulary battalions — were formed. In autumn 1941, the following constabulary battalions were in the Reichs Commissariate — here are only the Baltic Provinces:

Constabulary Battalion	5 (Latvian) in Riga,
Constabulary Battalion	37 (Estonian) in Dorpat,
Constabulary Battalion	38 (Estonian) in Fellin,
Constabulary Battalion	39 (Estonian) in Poltsaama,
Constabulary Battalion	40 (Estonian) in Pleskau
Constabulary Battalion	41 (Estonian) in Reval
Constabulary Battalion	42 (Estonian) in Reval,
Constabulary Battalion	270 (Latvian) in Abrene,
Constabulary Battalion	Lithuania (Lithuanian) in Kovno.

By the end of the German occupation there were 9,000 Estonian and 15,644 Latvian members of the constabulary battalions, which, at times, were commanded to participate at the front.[1]

The Baltic population, which at first greeted the Wehrmacht as liberators from the Bolshevik yoke, realized within a few months that, with the arrival of the German civil administration, freedom was not to be forthcoming.

The General Commissar of Estonia, SA Obergruppenfuehrer Litzmann, reported on his assigned area on 9/16/1942:

"The reasons for the decrease in morale of the population lay above all in the fact that the inhabitants have been excluded from economic life. Their almost complete elimination from economic life ... their still unfulfilled wish for reintroducing private enterprise, is having an extremely depressing effect on their morale, which will, sooner or later, lead to their passive resistance. ..."

This warning from the talented General Commissar in Ostland fell on deaf ears at the Reich Commissariate, as well as at the Reich Ministry for the Occupied Eastern Territories. As before, Ostland was treated as a colony, whose residents were a lower race of men.

The German-Baltic groups, which were in the Reich, were not, at first, allowed to return to their countries, even though contact between German and Baltic peoples was supposed to be guaranteed! At the end of 1942, 36,000 Baltic Germans were allowed to return to Lithuania. Nevertheless, they were not brought to established settlements, but had to work farms which were adjacent to the supply routes.

A second plan, which the Reich Ministry was considering, was just as pointless. This was to let Dutch farmers work 500,000 hectares of land near Libau. On 6/11/1942, a "Netherlands East Company" was formed in Rotterdam. However, nothing came of the settlement plan.

The greatest failure in the field of economics was in industry. Indeed, it was not dismantled under German rule. However, it did not progress, because no one in authority knew what they were doing. For example, in the large Estonian works at Kivioli the local national engineers were discharged and replaced by German novices, who had no technical experience at all!

The construction of the Estonian chief oil works occurred first in 1943 by a special order of the four year plan. Now they had to make up quickly what they had neglected in two years. The output for 1943 was 160,000 tons. An increase to 1.5 million tons was planned for.

The consumption of rations for the economic year 1942/43 was as follows:

Item	Army Group	Commissariate
Bread Grain	9,222 tons	131,526 tons
Meat	1,671 tons	47,074 tons
Fat	971 tons	13,954 tons
Potatoes	60,950 tons	202,760 tons

Additional alienation between German authorities and the population occurred over the work obligation for men and women. In the autumn of 1941, labor bureaus were established in all large cities. Their main duty was to recruit as many workers as possible for industrial operations in the Reich.

Chapter 7: The Interior

One statistic of the army group from 6/30/1944 indicates that, up to this time, a total of 128,724 men, including 50,475 Russians, were dispatched from the Reich Commissariate to Germany as forced laborers!

The Drifting apart of Germany and the Baltic Provinces became noticeable. Reich Commissar Lohse himself requested from the Reich Ministry an official clarification of the political goals in Ostland in a 51 page memorandum at the end of 1942. He received no answer; neither did General Commissar Litzmann, who constantly proposed that the Baltic people should be guaranteed their self-administration.

He received support from a side that he had never counted upon. In autumn 1943, the Reichsfuehrer SS intervened even more into the administration of Ostland. The SS wanted the expansion of independent local national authority, because so many Baltic volunteers reported for duty in the armed forces. Himmler himself decided to come to Estonia. Then Hitler intervened — and all remained as it was!

In 1944, as Army Group North withdrew to the border of Ostland, Berlin decided to grant the Baltic people more independence. General Commissar Litzmann dismissed his staff and, in January 1944, called into being an Estonian administration.

On 1/31/1944, the new authority of the land called all who were born from 1904-1923 to arms!

The jurisdiction of the Estonian and later also the Latvian self-administration was officially recognized on 3/18/1944 and expanded!

However — it was too late!

The war had returned to Ostland.

Estonia and Latvia were overran by Soviet tanks!

Reich Commissar Lohse left his area, which he had ruled for three years like a patriarch of the middle ages, on 7/28/1944 — without notifying the commander of Army Group North.

Gauleiter Koch was appointed his successor, but never once crossed the East Prussian border. Nevertheless, the border was hermetically sealed, so that the Estonian and Latvian refugees were left behind and fell into the hands of the Soviets. After an energetic protest from General Schoerner to the Reichsfuehrer SS, the border was re-opened!

In autumn 1944, the Reich Commissariate Ostland no longer existed! The blame lay not with the situation on the front, but with the German administration. As a Baltic saying goes: "I can govern a land like Estonia with 12 men, with 120 men administer it poorly, with 1200 men destroy it!"

Finally Kurland was still occupied by the Germans and administered by the German civil authorities. As representative of the Reich Commissar (the Reich Commissariate was not officially disbanded!) Vice Chief Matthiessen administered Kurland. To him was subordinate the territorial director of Latvia, Engels, and as the last district chief, the Regional Commissar of Libau, Hansen.

The strong political position of these agencies is documented by the fact that, on 12/16/1944, the army group commander appointed the General Inspector of the Latvian volunteers, SS Gruppenfuehrer Bangerskis, as territorial director of Kurland. Vice Chief Matthiessen immediately protested against these measures. The army group had to give in! The German civil administration maintained its luster...even as it fell to pieces.

The "Special Principles for Directive Nr. 21" made the following reference in section 2b:

"In the Army operations area, the Reichsfuehrer SS has the special task of preparing the political administration, which in the course of combat, will produce two opposing political systems. ..."

The special tasks were not directed against military personnel, but were naturally confined to the interior and, therefore, the civilians. A Führer Decree of 5/13/1941 outlined the war jurisdiction in these regions as follows:

"1. Offenses by enemy civilian personnel come under the jurisdiction of courts-marshal.

2. ...

3. Also, all other attacks of enemy civilian personnel ... are to be suppressed by the troops on the spot, with whatever means available, to destroy the attackers.

4. ...against towns, from which the Wehrmacht has been insidiously attacked, immediate measures will be taken collectively, when the individual culprits cannot be identified. ..."

This "license" for reprisal was expanded upon in a supplement to Führer Directive Nr. 31 from 7/23/1941:

"... all resistance is not only punishable by trial, but when the defendants have partaken in some form of terror, then the populace will suffer retribution!"

Einsatzkommandos and elements of the SD (Sicherheitsdienste) Tilsit crossed the border on 6/23. Their mission, which was at first known only to the unit leaders, was directed against the Jewish population. The horrible balance sheet for the first week of the campaign was published in a "report of successes":

on 6/23:	in Garsden	=	210 executed,
on 6/26:	in Krottingen	=	214 executed,
on 6/26	in Augustovo	=	316 executed,
on 6/28:	in Krottingen	=	63 executed,
on 6/30:	in Polangen	=	111 executed.

The mission of the SD was not finished at this time. It continued far into the month of August — and 1480 more people lost their lives.

The commitment of these execution commandos was not done arbitrarily, but according to a "master plan." The chief of the security police and the SD, SS Gruppenfuehrer Heydrich, informed the Führer in mid June of the newly established SS Einsatzgruppen and their special mission.

Einsatzgruppe A, under SS Brigadefuehrer Dr. Stahlecker, was committed in the operations area of Army Group North. There were four

Einsatzkommandos subordinate to this group: IA (SS Standartenfuehrer Dr. Sandberger) for the area of the 18th Army; IB (SS Oberfuehrer Ehrlinger) for the rear area of the 16th Army; II (SS Obersturmbannfuehrer Strauch) in Latvia and Belorussia; and III (SS Standartenfuehrer Jaeger) in Lithuania. The Einsatzkommando Tilsit (SS Sturmbannfuehrer Boehme) was only committed for a short time in a 25 kilometer wide strip on the far side of the Reich border.

The activities of the Einsatzkommandos ended on the day the civilian administration was established. However, up to that time, the Einsatz-kommandos had caused quite enough terror.

The activities of the Einsatzkommandos were known to the German leadership. The reports of SS Brigadefuehrer Dr. Stahlecker referred several times to the good relations between his staff and the army command-ers', as well as with the commander of the 4th Panzer Group.

The Einsatzkommandos made use of the local nationals' anti-semitism and organized pogroms. Alone during the night of 6/26, in Kovno, 1500 Jews were removed from Lithuania, and several synagogues and 60 residences were set afire. The "Lithuanian Security and Criminal Police" advanced rigorously, egged on by their German instigators. Through such pogroms in Latvia and Lithuania, 5,500 people were killed. SD Tilsit likewise executed 5,500 Jews and Communists in the border sector.

A list of executions performed by Einsatzgruppe A from 10/15/1941 follows:

Lithuania -	Kovno area:	31,914 Jews, 80 Communists;
	Shaulen area:	41,382 Jews, 763 Communists;
	Vilna area:	7,015 Jews, 860 Communists;
Latvia -	Riga area:	6,378 Jews and Communists;
	Mitau area:	3,576 Jews and Communists;
	Libau area:	11,860 Jews and Communists;
	Wolmar area:	209 Jews and Communists;
	Duenaburg area:	9,845 Jews and Communists;
Estonia -	Estonian region:	474 Jews, 684 Communists.

Chapter 7: The Interior

The majority of the Jewish population were stuck in ghettos for later shipment to concentration camps in Poland. The ghettos in Riga and Vilna were established in September 1941 and held approximately 15,000 people. In the summer of 1943, the Riga ghetto was dissolved, and the last inmates were transported to Poland.

The persecution of the Jewish population did not end with the coming of the civil administration. The eradication of the so-called "enemy of the people" took such horrible forms, that, in October 1941, Reich Commissar Lohse protested to the Chief of the Security Police. A month later, the Wehrmacht reported: "The Senior SS and Police Commander has, in the meantime, aggressively pursued a policy of execution and, on Sunday, 11/30/1941, eliminated approximately 4000 Jews from the Riga ghetto!"

When the Einsatzkommandos of the SD were no longer active in the Reich Commissariate, the organs of the Senior SS and Police Commander took up the macabre "work."

The German occupying power, whose authority exhibited such methods, could not make friends with the local populations in the long run. These activities were the reason for the war's expansion to the interior just a few weeks after the beginning of the Eastern Campaign. The partisan war — which was not that noticeable in Reich Commissariate Ostland during the first years — turned the Eastern Campaign into a war without fronts. It was a struggle in which friend and enemy were unrecognizable.

"The partisans had inconspicuous guards in front of their camps, harmless peasants, which could emerge in the towns and among the German troops. The Landser did not know which of the farmers on the side of a hill, on the farms, in the stables, or which women at the water trough were enemies. Who anticipated the smoke from a chimney, the significance of a fire in a field, what was in a tobacco pouch or what was in the horse-drawn carriage that was standing in one place for so long!"[2]

The directive of the Central Committee of the Communist Party of the Soviet Union of 6/29 read:

"In the regions occupied by the enemy, partisan detachments and division groups are created for the struggle against the units of the fascist army and provoke the partisan war throughout..."

Three weeks later, the Central Committee issued another proclamation:

"The task is to create insufferable conditions for the German interloper, disrupt his communications, supply, and the troop formations themselves, sabotage his efforts, destroy the invader and his collaborators, establish partisan groups on horseback and on foot, with whatever means available..."

The Regional Committee of the Communist Party of the Soviet Union in Leningrad established an organizational detachment for partisans in July 1941. The first 191 partisan detachments came into being and reached the Leningrad area before the combat vehicles of the 4th Panzer Group did. In September, there were 400 detachments with 18,000 men in the Leningrad area! By the end of the same month, these detachments reported the following successes: 1,713 Germans killed; destroyed: 8 tanks, 178 vehicles, 47 bridges, 101 motorcycles, among others.

In 1941, the main area of partisan operations was Pleskau, Novgorod, and Staraya Russa. The activity of the groups suffered during the strong winter, but increased in the spring of 1942. The first partisan brigades were organized by the political leaders of the staffs of the Northwest Front, later known as the Leningrad Front.

The three Leningrad partisan brigades, under their leaders Buinov, German, and Glebov, and the partisan regiment under Laivin concentrated during the summer of 1942 on their main effort, the destruction of lines of communications. The Pleskau-Dno and Dno-Staraya Russa rail lines were destroyed many times. 115 military trains were blown into the air in nine months.

The partisan war went further in 1943. During this year, the first organized groups operated in the Reich Commissariate itself, which had been spared partisan attacks before this time. At the same time, illegal local chapters of the Communist Party of the Soviet Union appeared in all of the General Commissariates. In Lithuania, 20 of these local chapters existed, and 8 in Latvia.

The first noteworthy appearance of partisans in the Baltic area occurred on 9/1/1943 in Kovno, when an ammunition dump was blown into the air and 22 locomotives were destroyed. On 11/16/1943, they even reached Riga, the seat of the Reich Commissar, when a political rally on the city hall square was bombed.

That was the first evidence that the partisan movement had a foothold in the German administrative cities.

As before, the main operation area of the partisans was the area behind the front. The situation map of the army group commander showed the following commitment areas in May 1943: the rear area of the 18th Army was secured by one German security battalion, one Ostland battalion, 12 independent Ostland companies, and 8 Baltic companies. The main effort lay on the Luga-Krasnovardeisk, Narva-Krasnovardeisk, Soltsy-Pushkin, and Luga-Novgorod rail lines. A partisan brigade reportedly blew up the latter stretch twice in one month.

The interior area of the 16th Army was guarded by 6 German security battalions, 10 security companies, 23 Ostland, and 8 Baltic companies. The Novosokolniki-Dno, Pleskau-Staraya Russa rail lines and the marsh area south of Dno were the disposition points of 5 partisan brigades, which blew the Novosokolniki-Dno stretch three times in May and, on the same stretch, derailed three transport trains.

The Army rear area was occupied by three security divisions. The 207th Security Division, with 7 subordinate Baltic and 6 Ostland companies, was located in the Pleskau-Narva-Kingisepp area. In this region they ran into only limited partisan groups. Nevertheless, the Pleskau-Kingisepp rail line was mined in eleven places.

The 285th Security Division was in combat with 5 partisan brigades, which operated primarily in the Pleskau area. The Luga -Pleskau rail line was destroyed five times in May. The 281st Security Division, which was quartered between the Ostrov-Rositten -Latvian border, faced 12 enemy brigades. The main location threatened was the Rositten-Pleskau rail line, which was mined several times in May, so that eight trains were derailed.

There was a noticeable increase in partisan attacks in fall of 1943 throughout the rear of Army Group North. German strong points, police stations, and local administrative authorities were attacked in Plyussa, Utorgosh, Soltsy, Luga, Dno, Porkhov, Gdov, Pleskau, Seredka, and the defenders overpowered. The Siverskaya-Chudovo rail line was blown 208 times, as 219 trains ran over mines. The Pleskau-Dno stretch was severed in 319 places, and the Pleskau-Narva line in 447 places! The last three months of the year 1943 recorded a total of 3,079 blown stretches in the Army rear area!

Partisan activity reached a climax at the beginning of the Soviet summer offensive in 1944. The enemy leadership directed the partisan detachments and brigades against sensitive lines of communications, which were to be destroyed on the day of the attack. The first planned commitment occurred on the night of 20 June on the right flank of the 16th Army, as well as on the seam with Army group Center. At the same time, at several locations, the tracks of the Duenaburg-Polozk and Vilna-Duenaburg rail lines were blown into the air.

The destruction in the rear of the German front increased at the beginning of the offensive. According to Soviet sources, 58,563 stretches of track and 300 bridges were blown at this time, 133 trains were derailed, 1,620 trucks were captured, and 15 railroad stations were destroyed. A special achievement of the Latvian partisans was the fire bombing of the Riga communications bureau on 6/28, which was not re-established until the end of the war.

The withdrawal of the army group into the Baltic Provinces, naturally, reduced the threat from partisans the closer the front came to the border of the Reich Commissariate. In September 1944 there were no more reports of unified partisan detachments! Obviously, however, there were small groups everywhere which operated in isolation. Thus, in the Latvian area there were three groups primarily southeast of Riga, and in Lithuania there were several individual bands reported.

After withdrawing into the Kurland area, the army group formed a special combat group, which was to hunt down the remaining partisan bands and destroy them. SS Obergruppenfuehrer Jeckeln and his Chief of Staff, Colonel von Braunschweig, were tasked directly by the army group commander. The staff of the 16th Police Regiment took control. (All other German police staffs were back in the homeland.)

Two battalions, under Captain Held and SS Hauptsturmbannfuehrer Schatz, each with three companies, were organized into a combat group. The battalions were motorized and each had 4 medium mortars, two heavy, and two medium anti-tank guns. The battalion of SS Hauptsturmbannfuehrer Schatz was the search battalion, while the battalion of Captain Held was the attack battalion. Both battalions were quartered in the Talsen area.

In Kurland there were no battles with partisans. Ultimately, there were only groups of Latvian deserters that lived only by robbery and murder, with few having the inclination to cause harm to the Germans. The last commitment of the combat group of SS Obergruppenfuehrer Jeckeln occurred at the end of October west of Engure, 23 kilometers north of Tuckum. After the destruction of this group, the partisan war in the Army Group North area was over. Battalion Schatz was dissolved.

A tragi-comic episode closed the chapter on the "partisan war."

At the beginning of November 1944, the army group commander planned the creation of a special formation under the Latvian General Kureils, who had formerly worked for the German Abwehr. This formation was to infiltrate behind the enemy front and disrupt Soviet lines of communication, report on troop movements, etc.

The 16th Army commander, who was to lead the way in the formation of the formation, soon began his endeavor. It soon became obvious, though, that the majority of the volunteers for this unit were deserters, who saw it as a chance to get to the other side as quickly as possible. The Kureils formation was disbanded on 11/14. 595 officers and soldiers were arrested and General Kureils was sent to Germany.

The army group no longer thought of organizing such a formation. It now had enough to keep it busy. It had to prepare for the final battle of Kurland...

NOTES:

[1] In this work there is no reference to the Baltic volunteers, which fought as members of the Waffen SS on all fronts. Their history extends beyond the scope of this book.
[2] *290th Infantry Division. 1940-1945*. Bad Nauheim: Podzun 1960. 428 pages.

8

THE SURRENDER
The Final Battle in Kurland

"The enemy's Kurland Group continued to block on the peninsula until the end of the war and surrendered in May 1945."

This sentence is found in the official work of the Soviet Ministry of Defense about the 2nd World War. 16 words reported about the last seven months of war in the Kurland area. A single insignificant sentence handles the commitment of two German armies and an army group. 16 words to also describe the battle of three enemy army groups with, at times, 19 armies![1]

The war in Kurland between October 1944 and May 1945 was either insignificant to the writer of the history, or it was senseless. Which was it?

In mid October 1944, the Red Army stood on a 120 kilometer front between the mouth of the Memel and the coast, several kilometers south of Libau on the Baltic Sea. Only the XXVIII German Army Corps, along with the "Grossdeutschland" Armored Infantry Division, 7th Panzer Division, and 58th ID clung to the city of Memel.

Army Group North was decisively cut off from the Reich!

The OKH ordered that the Memel bridgehead must be freed at all costs. Army Group North was to begin the attack — "Operation Geier" — on 10/ 17. The XXXIX Panzer Corps (General of Panzer Troops von Saucken) had to force the breakthrough to Memel and further to East Prussia, with the 4th, 12th, 14th Panzer Divisions, and the 11th and 126th ID. Contact with Army Group Center was the goal!

General of Infantry Boege, commander of the 18th Army, conducted the necessary commitment briefing with the responsible commanders in his headquarters near Hasenpoth on 10/15. It was, in this manner, established, that the enemy in front of the army was preparing for a new offensive. Therefore, the initiation of the operation had to be hastened. The three panzer divisions were quickly ordered to their assembly areas — 4th Panzer Division in Grobin, 14th Panzer Division in Preekuln, and 12th Panzer Division southeast of Hasenpoth.

The Red Army was, at the same time, preparing for the last attack against Army Group North. The 2nd Baltic Front (Army General Eremenko) had the 3rd Shock and the 42nd and 22nd Armies attacking out of the Doblen area to the west, with the 1st Shock Army along the coast. The 1st Baltic Front (Army General Bagramyan) was to break through from Vainode-Skuodas to Libau with the 6th Guards and 51st Armies. The 61st Army and 5th Guards Tank Army were to supply reinforcements.

The 1st Battle of Kurland began on 10/16.

The main effort of the enemy offensive lay on the right flank. The Soviet armies assaulted between the Gulf of Riga and the Windau against the positions of the 16th Army and Army Detachment Grasser. The 1st Shock Army (Lieutenant General Sakhvataev) attacked out of the Schlock area against the extreme left German flank. The defenders resisted fiercely. The tanks and infantrymen advanced only slowly. On 10/18 they were able to occupy Kemmern; the next day they bogged down 10 kilometers east of Tuckum!

The secondary effort was the area on either side of Doblen. Here, the enemy not only wanted to separate the 16th Army and Army Detachment Grasser, but, with a breakthrough between Autz and Frauenburg, collapse the front of the army group. The two Russian corps — XII and CXXII — fought 13 divisions for three days against three German divisions. The 24th, 93rd, and 122nd ID resisted the enemy with all of their strength. During this time, the three divisions lost 1,050 men, but still held!

Now the 1st Baltic Front attacked.

Fighter-bomber aircraft and barrage fire initiated the battle between Moscheiken and Skuodas, a battle which was to end in the conquest of Libau. The attack near Moscheiken was stopped by the 12th Panzer Division (Lieutenant General Baron von Bodenhausen). The 30th ID and SS "Nordland" Division repulsed the enemy between Vainode and Skuodas. A gap between the divisions was closed by the 4th Panzer Division (Major General Betzel). The 14th Panzer Division and 563rd ID later strengthened the main combat line.

The enemy was unable to break through anywhere!

Their only gain in ground was on the extreme right flank near Kemmern and on both sides of Doblen.

The Soviet attack momentum diminished.

They would not be able to overrun Army Group North so easily.

The 1st Battle of Kurland fizzled out on 20 October.

In spite of this, the Soviets registered a success: they had prevented the breakout of the army group to East Prussia! The German leadership had to realize that "Operation Geier" could no longer be executed. The XXXIX Panzer Corps, the remnants of the 58th and 61st ID, and the "Grossdeutschland" Armored Infantry Division were transported to the homeland.

The army group commander issued the following order on 10/21:

"The Führer has ordered that Kurland be held and that we transition to the defense in our present positions. Our mission is to not give up one foot of ground, to tie up 150 opposing enemy formations, to batter them wherever we have the opportunity and, thereby, facilitate the defense of the homeland.

We will immediately exhaust all means available to strengthen our defense. It must cover the entire depth of the battlefield and be insurmountable. In addition, we must build, build and build some more! Each soldier, that is not committed to a position with a weapon in his hand, must be working with a spade. We cannot work enough on the main battlefield, on the streets and on the roads! 2nd and 3rd defensive belts, road blocks, obstacles, bunkers must be constructed in the shortest period of time. Engineers must be pulled from the main line of combat and committed to construction, the civilian population must be immediately mobilized! ..."

On the next day, the OKH issued further instructions to the army group, and its last order was short and precise: "Hold your present positions! Learn how to commit replacements in combat and shoot down aircraft! Your mission in a nutshell: Tie up forces!"

The dispositions of Army Group North at this time, from left to right, was as follows:

The 16th Army (General of Infantry Hilpert) was in the north. The XLIII Army Corps was responsible for coastal protection and the Baltic islands. The 23rd and 218th ID defended Sworbe, the 207th Security Division covered the coast on both sides of Windau, the 12th Luftwaffe Field Division and North Field Construction [Battalion] the northern tip of Kurland, and the 83rd ID the coast on Riga Bay. Corps Group Lieutenant General von Mellenthin (previously Corps Group Kleffel) stood with the 205th, 227th ID, and 281st Security Division east and southeast of Tuckum. The VI SS Corps was deployed in the Dzukste-Doblen area with the 290th ID, 19th SS Division, and 389th ID.

Army Detachment General of Infantry Grasser occupied the main combat line between Doblen and the Windau. The front ran from Lake Zeres in the north, directly west of Bene, east from Autz, to Vieksniai on the Windau and bowed here toward Moscheiken. The L Army Corps held the left with the 24th, 122nd, 121st, and 329th ID, while the XXXVIII Army Corps held the right sector with the 81st ID, 21st Luftwaffe Field Division, 201st Security Division, and the 32nd and 225th ID. The 93rd and 215th ID were removed and were in the interior marching to the southwest.

The front from the Windau to the coast was the operational area of the 18th Army (General of Infantry Boege). The II Army Corps, with the 12th Panzer Division, 132nd, 263rd, and 31st ID, fought in the area between Moscheiken and Vainode. The X Army Corps was deployed near Vainode with the 563rd and 30th ID, as well as the 4th Panzer Division. The III SS Panzer Corps fought south and southwest of Preekuln with the "Nordland"

and "Nederlande" Divisions. The I Army Corps secured the area south of Libau with the 87th and 126th ID.

Here, on the coast, was the most threatened cornerstone of the entire front. If the Soviets were able to break through and occupy Libau, then the army group was lost. Libau, the city of 50,000, was the junction of all of the Kurland defensive lines. The harbor was an emporium for the Army, Luftwaffe, and civil administration. Each ship that arrived from the homeland with men and equipment strengthened the friendly front.

The 18th Army was able to master its mission. The army launched a limited attack to improve the main combat line on 10/24 in the Vainode sector. The X Army Corps (General of Infantry Foertsch) advanced on a 10 kilometer wide strip against the enemy positions with the 31st, 563rd ID, and 14th Panzer Division.

The first day they gained about 3 kilometers of ground, took 200 prisoners, and destroyed 38 guns. The divisions chewed their way through the Soviet trenches and fought their way to the firing positions — and bogged down under strong defensive fire on 10/26!

The success of this operation led to the bitter recognition that the Soviet front had been reinforced by additional troop formations. It was known that the 1st Baltic Front was preparing for a new offensive.

The objective was clear!

A surprise air attack had pointed it out. On the afternoon of 10/22, strong Soviet combat air formations attacked Libau. Blocks of houses burst into flames. The weapons bureau was included among them. The most damage was suffered by the harbor area. Bombs tore through the torpedo boat "T-23", the steamer "Diedenhofen" (6,621 tons), a tug boat, and two naval ferries. The flames were still rising into the evening sky when the second bombing attack occurred.

The 2nd Battle of Kurland began five days later.

2000 guns of all calibers conducted a 1.5 hour barrage fire on the positions of the 18th Army and Army Detachment Grasser at 0600 hours on 10/27. 60 Soviet divisions attacked. The front between the coast and the Windau, between Autz and Doblen, burst into flames that morning!

The 5th Guards Tank Army (Marshal Rotmistrov) committed 400 combat vehicles between Skuodas and Vainode. The thin German lines could

not offer these masses of forces any resistance. The first penetration occurred. Immediately tanks were shoved into the gaps and rolled toward the
trenches of the III SS Panzer Corps and X Army Corps.

"The small bunkers rocked like boats on the sea. Wood splintered,
entire tree-tops were torn off and slammed down on top of the foxholes
and trenches. The positions could no longer be recognized in the dense
smoke of the battle. No one knew, where the Russians attacked first,
where they had already penetrated and which of the soldiers from the
infantry companies still lived. Gradually they could tell from reports
that they had broken through at many locations throughout the front. ...
Two hours after the start of the barrage fire a radio message came
in from the 2/215 Fusilier Battalion: 'The Russians are attacking Hill
94.1 with three tanks. The company has suffered heavy losses. Lieutenant Schmid is dead.' A half hour later: 'The Russians have broken
through near 94.1!' Another half hour later: 'The main combat line is
restored by a counterattack!
After a fierce fire fight, the 1/215 Fusilier Battalion sent a radio
message: 'The enemy attacked on a wide front. We are holding!' Shortly
after that another radio message: 'The enemy is attacking with 20 tanks
...' Here, the radio message was interrupted. It was the last message
from this company. ..."[2]

Local, limited counterattacks brought passing success, but the enemy
was stronger. His III Guards and XIX Tank Corps tore through the main
combat line of the 30th ID (Colonel Barth) and pushed the infantrymen
back to the forested hills of Mikeli. A breakthrough was not achieved. Pouring rain turned the terrain into a porridge of sand and clay. Then the "T-34"
and "Stalin" tanks got stuck.
The second attack point on this day lay near Autz. The 10th Guards
Army (Lieutenant General Korotkov) attacked here. The 21st Luftwaffe
Field Division (Major General Henze) could not resist this attack and broke
apart. Elements defended themselves in the city of Autz, which was encircled by the enemy. The army group commander immediately set the

12th Panzer Division and combat groups of the 389th ID in march to this threatened position.

The battle continued with extreme ferocity on 10/28. During the night, the Soviets shoved new tank forces into the front. These were to decisively tear through the German main combat line on the following day. The battle centered around individual farms, strong points, and intersections. Infantrymen, engineers, and communicators advanced against the tanks with bazookas and magnetic anti-tank hollow charges after they lost the anti-tank guns.

The men of the 6th Infantry Regiment (Colonel Hoffmeister) of the 30th ID destroyed 21 combat vehicles in close combat. Four "Tiger" tanks of the 510th Panzer Battalion (Senior Lieutenant Gerlach) conducted a six hour battle against enemy combat vehicles on the Auderi-Asite-Bruvelini road. 14 "Stalin" and "T-34" tanks were destroyed.

Just as here, the front exploded between Autz and Skuodas for the entire day and night.

10/29 was a day of fierce combat like no other before. Enemy guns and mortars initiated the attack. Strong formations of the air force supported the ground troops. 1,817 aircraft with the red stars flew between Libau and Autz into the interior, bombing railroad stations, roads, and troop columns. The few fighters of the 54th Fighter Group attacked the Russian squadrons. On 10/27 they shot down 57 aircraft. Major Rudorffer, commander of the 3/54 Fighter Group, alone shot down eleven bombers on 10/29 and raised his total air victories to 206.

The fiercest combat took place in the area of the 18th Army near Preekuln and north of Skuodas. The 30th, 31st ID, SS "Nordland" Division, and 14th Panzer Division stood in the center of the battle. The divisions lost 1,440 men in two days. The few tanks of the 14th Panzer Division (Colonel Munzel) had to be committed as the last reserve. The combat vehicles of the 36th Panzer Regiment (Major Molinari) held off the "Stalin" tanks between Jagmani and Bruvelini. An air defense battery near Dinzdurbe fired until the last gun fell. This battle allowed the main first aid station to be rescued. The 4th Panzer Division (Major General Betzel) stopped an attack on the Letila Hills and destroyed 73 enemy tanks.

Army Detachment Glasser, which was taken over by General of Cavalry Kleffel on 10/29, defended just as desperately as the 18th Army. The main effort lay on either side of Autz, which was lost on this day. Contact between the divisions was broken. The regiments were separated from each other, and companies were separated from their battalions. The desperate attempts to re-establish contact during the night met with no success.

The ferocity of the combat is documented by the number of destroyed tanks. During the time period from 10/1 to 10/31, the 18th Army destroyed 681, the 16th Army 246, and Army Detachment Kleffel 216 combat vehicles!

On 11/1, the Soviets took a short breather. They resumed their attack in the afternoon against the 18th Army and Army Detachment Kleffel. The XXXVIII Army Corps (General of Artillery Herzog) repulsed fierce attacks between Lakes Lielauce and Zebres. The 83rd, 329th ID, and 21st Luftwaffe Field Division withdrew slowly to the "Brunhilde Positions" between the lakes. There, the corps stopped the enemy offensive.

The battle near Preekuln was similarly fierce. The X Army Corps (General of Infantry Foertsch) held off the 5th Guards Tank Army with the 4th, 14th Panzer Divisions, 30th, 31st, 263rd, adn 563rd ID, and the 60th Air Defense Regiment. The OKW reported:

"... In the area southeast of Libau, the aspired Soviet breakthrough was frustrated by our troops, 62 tanks were destroyed."

It was a wonder: the Soviets gave up! Silence lay over the trenches, which were sinking in the rain and mud. Feverishly they worked on reinforcing the main combat line, new shelters were built, munitions stores were refilled, 10% of all officers and men were removed from the staffs and sent to the front.

The X Army Corps, which stood on the main effort of the enemy offensive from 10/27 to 11/2, lost 4,012 men during this period, and that was 50% of its combat strength! The flow of wounded to the main first aid stations of the army group were indicative of the severity of the battle:

27/10 = 776 wounded,	31/10 = 883 wounded,
28/10 = 480 wounded,	1/11 = 662 wounded,
29/10 = 560 wounded,	2/11 = 1,017 wounded,
30/10 = 450 wounded,	3/11 = 566 wounded.

The total losses from 10/1 to 11/7 came to 44,000 officers and men, of which 19,000 were registered after 1/11. The army group was allotted supplies from the homeland. However, between 10/1 and 11/7 only 28,000 personnel replacements arrived! A heavy loss for Kurland was the sinking of the steamer "Schiffbeck" before Libau, with 12 light field howitzers, 3 heavy field howitzers, one 15 cm canon, 6 heavy infantry guns, 17 2 cm air defense guns, and 1,800 machine pistols on board.

The army group found the time to regroup. The staff and army troops of Army Detachment Kleffel loaded up in Libau and Windau for shipment to Danzig and Gotenhafen. The staff was further transferred to Holland and formed the XXX Army Corps. Major General Walter, the former 182nd Field Commandant, was charged with the command off all convoys and other formations arriving in Danzig. Corps Group Lieutenant General von Mellenthin was re-designated the XVI Army Corps. The 207th and 285th Security Divisions were disbanded. Their regiments were sent to the front lines. The remnants of the 23rd ID coming from Sworbe were subordinated to the 218th ID, which then took over the protection of the coast in northern Kurland. The 21st Luftwaffe Field Division no longer existed, since only the staff remained. The three panzer divisions — the 4th, 12th, and 14th Panzer Divisions — left the main combat line. They formed the mobile reserve of the army group. Libau was fortified. Stocks were ordered for 40,000 men for three months. The army group transport officer, Lieutenant Colonel Fester, had the responsibility here. Lieutenant General Baron Digeon von Monteton was named fortress commandant. The rear area was organized for defense. The supply lines and lines of communication were improved. Engineer forces constructed a rail line between Libau and Windau, which became operational on 11/15.

The Soviets also made good use of the combat pause. On 11/19, they completed their regrouping. On this day at 1030 hours, fierce barrage fire suppressed the positions of the 18th Army between Engelspusi and the

Windau. This was the exact seam between the two armies (the operations area of the 16th Army had been extended prior to this, after the staff of Army Detachment Kleffel departed).

The fire of guns, "Stalin Organs", and the hail of bombs rained down on the trenches of the 31st, 32nd, 121st, and 263rd ID. An hour later, the Soviet divisions attacked. The attack was repulsed. However, between Lake Sepeni, Dzelgaleskrogs, and Engelspusi yawned a gap!

Combat groups counterattacked. Bloodied and exhausted, the German soldiers worked their way through icy water and swampy marshes. For hundreds of such counterattacks, the relation of one will have to suffice: Hill 107.5 was lost on Lake Sepeni. They had to take it during the following night. Batteries of the 30th Artillery Regiment (30th ID) fired to create an assault lane. While the last shells were still falling, the combat group of Captain Stein — an engineer platoon and group of officer cadets, which were experiencing their first engagement — shoved into the forest. The men were only equipped with machine pistols, and they kept an eye on each other so that they would not lose anybody in one of the numerous water-filled trenches. Then they assaulted the Hill!

The Soviets were stubborn. If they did not achieve a breakthrough here, then they would try some place else. The 4th Shock Army (Lieutenant General Malyshev) assaulted the Venta. The enemy utilized the inclement weather. They penetrated into the positions of the 83rd, 132nd, and 225th ID on the left flank of the army.

The army group commander tasked the Senior Artillery Commander, Lieutenant General Thomaschki, with Colonel Reinhardt as the Chief of Staff, to take command in the threatened area. However, what was the use of bravery, when, on 11/21 alone, 35,000 shells battered the main combat line of the II Army Corps? The Soviets penetrated the Venta on a 5 kilometer wide front and achieved a depth of 2 kilometers!

Enemy fire increased even more on the next day. Now the 6th Guards (General Chistyakov) and 5th Guards Tank Armies (Marshal Rotmistrov) attacked between Preekuln and the Windau. At the same time, 15 rifle divisions assaulted against the XXXVIII German Army Corps. This enemy group had Frauenburg as its objective.

The 290th ID had to face the fiercest combat in its history. The infantrymen of the 215th ID and the 5th Armored Infantry Regiment (12th Panzer Division) raged around the Kalvas Hills all day long. The battalions of the 24th ID and 12th Panzer Division withdrew into the forests on Lakes Zebres and Lielauce. The 205th ID repulsed six enemy divisions south of Frauenburg!

The situation was critical. The army group had no reserves left! Every clerk and radioman, every medic and driver had to take up rifles and bazookas in the front lines. No one knew where they would end up. The situation changed by the hour. First the Russians would take a hill, then the Germans would retake it, then finally the enemy again.

Losses on both sides were enormous. The main first aid stations of the XXXVIII and L Army Corps reported from 11/22 to 11/24 the arrival of 1,413 men! The X Army Corps consisted of no more than a combat group. The armored personnel carrier battalion of the 14th Panzer Division totaled 40 men. The battalions of the 32nd ID gave the following daily report for 11/28: 1/4 Infantry Regiment = 80; 2/4 Infantry Regiment = 40; 1/94 Infantry Regiment = 90; 1/96 Infantry Regiment = 105 men; and the 2/94 Infantry Regiment and 2/96 Infantry Regiment had already been dissolved!

Heavy rain fell on the land during the last few days, and it prevented further fighting. The terrain in and around the main combat line was a swamp. Even the Soviets had to give in! The Russians even gave up some territory and withdrew between Vainode and Pikeliai. The enemy gave up on the 2nd Battle of Kurland!

The army group reported its losses from 11/1 to 11/30: 33,181 officers, non-commissioned officers, and men were killed, wounded, or missing. Weapons losses included: 1,226 pistols, 733 machine pistols, 5,760 carbines, 1,181 machine-guns, 96 light and 27 heavy mortars, 92 anti-tank guns, 18 infantry guns, 19 air defense guns, and 34 light and 14 heavy field howitzers.

Enemy losses — as far as the German side was able to establish — ran 4,410 counted dead, 12,550 estimated dead, 25,100 estimated wounded, and 961 prisoners, including 105 deserters. Additionally, reported as either destroyed or captured were: 23 guns, 166 tanks, 82 anti-tank guns, 303 machine-guns, and 8 mortars. The total losses of enemy combat vehicles in the sector of Army Group North since 6/22/1944 was 4,722.

The troops were exhausted. The main combat line consisted mostly of holes in the ground filled with melted snow water. In the days of crises, the supplies did not make it forward. There were many dysentery patients during these weeks. As soon as there was a pause on the front, the soldiers attacked with spades and shovels. The slogan of the army group was"

"Trenches instead of Graves!"

The few days and weeks the Soviets did not conduct a major attack were utilized to remove, shift, transport to the homeland, and deploy new replacements. At the end of November, "Operation Autoklau" was conducted. All vehicles not needed by the front troops were assembled and shipped to the homeland. Thus, on 11/25, four steamers left Libau for Danzig with 91 heavy trucks, 70 light trucks, and 39 motorcycles.

The following groups of personnel left the army group area between 9/24 to 11/25: 69,409 soldiers, 68,562 wounded, 7,558 Latvian recruits, 3,108 Latvian and Estonian soldiers, 5,809 OT men, 75,319 evacuated Baltics, and 1,791 evacuated Russians. At the same time, 11,626 horses, 6,432 vehicles, and 290 guns were transported to the Reich.

Luftflotte 1 (commander: General of Aviation Pflugbeil), in spite of their overwhelming inferiority, supported the combat of the two armies during the two battles of Kurland as well as their units were able to. From 7/25 to 9/23, the Luftflotte had made available to the Army an additional 5,643 officers and men. Those ground commands no longer needed were sent to Germany in October. All that remained at the airfields in Kurland were the air crews and the necessary technical personnel.

The Luftflotte had no more bombers left. Only the 54th Fighter Group and several reconnaissance squadrons were left in the army group area. In November, the 54th Fighter Group had the 1st Squadron stationed in Tuckum, and later in Cirava. The 2nd and 3rd Squadrons were deployed near Libau.

The Soviet Air Force had unlimited superiority in the air. Day and night, their bomber squadrons flew the transport routes and bombed railroad stations, roads, and harbors. The few friendly fighters were on constant battle readiness.

On 12/14, 60 enemy aircraft attacked the city and harbor of Libau in two waves. The first wave caused considerable damage between 1100 and 1200 hours. Seven ships were sunk! The second attack was flown between 1650 and 1800 hours. This time four ships were damaged. The German "FW-190's" immediately took off. On this day, they shot down 44 aircraft! The Soviets repeated their attack on Libau on 12/15. This time 200 aircraft burst forth and dropped bombs on the railroad station area and on the Libau and Grobin airfields. The 54th Fighter Group (Lieutenant Colonel Hrabak) shot down 56 enemy aircraft. Eleven friendly aircraft were lost on the airfields to the bombings.

The decimated batteries of the 6th Air Defense Division were also able to shoot down 110 Soviet aircraft from 10/29 to 11/7. The Luftflotte had made several batteries available to the Army. The 1/2 Air Defense Regiment was attached to the 18th Army, and the 1/51 Air Defense Regiment to the 16th Army. The 219th Air Defense Battalion was responsible for the air defense over Windau.

December had arrived. The weather worsened. Frost arrived mid month. The mud froze into stone hard ground. Roads were again passable. Combat activity revived throughout. Assault troops of the 3rd Guards and 4th Shock Armies conducted reconnaissance in force near Schrunden. German artillery and the counterattacks of the infantry repulsed the first foreboding of a new offensive.

On 12/1, the German forces in Kurland numbered:

	Army	SS & Police	Luftwaffe	Navy	Total
16th Army	126,011	19,731	7,680	4	153,426
18th Army	302,179	18,716	25,039	6,186	352,120
Totals	428,190	38,447	32,719	6,190	505,546

The Soviets took a longer time before they completed the preparations for the 3rd Battle of Kurland. On 12/21 at 0720 hours they let loose a fire hurricane on a 35 kilometer front. 170,000 shells of all calibers fell onto the positions of the I and XXXVIII Army Corps. The trenches and bunkers of the 205th, 215th, 225th, and 563rd ID were plowed up on this morning. Then — at 0830 hours — the 3rd Shock (General Kasakov), 4th Shock (Lieutenant General Malyshev), 10th Guards (Lieutenant General Korotkov), and 42nd Armies (Lieutenant General Sviridov) attacked. The objective was to reach Frauenburg and Libau.

Already one half hour after the start of the attack, contact with the 225th ID was lost. At the same time, the 329th ID had to defend against an overwhelming tank attack. The 205th ID collapsed under the blows of enemy combat vehicles and infantry near Frauenburg.

Hastily, the army group transferred the 12th Panzer Division and the 227th ID toward Frauenburg into the threatened area. The counterattack was ineffective, even though the men of the 5th and 25th Armored Infantry Regiments fought so bravely. The enemy was stronger!

The Soviet main effort was clearly in the Pampali area, south of Frauenburg. From here, they wanted to attack to the northwest, capture the Frauenburg-Libau rail line and, therefore, separate the two German armies. Tanks with the red stars advanced to a depth of 4 kilometers. They came to their first halt before the guns of the 912th Assault Gun Brigade (Captain Brandner). The 1st Battery (Senior Lieutenant Schubert) destroyed 37 "T-34" and "Stalin" tanks in the next few days. The 132nd ID (Lieutenant General Wagner) could not hold and withdrew before the bulk of the advancing tanks. The 438th Infantry Regiment (Colonel Sierts) was pushed back to Pampali.

"...The completion of the encirclement occurred in the afternoon hours. The number of dead and wounded constantly rose. Ammunition, bandages and rations declined. Contact with the regiment and the division was no longer possible over radio. The order to halt was repeatedly transmitted. The ring tightened. Defenses were formed around the command post. The defense was suspended at 2400 hours and an attempt to withdraw the division was announced, without ammunition, no heavy weapons, and, on top of everything, a large number of wounded. We received no reply. Radio communications were lost. We waited until 0300 hours. Finally, we decided to breakout before dawn.

The wounded were distributed among the columns. Several sleds were organized, the rest went in tents. We were ready. ..."[3]

The Soviets were penetrating near the I and XXXVIII Army Corps. The 11th ID was shoved between the 132nd and 225th ID, both of which had suffered heavy losses. The 12th Panzer Division was able to close the gap between the 215th and 290th ID during the night. There were still no breakthroughs anywhere. Throughout, the German main combat line was stretched to the maximum.

The counterattacks of the two armies on the next day did not succeed. Enemy dive bombers, tanks, and artillery would not allow the German soldiers to get out of their own trenches. On the first day of the battle, 2,491 aircraft of the Red Air Force were over the lines of the army group. 42 were shot down. On the next day, 1,800 combat aircraft flew to attack the positions in Kurland, and of these 39 were lost. 12/23 showed an increase in Soviet air activity. This time 2,415 aircraft flew!

As before, the enemy main effort lay in the area south of Frauenburg. The 4th Shock Army attacked against the thin lines of the 18th Army main combat line on both sides of Pampili with the 119th, 360th, 357th, 378th, 145th, 239th, 306th, 164th, and 158th Rifle Divisions.

The 16th Army defended itself in the Zvardes area against the 10th Guards Army, with the 56th, 65th, 53rd, 85th, 30th, 29th, 119th, and 7th Guards Divisions and against the 42nd Army, which had committed the 2nd, 268th, 256th, and 48th Rifle Divisions.

The superiority was enormous. German infantrymen, engineers, artillerymen, tank drivers, radiomen, and medics defended. Out of the many different commitments we will single out the following: the Baden-Wuerttemberger 205th ID (Lieutenant General von Mellenthin) defended against an attack by three enemy divisions. The North German 290th ID (Major General Baurmeister) beat back 52 enemy advances. The 11th East Prussian ID (Major General Feyerabend) smashed 11 tank attacks in front of its main combat line.

Finally, during the night of 12/23, the German front re-stabilized!

Then the Soviets began to increase the strength of their offensive. The 22nd Army (Lieutenant General Yushkevitz) attacked the VI SS Corps (SS

Obergruppenfuehrer Frueger) north of Doblen. here, the enemy was able to push back the German front to a depth of 3 kilometers. The 19th SS Division — the Latvian volunteers — defended bitterly. The attack was stopped directly east of Dzukste.

The next day was the 24th of December.

However, neither friend nor foe had the time to look at the calendar. Soviet artillery boomed, Russian tanks moved, German machine-guns spattered, the wounded moaned, and orders were written — the battle continued.

"At approximately 1700 hours, the Russian fire suddenly stopped. The noises of combat grew silent. The unearthly quiet continued, but it did not exclude the anticipation of another attack. However, the Christmas spirit covered the entire sector. Near Pinkas, Pastor Sauerbeck assembled a small audience. The division commander visited his regiments in their positions. Through the quiet of the starry clear night rang "Silent Night, Holy Night" as the fusilier battalion sang the song in the forward line. An entire company, which was quite small due to losses, assembled in a small bunker, in order to light an advent candle for their wounded commander, while another company decorated a Christmas tree near the command post. This is how the soldiers spent their 6th Christmas, the last and most moving."[4]

Christmas Eve 1944 brought peace — the war caught its breath for a few hours.

The Soviet guns roared again on 12/25.

This time, the main effort of the new offensive was Dzukste south of Tuckum. While the 227th ID (Major General Wengler), 81st ID (Major General von Bentivengi), 12th Luftwaffe Field Division (Major General Weber), and the Latvian SS Formation (Major General Henze) opposed the attacking Soviets with all of their strength, an attack was launched on another sector of the front!

The 6th Guards Army (General Chistyakov) attacked Libau from the south. The II Army Corps (General of Infantry Hasse) stood here with the 126th ID (Lieutenant General Fischer), 31st ID (Major General von

Stolzmann), and 14th Panzer Division (Lieutenant General Unrein). The three defending divisions did not give up one foot of ground. They only allowed the 6th Guards Army to come into the initial trenches, and no further! The front before Libau stood firm!

The situation in the Dzukste area developed more unpleasantly. Here, after a barrage fire by 60 batteries, the Soviet V and XIX Tank Corps, with the 101st and 202nd Tank Brigades, overran the 19th SS Division. The 16th Army commander immediately dispatched all elements of the front attack reserve to alleviate the critical situation. The 272nd Infantry Regiment (93rd ID), 366th Infantry Regiment (227th ID), and 24th Luftwaffe Light Infantry Regiment (12th Luftwaffe Field Division) prevented the collapse of the front before Dzukste on the first day of Christmas! During the evening, the first elements of the 4th Panzer Division arrived and reinforced Machine-gun Battalion "Stettin" in Libau that morning.

The battle continued on the next day. The Soviets searched for a weak spot on the front. Shells rooted up the earth, tanks rolled on, flame throwers smoked out shelters, and bombers shredded roads. The battle see-sawed. The 22nd Soviet Guards Division had a special combat mission on this day. They attacked the 205th ID. The first wave of the attacking infantrymen wore German uniforms! Therefore, the outposts were deceived. The anti-tankers were, however, at their posts. They destroyed 18 of the following combat vehicles.

On this day, the army group destroyed a total of 111 enemy tanks!

The battle for Dzukste was fought on 12/27 with the same ferocity as it was on the previous day. The Soviets wanted to achieve a success at any cost, especially after they were frustrated before Frauenburg and Libau. This time they did not take any breaks. Tank after tank was thrown into the battle. Losses rose. The main combat line tore at several locations. The enemy broke through to a depth of 2 kilometers. Throughout the battlefield, strong points held and fought to their last bullet. The division command posts of the 19th SS Division (SS Brigadefuehrer Streckenbach) and the 227th ID (Major General Wengler) were bitterly defended. The 24th Luftwaffe Light Infantry Regiment under its excellent commander, Colonel Kretzschmar, stood like a rock in the surf. The Luftwaffe soldiers gave no ground without exacting a price. Colonel Kretzschmar died a soldier's death with his weapon in his hand.

The battle died down in the evening.

The Soviets ceased their breakthrough attempts.

The 3rd Battle of Kurland was over!

On the last day of the year, the OKW reported the results:

> "Army Group Kurland has destroyed 513 tanks, 79 guns and 267 machine-guns of the Red Army and shot down 145 aircraft!"

The losses for this last battle of the year in the 16th Army totaled 15,237 dead, wounded, and missing. The 18th Army lost 11,907 officers and men.

In general, the winter was mild, with less snow fall. The exhausted troops again began to deepen and improve their positions. The soldiers were satisfied with the enemy and the weather, but not with the situation as a whole. They knew that contact with the homeland and, therefore, their salvation was by sea. The little news that the men of the 16th and 18th Armies and Luftflotte 1 received from Germany was becoming sparser by the week. Only the Wehrmacht reports, reports from the army group transmitter in Libau, front newspapers, and reports from the NSFO [National Socialist Guidance Officer] provided information about the bombings at home and the events in the world at large.

"Fortress Kurland" (Officially, this designation was never applied!) was on its own at the beginning of the new year, 1945.

The army group was ordered to hold. During the situation briefings, Hitler repeatedly said: "The army group stays where it is. I am expecting a change in the situation soon, then we will deal with Kurland..."

General Guderian, Chief of the General Staff of the OKH, was powerless to oppose this "Führer Directive", although he continued to request transporting the army group back to the Reich. He was able to move some elements back to the homeland. At the end of 1944, the 83rd ID was loaded in Libau. In January followed the 4th Panzer Division, 32nd, 227th, 389th, 15th Latvian SS Divisions, and the III SS Panzer Corps.

General Schoerner, commander of Army Group North, received the Swords and Diamonds to the Oak Leaves of the Knight's Cross for the combat of his troops at the beginning of January. Several days later he left Kurland with his Chief of Staff, Major General von Natzmer. He took command of Army Group Center. General Dr. Rendulic, the former commander of the 20th Mountain Army in Norway, was the new commander of Army Group North. Major General Foertsch, the former Chief of Staff of the 18th Army, was now Chief of Staff of the army group.

On 1/25/1945, the army group was designated "Army Group Kurland."

The formations of the 2nd and 4th Armies, encircled in East Prussia, were formed into Army Group North under the command of General Reinhardt (the history of these two armies is covered considerably in the literature and, therefore, will not be referenced in this book. The Battle for East Prussia and the Danzig-Gotenhafen area took place in the former operations area of Army Group Center and must be looked at in that context).

The "Kurland" sleeve stripe was established as an award for soldiers between Libau and Tuckum. This band was domestically woven in gold. Latvian women sewed many hours at home to produce the last German war decoration. The 3.8 cm band bore, in silver-gray material, the Grand Master Coat of Arms of the Knights' Order and the elk's head from the coat of arms of the city of Mitau. In between is the word KURLAND.

The army group's strength report for January 1945 read:

Army	357,000 men
Luftwaffe	20,500 men
SS & Police	12,000 men
Civilians	10,000 men
Total	399,500 men.

The Army had 10,050 vehicles and the Luftwaffe 2,265. There were 8,778 horses on hand. Additionally, there were about 10,000 prisoners of war in the custody of the army group.

The front of the army group ran from the coast, 20 kilometers south of Libau, 10 kilometers to the east, then turned sharply to the northeast directly south of Durben and Schrunden into the Frauenburg hills, and from there the main combat line returned to the northeast, passed directly east of Tuckum, and on to Klapkalnice on the Gulf of Riga.

Chapter 8: The Surrender

The Soviet forces had also undergone changes in the beginning of January. By mid January, there remained in the three large sectors of the Kurland front, under the command of Marshal Govorov:

Libau area:	51st Army with 11 divisions,
	6th Guards Army with 10 divisions,
	4th Shock Army with 7 divisions,
	III Guards Mech Corps with 18 brigades.
Pampali area:	42nd Army with 7 divisions,
	10th Guards Army with 12 divisions,
	XIV Guards Rifle Corps with 3 divisions,
	XIX Tank Corps with 2 brigades.
Tuckum area:	22nd Army with 5 divisions,
	1st Shock Army with 5 divisions,
	67th Army with 5 divisions,
	V Tank Corps with 2 brigades.

The re-organization of the enemy forces was completed in the second half of January. Then the 4th Battle of Kurland began.

A short but heavy fire strike by Soviet artillery on the morning of 1/24 initiated the new offensive.

Eleven rifle divisions crashed against the German front on both sides of Preekuln. As before, the target remained Libau and, additionally, the separation of the two armies on the Schrunden-Frauenburg road. The weight of the first attack hit the 30th ID (Major General Barth) and the SS "Nordland" Division (SS Brigadefuehrer Ziegler). The enemy penetrated into the main combat line in order to conduct bitter hand to hand combat.

The battle wavered for three long days, and neither friend nor foe would give any quarter. The defenders withdrew to the second defensive belt. There the German reserve attacked. At the very beginning of the offensive, the army group had alerted the 14th Panzer Division and set it in march.

At midday, the regiments left their assigned assembly areas. It was a variegated and strange assembly of vehicles that rolled through the forest trails and corduroy roads to the main highway: Volkswagon Jeeps, amphibious cars, several motorcycles with sidecars; prime movers and "Mules", in addition to German Opels, Fords, Henschels, and Kruppwagons; French Peugeots, Berliets, and Renaults; and English and American Morris, Badford, MG, and Studebaker vehicles that were captured. All were loaded to capacity with weapons, ammunition, and equipment. Everything that was needed to construct positions and bunkers was taken: construction equipment, crowbars, shovels, picks, saws, axes, stoves..."On top of everything — where there was still some room between the cargo and the roof of the vehicles — rode the armored infantrymen..."[5]

The men of the Saxon 14th Panzer Division, supported by "Tigers" from the 510th Panzer Battalion (Major Gilbert), counterattacked into the Kaleti and Purmsati forests south of Preekuln on 1/25. They restored the old main combat line by that evening. 63 Russian tanks lay as wrecks along the way!

Here, the battle came to a standstill. The Soviets again re-grouped. They prepared the second part of their offensive with intensive mortar fire. The defenders were so weakened from losses that they lost the main combat line a second time. Enemy tanks drove to the high ground on the Vartaya and established two bridgeheads. At the same time, combat vehicles and infantrymen attacked north of Preekuln. Here the attackers were stopped by the 121st (Major General Rank) and 126th ID (Colonel Haehling).

The breakthrough to Libau did not result from these initial successes!

Again the Soviets tried their luck at Frauenburg. They wanted to utilize the rail line to Libau as the guide for their offensive. Nine rifle divisions raged against the two Baden-Wuerttemberger divisions, as well as the 205th (Lieutenant General von Mellenthin) and 215th ID (Lieutenant General Frankewitz) — in vain! The 205th ID destroyed 117 combat vehicles within five days! The 225th (Lieutenant General Risse) and 122nd ID (Lieutenant General Fangohr) fought outstandingly. The Upper Silesians of the 81st ID (Lieutenant General von Bentivengi) and elements of the 12th Panzer Division (Lieutenant General Baron von Bodenhausen) removed a penetration south of Tuckum.

At the end of January, the 4th Battle of Kurland bogged down in snow and the first mud.

Chapter 8: The Surrender

The Soviets transitioned to the defense! Between 1/24 and 2/3, they lost approximately 40,000 men, 541 tanks, and 178 aircraft.

Army Group Kurland had achieved another marked success. Nevertheless, the losses were so high that it was just a question of time as to how long they could hold out. It was almost certain that the two armies could no longer withstand the major enemy offensives. The loss of men and equipment could not be made up for by the courageous efforts of the transport ships and the 9th Naval Security Division. In the time period from 2/1 to 2/13, only 13,000 tons of supplies made it to Kurland by sea. This was not enough!

General von Vietinghoff took command of the army group on 1/29. At the very beginning, he outlined a new study, which included the transport of the army group by sea. During the next few days, Colonel Hoefer from the army group proposed the study "Laura", which purported:

> "By adhering to the former mission, there is a great danger of the gradual sapping of the army group, so that the Russians will gain time ... to be able to breakthrough the thin friendly security lines. ... The breakout to the south becomes meaningless after the surrender of Memel and the withdrawal of the front in East Prussia. It comes down to the question of reducing the bridgehead by transporting as many divisions with their full equipment load as possible.
>
> ...The withdrawal to a large bridgehead at Libau will free up most of the forces. ...and to a smaller bridgehead at Windau ... Going to Libau: the 18th Army and the three right hand corps of the 16th Army; to Windau: XVI Army Corps and the coastal protection."

The study went on to address the transport plan, according to which the army group could be loaded with all vehicles within 15 days on daily ship runs of three transports and nine freighters.

This plan was sent to Berlin and formed the basis of discussions on 2/15 and 2/17, and in General Guderian's opinion the withdrawal of the army group was most urgent. Grand Admiral Doenitz, commander of the Navy, agreed with this proposal. He said:

"The plan for the withdrawal has been worked out. Without considering the commitment of available ships, curbing all remaining requirements in the shipping area and strong Luftwaffe support, I figure it would take four weeks to withdraw the men and necessary equipment. ...The loading capacity at Windau and Libau is sufficient."

Hitler stared wordlessly at the Grand Admiral, then shifted his gaze to General Guderian:

"The withdrawal of the troops from Kurland is out of the question!"

The enemy in Kurland was becoming stronger by the day. His combat air squadrons controlled the entire air space. The squadrons repeatedly flew at the harbors of Libau, Windau, and the arriving supply trains. A major attack on Libau in February collapsed in the fire of the batteries of the 6th Air Defense Division (Lieutenant General Anton). 40 aircraft fell in flames before reaching their target. Then there were the "FW-190's" of the 1/54 Fighter Group (Major Eisenach). The group of "Green Hearted Squadrons" was the only air formation in Kurland! The fighters dived as usual onto the Soviets and shot down 60 aircraft. Senior Lieutenant Kittel, commander of the 2nd Company of the 54th Fighter Group — the most successful fighter pilot in the northern sector of the Eastern Front — achieved his 267th air victory! Then he was hit by a deadly bullet.

The air attack on Libau and Windau — over the harbors where 48 enemy aircraft dove in the past two days — foreboded an offensive. The army group had to adjust. Throughout, mobile reserves were separated, and they were placed in the 2nd and 3rd defensive belts. The main combat line was only occupied in a strong point-like manner.

New units — such as the Kurland Panzer Brigade, the Kurland Officer Cadet Regiment, and the Kurland Field Construction Division — were formed. They were to be utilized as motorized attack formations when the attack began.

It happened on 2/20!

Chapter 8: The Surrender

At 0700 hours in the morning, the Soviet guns between Dzukste and Preekuln roared. The 5th Battle of Kurland began.

The main effort was again in the south near Preekuln. From here lay the shortest route to Libau. 21 rifle divisions and several tank brigades assaulted under the fire cover of numerous batteries and mortars against the main combat line on both sides of Preekuln. The soldiers of the 12th Luftwaffe Field Division, as well as the 121st, 126th, 263rd, and 290th ID took the weight of the offensive.

The 126th ID (Major General Haehling) fought around Preekuln. The soldiers from the Rheinland and Westphalia were forced to give in by the overwhelming enemy. The 426th Infantry Regiment (Colonel Daubert) was jammed into a gravel pit and defended here for three full days. The 422nd and 424th Infantry Regiments were to hold Preekuln as a fortress. The enemy had long passed by the city. The remnants of the regiments were ordered to fight their way to the west during the night of 2/22.

The German front stabilized on the hills before Vartaya. This time the enemy could not get through. North of Preekuln the 11th ID (Major General Feyerabend), 14th Panzer Division (Lieutenant General Unrein), and the 912th Assault Gun Brigade (Major Bradner) inflicted heavy losses on him. The 121st ID (Major General Rank) gradually withdrew. The division had enormous losses. All of the battalion commanders had fallen. The soldiers from East Prussia did not give up. In this battle, they destroyed 250 tanks and vehicles!

The 18th Army commander shoved the 132nd (Colonel Demme) and 225th ID (Lieutenant General Risse) to the front on the Vartaya. The Soviets bogged down far from the river. They could only negotiate the steep bank near Krote. Therefore, they were exhausted! The 18th Army bemoaned the loss of 5,400 men, of which 41% were from the I Army Corps. As before, the Soviet troops were not allowed to break through to Libau!

On 3/1, the Red Army tried to change their luck near Frauenburg. The VI SS Corps (SS Obergruppenfuehrer Krueger) held the main combat line on both sides of the city. The 122nd ID (Lieutenant General Fangohr) was pushed back to Lake Lemzere during a day-long battle in biting frost. The 24th ID (Major General Schulz), 19th SS Division (SS Brigadefuehrer Streckenbach), and the Kurland Panzer Brigade (Colonel von Usedom) stopped the enemy attack in the thick forests near Lieblidiene and Upesmuiza, as well as on the Doblen-Frauenburg rail line. The 21st Luftwaffe Field Division (Major General Barth) bitterly defended the area around Dungaga.

In mid March, a surprising thaw occurred. Within a few hours, the land turned to mud. Tanks, guns, and trucks became hopelessly stuck. The Soviets broke off the battle! They had lost 70,000 soldiers, 608 tanks, 436 guns, and 178 aircraft. Their only success was the capture of the city of Dzukste.

Things were quiet for several days. The army group re-ordered its heavily battered formations. The two SS divisions "Nordland" and "Nederlande", and the 215th ID were transferred home. No new formations replaced them.

Naval ships and transport steamers continued to arrive at Libau and Windau. They brought ammunition, weapons, and rations. The war at sea was also getting harder. The ships not only had to defend against numerous air attacks, but Soviet submarines and motor torpedo boats were also active. The German U-Boats were no longer operational. By the beginning of 1945, 14 U-Boats were operating in the eastern Baltic Sea, but by the end of January there were only five: U-242, 370, 475, 676, and 745. The others returned to their bases to be fitted with snorkels. "U-475" was the last U-Boat to leave the Baltic Sea on 3/17.

During a situation briefing in the Führer Headquarters on 3/18, Grand Admiral Doenitz submitted the plans for the final withdrawal of the army group. He still had 28 ships with 110,729 tons available. These steamers could return 23,250 men, 4,520 horses, and 3,610 vehicles in 9 days. Hitler again refused.

Therefore, the fate of the army group was sealed!

General von Vietinghoff was transferred to Italy. General Rendulic returned to Kurland. He stayed only 24 hours. The OKH again ordered him to northern Norway. General of Infantry Hilpert, the former commander of the 16th Army, took command of the army group on 3/14. General of Infantry von Krosigk took his place as commander of the 16th Army, and he was killed on the next day during an air attack. General of Mountain Troops Volckamer von Kirchensittenbach became commander of the 16th Army.

Chapter 8: The Surrender

The Soviet leadership wanted to decisively eliminate Army Group Kurland. At the beginning of March they planned an offensive that was directed through Frauenburg directly to the west in the direction of Libau. The 10th Guards Army (Lieutenant General Korotkov) was committed with a full complement of rifle divisions and tank brigades. Strong air formations were prepared, which were to try to paralyze the lines of communications in the interior during the planned harassment attacks.

3/18 was a day of horror, fire, and death. Hundreds of batteries hurled their shells onto the positions between Dangas and Skutini. Even before the smoke settled on the mortally wounded earth, tanks and infantry advanced. The enemy artillery spared those positions on the German main combat line, through which the "T-34" and "Stalin" tanks were rolling.

The exhausted defenders found no more strength to hold on. The first penetrations occurred. The Soviets shoved new groups of tanks into the gaps and rolled over the trenches. The army group commander directed reserves here from all sectors of the wide front. These were the ever-active "fire fighters": the East Prussian 11th ID (Lieutenant General Feyerabend), the Pomeranian 12th Panzer Division (Lieutenant General Baron von Bodenhausen), and the Saxon 14th Panzer Division (Lieutenant General Unrein).

The motorized formations formed a defensive blocking position, which held for the time being. However, soon communications were lost throughout. Individual battalions and strong points were split apart. They fought all day and night in the forests on either side of the road to Frauenburg.

The Soviets had concentrated their main effort there — and, after the first day of battle, there lay 92 tanks burning and destroyed.

The 10th Guards Army did not give up! They repeated their breakthrough attempt during the following days. The XXXVIII Army Corps (General of Infantry Herzog) got into trouble in a battle south of Frauenburg. The battle disintegrated into individual combat. It was relentlessly fought in the forests, and it burned down farmhouses, intersections, and bunkers. The 44th Infantry Regiment (Lieutenant Colonel Laebe) of the 11th ID defended the small town of Bezzobiy like it was a fortress. The 386th Infantry Regiment (Colonel Reuter) of the 218th ID was encircled in Struteli.

They formed a breaker in the surging flood. The 12th Panzer Division held off a tank breakthrough near Mezalazi.

The bloody losses were equally high for friend and foe. The 10th Guards Army felt squeamish. Its commander stopped the troops south of Frauenburg on 3/23. The battle died out.

The battle in the north of the city raged on. Here, the enemy was able to cut the Doblen-Frauenburg rail line. The defenders withdrew to the "Burg Positions" on the Viesate. Elements of the 24th ID (Major General Schultz) entrenched themselves at the Josta railroad station for four days as the rear guard. Therefore, they prevented the collapse of the front.

Then, the Soviets also gave up here.

They left 533 prisoners in German hands and lost 263 tanks, 249 machine-guns, 185 guns, 29 mortars, and 27 aircraft.

The 6th battle of Kurland ended at the end of March.

On 4/1, the army group commander sent an estimation of the combat effectiveness of his divisions to the OKH. The report (Ia Nr. 46/45 gKdos Chefs) sheds light on the heavy commitment in the last six Kurland battles. The classification of the divisions was as follows:

Group 1 (very good): 11th ID - A particularly trustworthy division in times of crises with high morale. In the last battle, was constantly reliable. Combat experienced, efficient leadership.

Group 2 (good): 12th PD - Experienced, reliable PD with excellent spirited commanders; 24th ID - in the last battle showed steadfastness. Good secure leadership; 81st ID - In the crisis situations of the 5th and 6th Kurland battles was completely reliable. Solid and clear leadership; 121st ID - Reliable in crisis situations. Secure, agile leadership; 126th ID - The division again proved reliable. Combat morale has increased. Dependable, agile leadership; 205th ID - Reliable division ... firm, agile leadership; 225th ID - Steadfast, tenacious division of excellent spirit and bearing. Firm and decisive leadership, confident and stable; 263rd ID - Strong and formidable. Dependable, firm leadership; 329th ID - ...clear, secure and firm leadership.

Group 3 (sufficient): Here were classified the 30th, 122nd, 132nd, 218th, 290th ID, 19th SS Div, 14th PD.

Group 4 (insufficient): 563rd ID (The 563rd ID was battered in hard combat during the last battle and had partially lost its integrity. On its front was the first and only deserter reported, who willingly went over to the Soviets!)

In spite of all privations and the oppressive physical and mental molestations, there was only one loss of discipline in Kurland. The crew of Harbor Patrol Boat "31" mutinied on 3/16. The five sailors murdered their young commander and fled with the boat to Sweden.

General of Infantry Hilpert sent a similar briefing to the commander of Luftflotte 1 and the Latvian Naval Commandant. He asked them to give up units for ground combat. The losses of the army group could no longer be made up for by replacements from the homeland.

General of Infantry Hilpert wrote (Ia Nr. 49/45 gKdos Chefs):

"...The mission of Army Group Kurland has remained unchanged, that is, to fight with all available means and, therefore, weaken the Russian man-power and prevent the attack of further Russian forces into the Reich itself. ..."

A day later, an order arrived from the OKH concerning the combat leadership. It said:

"2) To make the 7th Battle of Kurland another defensive success, the army group must take considerable risk on non-threatened sectors of the front, in order to strengthen the areas in the main effort, especially in the area east of Libau. ..."

On 4/14, the army group radioed its plan and requirements to Berlin:

"1) In general: Meeting the coming battle in present positions. The army group decides to maintain the present front by tenacious defense and active combat leadership. Conditional to sufficient ammunition and fuel.

2) In specific:

a) The area northwest and northeast of Preekuln: Reinforcement of infantry defensive forces by committing the next arriving replacements here. Prepare for the commitment of the 14th Panzer Division, including the 510th Panzer Company and 126th ID. ...

b) Area southwest of Frauenburg: Hold one infantry regiment of 11th ID as army group reserve. Special support by artillery, air defense, assault guns. ... Create no special strong points, because of the shortage of infantrymen..."

The shortage was so enormous that the front could no longer be unified. At many locations, there were only double outposts at 100 meter intervals! The Soviets often infiltrated through these gaps and caused unrest in the interior.

In April, Luftflotte 1 organized another 17 battalions from its ranks in order to offer them to the ground battle. These totaled 257 officers, 6,735 non-commissioned officers and men, as well as 127 clerks. The battalions were predominantly committed to the protection of airfields and targets, while one battalion had taken over an engineer mission and was distributed over the entire area.

There would be no 7th Battle of Kurland!

The Soviets had withdrawn the majority of their troops. In the Kurland area, they left only: the 1st Shock Army between the Gulf of Riga and Tuckum, the 22nd Army west of Dzukste, the 42nd Army in front of Frauenburg, the 4th Shock Army on either side of the Windau, the 6th Guards Army between Vainode and Skuodas, and the 51st Army south of Libau.

These armies stood at "parade rest." They could wait. Kurland must fall like a ripe fruit into their hands. The decisive game was being played out in Germany!

On 5/1, Soviet loudspeakers roared out to the front. They broke the news that Hitler was dead! Two days later, new music droned through the ether, then the words rang out, "Berlin is ours!.

The war was over!

Grand Admiral Doenitz, the new Supreme Commander of the Wehrmacht, transmitted the following radio message to the headquarters of General (he was promoted to this rank on 5/1) Hilpert at the Pelci Palace on 5/3 at 1930 hours:

"The changing situation in the Reich requires the rapid removal of numerous troop units from out of the East and West Prussian areas, as well as Kurland. The combat leadership of the armies of east Prussia and Army Group Kurland have to adjust to these requirements.

The personnel of the withdrawing troop units are to be equipped with light infantry weapons. All other materials, including horses, are to be left behind and destroyed. Army Group Kurland receives the operational freedom to withdraw the main combat line into the assigned bridgeheads around the harbors of Libau and Windau."

The army group would not be able to conduct the withdrawal, because there were no ships available. Only the 16th Army was ordered to evacuate Tuckum on 5/6 and occupy a line in the rear. The 18th Army gave up their front salient as a precautionary measure. Elements of their formations withdrew to the Vartaya sector.

The army group awaited the transport ships.

They did not come! Against all agreements, the government of Sweden stopped the necessary coal shipments. The steamers were stuck in Mecklenburg and Schleswig-Holstein ports!

Then reports reached Kurland that German and British commanders concluded a truce. General Hilpert then issued an order of the day:

"...The war in the east continues! The officers and men must preserve their confidence!"

In the meantime, the small and smallest ships of the 9th Naval Security Division loaded as many men and as much equipment as they could in Libau and Windau. The boats were overloaded. The Naval Commander of the Eastern Baltic Sea, Admiral Burchardi, left Libau on 5/5 and moved his staff to Hela in order to direct and organize the entire transport operation from there. S- and R- patrol boats, naval fishing smacks, and naval barges operated without pause. The 5th S-Boat Flotilla ran into attacking Soviet motor torpedo boats during the night of 5/7, and one was sunk.

The German Wehrmacht surrendered on 7 May 1945.

The army group received a radio message:

"...Due to the surrender, all naval and security forces, as well as cargo ships, must leave the harbors in Kurland and Hela by 9 May at 0000 hours. Therefore, the transport of German men out of the east must be accomplished at great haste."

General Hilpert made contact with the commander of the Soviet forces in Kurland, Marshal Govorov, by radio telegraph. He offered the surrender of the army group!

The Soviets answered immediately. They were agreeable. The army group commander issued the last order to the troop units of the Army and Luftwaffe that night:

"To all! Marshal Govorov has agreed to begin a truce on 8 May at 1400 hours. The troops are to be immediately informed. White flags will be displayed in their positions. The commanders are expected to loyally execute this mission, because the future fate of all Kurland fighters depends upon it!"

Colonel von Amsberg, commander of the 502nd Infantry Regiment of the 290th ID, received the mission to cross the road to Pampili and prepare for the surrender. The colonel, a bugler, an interpreter, and a non-commissioned officer made it to the Soviet lines with a white flag at exactly 1400 hours.

Chapter 8: The Surrender

To the right and left of the road fluttered torn shirts, pieces of bandage, trousers — but no white flags!

The war was over!

The guns were silent!

Army Group Kurland laid down its weapons!

At noon on 5/8, they were the only German army group with a solid front! This ran and was occupied as follows:

18th Army: (Commander: General of Infantry Boege, Chief of Staff: Major General Merk)

X Army Corps: (General of Artillery Thomashki) south of Libau with the 30th (Lieutenant General Henze), 132nd (Major General Demme), 126th ID (Major General Haehling);

I Army Corps: (Lieutenant General Usinger) southwest of Durben with the 225th (Lieutenant General Risse), 87th ID (Lieutenant General Baron von Strachwitz);

II Army Corps: (Lieutenant General Gause) from southwest of Schrunden to Windau with the 263rd (Lieutenant General Hemmann, 563rd ID (Major General Neumann).

16th Army: (Commander: General of Mountain Troops Volckamer von Kirchensittenbach, Chief of Staff: Major General von Gersdorff)

XXXVIII AC: (General of Artillery Herzog) on either side of Frauenburg with the 290th (Colonel Frotscher), 329th (Lieutenant General Menkel), 122nd ID (Major General Schatz);

L Army Corps: (Lieutenant General von Bodenhausen) northeast of Frauenburg with the 218th (Major General Rank), 24th ID (Major General Schultz);

VI SS Corps: (SS Obergruppenfuehrer Krueger) southwest of Tuckum with the 19th SS (SS Brigadefuehrer Streckenbach), 205th ID (Major General Giese);

XVI Army Corps: (Lieutenant General Weber) from west of Tuckum to the sea with the 21st Luftwaffe Field Division (Major General Barth), 81st ID (Lieutenant General von Bentivegni), 300th ID (Major General Eberth).

Army Group North

The 12th Panzer Division (Colonel von Usedom) was the only reserve of the army group and was deployed north of Frauenburg.

The 14th Panzer Division (Colonel Graessel), 11th (Lieutenant General Feyerabend), and elements of the 126th ID were in Libau and Windau. These three divisions were assigned for shipment.

Six German escorts assembled under the leadership of Fregattenkapitaen von Blanc in Libau and Windau. The 1st Escort (patrol boat "1450" and 26 boats from the 14th Security Flotilla) had 2,900 men on board. The 2nd Escort ("M-3", 8 fishing smacks, 3 tugs, 1 tanker, 3 siebelfaehren, 2 naval barges, 1 barge, 2 ferries, 1 R-Boat, 1 motor boat, artillery barge "34", artillery boat "Nienburg", and the coastal motor boat "Kurland") brought 5,720 soldiers home. The 3rd Escort (the steamer "Tsingtau", 3 R-Boats, and 2 air defense boats) took on 3,780 men. The 4th Escort (1st, 2nd, and 5th S-Boat Flotillas) transported 2,000 soldiers to the west. The 5th and 6th Escorts (15 fishing smacks, 45 engineer landing boats, and the tanker "Rudolf Albrecht") were the last groups of the German Navy to leave Windau harbor with 11,300 men at midnight.

On the way, the six escorts were repeatedly attacked by Soviet aircraft and motor torpedo boats, even though a truce already existed! However, all escorts made it safely to the homeland, with very few losses. In Kurland it was 0000 hours on 9 May!

42 generals, 8,038 officers, and 181,032 non-commissioned officers and men of Army Group North and Luftflotte 1, as well as 14,000 Latvian volunteers, were left behind. They now heard the last Wehrmacht order over the radio:

"...our army group in Kurland, which had endured months of strongly superior Soviet tank and infantry formations and stood fast during six great battles, has achieved immortal fame. ..."

However, what good were words now?

The war was over!

The history of Army Group North was ended!

The march of 203,000 soldiers through the marshy forests into the unending expanse of the east had begun.

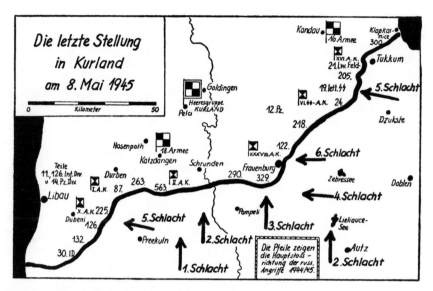

The last positions in Kurland on 8 May 1945
The arrows show the main attack directions of the Russian armies 1944/1945.

NOTES:

[1] *History of the Great Patriotic War of the Soviet Union, 1941-1945.* Vol. 4, page 363. Moscow: Voennoe Izdat. Ministry of Defense USSR 1962.
[2] Schelm, W. and H. Mehrle: *From the Battles of the Wuerrtemberger - Baden Infantry Division.* Bad Nauheim: Podzun 1955. 334 pages.
[3] Bidermann, G. H.: *Crimea - Kurland. With the 132nd Infantry Division.* Bad Nauheim: Podzun 1966. 360 pages.
[4] Buxa, W.: *Route and Fate of the 11th Infantry Division.* 2nd Edition. Bad Nauheim: Podzun 1963. 163 pages.
[5] Grams, R.: *The 14th Panzer Division, 1940-1945.* - Bad Nauheim: Podzun 1957. 359 pages.

Appendixes

APPENDIX 1
German Commanders

a) Das Heeresgruppenkommando Nord

	22. 6. 1941	15. 12. 1942	15. 12. 1943	8. 5. 1945
OB.	Ritter v. Leeb Feldmarschall	von Küchler Feldmarschall	von Küchler Feldmarschall	Hilpert Gen.Ob.
Chef d. Gen.St.	Brennecke Glt.	Kinzel Glt.	Kinzel Glt.	Foertsch Glt.
Ia	Hermann Oberstlt. i. G.	v. Gersdorff Ob. i. G.	v. Gersdorff Ob. i. G.	Richter Ob. i. G.
Ic	Jessel Mj. i. G.	Frhr. v. Süßkind Ob. i. G.	Frhr. v. Süßkind Ob. i. G.	Frhr. v. d. Recke Mj.
OQu.	Toppe Mj. i. G.	Bucher Ob. i. G.	Rauser Ob. i. G.	Rauser Gm.
Nachr.Fhr.	Schrader Gm.	Schrader Glt.	Schrader Glt.	Negendanck Gm.
Gen.d.Pi.	van Schaewen Glt.	Medem Glt.	Medem Glt.	Medem Glt.
Gen. zbV.	— —	Veith Glt.	Veith Glt.	Pawel Gm.
HGr.Arzt	Dr. Uter O.St.Arzt	Dr. Gunderloch GenSt.Arzt	Dr. Wagner GenSt.Arzt	Dr. Wagner GenSt.Arzt
HGr.Vet.	Dr. Klingler GenSt.Vet.	Dr. Klingler GenSt.Vet.	Dr. Klingler GenSt.Vet.	Dr. Köhler GenSt.Vet.
HGr.Intend.	Schreiner GenSt.Int.	Schreiner GenSt.Int.	Schreiner GenSt.Int.	Schreiner GenSt.Int.
HGr.Richter	Hentschel Ob.Kr.Ger.R.	Wunderlich Gen.Richter	Wunderlich Gen.Richter	Wunderlich Gen.Richter

b) Die Oberbefehlshaber der Heeresgrupppe

Feldmarschall Ritter von Leeb	22. 4. 1941 — 16. 1. 1942
Feldmarschall von Küchler	17. 1. 1942 — 8. 1. 1944
Feldmarschall Model	9. 1. 1944 — 30. 3. 1944
Generaloberst Lindemann	31. 3. 1944 — 4. 7. 1944
Generaloberst Frießner	5. 7. 1944 — 24. 7. 1944
Generaloberst Schörner	25. 7. 1944 — 14. 1. 1945
Generaloberst Rendulic	15. 1. 1945 — 25. 1. 1945
Generaloberst von Vietinghoff-Scheel	26. 1. 1945 — 9. 3. 1945
Generaloberst Rendulic	10. 3. 1945 — 14. 3. 1945
Generaloberst Hilpert	15. 3. 1945 — 8. 5. 1945

c) Die Chefs des Generalstabes der Heeresgruppe

Generalleutnant Brennecke	22. 4. 1941 — 17. 1. 1942
Generalmajor Hasse	18. 1. 1942 — 30. 11. 1942
Generalleutnant Kinzel	1. 12. 1942 — 18. 7. 1944
Generalmajor von Natzmer	19. 7. 1944 — 27. 1. 1945
Generalleutnant Foertsch	28. 1. 1945 — 8. 5. 1945

d) Die Oberbefehlshaber der Armeen und der Luftflotte

16. Armee:

Feldmarschall Busch	Febr. 1940 — 11. 10. 1943
General d. Art. Hansen	12. 10. 1943 — 1. 7. 1944
General d. Inf. Laux	2. 7. 1944 — 3. 9. 1944
General d. Inf. Hilpert	4. 9. 1944 — 14. 3. 1945
General d. Inf. von Krosigk	15. 3. 1945 — 16. 3. 1945
General d. Geb.Tr.	
Volckamer von Kirchensittenbach	17. 3. 1945 — 8. 5. 1945

18. Armee:

Generaloberst von Küchler	Nov. 1939 — 16. 1. 1942
Generaloberst Lindemann	17. 1. 1942 — 30. 3. 1944
General d. Art. Loch	31. 3. 1944 — 4. 9. 1944
General d. Inf. Boege	5. 9. 1944 — 8. 5. 1945

zeitweise unterstellt

11. Armee:

Feldmarschall von Manstein	Sommer — Herbst 1942

3. Pz.Armee:

Generaloberst Raus	Sommer — Herbst 1944

Pz.Gruppe 4:

Generaloberst Hoepner   Sommer — Herbst 1941

Luftflotte 1:

Generaloberst Keller   Febr. 1941 — 31. 7. 1941
General d. Flieger Korten   1. 8. 1941 — 23. 8. 1943
General d. Flieger Pflugbeil   24. 8. 1943 — 8. 5. 1945

e) Die Befehlshaber der rückwärtigen Gebiete

Befehlshaber des rückwärtigen Heeresgebiets [ab 1942:] *Kommandierender
General der Sicherungstruppen und Befehlshaber im rückw. Heeresgebiet:*

General d. Inf. von Roques   15. 3. 1941 — 31. 3. 1943
General d. Inf. von Both   1. 4. 1943 — 26. 3. 1944

Kommandeure der rückwärtigen Armeegebiete:

Korück 583 (18. Armee):

Generalleutnant Knuth   20. 1. 1941 — 20. 6. 1943
Generalleutnant van Ginkel   21. 6. 1943 — 8. 5. 1945

Korück 584 (16. Armee):

Generalleutnant Spemann   1. 9. 1939 — 24. 7. 1943
Generalleutnant Pflugradt   25. 7. 1943 — 31. 8. 1943
Generalleutnant von Krenzki   1. 9. 1943 — 31. 10. 1944
Generalleutnant Fischer   1. 11. 1944 — 8. 5. 1945

Appendixes

APPENDIX 2

Organization of Army Group North

a) 22. Juni 1941

Heeresgruppenkommando
Reserve: XXIII. AK. (nur Gen.Kdo.)

AOK 16
Reserve: 206., 251., 253. ID.

II. AK. mit 12., 32., 121. ID.
X. AK. mit 30., 126. ID.
XXVIII. AK. mit 122., 123. ID.

AOK 18
Reserve: XXXVIII. AK. mit 58., 254. ID.

I. AK. mit 1., 11., 21. ID.
XXVI. AK. mit 61., 217. ID.
291. ID. (direkt unterstellt)

Pz.Gr. 4

Reserve: 3., 36. ID.mot., SS-T-D.
XXXXI. AK. mot. mit 1., 6. PD., 269. ID.
LVI. AK. mot. mit 8. PD., 290. ID.

Gen.Kdo. rückw. Heeresgebiet 101
mit 207., 281., 285. Sich.D.

b) 30. Juni 1942

Heeresgruppenkommando
Reserve: 12. PD.

AOK 18

Reserve: SS-Pol.-D.
I. AK. mit 11., 21., 93., 96., 217., 269. ID.
XXVI. AK. mit 223., 227. ID.
XXVIII. AK. mit 61., 121., 215., 254., 291. ID.
XXXVIII. AK. mit 58., 126., 250. ID., 2. SS-Br.
L. AK. mit 212., 225. ID., 5. Geb.D., Gr. Jeckeln

AOK 16
> II. AK. mit 12., 30., 32., 123., 290. ID., SS-T-D.
> X. AK. mit 81., 122., 329. ID., 18. ID.mot., 5., 8. Jäg.D., 21. LwFD.
XXXIX. AK.mot. mit 8. PD., 218. ID.

Befh. rückw. Heeresgebiet
> 207., 281., 285. Sich.D., Landes-Schtz.R. 107

c) 30. Juni 1943

Heeresgruppenkommando
Reserve: 18. Pz.Gr.D.

AOK 18
Reserve: 23., 121. ID.

> I. AK. mit 1., 69., 212., 290. ID., 5. Geb.D., 28. Jäg.D.
> XXVI. AK. mit 61., 81., 96., 132., 225. ID., 12. LwFD.
> L. AK. mit 170., 215., 250. ID.
> LIV. AK. mit 21., 24., 58., 254. ID., SS-Pol.-D.
> III. LwFK. mit 9., 10. LwFD.

AOK 16
Reserve: 223. ID., 8. Jäg.D.
> II. AK. mit 12., 93., 123., 218., 331. ID.
> X. AK. mit 30., 329. ID., 5. Jäg.D.
> K.G. Höhne mit 32., 122. ID., 21. LwFD.

Befh. rückw. Heeresgebiet
> 207., 281., 285. Sich.D.

d) 13. Oktober 1944

Heeresgruppenkommando
Reserve: III. SS-PzK. mit SS-Pz.Gr.D. „Nordland",
> 20. SS-Gr.D., SS-Pz.Gr.Br. „Nederland",
Feld-Ausb.D. Nord

AOK 18
> I. AK. mit 11., 126. ID.
> X. AK. mit 30. ID., 14. PD.
> XXXIX. PzK. mit 61., 225. ID., 4., 12. PD.

AOK 16

Reserve: 24.,. 31., 87., 132., 263. ID., Div. zbV 300
> II. AK. mit 227., 563. ID.
> XXXXIII. AK. mit 23., 83., 218. ID., 12. LwFD., 207., 390. Sich.D.
> L. AK. mit 290. ID., 281. Sich.D
> K.Gr. Kleffel mit 19. SS-Gr.D.

Armee-Abt. Grasser
> XXXVIII. AK. mit 32., 81., 121., 122., 329. ID., 201. Sich.D., 21. LwFD.

e) 1. März 1945

Heeresgruppenkommando

Reserve: 201. Sich.D., Feld-Ausb.D. Nord

AOK 18

Reserve: 121. ID., 12., 14. PD., Fest. Libau
      I. AK. mit 132., 218. ID.
      II. AK. mit 263., 290., 563. ID.
      X. AK. mit 30., 87., 126. ID., 12. LwFD.
      L. AK. mit 11., 205., 215. ID.

AOK 16

    XVI. AK. mit 81. ID., Div. zbV. 300, 21. LwFD.
XXXVIII. AK. mit 122., 329. ID.
XXXXIII. AK. mit Fest. Windau, Kdt. Küste, 207. Sich.D.
    VI. SS.AK. mit 24. ID., 19. SS-Gr.D.

APPENDIX 3

Rear Area Services of Army Group North

a) Verbände des Oberquartiermeisters 1941 — 1944

Fahr-Div. 4 (Pleskau)
Feld-Eisenbahn-Kdo. 4 (Pleskau)
Nachschubführer 56 (Dünaburg), 207 (Pleskau), 507 (Luga), 550 (Reval)
Feldzeugamt für 16. Armee: 26 und 36 (Dorogostizy)
                18. Armee: 24 (Grjasno), 34 (Roshdjestweno)
Fahrkolonnen-Abt. 503 (Pleskau), 986 (Riga), 813 mot. (Riga)
Pionierpark TA-11 (Pleskau), TB-7 mot. (Krasnowardeisk)
Kraftfahrpark 564 (Cholm), 990 (Pleskau)
Kfz-Instands.Btl. 597 (Schimsk)

b) Verbände des Generals zbV 1941 — 1944

Kdr. d. Heeresstreifendienstes mit 3 mot. Offiziers- u. 5 mot. Feldwebelstreifen
Kdr. f. Urlaubsüberwachung (Urlaubersammelkompanien, Zugwachabteilung)
     Kdo. 1 (Riga), 3 (Pleskau), 4 (Luga), 5 (Reval), 51 (Libau),
         53 (Dünaburg), 54 (Walk), 102 (Rositten)
     Zugwachabt. 101 (Schaulen), 510 (Reval), 513 (Riga)
Kdr. d. Heeresbetreuungsabt. 5 (Dorpat)
Kdr. d. Frontleitstelle Nord (Pleskau) mit Frontleitstelle 2 (Pleskau),
     4 (Luga), 11 (Dünaburg), 21 (Riga), 62 (Dno)
Entlausungskompanien 52 (Pleskau), 61 (Dünaburg), 62 (Riga), 63 (Kowno),
     72 (Krasnowardeisk)
Propaganda-Kompanien 501 (für 16. Armee), 621 (für 18. Armee),
     694 (für Pz.Gr. 4)

c) Verbände des Höheren Nachrichtenführers 1941 — 1944

Heeresgruppen-Nachr.R. 639
Nachr.Abt. zbV. 685
Eisenbahn-Nachr.Abt. zbV. 314
Armee-Nachr.Rgter 501 (AOK 16), 520 (AOK 18), 558 (AOK 11),
Pz.Gr.Nachr.R. 4 (Pz.Gr. 4)

Appendixes

Organization of Air Fleet 1

a) 22. Juni 1941

Luftflottenkdo.

I. Fl.K.

JG. 54 mit I.—III./JG. 54, II./JG. 53
KG. 1 mit II., III./KG. 1
KG. 76 mit I.—III./KG. 76
KG. 77 mit I.—III./KG. 77
Aufkl.St. 5 (F)/122

Fliegerführer Ostsee

KGr. 806
Aufkl.Gr. 125

Flak-Verbände

Flak-R. 133 mit I./3, II./23, II./36, lei. 83., lei. 92, II./411
Flak-R. 151 mit I./13, I.,/291, I./411
Flak-R. 164 mit I./51

Nachrichtenverbände

Luft-Nachr.R. 1, 10, 11, 21, 31

b) 31. März 1942

Luftflottenkdo.

JG. 54 mit I.—III./JG. 54, I./JG. 51, III./JG. 3
KG. 1 mit II., III./KG. 1, I./KG. 3, I./KG. 77
KG. 4 mit I., II./KG. 4, I./KG. 53, II./KG. 27
Stuka-G. 1 mit III./St.G. 1, I., II./St.G. 2
Aufkl.St. 3. (F)/22, 5. (F)/122, 3./Ob.d.L., 3. Nacht/3
Wettererk.St. 1
San.St. 1
Transport-Gr. II./1, 4, 5, 8, 9, I./172, 211, 600, 700, 900, 999,
Öls, Posen

2. Flak-D.

Flak-R. 41 mit Abt. 116, 127, 245, 323, 431, 517, lei. 92, 743, 745,
833, 994
Flak-R. 151 mit Abt. I./13, I./111, I./411
Flak-R. 164 mot. mit Abt. I./51, II./36, I./291, lei. 75

c) 22. Juni 1943

Luftflottenkdo.

3. Flieger-D.

JG. 54 mit I., II./JG. 54
KG. 53 mit I., III./KG. 53, II./KG. 101
KG. 102 mit IV./KG. 1
Stuka-G. 1 mit I., II./St.G. 1
1./Störkampf-Gr.
Fern-Aufkl.Gr. 1
Nah-Aufkl.Gr. 8, 11, 127
Seenotverb. 7
Verb.St. 5, 51, 2./zbV. 7
Kurierst. 2, 9, 12

2. Flak-D.

Flak-R. 43 mit Abt. 245, 323, 341, lei. 833
Flak-R. 41 mit Abt. 116, lei. 745, lei. 834, lei. 994
Flak-R. 182 mit Abt. 127, 431, 517

6. Flak-D.

Flak-R. 151 mit Abt. I./13, I./411, I./111, lei. 92
Flak-R. 164 mot. mit Abt. I./51, II./36, I./291, lei. 75

d) 1. Oktober 1944

Luftflottenkdo.

3. Flieger-D.

JG. 54 mit I., II./JG. 54
Schlacht-G. 3 mit II., III./SG. 3, III./SG. 4
Nacht-Schlacht-Gr. 3
Nah-Aufkl.-Gr. 5

2. Flak-D.

[Gliederung wie oben]

6. Flak-D.

[Gliederung wie oben]

Flak-Gr. Ostland

e) Stellenbesetzung der Luftflotte am 22. 6. 1941

Luftflottenkdo.	Befh.	Generaloberst Keller
	Chef d. GenSt.	Ob. i. G. Rieckhoff
	O.Qu.	Ob. i. G. von Criegern
	Höh.Nachr.Fhr.	Glt. Fahnert
I. Flieger-K.	Kdr.Gen.	General d. Flieger Förster
	Chef d. GenSt.	Ob. i. G. Boenicke
	Ia	Oberstlt. i. G. Kreipe
	Nachr.Fhr.	Oberstlt. Pusch

	JG. 54	Major Trautloft
	KG. 1	Gm. Angerstein
	KG. 76	Ob. Bormann
	KG. 77	Ob. Raithel

Flieger-Fhr. Ostsee	Kdr.	Oberstlt. von Wild
	KGr. 806	Oberstlt. Emig
	Aufkl.Gr. 125	Oberstlt. Kolbe

Luft-Nachr.-Rgt.	1	Oberstlt. Schlabach
	10	Ob. Schleich
	11	Oberstlt. Köhler
	21	Oberstlt. Eckstein
	31	Oberstlt. Pusch

Stellenbesetzung des Luftflottenkommandos, Ende September 1944

Befh.	General d. Flieger Pflugbeil
Chef d. GenSt.	Gm. Uebe
Ia/op.	Oberstlt. i. G. Hozzel
Ia/Flieger	Oberstlt. i. G. Wöhlermann
Ia/Flak	Oberstlt. i. G. Wendt
Ic	Oberstlt. i. G. Allolio
O.Qu.	Oberstlt. i. G. Pape
Höh.Nachr.Fhr.	Glt. Sattler
Kdr. der 3. Flieger-D.	Gm. Frhr. von Falkenstein
Kdr. der 2. Flak-D.	Glt. Luczny
Kdr. der 6. Flak-D.	Glt. Anton

f) Stellenbesetzung und Erfolge des Jagdgeschwaders 54

1. Die Kommodore

Ob. Trautloft	14. 8.1940 — 14. 7.1943
Mj. von Bonin	15. 7.1943 — 17.12.1943
Oberstlt. Mader	18.12.1943 — Okt. 1944
Ob. Hrabak	Okt. 1944 — 8. 5.1945

2. Die Gruppenkommandeure

	22. 6. 1941	1. 5. 1943
I./54	Hptm. von Bonin	Mj. Seiler
II./54	Hptm. Hrabak	Hptm. Jung
III./54	Hptm. Lignitz	Hptm. Schnell
II./53	Hptm. Bretnütz	— —

3. Die Kommandeure der I./JG. 54

Hptm. von Bonin	[bis 1. 7.1941]	Mj. Hohmuth	[ab 2. 8.1943]
Hptm. von Selle	[ab 2. 7.1941]	Hptm. Nowotny	[ab 1. 9.1943]
Hptm. Eckerle	[ab 18.12.1941]	Hptm. Ademeit	[ab 5. 2.1944]
Mj. Philipp	[ab 17. 2.1942]	Mj. Eisenach	[ab 21. 8.1944]
Mj. Seiler	[ab 15. 5.1943]		

4. Die erfolgreichsten Jagdflieger des Geschwaders

14. 4. 1943

Mj. Philipp	203 Abschüsse
Oblt. Stotz	161 Abschüsse
Oblt. Beißwenger	152 Abschüsse
Mj. Hahn	108 Abschüsse
Oblt. Ostermann	102 Abschüsse
Lt. Hannig	90 Abschüsse
Mj. Seiler	82 Abschüsse
Oblt. Nowotny	81 Abschüsse
Hptm. Späte	80 Abschüsse

31. 12. 1944

Oblt. Kittel	264 Abschüsse
Mj. Nowotny	255 Abschüsse
Hptm. Rudorffer	212 Abschüsse
Oberstlt. Philipp	203 Abschüsse
Hptm. Stotz	182 Abschüsse
Mj. Ademeit	166 Abschüsse
Hptm. Lang	159 Abschüsse
Oblt. Beißwenger	152 Abschüsse
Lt. Wolf	142 Abschüsse

5. Die Luftsiege des Geschwaders

am 1. 8. 1941	der 1 000. Abschuß
am 4. 4. 1942	der 2 000. Abschuß
am 23. 2. 1943	der 4 000. Abschuß
am 11. 10. 1943	der 6 000. Abschuß
am 31. 12. 1944	der 9 141. Abschuß

APPENDIX 5
Organization of the Navy in the Ost Sea Area

a) 22. Juni 1941

Marinegruppenkdo. Nord	OB.	Generaladm. Carls
	Chef d. Adm.St.	K.Adm. Klüber
	1. Adm.St.Off.	Kpt.z.S. Freymadl
Befh. d. Kreuzer	Befh.	V.Adm. Schmundt
	1. Adm.St.Off.	K.Kpt. Marks
Fhr. d. Torpedoboote	FdT.	Kpt.z.S. Bütow
	1. Adm.St.Off.	K.Kpt. Schultz

Minenschiffgruppe COBRA (K.Kpt. Dr. Brill)
  mit „Cobra", „Kaiser", „Königin Luise"
Minenschiffgruppe NORD (F.Kpt. von Schönermark)
  mit „Tannenberg", „Brummer",
  „Hansestadt Danzig"

Schnellbootflottillen 1, 2, 3, 6
Räumbootflottille 5
U-Jagdflottille 11
Vorpostenbootsflottille 3

Fhr. d. Minensuchstreitkräfte Nord		
	FdM.	Kpt.z.S. Böhmer
	1. Adm.St.Off.	K.Kpt. von Grumbkow

Minensuchflottillen 5, 15, 17, 18, 31
Räumbootflottille 1
Sperrbrecher 6, 11, 138
Minenräumschiffe 11, 12

Fhr. d. Minenschiffe	FdM.	Kpt.z.S. Bentlage
	1. Adm.St.Off.	Kptlt. Engel

Minenschiffe „Preußen", „Grille", „Versailles", „Skagerrak"

selbständig operierend:
Linienschiff „Schlesien"   (Kpt.z.S. Lindenau)
Linienschiff „Schleswig-Holstein" (Kpt.z.S. Hennecke)
U-Bootflottille 22   (K.Kpt. Ambrosius)

b) Juni 1944 — Mai 1945

Der Kommandierende Admiral Östliche Ostsee		
	Kdr.Adm.:	Admiral Burchardi
		V.Adm. Thiele [ab April 1945]
	Chef d. St.:	F.Kpt. Forstmann

unmittelbar unterstellt: Hafenkommandantur **Riga**
                                            Küstenschutzflottille Ostland
                                            4. Artillerieträgerflottille
                                            5. Marineflugmeldeabteilung
                                            Inselkommandantur Tyttärsaari

Kommandant Seeverteidigung Estland [nur bis Sept. 1944]
                    Kdt.:   Kapt.z.S. Mulsow
                    AI: Kptlt. Köster
unmittelbar unterstellt: Hafenkommandant **Reval**
                                            Marine-Art. Abt. 530, 532
                                            Marine-Flak-Abt. 239, 711
                                            Marineausrüstungsstelle Reval
                                            Marineartilleriearsenal Reval

Kommandant Seeverteidigung Baltische Inseln [Sept. — Nov. 1944]
                    Kdt.:   Kpt.z.S. Mulsow
                    AI: F.Kpt. Schmeling
unmittelbar unterstellt: Marineeinsatz-Abt. Ostland
                                            Marine-Art.-Abt. 531, 532
                                            Marine-Flak-Abt. 239

Kommandant Seeverteidigung Lettland
                    Kdt.:   Kpt.z.S. Karstens
                            K.Adm. v. Arnswaldt [ab Aug. 1944]
                    AI: K.Kpt. Steeckicht
                            K.Kpt. Soiné [ab Oktober 1944]
                            F.Kpt. Schmeling [ab. Nov. 1944]
unmittelbar unterstellt: Hafenkommandant Libau, Windau
                                            Marine-Art.-R. 10
                                            Marine-Flak-Abt. 712
                                            9. Marine-Kraftfahr-Abt.
                                            Marine-Fest.Pi.Btl. 321
                                            Marineausrüstungsstelle Libau
                                            Marine-Artilleriearsenal Libau

9. Marine-Sicherungsdivision
                    Chef: F.Kpt. von Blanc
unterstellt: Minensuchflottillen 1, 3, 12, 25, 31
                                            Räumbootflottillen 1, 17
                                            Vorpostenbootflottillen 3, 9, 17
                                            Sicherungsflottillen 3, 14
                                            Landungsflottillen 13, 21, 24
                                            Artillerieträgerflottille 7
                                            U-Jagdflottillen 3, 11
                                            S-Boot-Schulflottillen 1, 2, 3

[Ferner gehörten zum Befehlsbereich des Kommandierenden Admirals noch folgende Dienststellungen, die nicht zum Operationsgebiet der Heeresgruppe Nord, später Kurland, gehörten:

Kommandant der Seeverteidigung Ost- und Westpreußen,
Kommandant im Abschnitt Memel;

es fanden keine Erwähnung die zeitweise unterstellten Transportflottillen, Lazarettschiffe, Marinelazarette u.a.m.]

APPENDIX 6

Organization of the Red Army in the Northern Sector

a) 22. Juni 1941

Baltischer Besonderer Militärbezirk

OB.:	Gen.Ob. Kusnecov
Kriegsrat:	Dibrova
Chef d. GenSt.:	Gm. Kljonov

AOK 8 (OB.: Gm. Sobennikov)

XVI. Schtz.K.	mit 67., 181. SD.
XXIV. Schtz.K.	mit 5. SD., 33. SD. mot.
III. mech.K.	mit 2., 23., 84. PzBr., 23. SD.
XII. mech.K.	mit 28., 202. Pz.Br.
direkt unterstellt:	10., 90., 125. SD.

AOK 11 (OB.: Glt. Morosov)

II. Schtz.K.	mit 126., 128., 188. SD., 5. Pz.Br.
XI. Schtz.K.	mit 179., 184. SD.
XXIX. Schtz.K.	mit 56.,. 129. SD.

AOK 27 (OB.: Gm. Bersarin)

XXII. Schtz.K.	mit 180., 182. SD.
LXV. Schtz.K.	mit 16. SD., 12., 18. Pz.Br.
I. mech. K.	mit 1., 3. PzBr.,. 163. SD., 25., 30. KD.

b) 30. September 1942

Leningrader Front (OB.: Glt. Goworow)

AOK Primorski (Oranienbaum)
   mit 48., 168. SD., 3., 50., 71. SBr., 2., 5. Mar.Br.

AOK 42 (OB.: Gm. Nikolaev)
   mit 48., 168. SD., 3., 50., 71. SBr., 2., 5. Mar.Br.

AOK 55 (OB.: Glt. Sviridov)
   mit 43., 46., 56., 72., 85., 125., 136., 268. SD.

Armee-Abt. Newa
   mit 70., 142. SD., 11., 86. SBr., 220. Pz.Br.

Wolchowfront (OB.: Armeegen. Meretzkov)

AOK 8　(OB.: Gm. Stanikow)
　　　　19., 24. Gd.-D., 11., 36., 191., 259., 265., 286., 318. SD., 22., 23., 32.,
　　　　33., 53., 73. SBr., 16., 21., 29., 98., 122. Pz.Br.

AOK 2. *Stoß-A.* (OB.: Glt. Klykov)
　　　　mit 294., 314., 327., 372., 374., 376. SD., 1. Gd.-Br., 137., 140. SBr.

AOK 54　(OB.: Gm. Suchomlin)
　　　　mit 115., 177., 198., 281., 285., 311. SD., 80., 124. SBr., 2. Mar.Br.

AOK 4　(OB.: Gm. Gusev)
　　　　mit 44., 288., 310. SD., 20. KD., 7. Gd.-Pz.Br., 126. Pz.Br.,
　　　　24., 58. SBr.

AOK 59　(OB.: Gm. Korovnikov)
　　　　mit 2., 377., 378., 382. SD., 193. Pz.Btl.

AOK 52　(OB.: Gm. Klykov)
　　　　mit 65., 225. SD., 165., 305. SBr., 336., 377. SBtl., 340., 345. MG-Btl.

Nordwestfront (OB.: Marschall Timoschenko)

AOK 27　(OB.: Gm. Ozerov)
　　　　mit 26., 162., 188., 254. SD., 38., 117., 177. Pz.Br.

AOK 11　(OB.: Glt. Morozov)
　　　　mit 22., 28. Gd.-D., 32., 55., 200., 201., 202., 282., 370., 384. SD.,
　　　　127., 145. SBr.

AOK 34　(OB.: Gm. Bersarin)
　　　　mit 133., 163., 170., 245. SD., 19., 37., 46., 126., 144., 147., 151.,
　　　　245. SBr., 83., 105. Pz.Br., 4. Mar.Br.

AOK 53　(OB.: Gm. Knesofontov)
　　　　mit 166., 235., 241., 250. SD., 86. SBr.

AOK 1. *Stoß-A.* (OB.: Gm. Korotkov)
　　　　mit 7. Gd.-D., 129., 130., 364., 391., 397. SD., 14., 44., 45., 47.,
　　　　121. SBr.

II. *Gd.K.* mit 8. Gd.-D., 33., 117. SD., 54. SBr.

c) 20. November 1944

1. *Baltische Front* (OB.: Armeegen. Bagramjan)

AOK 43　(OB.: Glt. Beloborodov)
　　　　mit 26., 32., 70., 145., 179., 182., 235., 344. SD.
　　　　Reserve: 222., 357. SD., 8. Art.D., 2. Gd.Gr.W.D.,
　　　　　　　　　10. Gd.Pz.D., Stu.Gesch.Rgt. 306, 377, 1203

AOK 51　(OB.: Glt. Krejser)
　　　　mit 77., 87., 91., 156., 204., 257., 267., 279., 346., 347., 417. SD.
　　　　Reserve: 315. SD., 15. Gd.D., Stu.Gesch.Rgt. 1052, 1102, 1489, 1492

AOK 61　(OB.: Gen.Ob. Belov)
　　　　mit 12. Gd.D., 23., 82., 217., 356., 397., 415. SD., 2. Art.D.

AOK 6. *Gd.A.* (OB.: Gen.Ob. Tschistjakov)
　　　　mit 9., 46., 47., 51., 67., 71., 90. Gd.D., 154., 166., 270. SD.

AOK 2. *Gd.A.* (OB.: Glt. Tschantschibadse)
 mit 16. lit. D., 32., 33. Gd.D.
 Reserve: 2., 24, 87. Gd.D., 126., 208., 263. SD.

AOK 5. *Gd.Pz.A.* (OB.: Marschall Rotmistrov)
 mit III. Gd.PK. (3., 18. Gd.D., 2. Gd.D.mot., 19. Gd.Pz.Br.)
  XXIX. PK. (25., 31., 32. Pz.Br., 53. mech.Br.)
 Reserve: 47. Pz.Br.

AOK 4. *Stoß-A.* (OB.: Glt. Malyschev)
 mit 119., 158., 164., 216., 239., 251., 311., 332., 334., 360., 378. SD.,
 20. Art.D.
selbständig: I. PK. (89., 117., 159. Pz.Br., 44. mech.Br.)
 Reserve: 39. Gd.Pz.Br., Stu.Gesch.Rgt. 1437, 1491
 XIX. PK. (28., 79., 101., 202. Pz.Br., 26. mech.Br.
 Reserve: 29., 105. SD., 24. Gd.D., 14., 34. Pz.Br., Stu.Gesch.Rgt. 867,
    1048, 1049, 1050, 1452, 1824
 III. Gd.mech.K. (7., 8. GD., 35. Gd.PD., 9. Gd.mech.Br.)

2. *Baltische Front* (OB.: Armeegen. Eremenko)

AOK 22 (OB.: Glt. Juschlewitsch)
 mit 21. Gd.D., 200., 391. SD., Stu.Gesch.Rgt. 15, 1476
 Reserve: 2., 28. SD., 43. Gd.D., 219., 308. SD.

AOK 42 (OB.: Glt. Sviridov)
 mit 11., 43., 48., 123., 168., 256., 288. SD.
 Reserve: 37. SD., 19. Sturm-Pi.Br.

AOK 3. *Stoß-A.* (OB.: Gen.Ob. Kasakov)
 mit 23., 52., 53. Gd.D., 146., 150., 171., 198., 207., 265., 364. SD.,
 78. Pz.Br.
 Reserve: 33., 229., 379. SD., 21. Art.D.

AOK 10. *Gd.A.* (OB.: Glt. Korotkov)
 mit 7., 8., 29., 30., 85., 119. Gd.D., 27. SD.
 V. PK. (24., 41., 70. Pz.Br., 5. mech.Br.)
 X. PK. (176., 183., 186. Pz.Br., 11. mech.Br., Stu.Gesch.Rgt. 1199)
 Reserve: 22., 29., 48., 56., 65. Gd.D., 6. mech.Gd.Br., 37., 227., 236.,
 239., 249. SD., 221. Art.D., Stu.Gesch.Rgt. 1261, 1281, 1297, 1453,
 1498, 1515

3. *Baltische Front* (OB.: Armeegen. Masslenikov)

AOK 54 (OB.: Glt. Roginskij)
 mit 98., 374., 376., 377. SD.
 Reserve: 225., 285. SD., 2. Art.Br.

AOK 67 (OB.:   )
 mit 85., 189., 196. SD., 16. Pz.Br., Stu.Gesch.Rgt. 1047, 1450

AOK 1. *Stoß-A.* (OB.: Glt. Sachwatajev)
 mit 191., 354., 364., 395., 417., 487. SD., 155. Fest.Br., 336. MG-Br.
 Reserve: 33., 229., 379. SD., 21. Art.D.

AOK 2. *Stoß-A.* (OB.: Glt. Fedjuninskij)
 mit 44., 352., 396., 523., 525., 526. SD., 118. Pz.Br.
 Reserve: 64., 72., 86., 90., 128., 282., 291., 321., 326., 327. SD.,
    14. Fest.Br., 125. Pz.Br., Stu.Gesch.Rgt. 1453

AOK 23 (OB.: Glt. Tscherepanow)
    mit 10.. 13., 92., 142., 286., 327., 381. SD.

AOK 8 (OB.: Glt. Starikov)
    mit 64. Gd.D., 109., 131. SD., 249. estn.D.
    Reserve: 30., 45. Gd.D., 7. estn.D., 1., 120., 125., 152. SD., 23. Art.D,,
    80. Art.Br., 16. Fest.Br.,
    220. Pz.Br., Stu.Gesch.Rgt. 12, 397, 1811

d) Stellenbesetzung der Fronten und Armeen am 31. 12. 1941

Nordwestfront	OB.:	Glt. Kurotschkin
	Kriegsrat:	Korpskomm. Bogatkin
	Chef d. St.:	Glt. Watutin
Leningrader Front	OB.:	Glt. Chosin
	Kriegsrat:	Armeekomm. Shdanow
	Chef d. St.:	Gm. Gusew
Wolchowfront	OB.:	Armeegen. Meretzkov
	Kriegsrat:	Korpskomm. Zaporoschetz
	Chef d. St.:	Gm. Stelmach

Armee	OB.	Chef d. St.	Kriegsrat
4.	Glt. Ivanov	Ob. Alferov	Zelenkov
8.	Glt. Schevaldin	Ob. Smirnov	Tschuchnov
11.	Glt. Morozov	Gm. Schlemin	Kolonin
23.	Glt. Gerasimov	Gm. Ivanov	Pojidaev
34.	Gm. Bersarin	Gm. Jarmoschkevitz	Bazilevskij
42.	Gm. Nikolaev	Gm. Buchovetz	Klementev
52.	Glt. Klykov	Ob. Rojdestvenskij	Pantas
54.	Gm. Suchomlin	Gm. Beresinskij	Sytschev
55.	Gm. Sviridov	Gm. Ljubbovtschev	Kurotschkin
59.	Gm. Galanin	Gm. Tokarev	Dubrova
2. Stoß	Glt. Sokolov	Gm. Vizjalin	Michailov

e) Stellenbesetzung der Luftarmeen 1942 — 1944

7. Luftarmee (1. 12. 1942 — 10. 8. 1944)
                OB.:   Gm. Sokolov
           Chef. d. St.:   Ob. Belov
                      Ob. Sveschnikov [ab 3. 2. 1943]
                      Gm. Belov [ab 30. 6. 1944]

13. Luftarmee   (25. 11. 1942 — 10. 8. 1944)
                OB.:   Gm. Rybaltschenko
           Chef d. St.:   Ob. Alekseev
                      Gm. Lavrik [ab 11. 7. 1944]

14. Luftarmee   (15. 8. 1942 — 1. 3. 1944)
                OB.:   Gm. Tschuravlev
           Chef d. St.:   Ob. Murgonov
                      Ob. Abramov [ab Febr. 1943]
                      Gm. Storotschenko [ab Dez. 1943]
                      Gm. Gluchov [ab 27. 2. 1944]

15. Luftarmee   (20. 10. 1943 — 1. 3. 1944)
                OB.:   Glt. Naumenko
           Chef d. St.:   Gm. Sakornin

Appendixes

Organization of the Baltic Red Banner Fleet on 22/6/1941

Stab:	Befh.:	V.Adm. Tribuc
	Chef d. St.:	K.Adm. Panteleev
	Kriegsrat:	Div.Komm. Lebedev
Geschwader:	Befh.:	K.Adm. Vdovičenko

Linienschiffbrigade mit Linienschiffe „Marat", „Oktjabrskaja Revoljuzija"
Sicherungsdivision mit Wachboote „Taifun", „Sneg", „Tuča", „Ciklon",
„Burja", „Vicht"
Kreuzerbrigade mit Schwere Kreuzer „Kirov", „Maksim Gorkij"
1. Zerstörerdivision mit Zerstörer „Gnevnyj", „Grozjaščij", „Gordyj",
„Smetlivyj", „Stereguščij"

Leichte Seestreitkräfte: Befh.: K.Adm. Drozd
Flottillenführer „Leningrad", „Minsk"

2. Zerstörerdivision mit Zerstörer „Stojkij", „Silnyj", „Serdityj", „Surovyj",
„Smelyj", „Storoževoy"

3. Zerstörerdivision mit Zerstörer „Strašnyj", „Statnyj", „Slavnyj", „Skoryj",
„Strogyj", „Svirepyj", „Opytnyj"

4. Zerstörerdivision mit Zerstörer „Jakov Sverdlov", „Artem", „Engels", „Lenin",
„Volodarskij", „Kalinin", „Karl Marks"

direkt unterstellt
U-Bootbrigade 1, 2, 3, 4
Torpedokutter-Brigade 1, 2
Küstenschutzverband mit Minenkreuzer „Martij", Minenschiffe „Amur", „Ural"
und vier kleinere Minenleger
Minensuchbrigade mit Minensuchdivision 1, 2, 5 und Minenräumdivision.

APPENDIX 8
Statistical Data

a) Iststärke der Heeresgruppe am 1. Juni 1944

	Iststärke	*Fehlstellen*
16. Armee	265 432 Soldaten	5 867 Soldaten
	18 450 Hilfswillige	18 585 Hilfswillige
18. Armee	195 303 Soldaten	3 269 Soldaten
	13 560 Hilfswillige	10 659 Hilfswillige
Armee-Abt. Narwa	156 942 Soldaten	1 029 Soldaten
	10 089 Hilfswillige	7 888 Hilfswillige
unterst.	77 850 Soldaten	5 937 Soldaten
Einheiten	13 396 Hilfswillige	4 256 Hilfswillige
	695 527 Soldaten	16 102 Soldaten
	55 495 Hilfswillige	41 388 Hilfswillige

b) Verluste und Ersatz der Heeresgruppe im Jahr 1942

	16. Armee		18. Armee	
	Verlust	Ersatz	Verlust	Ersatz
Januar	17 500	650	9 300	2 250
Februar	16 280	5 700	15 200	20 300
März	16 700	13 250	20 200	24 600
April	14 000	5 150	16 650	16 800
Mai	11 100	16 200	11 000	18 450
Juni	9 350	25 750	16 400	20 100
Juli	10 400	15 400	8 150	17 800
August	11 050	9 250	7 150	6 600
September	8 500	9 250	3 550	7 800
Oktober	8 750	9 850	2 000	5 750
November	6 000	5 750	4 750	11 000
Dezember	11 400	9 400	3 600	10 750
	141 000	125 600	118 950	162 200

Heeresgruppe insgesamt = **259 950** Verlust, **287 800** Ersatz

c) Verluste und Ersatz der Heeresgruppe im Jahr 1943

	16. Armee		18. Armee	
	Verlust	Ersatz	Verlust	Ersatz
Januar	9 100	9 200	23 200	12 400
Februar	8 100	6 600	28 400	27 000
März	16 500	17 600	21 000	33 500
April	2 450	22 100	9 200	23 800
Mai	3 200	19 000	8 400	30 600
Juni	2 800	8 400	7 400	17 600
Juli	2 600	7 200	18 800	15 800
August	6 200	6 600	20 400	15 400
September	2 200	7 800	11 800	22 400
Oktober	7 600	8 400	9 200	10 800
November	8 800	8 800	4 500	10 800
Dezember	12 600	10 600	4 200	8 000
	82 150	132 300	166 500	228 100

Heeresgruppe insgesamt = Verluste 248 650, Ersatz 360 400

d) Munitionsverbrauch der Heeresgruppe 1942/43

	16. Armee		18. Armee	
	1942	1943	1942	1943
Januar	10 050 t	20 641 t	18 831 t	40 794 t
Februar	10 780 t	20 913 t	21 619 t	49 099 t
März	11 891 t	23 798 t	30 302 t	44 629 t
April	9 374 t	6 250 t	21 632 t	21 145 t
Mai	9 823 t	8 065 t	16 664 t	16 915 t
Juni	7 696 t	6 594 t	22 690 t	17 524 t
Juli	9 514 t	6 322 t	14 019 t	40 645 t
August	12 399 t	14 850 t	37 842 t	43 178 t
September	12 596 t	8 077 t	40 980 t	23 813 t
Oktober	11 124 t	12 801 t	21 830 t	24 134 t
November	8 736 t	14 019 t	15 512 t	12 082 t
Dezember	19 453 t	14 136 t	14 075 t	11 527 t

Heeresgruppe 1942 Verbrauch   397 034 t
           1943 Verbrauch   501 951 t

e) Deutsche Gefangene nach der Kapitulation 1945

     42 Generale
  8 038 Offiziere
181 032 Soldaten
 14 000 lettische SS-Freiwillige

f) **Von den Sowjets nach der Kapitulation erbeutetes Material**

325 Selbstfahrlafetten und Sturmgeschütze

136 Flugzeuge	224 gepanzerte Fahrzeuge
1 548 Geschütze	310 Funkanlagen
557 Granatwerfer	5 825 Kraftfahrzeuge
4 363 MGs	240 Zugmaschinen
57 646 Gewehre	3 442 Gespanne
	16 543 Pferde

g) **Iststärke der Sowjets im Januar 1944**

Leningrader Front = 33 Divisionen, 12 Brigaden
Wolchowfront = 22 Divisionen, 12 Brigaden
Beide Fronten verfügten über

375 000 Mann
14 300 Geschütze
1 200 Panzer
1 240 Flugzeuge

h) **Sowjetische Verluste Oktober 1944 — Mai 1945**

90 000 Gefallene	2 651 Panzer
300 000 Verwundete	1 389 MGs
4 000 Gefangene	1 091 Geschütze
	722 Flugzeuge

APPENDIX 9

The Reich Commissariat Ostland

a) Die Verwaltungsbezirke, Stand 1. 1. 1944

Generalbezirke und Kreisgebiete	Zahl der Stadt- kreise	Zahl der Land- kreise	Umfang in qkm	Einwohner zahl
I. *Estland* [2])	4	11	47 549	1 017 811 [1])
1. Reval/Stadt	1	—	87	140 911
2. Reval/Land	—	2	8 582	132 344
3. Dorpat/Land	1	3	12 573	272 164
4. Pernau/Land	1	2	9 285	156 124
5. Narwa/Land	1	1	7 387	126 307
6. Arensburg	—	2	7 744	112 803
7. Petschur	—	1	1 891	59 231
II. *Lettland* [3])	4	19	65 791	1 803 104
8. Riga/Stadt	1	—	210	308 342
9. Riga/Land	—	2	10 424	187 447
10. Wolmar/Land	—	3	12 646	222 918
11. Mitau/Land	1	5	14 184	316 510
12. Libau/Land	1	5	13 210	267 964
13. Dünaburg/Land	1	4	15 117	499 923
III. *Litauen* [4])	4	25	67 199	2 797 840
14. Wilna/Stadt	1	—	104	146 273
15. Wilna/Land	—	6	15 840	600 161
16. Kauen/Stadt	1	—	40	113 870
17. Kauen/Land	—	7	14 801	614 829
18. Schaulen/Land	1	6	19 628	720 818
19. Ponewesch/Land	1	6	16 786	601 889
IV. *Weißruthenien* [5])	1	69	53 662	2 411 333
20. Minsk/Stadt	1	—	42	103 110
21. Minsk/Land	—	9	5 429	304 241
22. Slonim/Land	—	5	4 704	171 563
23. Sluzk/Land	—	8	5 242	220 603
24. Wilejka/Land	—	8	7 530	299 553
25. Lida/Land	—	8	4 641	278 508
26. Barisau/Land	—	5	1 248	32 717
27. Hancewitze/Land	—	4	6 085	114 595
28. Glubokoje/Land	—	10	8 746	340 217
29. Baranowitschi	—	7	5 694	341 522
30. Nowogrodek/Land	—	5	4 301	194 504
5 Stadtkreisgebiete	5	—	483	812 506
25 Landkreisgebiete	8	124	233 718	7 217 582
Ostland zusammen	13	124	234 201	8 030 088

[1]) Die Speziellgezählten 17 927 sind nicht in Kreisgebiete aufgeteilt.
[5]) Einwohnerzahlen nach dem Stand von Ende 1942 / Anfang 1943.
[3]) Einwohnerzahlen nach der Volkszählung vom 24. 2. 1943.
[4]) Einwohnerzahlen nach der Volkszählung vom 27. 5. 1942.
[2]) Einwohnerzahlen nach dem Stande vom 1. 12. 1941.

b) Die Behörde des Reichskommissars (Sitz Riga)

Der Reichskommissar:	Gauleiter Lohse
Stellvertreter im Amt:	Ministerialrat Fruend
	NSKK-OGruf. Pröhl
	Ministerialrat Burmeister
Landesverwaltungspräsident:	Ministerialrat Burmeister
	Kriegsverw.Vizechef Mathiesen
Landesleiter der NSDAP:	Gauleiter Lohse
Stellvertreter des Landesleiters:	Reichsleiter Ziegenbein
Höh. SS- und Polizeiführer:	Glt. d. Waffen-SS Jeckeln
Befh. d. Ordnungspolizei:	Glt. d. Ordn.-Pol. Jedicke
Inspekteur d. RAD-Insp. I.:	Gen.Arb.Fhr. Eisenbeck
DRK-Beauftragter Ostland:	Generalfhr. Boehm-Tettelbach
Einsatzleiter Organisation Todt:	Generalingenieur Klugar
	Hauptbauleiter Ludewig
Generaldirektor Baltöl-Werke:	Generaldir. Schröder

c) Generalkommissare und Chefs der Landeseigenen Verwaltung

Generalkommissariat Litauen (Sitz Kowno)

Generalkomm.:	Reichshauptamtsleiter Dr. v. Rentelen
1. Generalrat:	General Kubiliunas

Generalkommissariat Lettland (Sitz Riga)

Generalkomm.:	Oberbürgermeister Dr. Drechsler
Generaldirektor:	General Dankers

Generalkommissariat Estland (Sitz Reval)

Generalkomm.:	SA-OGruf. Litzmann
1. Landesdirektor:	Dr. Mäe

Generalkommissariat Weißruthenien (Sitz Minsk)
[wurde hier nicht genannt, da es in den Operationsbereich der Heeresgruppe Mitte gehörte]

d) Stab Wehrmachtbefehlshaber Ostland

Der Befehlshaber:	General d. Kav. Braemer [bis 30. 4. 1944]
	General d. Pz.Tr. Kempf [bis 31. 8. 1944]
	General d. Inf. Grasser [bis 25. 9. 1944]

Stellenbesetzung am 10. 6. 1944

Der Befehlshaber:	General d. Pz.Tr. Kempf
Der Stellvertreter:	General d. Art. Ziegler
Der Chef d. Stabes:	Gm. (Lw.) Vodepp
Inspekteur Küstenschutz:	Glt. Scherer
Ia (Operationsabt.):	Oberstlt. Schallehn
IIa (Adjutantur):	Oberstlt. Sellin

Abbreviations

Zusammengesetzte Abkürzungen sind nicht aufgeführt, können aber selbständig aufgeschlüsselt werden.

AA.	— Aufklärungs-Abteilung		GR.	— Grenadier-Regiment
Abt.	— Abteilung		Gren.D.	— Grenadier-Division
Adm.	— Admiral		Gruf.	— Gruppenführer
AK.	— Armeekorps		H./	— Heeres-
AOK.	— Armee-Ober-kommando		Harko.	— Höherer Artillerie-Kommandeur
AR.	— Artillerie-Regiment		HGr.	— Heeresgruppe
Arko.	— Artillerie-kommandeur		HKL.	— Hauptkampflinie
			Hptm.	— Hauptmann
Art.	— Artillerie-		HQu.	— Hauptquartier
Aufkl.	— Aufklärung		I	— Infanterie-
Batt.	— Batterie		ID.	— Infanteriedivision
Befh.	— Befehlshaber		ID.mot.	— Infanteriedivision motorisiert
Br.	— Brigade		IG.	— Infanteriegeschütz
Brig.Fhr.	— Brigadeführer		i.G.	— im Generalstab
Btl.	— Bataillon		Inf.	— Infanterie-
D.	— Division		IR.	— Infanterie-Regiment
F.d.M.	— Führer d. Minensuchkräfte		JG.	— Jäger-
			K.	— Jagdgeschwader
F.d.T.	— Führer d. Torpedoboote		Jäg.	— Korps
			K.Adm.	— Konteradmiral
F.Kapt.	— Fregattenkapitän		Kapt.	— Kapitän
Fla.	— Heeresflak		Kaptlt.	— Kapitänleutnant
Füs.	— Füsilier-		Kdr.	— Kommandeur
Fw.	— Feldwebel		Kdtr.	— Kommandantur
G.	— Geschwader		Kfz.	— Kraftfahrzeug
Gd.	— Garde-		KG.	— Kampfflieger-geschwader
Geb.	— Gebirgs-			
Gefr.	— Gefreiter		KGr.	— Kampffliegergruppe
Gen.Adm.	— Generaladmiral		K.Kapt.	— Korvettenkapitän
Gen.d.	— General d.		Komm.Gen.	— Kommandierender General
Gen.Kdo.	— Generalkommando			
Gen.Ob.	— Generaloberst		Kp.	— Kompanie
Gen.St.	— Generalstab		lFH.	— leichte Feldhaubitze
Glt.	— Generalleutnant		Lkw.	— Lastkraftwagen
Gm.	— Generalmajor		Lt.	— Leutnant

Lw.	— Luftwaffe	Pz.Jäg.	— Panzerjäger
Lw.FD.	— Luftwaffen- Felddivision	Pz.K. R.	— Panzerkorps — Panzertruppe
mech.	— mechanisiert		— Regiment (nur bei
MG.	— Maschinengewehr	Pz.Tr.	Zusammen-
mot.	— motorisiert		setzungen)
MPi.	— Maschinenpistole	RAD.	— Reichsarbeitsdienst
Nachr.	— Nachrichten-	Radf.	— Radfahrer-
OB.	— Oberbefehlshaber	Rgt.	— Regiment
Ob.	— Oberst	rückw.	— rückwärtig
Oberstlt.	— Oberstleutnant	San.	— Sanitäts-
Oblt.	— Oberleutnant	Schlacht-G.	— Schlachtgeschwader
Ofw.	— Oberfeldwebel	schw.	— schwer
OGruf.	— Obergruppenführer	SD.	— Sicherheitsdienst
OKH.	— Oberkommado d. Heeres	sFH. Sfl.	— schwere Feldhaubitze — Selbstfahrlafette
OKL.	— Oberkommando d. Luftwaffe	Sich.D. Skl.	— Sicherungsdivision — Seekriegsleitung
OKM.	— Oberkommando d. Kriegsmarine	sowj. SS.	— sowjetisch — Waffen-SS
OKW.	— Oberkommando d. Wehrmacht	SS-Pol.D. SS-T-D.	— SS-Polizeidivision — SS-Totenkopfdivision
OQu.	— Oberquartiermeister	Stand.Fhr.	— Standartenführer
OT.	— Organisation Todt	Sturmbannf.	— Sturmbannführer
PD.	— Panzerdivision	Uffz.	— Unteroffizier
Pi.	— Pionier-	V-Abt.	— Vorausabteilung
PK.	— Propagandakompanie	V-Adm.	— Vizeadmiral
Pol.	— Polizei-	VB.	— Vorgeschobener
Pz.	— Panzer-		Beobachter
Pz.Gren.	— Panzergrenadier-	z.S.	— zur See

Bezeichnungen der Schiffsgattungen:

M	— Minensuchboot
R	— Räumboot
S	— Schnellboot
T	— Torpedoboot
U	— Unterseeboot
UJ	— Unterseebootsjäger
V	— Vorpostenboot
Z	— Zerstörer

Bibliography

Die nachfolgende Auswahl der Quellen- und Buchliteratur kann keine zusammenfassende Bibliographie zur Geschichte der Heeresgruppe Nord sein. Es wurden bei der Aufzählung absichtlich außer acht gelassen: Allgemeine Geschichte des 2. Weltkrieges, Erlebnisberichte, historische Erzählungen, Truppengeschichten, Zeitschriften- und Zeitungsartikel.

Die Aufzählung dieser Literaturgattungen würde den Rahmen des Buches sprengen. Es darf nur darauf hingewiesen werden, daß heute bereits weit über 100 Divisions- und Regimentsgeschichten der deutschen und sowjetischen Armee vorliegen.

Der Verfasser dankt für die Zurverfügungstellung der benutzten Buch- und Quellenliteratur ganz besonders der Bibliothek für Zeitgeschichte in Stuttgart und dem Bundesarchiv/Militärarchiv in Koblenz.

Ferner ist der Autor vielen ehemaligen Angehörigen der Heeresgruppe Nord, Luftflotte 1 und der Kriegsmarine zu Dank verpflichtet, die ihm bei der Abfassung seiner Arbeiten durch Hinweise, Briefe, persönliche Tagebücher, Aufzeichnungen oder in Gesprächen unterstützten. Der Dank gilt gleichermaßen dem Herrn Großadmiral, den Oberbefehlshabern der Heeresgruppe und Armeen, den Kommandierenden Generalen, den Kommandeuren der verschiedensten Einheiten, den Kompanie-, Zug-, Gruppenführern und einfachen Soldaten, die alle irgendwie beitrugen, daß die Geschichte der Heeresgruppe Nord entstehen konnte.

1. Unveröffentlichte Quellen

Heeresgruppe Nord: Der Feldzug gegen die Sowjetunion. Karten- und Textband. Für das Jahr 1941, 1942, 1943;
Kriegstagebuch für das 2. Halbjahr 1944;
Kriegstagebuch OQu vom August 1942 — März 1943;
Akte gKdos, Chefsache, April 1945;
Kriegslagekarten Estland 1941;
Lagekarten Juli 1944;
Lagekarten während der 5 Kurlandschlachten;
Studie „Laura" (Seetransport) vom 30. 1. 1945.

AOK 16: Armeebefehle 1941;
Studie über die Kämpfe um die Landbrücke Demjansk.

AOK 18: Hauptdaten Ostfeldzug;

Befehlsgliederung Ostfeldzug;
Übersichtskarten zum Ostfeldzug;
Kampf um Leningrad (Studie);
Kriegstagebuch 1. 1. — 31. 3. 1945.

OKM: Skl/Lagebetrachtung für den Fall „Barbarossa";
Skl/Stellungnahme Großadmiral Raeder zu
„Seelöwe" und „Baubarossa";
Kriegswissensch. Abt./Operationen und Taktik. H. 12.
Der Ostseekrieg gegen Rußland 1941.

ferner Kriegstagebücher (auch im Auszug) von verschie-
denen Armeekorps, Divisionen, Jagd-Geschwader 54,
des Lufttransportführers, sowie private Tagebücher.

2. Memoiren

E r e m e n k o, A. I.: Na zapadnom napravlenii. — Moskva: Voennoe
Izd. Minist. Oborony SSSR 1959. 188 S.

F e d j u n i n s k i j, I. I.: Podnjatye po trevoge. Izd. 2. — Moskva:
Voennoe Izd. Minist. Oborony SSSR 1964. 245 S.

G u d e r i a n, H.: Erinnerungen eines Soldaten. — Heidelberg:
Vowinckel 1951. 464 S.

H a l d e r, Fr.: Kriegstagebuch. Tägliche Aufzeichnungen des Chefs des
Generalstabes des Heeres 1939 — 1942. Bd. 2. 3. — Stuttgart: Kohlhammer 1962 — 1963. XII, 503, 589 S.

K u r z e n k o v, S. G.: Pod nami — zemlja i more. — Moskva: Voennoe
Izd. Minist. Oborony SSSR 1960. 160 S.

K u z n e c o v, P. G.: Dni boevye. — Moskva: Voennoe Izd. Minist.
Oborony SSSR 1964. 324 S.

Generaloberst a. D. Georg L i n d e m a n n. [Daten und milit. Laufbahn.]
Freudenstadt 1955. 14 S.

M a n s t e i n, E. v.: Verlorene Siege. — Bonn: Athenäum 1955. 664 S.

R e n d u l i c, L.: Gekämpft, gesiegt, geschlagen. — Wels, Heidelberg:
Welsermühl 1952. 384 S.

T r i b u c, V. F.: Podvodniki Baltiki atakujut. Voennye memuary. —
Leningrad: Lenizdat 1963. 333 S.

W a g n e r, E.: Der Generalquartiermeister. Briefe und Tagebuchauf-
zeichnungen d. Generalquartiermeister. d. Heeres. — München, Wien:
Olzog 1963. 318 S.

W a r l i m o n t, W.: Im Hauptquartier der deutschen Wehrmacht
1939 — 1945. Grundlagen, Formen, Gestalten. — Frankfurt/M.:
Bernard u. Graefe 1962. 570 S.

3. Allgemeine Werke

The German C a m p a i g n in Russia. Planning and operations (1940 —
1942). — Washington: Department of the Army 1955. VIII, 187 S.

C a r e l l, P.: Unternehmen Barbarossa. Der Marsch nach Rußland. —
Frankfurt/M., Berlin, Wien: Ullstein 1963. 559 S.

C l a r k, A.: Barbarossa. The Russian-German conflict 1941 — 45. —
New York: Morrow 1965. XXII, 522 S.

Appendixes

D e b o r i n , G. A.: Vtoraja Mirovaja Vojna. Voenno-polit. očerk. — Moskva: Voennoe Izd. Minist. Oborony SSSR 1958. 430 S.

D e s r o c h e s , A.: La Campagne de Russie d'Adolf Hitler. — Paris: Maisonneuve et Larose 1964. 295 S.

D e u t s c h l a n d im Kampf. Hrsg. von A. I. Berndt u. H. v. Wedel. Nr. 43—116. — Berlin: Stolberg 1941—1944. Getr.Pag.

G o l i k o v , S.: Vydajuščiesja Pobedy sovetskoj armii v Velikoj Otečestvennoj Vojne. — Moskva: Gosud. Izd. Polit. Liter. 1952. 278 S.

G u i l l a u m e , A. La Guerre germano—soviétique 1941 — 45. — Paris: Payot 1949. 219 S.

H i l l g r u b e r , A.: Hitlers Strategie. Politik und Kriegführung 1940 — 1941. — Frankfurt/M.: Bernard u. Graefe 1965. 715 S.

J a c o b s e n , H.-A.: 1939 — 1945. Der Zweite Weltkrieg in Chronik und Dokumenten. 5. Aufl. — Darmstadt: Wehr u. Wissen 1961. 764 S.

I s t o r i j a Velikoj Otečestvennoj Vojny Sovetskogo Sojuza 1941—1945. Tom 1—6. Moskva: Voennoe Izd. Minist. Oborony SSSR 1960—1965.

K r i e g s t a g e b u c h des Oberkommandos der Wehrmacht 1940—1945. Bd. 1—4. — Frankfurt/M.: Bernard u. Graefe 1961—1965. Getr.Pag.

Hitlers L a g e b e s p r e c h u n g e n. Die Protokollfragmente seiner militärischen Konferenzen 1942 — 1945. Hrsg. v. H. Heiber. — Stuttgart: Deutsche Verlagsanstalt 1962. 970 S.

M u r a w s k i , E.: Der deutsche Wehrmachtsbericht 1939 — 1945. Ein Beitrag zur Unters. d. geistigen Kriegführung. — Boppard a. Rh.: Boldt 1962. IX, 768 S. (Schriften des Bundesarchivs. Bd. 9.)

O č e r k i istorii Velikoj Otečestvennoj Vojny 1941—1945. — Moskva: Izd. Akademii Nauk SSSR 1955. 534 S.

Važnejšie O p e r a c i i Velikoj Otečestvennoj Vojny 1941 — 1945 gg. — Moskva: Voennoe Izd. Minist. Oborony Sojuza SSSR 1956. 622 S.

P h i l i p p i , A. u. H e i m , F.: Der Feldzug gegen Sowjetrußland 1941 bis 1945. Ein operativer Überblick. — Stuttgart: Kohlhammer 1962. 293 S.

S t a l i n , I. V.: O Velikoj Otečestvennoj Vojne Sovetskogo Sojuza. — Moskva: Ogiz Gos. Izd. Polit. Lit. 1946. 182 S.

T e l ' p u c h o v s k i j , V. S.: Velikaja Otečestvennaja Vojna Sovetskogo Sojuza 1941—1945. — Moskva: Gos. Izd. Polit. Lit. 1959. 574 S.

Velikaja Otečestvennaja V o j n a Sovetskogo Sojuza 1941 — 1945. — Moskva: Voennoe Izd. Minist. Oborony SSSR 1965. 617 S.

(V t o r a j a Mirovaja Vojna 1939 — 1945, [Dt.]). Geschichte des Zweiten Weltkrieges 1939 — 1945. Bd. 1—6. — Berlin: Dt. Militärverlag 1961 — 1966. Getr.Pag.

W e r t h , A.: Russia at war 1941 — 1945. — New York: Dutton 1964. XXV, 1100 S.

4. Werke zu einzelnen Themen

A n f i l o v , V. A.: Načalo Velikoj Otečestvennoj Vojny. — Moskva: Voenne Izd. Minist. Oborony SSSR 1962. 221 S.

C o m b a t in Russian forests and swamps. — Washington: U. S. Gov. Pr. Off. 1951. VII, 39 S.

German D e f e n s e T a c t i c s against Russian break-throughs. —

V D n i vojny. (Iz istoriii Latvii perioda Velikoj Otečestvennoj Vojny 1941—1945 gg.) — Riga: Izd. Akad. Nauk Latvijskoj SSSR 1964. 292 S.

H e y s i n g , G.: Nordpfeiler der Ostfront. — Berlin-Schöneberg: Riffarth 1944. 123 S.

J u n i 1941. Beiträge zur Geschichte des hitlerfaschistischen Überfalls auf die Sowjetunion. Red.: A. Anderle u. W. Basler. — Berlin: Rütten u. Loening 1961. 367 S.

M i d d e l d o r f , E.: Taktik im Rußlandfeldzug. — Darmstadt: Mittler 1956. 239 S.

P o t t g i e s s e r , H.: Die Deutsche Reichsbahn im Ostfeldzug 1939— 1944. — Neckargemünd: Scharnhorst Buchkameradschaft 1960. 152 S.

Eesti R i i k ja rahvas teises maailmasojas. [Bd] 1 — 10. — Stockholm: Kirjastus EMP. 1954 — 1962.

S a m s o n o v , A. M.: Ot Volgi do Baltiki. Očerk istorii 3-go Gvardejs-kogo mechanizirovannog Korpusa 1942 — 1945 gg. — Moskva: Izd. Akad. Nauk SSSR 1963. 448 S.

B r ä u t i g a m , O.: Überblick über die besetzten Ostgebiete während des 2. Weltkrieges. — Tübingen: Institut für Besatzungsfragen 1954. VI, 97 Bl.

B y č k o v , L. N.: Partizanskoe dviženie v gody Velikoj Otečestvennoj Vojny 1941 — 1945. — Moskva: Izd. Soc.-ekonom. Liter. „Mysl'" 1965. 453 S.

D a l l i n , A.: Deutsche Herrschaft in Rußland 1941—1945. — Düssel-dorf: Droste 1958. 727 S.

T o s a n k a , F. W.: Modern Guerrilla Warfare. Fighting Communist guerrilla movements, 1961—1961. — New York: Free Press of Glencoe 1962. XXII, 519 S.

H e r z o g , R.: Grundzüge der deutschen Besatzungsverwaltung in den ost- und südosteuropäischen Ländern während des 2. Weltkrieges. — Tübingen: Institut f. Besatzungsfragen 1955. XXII, 200 Bl.

H o w e l l , E. M.: The Soviet Partisan Movement 1941 — 1944. — Washington: Dep. of the Army 1956. X, 217 S.

K ü h n r i c h , H.: Der Partisanenkrieg in Europa 1939—1945. — Berlin: Dietz 1965. 603 S.

Morvarid M a s k i t a . — Tallinn: Eesti Riiklik Kirjastus 1961. 155 S.

Hitlerine O k u p a c i j a Lietuvoje. — Vilnius: Gospolitnaučizdat Lit. SSR 1961. 544 S.

R e i t l i n g e r , G.: The House built on sand. The conflicts of German policy in Russia, 1939—1945. — London: Weidenfeld and Nicolson 1960. 459 S.

A č k a s o v , V. I. u. V a j n e r , B. A.: Krasnoznamennyi Baltijskij Flot v Velikoj Otečestvennoj Vojne. — Moskva: Voennoe Izd. Minist. Obor. SSSR 1957. 399 S.

Appendixes

B e k k e r , Ostsee — deutsches Schicksal 1944/45. — Oldenburg, Hamburg: Stalling 1959. 319 S.

Krylatye B o g a t-y r.i . — Leningrad: Lenizdat 1965. 349 S.

G r e č a n j u k , N.: Baltijskij Flot. Istoričeskij očerk. — Moskva: Voennoe Izd. Minist. Oborony SSSR 1960. 373 S.

I s a k o v , I. S.: The Red Fleet in the Second World War — London: Hutchinson. 124 S.

M e i s t e r , J.: Der Seekrieg in den osteuropäischen Gewässern 1941 — 45. — München: Lehmann 1958. 392 S.

O p e r a t i o n s g e b i e t östliche Ostsee und der finnisch-baltische Raum 1944. — Stuttgart: Dt. Verl.-Anst. 1961. 186 S.
(Beiträge zur Militär- und Kriegsgeschichte. Bd. 2.)

P i t e r s k i j , N. A.: Die Sowjetflotte im Zweiten Weltkrieg. [Dt.] Im Auftr. d. Arbeitskreises f. Wehrforschung hrsg. . . . von J. Rohwer. — Oldenburg: Stalling 1966. 530 S.

Boevoj P u t ' Sovetskogo voenno-morskogo flota. Avtorskij Kollektiv: V. I. Ačkasov. — Moskva: Voennoe Izd. Minist. Oborony SSSR 1964. 620 S.

Š a d s k i j , P. I.: Sovetskaja aviacija v bojach za rodinu. — Moskva: Izd. Dosaaf 1958. 84 S.

W i r kämpften gegen die Sowjets. 1941/42. VIII. Fliegerkorps. Dresden 1942: Güntz-Druck. 248 S.

5. Werke zu einzelnen Schlachten usw.

A b w e h r k ä m p f e am Nordflügel der Ostfront 1944 — 1945. Hrsg.: H. Meier-Welcker. — Stuttgart: Deutsche Verlags-Anstalt 1963. 459 S. (Beiträge zur Militär- und Kriegsgeschichte. Bd. 5.)

B a r b a š i n , I.P. u. C h a r i t o n o w , A.D.: Boevye dejstvija sovetskoj armii pod Tichvinom v. 1941 g. — Moskva: Voennoe Izd. Minist. Oborony SSSR 1958. 78 S.

B a r b a š i n , I. P. [u. a.]: Bitva za Leningrad 1941 — 1944. — Moskva: Voennoe Izd. Minist. Oborony SSSR 1964. 607 S.

B y č e v s k i j , B. V.: Gorod-front. O bojach pod Leningradom v 1941 — 1943 gg. — Moskva: Voennoe Izd. Minist. Oborony SSSR 1963. 197 S.

Č e r n o v , J.: Oni oboronjali Moonzund. — Moskva: Gosud. Izd. Polit. Lit. 1959. 86 S.

C h a l e s d e B e a u l i e u , W.: Der Vorstoß der Panzergruppe 4 auf Leningrad. — Neckargemünd: Vowinckel 1961. 175 S. (Die Wehrmacht im Kampf. Bd. 29.)

The D e f e n c e of Leningrad. Eye-witness accounts of the siege (1942/43). — London: Hutchinson 1943. 136 S.

D m i t r i e v , V. I.: Saljut Leningrada. — Moskva: Voennoe Izd. Minist. Oborony SSSR 1959. 160 S.

Devjat'sot D n e j. Literaturno-chudožestvennyj i dokumental'nyj sbornik, posvjaščennyj geroičeskoj oborone Leningrada. [Hrsg.:] Michajlovskij, N. G. — Leningrad: Lenizdat. 1957. 595 S.

F r e i v a l d s , O.: Kurzemes Cietoksnis. Bd. 1. 2. — Kopenhagena: Imanta 1954. 183, 219 S.

G o u r e , L.: The Siege of Leningrad. — Stanford: Stanford Univ. Press 1962. XII, 563 S.

H a u p t , W.: Baltikum 1941. Die Geschichte eines ungelösten Problems. — Neckargemünd: Scharnhorst Buchkameradschaft 1963. 200 S. (Die Wehrmacht im Kampf. Bd. 37.)

H a u p t , W.: Demjansk 1942. Ein Bollwerk im Osten. 2. Aufl. — Bad Nauheim: Podzun-Verlag 1963. 230 S.

H a u p t , W.: Kurland. Die letzte Front — Schicksal für zwei Armeen. 4. Aufl. — Bad Nauheim: Podzun 1964. 134 S.

J a r c h u n o v , V. M.: Čerez Nevu. — Moskva: Voennoe Izd. Minist. Oborony SSSR 1960. 94 S.

K a r a e v , G. N.: Geroičeskaja Oborona Leningrada. — Leningrad: Gosud. Izd. Detskoj Lit. Minist. Prosveščenija RSFSR 1960. 110 S.

K a r a s e v , A. V.: Leningradcy v gody blokady 1941 — 1943. — Moskva: Izd. Akad. Nauk SSSR 1959. 313 S.

K o r o v n i k o v , I. T.: Novgorodsko-Lužskaja Operacija. Nastuplenie vojs 59-j armii. — Moskva: Voennoe Izd. Minist. Oborony SSSR 1960. 177 S.

Südlich des L a d o g a s e e s . Winter 1943. Hrsg. von d. Armee vor Leningrad. — Riga 1943: Tevija. 223 S.

L u k n i c k i j , P. N.: Na Beregach Nevy. — Moskva: Voennoe Izd. Minist. Oborony SSSR 1961. 262 S.

L u k n i c k i j , P. N.: Skvoz vsju Blokadu. — Leningrad: Lenizdat 1964. 605 S.

M e l z e r , W.: Kampf um die Baltischen Inseln 1917 — 1941 — 1944. — Neckargemünd: Scharnhorst Buchkameradschaft 1960. 197 S. (Die Wehrmacht im Kampf. Bd. 24.)

M u c k , R.: Kampfgruppe Scherer 105 Tage eingeschlossen. — Oldenburg: Stalling 1943. 130 S.

P o h l m a n , H.: Wolchow. 900 Tage Kampf um Leningrad 1941 bis 1944. — Bad Nauheim: Podzun-Verlag 1962. 136 S.

S a c h s , G.: Südlich des Ilmensees. Ein Kriegsbericht. — Berlin: West-Ost-Verlag 1943. 227 S.

S c h l a c h t am Wolchow. Hrsg. v. d. Propaganda-Kompanie einer Armee. — Riga 1942: 210 S.

S i r o t a , F. I.: Leningrad gorod-geroj. — Leningrad: Lenizdat 1960. 181 S.

W e r t h , A.: Leningrad.. — London: Hamilton 1944. 189 S.

S v i r i d o v , V. P., J a k u t o v i c , V. P., V a s i l e n k o , V. E.: Bitva za Leningrad. — Leningrad: Lenizdat 1962. 553 S.

Z u b a k o v , V. E.: Proryv blokady Leningrada. — Moskva: Voennoe Izd. Minist. Oborony SSSR 1963. 47 S.

Z u b a k o v , V. E.: Nevskaja Tverdynja. Bitva za Leningrad v gody Velikoj Oteč. Vojny 1941 — 1944. — Moskva: Voennoe Izd. Minist. Oborony SSSR 1960. 201 S.

Also from the Publisher

SCORCHED EARTH Paul Carell. The classic! This new edition of Paul Carell's eastern front study picks up where *Hitler Moves East* left off. Beginning with the battle of Kursk in July 1943, Carell traverses the vast expanse of the Russian War, from the siege of Leningrad and the fierce battles of the northern front, to the fourth battle of Kharkov, and the evacuation of the Crimea, a withdrawal forbidden by Hitler. The book ends in June of 1944 when the Soviet Armies reach the East Prussian frontier. Hundreds of photographs, situation and campaign maps, complete index, and comprehensive bibliography add to this impressive account. This edition includes a new preface by the author. Paul Carell is also the author of *Foxes of the Desert*; *Invasion! They're Coming*; *Operation Barbarossa In Photographs*; and *Stalingrad - The Defeat of the German 6th Army* (all four titles are available from Schiffer Military/Aviation History).
Size: 6" x 9"
b/w photographs, maps   600 pages, hard cover
ISBN: 0-88740-598-3 $39.95

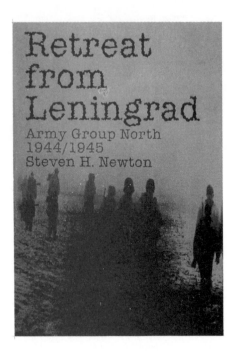

RETREAT FROM LENINGRAD: ARMY GROUP NORTH 1944/1945 STEVEN H. NEWTON. Most histories of the northern sector of the Russian front concentrate on the siege of Leningrad, and focus little attention on the heavy fighting during the Wehrmacht's withdrawal into the Baltic countries. *Retreat from Leningrad* begins where those books end, with the massive January 1944 Soviet offensive which was designed not only to break the siege completely but also to destroy Army Group North. Enjoying huge superiorities in men and material, the Red Army attempted to crush two German armies which lacked more than a handful of tanks, contained a high percentage of unreliable foreign volunteers, and were hampered by Adolph Hitler's inflexible "no retreat" strategy. This untold story is recovered here in great detail, primarily as told by the German officers who served as commanders and chiefs of staff for Army Group North and its constituent armies. Their accounts were drafted soon after the war ended at the request of the United States Army, but have languished in poorly translated manuscripts until Professor Steven H. Newton re-translated, corrected, and annotated them, as well as providing substantial amounts of new material direct from the army group's operational records. The result is the most comprehensive and detailed operational study of sustained combat in the northern sector of the Russian front ever published in English.

Size: 6" x 9"   maps

328 pages, hard cover

ISBN: 0-88740-806-0 $24.95

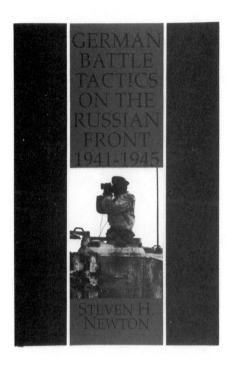

GERMAN BATTLE TACTICS ON THE RUSSIAN FRONT, 1941-1945 Steven H. Newton. In this new book, Professor Steven H. Newton has retrieved, retranslated, and annotated the detailed tactical accounts of combat in Russia that German officers provided their American captors after the war. In this collection of ten essays, the Chief of Staff of the XXXXI Panzer Corps describes the final furious dash toward Moscow. One of the commanders of the relief force narrates the rescue of the troops trapped in the Demyansk pocket. A corps commander on Manstein's right flank at Kursk analyzes the tactical failures of the battle. And in one of the more controversial documents in the early cold war, the last commander of Army Group South recalls his futile attempt to interest General Patton in assisting in the war against the Soviets. A wide variety of tactical situations – from winter warfare to desperate infantry defenses, and unit types – from panzer divisions to cavalry brigades – are covered in this collection.

Size: 6" x 9"

20 maps 320 pages, hard cover

ISBN: 0-88740-582-7 $24.95

RED ARMY TANK COMMANDERS: THE ARMORED GUARDS Colonel Richard N. Armstrong. This new book profiles six Soviet commanders who rose to lead six tank armies created by the Red Army on the eastern front during the Second World War: Mikhail Efimov Katukov, Semen Il'ich Bogdanov, Pavel Semenovich Rybalko, Dmitri Danilovich Lelyushenko, Pavel Alekseevich Rotmistrov, and Andrei Grigorevich Kravchenko. Each tank commanders' combat career is examined, as is the rise of Red Army forces, and reveals these lesser known leaders and their operations to western military history readers.
Size: 6" x 9" 15 b/w photos, maps
476 pages, hard cover
ISBN: 0-88740-581-9 $24.95

RED ARMY LEGACIES: Essays on Forces, Capabilities & Personalities Richard N. Armstrong. For twenty-five years, it was the author's job to watch and examine the Soviet Army for a possible conflict, and to understand the Soviet Army's use of its combat experience. In Richard Armstrong's new book, *Red Army Legacies: Essays on Forces, Capabilities & Personalities*, eleven essays show how the Soviet Army used its "Red Army Legacy." Among the subjects covered are: **Part I - Forces**; Chapter One - Guards of Destruction; Chapter Two - The Bukrin Drop: Limits to Creativity; Chapter Three - Tank Corps Commander; Chapter Four - Mobile Groups: Prologue to MG: **Part II - Capabilities**; Chapter Five - Hunting Tongues; Chapter Si̸ - Battlefield Agility: The Soviet Legacy; Chapter Seven - Red Army Indicators; Chapter Eight - Repelling Cou̸ terattacks and Counterstrikes: **Part III - Personalities**; Chapter Nine - Nachalnik Razvedki: The Red ̸ Chapter Ten - Popel: The Fighting Commissar; Chapter Eleven - Radzievskii: The Thinking Warrior. ̸

Size: 6" x 9" maps
256 pages, hard cover
ISBN: 0-88740-805-2 $24.95

STALINGRAD The Defeat of the German 6th Army Paul Carell. In this 50th Anniversary book,
updates and revises the Stalingrad sections of *Hitler Moves East* and *Scorched Earth,* and reap-
tions of the 6th Army from the 1942 German summer offensive, through the fighting in the
the final defeat in January 1943.

and b/w photographs, 27 maps
$29.95